THE SWEEP OF AMERICAN HISTORY

Volume II

Third Edition

Edited by
ROBERT R. JONES
University of Southwestern Louisiana

GUSTAV L. SELIGMANN, JR.
North Texas State University

JOHN WILEY & SONS, INC.
New York • Chichester • Brisbane • Toronto

Copyright © 1969, 1974, 1981, by John Wiley & Sons, Inc.

All rights reserved. Published simultaneously in Canada.

Reproduction or translation of any part of
this work beyond that permitted by Sections
107 and 108 of the 1976 United States Copyright
Act without the permission of the copyright
owner is unlawful. Requests for permission
or further information should be addressed to the
Permissions Department, John Wiley & Sons.

Library of Congress Cataloging in Publication Data

Jones, Robert Rivers, 1934–   comp.
  The sweep of American history.

  Includes bibliographies and index.
    1. United States—History—Addresses,
essays, lectures. I. Seligmann, Gustav L.
II. Title.
E178.6.J582   1981   973   80-39484
ISBN 0-471-07898-0 (v. 1)
ISBN 0-471-07897-2 (v. 2)

Printed in the United States of America

10 9 8 7 6 5 4 3 2 1

TO
Our wives, Pat Jones and
Janelle Seligmann,
and our children, Tricia,
Bobby, Tommy, and Beth Jones
and Amy Seligmann Buesing

PREFACE

The assembling of this collection of readings began as part of a pedagogical experiment over a decade and a half ago. Our original plans did not include publication; our aim was merely to improve our own basic American history survey courses. Ultimately, however, we concluded that others teaching American history might like our approach and welcome the opportunity to use the outstanding articles and selections we had collected. Many apparently have. In this third edition we have revised our original work in response to the many suggestions of the users of the first two editions, the changes in emphases in historical research and writing over the past several years, and our own changing views of the nation's past.

Our intent in these volumes is to provide a series of readings that covers the sweep of American history from pre-European settlement times through the 1970s, utilizing selections from the works of some 52 historians and scholars whose writings well illustrate the great variety and richness of American historical study. These readings will introduce students to numerous historical subject fields, to differing approaches to historical study, and to the special insights and styles of some of the best historians writing in the field. In choosing these selections, we have consciously avoided the specialized and sophisticated studies that appear so frequently in professional historical and scholarly journals. Most selections are from major historical syntheses or historical monographs, and most employ a broadly interpretive approach that should help make American history more understandable to freshman and sophomore students. Several of the readings are from classic works, but most represent the most recent scholarship. Included are selections on topics of immense current interest, such as Indians, women, blacks, and various aspects of cultural, social, and psychohistory. In short, this revised collection will acquaint students with a good deal of the best that has been written in the field of American history.

Each of the revised volumes contains 27 major topics, arranged in chronological order, with a single reading on each topic. An introductory essay to each reading links the topics, places the reading in historical perspective, and suggests key points, questions, and additional readings for the student's consideration. All of the readings, we believe, are suited to the level of students in college survey courses.

We are most appreciative of the cooperation and aid of our colleagues and friends whose suggestions, both initially and for this edition, have broadened our historical horizons. Specifically we thank Professors Donald K. Pickens and Judith F. Gentry for their help and advice. We are grateful to Mrs. Eloise

Green and Mrs. Ann Doolin and their staffs, Ms. Cindy Carroll, Ms. Beth Broyles; Ms. Pat Loveless, and Ms. Kellye Reynolds, for their aid in preparing this manuscript. Also we appreciate the efforts of Wayne Anderson and his staff at Wiley, who were helpful during every stage of the project. Finally we thank all of our teachers, friends, and colleagues who have helped to make these volumes a contribution to the teaching of history.

Robert R. Jones
Gustav L. Seligmann, Jr.

CONTENTS

CHAPTER 1

THE CIVIL WAR AND NEGRO EQUALITY

One of the most crucial—perhaps *the* most crucial—of the domestic issues that have confronted the nation in the 1960s is the role of blacks in American life. It is not a new issue, but has roots deep in the American past. Before the Civil War, Americans differed strongly in their attitudes toward slavery, although there was general agreement that inherent Negro inferiority prevented blacks from participating fully in American society. At the outset of the Civil War, most Northerners regarded the question of slavery and the status of blacks as secondary to the issue of preserving the Union. But the course of the war, and its impact on both foreign and domestic affairs, prompted a continuing debate concerning Northern war aims, which eventually came to include freedom for blacks. This raised the associated question of equality. The people of the North gradually became firmly committed to the idea of emancipation, but the fate of equality was another story.

It is with this other story that C. Vann Woodward is concerned in his essay, "Equality: The Deferred Commitment." Professor Woodward suggests that Northern war aims were ill-defined in 1861, that numerous factors prompted the framing of broad objectives, and that the North ultimately embraced a total war with positive and revolutionary aims, including emancipation and equality for blacks, North and South. Woodward is careful to point out that the country never committed itself to equality to the same degree that it committed itself to freedom. But, he stresses, the commitment was made. Yet the commitment was not fulfilled during the war and Reconstruction. Only in the last half of the twentieth century has conscience begun to catch up with commitment and has the country begun to pay in full an almost forgotten debt.

The process by which Northern war aims were slowly and painfully defined, the role of Lincoln in that process, and the underlying causes for the ultimate deferral of the commitment to equality are treated fully by Woodward. But his essay raises other significant questions about American society and its

1

history. Why was the debt forgotten? Why did it take a hundred years for America's conscience to reawaken? Might one reason have been a tendency, hinted at by Woodward, for Americans to view their nation's history as the uninterrupted furtherance of "life, liberty, and the pursuit of happiness" and to ignore conflicts and contradictions that were harsh, painful, and ignoble?

The literature on this topic is varied and controversial. Interested students should see James M. McPherson, *The Struggle for Equality: Abolitionists and the Negro in the Civil War and Reconstruction** (1964); C. Vann Woodward, *The Strange Career of Jim Crow** (1955); and Kenneth M. Stampp, *The Era of Reconstruction, 1865–1877** (1965). The essays on Lincoln in Richard Hofstadter, *The American Political Tradition and the Men Who Made It** (1948), and Richard Current, *The Lincoln Nobody Knows** (1958), are also valuable. Woodward's latest contribution on the subject is *American Counterpoint: Slavery and Racism in the North-South Dialogue** (1971). See also Chapter 25 of Volume I of this collection of readings.

*Available in a paperback edition.

EQUALITY: THE DEFERRED COMMITMENT

C. VANN WOODWARD

Now that the drive is on to give accustomed cant about equality for the Negro some basis in fact and to deliver on promises nearly a century old, the temptation is strong to pretend that we have been in earnest all along. Such a pretense, successfully maintained, might stiffen resolution, put the forces of resistance further on the defensive, and in general further a good cause. Before we become so deeply committed to the pretense that we believe in it ourselves, however, it would be well to look soberly into the curious origins of the commitment to equality during the Civil War and into its subsequent abandonment.

The North had a much more difficult time defining its war aims than the South. The aims of the South were fixed and obvious from the start and remained constant until rendered hopeless—the establishment and defense of independence. The North moved gradually and gropingly toward a definition of its war aims. Its progress was obstructed by doubt and misgiving and characterized by much backing and filling. The debate and the outcome were shaped by the course of the war itself, by military necessities, foreign propaganda needs, and domestic morale demands, as well as by the exigencies of party politics and political ambitions.

As the North progressed toward the framing of war objectives, America was inched along from right to left. It moved from hesitant support of a limited war with essentially negative aims toward a positive war with total and revolutionary aims. The character of the war changed from a pragmatic struggle for power to a crusade for ideals. The struggle took on many aspects of an ideological war, and in some minds became a holy war, fought, financed, and supported by men who could feel themselves instruments of divine will.

It was far different at the outset. Lincoln was inaugurated President of a slaveholding republic. He had been elected on a platform firmly pledging him to the protection of the institution of slavery where it existed, and in his first inaugural address, while not abandoning his moral views of slavery, he explicitly denied that he entertained any "purpose, directly or indirectly, to interfere with the institution of slavery in the states where it exists." Not only had he

SOURCE. C. Vann Woodward, "Equality: The Deferred Commitment," *The American Scholar,* XXVII (1958), pp. 459–72. Reprinted by permission

no purpose, but he declared he had "no lawful right" and indeed, "no inclination to do so." He assured the people of the South that their property was not "in any wise endangered by the now incoming administration." His emphasis was upon the negative aim of preventing secession and the disruption of the Union.

Four and a half months later, after blood had been shed and the war was in full swing, Congress took a hand in defining war aims. On July 22 the House adopted, with only two negative votes, a resolution declaring that "this war is not waged . . . [for the] purpose of overthrowing or interfering with the . . . established institutions of those States, but to . . . maintain . . . the . . . States unimpaired; and that as soon as these objects are accomplished the war ought to cease." The Senate backed this sentiment up with a similar resolution, also adopted by a nearly unanimous vote. At this stage, so far as both President and Congress were able to formulate war aims, this was a war of narrowly limited objectives and no revolutionary purpose. It was to be a war against secession, a war to maintain the Union—that, and nothing more.

This negative phase did not last long. No mood lasted very long in the flux and change of the Civil War. Five months later the House voted down a motion to reaffirm the resolution of limited war aims. Already the movement was under way to extend those aims from mere Union to embrace freedom as well. The second war aim was not attained by a stroke of Lincoln's pen, as Lincoln was the first to admit. It was forced by events, by necessities, and those events and necessities first took the shape of thousands of pitiable fugitive slaves crowding into the Union lines. Their path toward freedom was tedious and rugged, filled with obstacles. Thousands wavered between freedom and slavery for years and were never quite sure when freedom came, or if it did. The majority only began their struggle for freedom after the war was over.

Freedom as a war aim was arrived at by a long succession of piecemeal decisions. There were orders by field commanders, some countermanded, some sustained; there were acts of state legislatures; and there was a long succession of bits and driblets of emancipation enacted by Congress, which did not get around to repealing the Fugitive Slave Act until June of 1864. And always there was the embarrassed and reluctant dragon of emancipation, the invading army. "Although war has not been waged against slavery," wrote Secretary Seward to Charles Francis Adams in 1862, "yet the army acts . . . as an emancipating crusade. To proclaim the crusade is unnecessary."

The crusade *was* eventually proclaimed, though the proclamation was not the President's. Lincoln never wanted to turn the war into a moral crusade. It is not necessary to retrace here the painful steps by which Lincoln arrived at his numerous decisions upon slavery and emancipation. It is sometimes forgotten, however, how often he deprecated the importance of his Proclamation of Emancipation. He characterized it was a war necessity, forced by events, ineffectual, inadequate, and of doubtful legality. It is plain that his heart was in his plan for gradual emancipation, which he repeatedly but unsuccessfully urged upon Congress and proposed as a Constitutional amendment. This was an extremely conservative plan for gradual and voluntary emancipation over a period of thirty-seven years, to be completed by 1900, to be administered by the slave states themselves, and to be assisted by the Federal government with compensation to slaveowners and foreign colonization of freedmen. Support was not forthcoming, and war developments underlined the impracticality of the plan.

When Lincoln finally resorted to the Proclamation, he presented it as a war measure, authorized by war powers and justified by military necessity. Again and again he repeated that it was a means to an end—the limited Lincolnian end of Union—and not an end in itself, that union and not freedom was the true war aim. Yet freedom had become a second war aim anyway, and for many the primary war aim. In spite of the fact that the Proclamation emancipated no slaves, it had a profound effect upon the war—more effect upon the war, in fact, than upon slavery.

For one thing, it helped to elevate the war to a new plane. It was still a war for union, but not as before—a war for union with slavery. It was no longer merely a war against something, but a war for something, a war for something greatly cherished in American tradition and creed, a war for freedom. What had started as a war for political ends had, by virtue of military necessity, undergone a metamorphosis into a higher and finer thing, a war for moral ends. What had commenced as a police action had been converted into a crusade. Some abolitionists professed disappointment in the Proclamation, but so ardent a believer as Theodore Tilton was in "a bewilderment of joy" with the new spirit "so racing up and down and through my blood that I am half crazy with enthusiasm."

The great majority of citizens in the North still abhorred any association with abolitionists, but many of them were now free to share the forbidden transports of the despised radicals at no cost to their reputation whatever. Conservative, humdrum, unheroic millions could now sing "John Brown's Body" in naive identification with the demented old hero and partake, vicariously and quite inexpensively, of his martyrdom. An aura of glory descended upon the common cause that sometimes lifted men out of themselves, exalted them, though it seems to have inspired civilians and noncombatants more often than soldiers. It could endow men with a sense of moral superiority and divine purpose that enabled them to regard the enemy with a new indignation and righteousness. It emboldened them to make messianic pronouncements with no apparent self-consciousness. The exuberant religiosity of the age was tapped for war propaganda and yielded riches. How otherwise could men, with no consciousness of blasphemy, lift their voices to sing, "As He died to make men holy, let us die to make men free"?

Before he issued the proclamation, Lincoln had written privately that he was holding the antislavery pressure "within bounds." He could no longer make that boast with assurance, for after the edict of January 1, 1963, antislavery sentiment could not always be kept in bounds. As Professor James G. Randall put it, "The concomitants of emancipation got out of Lincoln's hands. He could issue his proclamation, but he could not control the radicals." The "concomitant" of the second war aim of freedom was a third—equality. No sooner was the Union officially committed to the second war aim than the drive was on for commitment to the third.

It cannot be said that this drive was as successful as the movement for freedom, nor that by the end of the war the country was committed to equality in the same degree it was to freedom. There was no Equality Proclamation to match the Emancipation Proclamation. The third war aim never gained from Lincoln even the qualified support he gave to abolition. Without presidential blessing the commitment was eventually made, made piecemeal like that to freedom, and with full implications not spelled out until after the war—but it was made.

The formal commitment to the third war aim would never have been possible had the abolitionist minority not been able to appeal to more venerable and acceptable doctrine than their own. It would be preposterous to credit the abolitionists with surreptitiously introducing the idea of equality into America. The nation was born with the word on its tongue. The first of those "self-evident" truths of the Declaration was that "all men are created equal." Back of that was the heritage of natural rights doctrine, and back of that the great body of Christian dogma and the teaching that all men are equal in the sight of God.

There were, of course, less disinterested inducements in operation. If freedom was in part a military expedient, equality was in part a political and economic expedient. Equality of the franchise for freedmen was deemed essential to Republican supremacy, and Republican supremacy was considered necessary by influential classes to protect the new economic order.

Equality was advisable, not only politically and economically, but also from a psychological and religious standpoint. For fulfillment of abolitionist purposes it was almost a necessity. Abolitionists had grounded their whole crusade against slavery on the proposition that it was a "sin." It is not sufficient simply to abolish a sin; it has to be expiated, and the sinner purified. Purification and expiation involve penance and suffering. Equality had a punitive purpose: the infliction of a penance of humiliation upon the status of the sinner. For those with an uncomplicated interest in sheer vengeance upon a hated foe, equality had punitive uses of a simpler sort.

Even with all these resources at their command, however, the radicals could never have succeeded in their drive for the formal commitment to equality had it not been launched upon the mounting tide of war spirit and had the war not already been converted into a moral crusade. A moral crusade could only be justified by high moral aims, even if those aims were embraced by the great majority as an afterthought, by many with important mental reservations, and by others as expedients for extraneous ends having nothing whatever to do with the welfare of the freedmen.

So far as the abolitionist minority was concerned, the association of freedom and equality, as Jacobus tenBroek has demonstrated, was rooted in three decades of organized antislavery agitation. Antislavery congressmen carried this association of aims into the framing of the Thirteenth Amendment. Debates over the question in the Senate in the spring of 1864 and in the House of Representatives in January, 1865, contain evidence that the framers aimed at equality as well as emancipation. Both objectives were assumed by the opponents as well as the sponsors of the amendment during the debate. As one of the supporters, William D. Kelley of Pennsylvania, put it: "The proposed Amendment is designed . . . to accomplish . . . the abolition of slavery in the United States, and the political and social elevation of Negroes to all the rights of white men." His broad construction of the amendment was echoed with variations by numerous supporters. They did not include enfranchisement among the rights of Negroes, but they specifically and repeatedly mentioned equal protection of the laws, safeguard for privileges and immunities, and guarantee against deprivation of life, liberty, and property without due process of law. The main ground of opposition to the amendment was this very aim of equality. A constant complaint of opponents was that the amendment would not only free the Negroes but would "make them our equals before the law."

The broad construction of the Thirteenth Amendment to include equality as well as freedom was not sustained when put to test, and the radicals themselves abandoned the interpretation. But they did not abandon their aim of equality. Instead, they increased the scope of it. Responding to provocation of Southern aggression against Negro rights and to inducement of political gains as well, they proceeded to make equality as much the law of the land as freedom. In the Civil Rights Act of 1866 they gave sweeping protection to the rights of Negroes as citizens, guaranteeing them "full and equal benefit of all laws and proceedings for security of person and property, as is enjoyed by white citizens," regardless of any law to the contrary. When the President vetoed the bill, they passed it over his veto. When doubt was cast upon its constitutionality, they enacted most of its provisions into the Fourteenth Amendment. When the South balked at ratification, they stipulated its adoption as a condition of readmission to the Union. Later they extended Federal protection to the Negro franchise by the Fifteenth Amendment. They re-enacted the Civil Rights act, implementing protection of voters, and followed that by another bill to carry out rights established by the Fourteenth Amendment. To crown the achievement they passed still another Civil Rights Act in 1875 which provided sweepingly that "all persons within the jurisdiction of the United States shall be entitled to the full and equal enjoyment of the accommodations, advantages, facilities, and privileges of inns, public conveyances on land or water, theatres, and other places of public amusement, subject only to the conditions and limitations established by law and applicable alike to citizens of every race and color, regardless of any previous condition of servitude."

Thus, by every device of emphasis, repetition, re-enactment, and reiteration, the radical lawmakers and Constitution-amenders would seem to have nailed down all loose ends, banished all ambiguity, and left no doubt whatever about their intention to extend Federal protection to Negro equality. So far as it was humanly possible to do so by statute and constitutional amendment, America would seem to have been firmly committed to the principle of equality.

And yet we know that within a very short time after these imposing commitments were made they were broken. America reneged, shrugged off the obligation, and all but forgot about it for nearly a century. The commitments to the war aims of union and freedom were duly honored, but not the third commitment. In view of current concern over the default and belated effort to make amends, it might be of interest to inquire how and why it every occurred.

Equality was a far more revolutionary aim than freedom, though it may not have seemed so at first. Slavery seemed so formidable, so powerfully entrenched in law and property, and so fiercely defended by arms that it appeared far the greater obstacle. Yet slavery was property based on law. The law could be changed and the property expropriated. Not so inequality. Its entrenchments were deeper and subtler. The attainment of equality involved many more relationships than those between master and slave. It was a revolution that was not confined to the boundaries of the defeated and discredited South, as emancipation largely was. It was a revolution for the North as well. It involved such unpredictable and biased people as hotel clerks, railroad conductors, steamboat stewards, theater ushers, real estate agents, and policemen. In fact, it could involve almost anybody. It was clear from the start that this revolution was going to require enthusiastic and widespread support in the North to make it work.

Was there any such support? Who were the American people so firmly committed to this revolutionary change, and what degree of support were they prepared to lend it? For one thing, among the Union-supporting people were those of the border area, which included not only Kentucky, Missouri, and West Virginia but also the Southern parts of Ohio, Indiana, and Illinois. This area embraced a white population approximately equal to the number of whites in the Confederate states. And if Maryland be added, as I think it should be, that area included considerably more white people than the Confederacy. Most of those people were still living in slave states during the war, and many of their attitudes and habits were not very different from those of people in states to the southward. Their enthusiasm for the third war aim was a matter of some doubt.

What of the Republican party itself, the party responsible for enacting the commitment to equality? During the war it was, of course, exclusively a sectional party, a party of Northern people. Its membership was heavily recruited from the defunct Whig party, and the new party never shook off its Whiggish origins. Many of its members, to use Lincoln's phrase, disliked being "unwhigged." The essence of Whiggery was accommodation and compromise, compromise of many kinds, including the old type of sectional compromise. Before Reconstruction was over, Republicans were again seeking out their old Whig friends of the South with proffered compromise that would leave the solution of the race question in Southern hands.

Lincoln was fully aware of the limited moral resources of his party and his section of the country. He knew that there were limits beyond which popular conviction and conscience could not be pushed in his time. Whatever his personal convictions—and he may, as one historian has maintained, have been entirely color blind—when he spoke as President of the United States or as leader of his political party, he spoke with measured words. And he did not speak in one way to Negroes and another to whites. To a delegation of Negro leaders at the White House he said, "There is an unwillingness on the part of our people, harsh as it may be, for you free colored people to remain with us." He expressed deep sympathy for their wrongs as slaves. "But even when you cease to be slaves," he said, "you are yet far removed from being placed on an equality with the white race. . . . The aspiration of men is to enjoy equality with the best when free, but on this broad continent not a single man of your race is made the equal of a single man of our. . . . I cannot alter it if I would. It is a fact. . . . It is better for us both, therefore to be separated." This idea of separating the races led Lincoln to support the most impractical and illusory plan of his entire career, the plan for colonizing the freedmen abroad or settling them in segregated colonies at home.

What were the sentiments of the Federal Army—the army of liberation—about the issue of equality? That great body included eventually more than two million men. There appears to have been a lower proportion of men from the upper income and social classes, and a higher proportion of the lower economic and social order in the Federal than in the Confederate Army. But there were men of all kinds and all views. Among them were officers and enlisted men of deep and abiding conviction, dedicated spirits whose devotion to the moral aims of the war is borne out in their conduct and in their treatment of slaves, freedmen, and Negro soldiers.

Unfortunately it cannot be said that soldiers of this turn of mind were typical of the army sentiment, or even that they were very numerous. They seem, on the contrary, to have been quite untypical. "One who reads letters and diaries of Union soldiers," writes Professor Bell I. Wiley, who has indeed read many of them, "encounters an enormous amount of antipathy toward Negroes. Expressions of unfriendliness range from blunt statements bespeaking intense hatred to belittling remarks concerning dress and demeanor." Many of the Union soldiers brought their race prejudices with them from civilian life. Sometimes these prejudices were mitigated by contact with the Negro, but more often they appear to have been intensified and augmented by army experience. Men who endure the hardships and suffering and boredom of war have always sought scapegoats on which to heap their miseries. In the Civil War the Negroes who crowded into Union lines were made to order for the role of scapegoat. The treatment they often received at the hands of their liberators makes some of the darkest pages of war history. Another shameful chapter is the treatment of the 200,000 Negroes who served in the Union Army. Enlistment of Negroes in the first place appears to have been strongly opposed by the great majority of white troops. And even after their battle record proved, as Dudley T. Cornish says, "that Negro soldiers measured up to the standard set for American soldiers generally," they continued to be discriminated against by unequal pay, allowances, and opportunities. These inequalities lasted throughout the war. It would seem at times that the army of liberation marched southward on its crusade under the banner of White Supremacy.

One is driven by the evidence to the conclusion that the radicals committed the country to a guarantee of equality that popular convictions were not prepared to sustain, that legal commitments overreached moral persuasion. The lag between conviction and commitment could be illustrated by many more examples, including race riots and violent labor demonstrations against the Negro that broke out during the war in Cleveland, Cincinnati, Chicago, Detroit, Buffalo, Albany, Brooklyn, and New York. The tendency would also be revealed by the neglect, exclusion, or hostility that craft unions and national unions exhibited toward the Negro during the war years and afterward. Further illustration could be drawn from the measures adopted by Western states to discourage freedmen from settling or working within their boundaries, or going to school with their children. One should also recall that in all but a handful of Northern states suffrage was denied the Negro long after it was mandatory for freedmen in the South.

In concentrating on the North as a source of illustration of this moral lag on equality, I have certainly not intended to suggest that it was peculiar to the North. I have taken agreement for granted that the lag was even greater in the South and that resistance to fulfillment of the commitment was in that area even more widespread, stubborn, and effective. It *has* been my intention, however, to suggest that the default was not peculiar to the South.

When such a lag develops between popular convictions and constitutional commitments, and when that lapse cannot be conveniently rationalized by statutory or amendatory procedures, it becomes the embarrassing task of the Supreme Court of the United States to square ideals with practice, to effect a rationalization. The justices in this instance examined the words of the Fourteenth Amendment and, by what Justice John M. Harlan in a famous dissenting opinion called "subtle and ingenious verbal criticism," discovered that they did not at all mean what they seemed to mean, nor what their authors thought they meant. By a series of opinions beginning in 1873 the court constricted the Fourteenth Amendment by a narrow interpretation which proclaimed that privileges and immunities we call civil rights were not placed under federal protection at all. In effect, they found that the commitment to equality had never really been made.

The Union fought the Civil War on borrowed moral capital. With their noble belief in their purpose and their extravagant faith in the future, the radicals ran up a staggering war debt, a moral debt that was soon found to be beyond the country's capacity to pay, given the undeveloped state of its moral resources at the time. After making a few token payments during Reconstruction, the United States defaulted on the debt and unilaterally declared a moratorium that lasted more than eight decades. The country was only nominally spared the formality of bankruptcy by the injunctions of the Supreme Court that cast doubt on the validity of the debt. In the meantime, over the years, interest on the debt accumulated. The debt was further augmented by the shabby treatment of the forgotten creditors, our own Negro citizens.

Then in the middle of the twentieth century conscience finally began to catch up with commitment. Very suddenly, relatively speaking, it became clear that the almost forgotten Civil War debt had to be paid, paid in full, and without any more stalling than was necessary. As in the case of the commitment to emancipation during the Civil War, amoral forces and pressures such as the exigencies of foreign propaganda, power politics, and military necessities exercised a powerful influence upon the recommitment to equality. But also as in the case of emancipation, the voices of conscience, of national creed, and of religious conviction played their parts. In the second instance the demands of the Negroes themselves played a more important part in the pressure than before. Equality was at least an idea whose time, long deferred, had finally come.

Once again there was a lag between popular conviction and constitutional interpretation. Only this time the trend ran the opposite way, and it was the Constitution that dawdled behind conviction. Again it proved unfeasible to close the gap by statutory or amendatory procedures, and again it became the embarrassing task of the Supreme Court to effect an accommodation, a rationalization. Once more the justices scrutinized the words of the Fourteenth Amendment, and this time they discovered that those words really meant what they said, and presumably had all along. The old debt that the court had once declared invalid they now pronounced valid.

Although this was acknowledged to be a national debt, in the nature of things it would have to be paid by a special levy that fell with disproportionate heaviness upon one section of the country. The South had been called on before to bear the brunt of a guilty national conscience. It is now called on a second time. One could hope that the South's experience in these matters might stand it in good stead, that having learned to swallow its own words before, it might do so again with better grace, that it might perform what is required of it with forbearance and humility. I do not know. I can only admit that present indications are not very reassuring.

There is no apparent prospect of full compliance nor of an easy solution. The white South is resisting, and a reactionary part of it is defiant. The resistance is stubborn. A minority could become nasty and its defiance brutish. Already there is evidence that the patience of the rest of the country is not unlimited. There is a sense of frustration and a demand that there be no more faltering. The taunts and jeers of our foreign adversaries are a provocation, and so are the partisan rivalries of politicians. The demand for stern measures and the use of armed force is growing. An example has already been set and more could follow. But the center of resistance has scarcely been seriously challenged, and when it is, the prospect is likely to grow even darker. These are facts that no one can contemplate soberly without a sense of foreboding.

We are presently approaching the centennial anniversary of the Civil War. Simultaneously we are approaching the climax of a new crisis—a crisis that divides the country along much the same old sectional lines, over many of the same old sectional issues. It would be an ironic, not to say tragic, coincidence if the celebration of the anniversary took place in the midst of a crisis reminiscent of the one celebrated.

The historian who, in these circumstances, writes the commemorative volumes for the Civil War centennial would seem to have a special obligation of sobriety and fidelity to the record. If he writes in that spirit, he will flatter the self-righteousness of neither side. He will not picture the North as burning for equality since 1863 with a hard, gem-like flame. He will not picture the South as fighting for the eternal verities. He will not paint a holy war that ennobled its participants. And he will try to keep in mind the humility that prevented the central figure in the drama from ever falling in with the notion that he was the incarnation of the Archangel Michael.

CHAPTER 2

THE LEGACY OF THE CIVIL WAR

The American Civil War was not just another war. As suggested in an essay in Volume I of these readings, it was the first modern war—a war of ideas, of unlimited objectives, of mass armies, and of the mass production of new and more efficient instruments of death and destruction. Because it was at once a modern war and a civil war, the struggle between North and South intimately touched more American homes and intensely involved a greater number of Americans than perhaps any other war in the nation's history. As historian Carl Degler has observed, it was a "people's war," and as such it had a profound effect on America's history.

In this selection, Allan Nevins seeks to measure the impact of the Civil War on the American nation. The sheer magnitude of the war ensured that its effects would be profound. Indeed, Professor Nevins suggests that the changes brought about by the war constituted an actual revolution. When in 1927 historian Charles A. Beard first applied the concept of revolution to the Civil War, he was primarily thinking of the change in the poitical balance of power between the North and the South. With the advantage of much subsequent research in economic, social, and intellectual history, Professor Nevins is able to look at the war from a different perspective, and he suggests that the war's most revolutionary effect was the conversion of an unorganized nation into an organized nation.

While reading this essay, the student should keep this question constantly in mind: What was the impact of the Civil War on the American nation? If the war was not the glorious and romantic event chronicled in American history and literature, was it then a purposeless, meaningless, and complete tragedy? If not, what were its positive and beneficial results, and how does one explain the endurance of some results and the transitoriness of others? Finally, what lesson, if any, does the Civil War have for modern America?

For an excellent summary treatment of the major results of the Civil War

see Carl Degler, *Out of Our Past: The Forces that Shaped Modern America**
(1959), Chapter VII. Alan Barker, *The Civil War in America** (1961), Chapters
I and IX, and Don E. Fehrenbacher, "Disunion and Reunion" in John
Higham, ed., *The Reconstruction of American History** (1962), discuss the
importance of the Civil War in American history. A popular work that catches
the significance of the conflict is Bruce Catton's *This Hallowed Ground**
(1956).

*Available in a paperback edition.

A MAJOR RESULT OF THE CIVIL WAR

ALLAN NEVINS

Thomas Carlyle shrank in horror from our Civil War. The fact that multi-tudes of Americans should take to butchering one another seemed to him an indictment of our democracy; the issue of the Negroes' status struck him as far from justifying such a holocaust of lives and property. His remark that the war was a fire in a dirty chimney, and his little fable called "Ilias Americana in Nuce" deeply offended the North.

Among the Northern soldiers who gave their lives were two gallant young men, Robert Gould Shaw and Charles Russell Lowell, who had warmly ad-mired Carlyle. Shaw, leader of Massachusetts colored troops, died in trying to capture Fort Wagner; Lowell who had married Shaw's sister Josephine, was slain at Cedar Creek. Both were graduates of Harvard. Three years after the war short biographies of them, and of ninety-five others who had been killed, appeared in the *Harvard Memorial Biographies*, edited by Thomas Went-worth Higginson. Thereupon Charles Lowell's young widow, Mrs. Josephine Shaw Lowell, sent the volumes to Carlyle, with a note describing their admira-tion of him, and a request that he read their lives, and reconsider his views on the war. Carlyle replied, in a letter here published for the first time:

CHELSEA—10 March, 1870

DEAR MADAM

I rec'd your gentle, kind and beautiful message, and in obedience to so touching a command, soft to me as sunlight or moonlight, but imperative as few could be, I have read those lines you marked for me; with several of the others and intend to read the whole before I finish. Many thanks to you for these Volumes and that note. It would need a heart much harder than mine not to recognize the high and noble spirit that dwelt in these young men, their heroic readiness, complete devotedness, their patience, diligence, shining valour & virtue in the cause they saw to be the highest—while alas any difference I may feel on that latter point, only deepens to me the sorrowful and noble tragedy [that] each of their brief lives is. You may believe me, Madam, I would strew flowers on their graves along with you, and piously bid them rest in Hope. It is not doubtful to me that they also have added their mite to what is the eternal cause

SOURCE. Allan Nevins, "A Major Result of the Civil War," *Civil War History*, V (1959), pp. 237–250. Copyright 1959 by The University of Iowa; rights now held by Kent State University. Reprinted by permission of the publisher.

of God and man; or that, in circuitous but sure ways, all men, Black & White, will infallibly get their profit out of the same.

With many thanks & regards, dear Madam, I remain

Yrs sincerely T. CARLYLE.

They "added their mite" to the "eternal cause of God and man." So Francis Parkman had earlier written Mrs. Robert Gould Shaw, saying that he envied her husband his death, so eloquent of the highest consecration.

Many of the gains and losses of any great war are intangible and incomputable. . . . Other gains and losses, some material, some moral, can partly be appraised. But in looking at the effects of the war, it is safe to lay down two generalizations at the outset: The tremendous magnitude of the change it wrought was not anticipated in its early phases, and the nature of the change was not and could not be accurately analyzed when it closed in 1865.

To be sure, some of its consequences *were* foreseen. Shrewd men perceived in 1861 that if the war was protracted and ended in Northern victory, it would strengthen not only the Union and the federal government, but the spirit of national unity. They perceived that it would result in the destruction of slavery. John Quincy Adams, indeed, had predicted a generation earlier that if civil conflict began, the government would use its war powers to extinguish slavery. Shrewd men also foresaw in 1861 that a long civil war, and the arming of the United States, would profoundly alter the world position of the republic and augment its authority in world affairs. Other changes were anticipated, and men did not hesitate to predict that their total effect would be revolutionary. In fact, as early as the autumn of 1861 the *New York Herald* prophesied (November 24) just this in a column editorial headed "The Great Rebellion: A Great Revolution." The war, said the *Herald,* was not only a great revolution in itself, but was causing many minor revolutions. . . .

Verily, in its effects the Civil War did constitute a revolution. In politics, for example, the old domination of the government by an alliance of agrarian interests of the South and West was overturned by a new alliance of the industrial East and grain-growing Northwest. But some of the predictions of change which men made most confidently in 1861 were utterly erroneous, while the most important single change flowing from the war was not grasped at the time and is not fully comprehended even today.

To understand the effects of the conflict we must venture certain generalizations—very broad generalizations. The first is that the results of a victorious war lie in the main in the positive sphere, those of defeat in the negative sphere. Success arouses a spirit of confidence, optimism, and enterprise not seen in a defeated society. For evidence of this assertion we may point to the exuberant spirit of Elizabethan England after the defeat of the Great Armada; the exuberant and even arrogant spirit of Germany after the Franco-Prussian War. The effects of the Civil War were positive in the North, negative in the embittered and depressed South. The second broad generalization is this: that no effect of war, no matter how marked it may appear to be for a time, will last if it runs counter to a long-continued and deeply felt national tradition. The third generalization is the converse of the second: That effect is greatest which harmonizes with and carries forward some tendency in national life already partly developed and growing, though it may still lie beneath the surface. For example, the Revolution, in the currents it set flowing, chimed with the belief of Americans that they had a plastic society which they could and should change to fit their ideals,with their confidence that they alone knew the secret of true liberty, and with their conviction that they were the predestined teachers of this liberty to the whole of mankind. . . .

One false prediction of 1861 illustrates the second of our generalizations. A favorite assertion was that the United States would become militarized. "Whether this war shall be long or short," said the *Springfield Republican* of June 4, 1861, "it is evident that hereafter we shall be a more military people." Some even prophesied that militarism would infect our politics, "Mexicanizing them" as the phrase then went—introducing the military dictator. Such ideas proved absurd. Our huge armies in 1865 melted almost overnight into civil life; military expenditures sank almost to zero, and the standing army to only 25,000 men; and the one President, Grant, who was elected primarily because of his military exploits became an object of strong public condemnation. Why did we not become militarized? Partly because no *continuing* peril existed. Wavers of the bloody shirt after the war sometimes tried to conjure up a continued peril from rebel brigadiers, but sensible men laughed at them. In the second place, and more importantly, militarization went completely against the long national tradition—indeed, against an Anglo-American tradition of five centuries; the same tradition which discarded all militarist tendencies after the first world war, and effected rapid disarmament just after the second.

What was the most important effect of the Civil War upon the character of the American people and the texture of society? Nobody would venture to say; but certainly one of the most important effects was, in an essentially inadequate phrase, the conversion of an unorganized nation into an organized nation, with an irresistible impetus toward greater and greater organization.

The United States in 1860 stood in almost as primitive a state of organization, socially and economically, as China in 1940. It was an agricultural country with a long historic belief in individualism; far more attached to the principle of self-reliance than to that of association. The shrewd French observer, Auguste Laugel, who wrote a book on the United States during the war, correctly stated, "There is a horror of all trammels, system, and uniformity." The population still lived close to the soil. Of the 8,200,000 whose occupations were noted by the census of 1860, 3,300,000 were farmers, planters, farm laborers, or stockmen, while as many more were indirectly connected with agriculture.

A few facts are signficant of the lack of organization: The country as yet had no standard time—Boston, New York, Philadelphia, and Washington each had its own time. It had no accepted gauge for railroads; the eight or more gauges ranged from three to six feet. The postal system was so wretched that in New York in 1856, ten million letters were delivered privately in contrast to one million carried by the government. In 1860 the American population slightly exceeded that of Great Britain; but that year Americans posted 184 million letters, while Great Britain posted 564 million. It had no national labor union worthy of the name; the typographers, iron molders, and hat-makers possessed unions, but they were shadowy bodies which did little more than meet and pass resolutions. The panic of 1857, indeed, had paralyzed the infant movement toward labor organization. It had few other organizations. Not one state bar association had been formed. Only two American cities in 1865 had paid fire departments. In all of New England in 1860 there were only three hospitals; in the entire South, four or five. The American Medical Association was twelve years old, but when the hour struck to establish medical and surgical services for the war, it was so feeble that nobody thought of using it. Three trunk-line railways had been established, for the Pennsylvania, the New York Central, and the Baltimore & Ohio could be termed interstate railroads. But ninety-five per cent of such manufacturing as existed was on a local basis and managed in small units. In fact, state laws of the time generally forbade corporations to hold property outside their own states except by special charter. Most business firms were managed as family affairs. Another significant detail is that in a country where whole libraries now groan with books on business organization and management, down to 1860 not one book—not one pamphlet—had been published on these subjects.

Modern organization, apart from politics, education, and religion, is built mainly on the machine, which is effective only with and through it. A mechanized country is of necessity an organized country; a land without machines is unorganized. Great Britain in 1860, with approximately the same population as the United States, was much better equipped with machine industry, and in consequence far better organized. With us, the industrial revolution was hardly beyond its beginnings. The partially mechanized area extending from Boston to Philadelphia was learning what organization meant, but learning slowly.

In just one broad field can the nation be said to have developed a considerable degree of organization before 1860: the field of westward expansion. Since the main fact in American life was the movement of population toward the setting sun, the major energies of the nation were channeled into its promotion.

The building of highways, canals, steamboats, and railroads to carry people west; the manufacture of plows, axes, drills, and harvesters to maintain them there; the production of arms to help them deal with Indians and wild beasts; the extension of churches, schools, and post offices to keep them linked with the older communities—all this was fairly well organized. Yet westward expansion was itself to some extent a disorganizing process, spreading civilization thin and straining the bonds of society.

This sprawling, inchoate country, much of it a veritable jellyfish, suddenly had to pull itself together; raise armies which (for the North alone) numbered 2,300,000 individuals before the war ended; clothe, arm, transport, and feed them; hospitalize many of them; obtain more than four billion dollars in taxes and loans; and, in short, make an effort then almost unprecedented in human history. To describe this effort in administrative outline would require a volume. To translate it into statistical tables would rob it of meaning. To suggest its scope, complexity, and impact, we can perhaps best deal with it in terms of a single individual—Montgomery C. Meigs, one of the key figures of the momentous change, for as quartermaster general he had charge of the spending of one and one-half billion dollars, half of the direct cost of the war to the North.

In any just view of the Civil War record, Quartermaster General Meigs ought to stand in relief as a central personage. He had charge of the spending of a vast amount of money, which he directed into channels that largely remade America. . . .

To say that Meigs was quartermaster general is to say little, for few people have any idea of that functionary's duties. To say that he, with the chief of ordnance and the commissary general, divided the entire work of equipping the two million Union soldiers for camp and field, drill and battle, is to do little better. Of the three, Meigs bore by far the heaviest responsibility. His duties included the procurement and distribution of uniforms, tents, horses, harness, wagons, ambulances, shoes, blankets, knapsacks, forage and a vast miscellany of other articles. His authority covered three-quarters of Northern industry. The Northern government, in July 1861, issued a call for 500,000 men. These men wore out shoes in two months and uniforms in four. They therefore needed 3,000,000 pairs of shoes and 1,500,000 uniforms a year. They needed mountains of arms, a hundred miles of wagons, great base hospitals, and an incredible amount of miscellaneous supplies.

The national government, be it remembered, had no War Production Board, no Priorities and Allocations Board, no possibility of any of the great administrative agencies developed in the two world wars; it had no basis for them. It had no organized partnership with industry, with labor, with agriculture, or with transportation, for they were all unorganized. Meigs had to create organization where none existed. In shaping government contract policy, he shaped much of the future economy of the United States. What share of contract should go to small manufacturers, what to large? How much should go to New England, and how much to the West? What part of the arms contracts, with dire necessity pressing the government, should go to slow American makers, and what part to Europeans who could make quick deliveries? Meigs rose magnificently to the initial crisis of supplying the hundreds of thousands who rushed to the colors in 1861. . . .

It was Meigs who set new standards for American shoe manufacture, finished early in the war almost wholly by hand, and hence in small lots, but before the end of the war by machinery in carload lots. Uniforms were lifted to the same quantity plane. It was Meigs who insisted that the army abandon for field use the large Adams and Sibley tents, which had to be transported by wagon, and use the little shelter tent portable on a soldier's back. It was Meigs who adapted French mess equipment for American use. He decided that the Northern armies were heavily overwagoned, and helped reshape their transport equipment. He read lectures to McClellan and other generals on the cruel and wasteful destruction of horses by undisciplined troops. He built temporary barracks; he even bought coal for army steamers. He had command of Grant's supply base at Fredericksburg and Belle Plain in 1864; and he took personal charge of the refitting of Sherman's worn army at Savannah in January, 1865.

By the close of 1862 the North had more than 1000 regiments, full or incomplete; each had its regimental quartermaster, who was required to send a monthly report to Washington with accounts; thus 12,000 accounts a year had to be settled.

Meigs's reward for all this is casual mention in James Ford Rhodes, a misspelling of his name by Carl Russell Fish, and almost total silence by other historians. So far as this neglect means the overlooking merely of one talented and devoted individual, it is of no great importance. But it is very important indeed as a symptom of the neglect of one key aspect of the war, its organizational side. Meigs was one of the organizers not merely of the war effort but of the modern America about to emerge, for he helped stimulate industry, systematize its efforts, and bring it into efficient operation for victory and for larger services after victory. His labors helped change the American character.

For the formless, protoplasmic United States of 1861 emerged from the war in 1865 at least half-organized and clearly conscious of the paths it would take forward. Under the forcing blast provided by government contracts, protective tariffs, and inflation a thousand businesses trebled or quadrupled in size. Government offices swelled to what would previously have seemed incredible proportions. A national banking system was created. More trunkline railroads began to take form. Truly national industries, reaching out for national as distinguished from local markets, appeared in flour milling, meat packing, clothing and shoe manufacture, and the making of machinery. Sir Morton Peto, coming to the United States in 1865 and finding the nation in the great throes of a happy boom, was struck with the evidences that not only capital but organizing ability was being invested in business as never before. The colonel of every regiment had learned a great deal about organization; and Peto walked into large industrial offices to hear the manager pointing out executives with the words, "That man was a colonel—the one at that desk yonder a major." The one fault he discerned was that they were all eager for too quick results.

Of great significance in this growth of organization was the instruction which Americans had received in the principles of capital formation and in the use of credit. While the national banking system was being organized, the government was floating its large bond issues. Jay Cooke, when the normal market was exhausted, undertook selling them in every street and hamlet. His canvassers sought far and wide for buyers; never before had so many men purchased securities. The greenbacks, the national bank notes used on bonds, and the ready extension of bank credit gave a powerful impetus to the industrial revolution and helped change the whole outlook of Americans.

The acceleration of investment and industrial expansion lasted until 1873, producing a remarkable array of new business captains, and accustoming the people to broader and bolder concepts of affairs. Not hitherto a nation, as Langel said, of "joiners," they had learned much from association in regiment and armies, in Union League Clubs and relief societies. They began to develop a spirit of voluntary combination which within a few years ran the gamut from the trusts and the grange to the GAR. By 1885 one of the most powerful organizers of modern times, John D. Rockefeller, was able to make his momentous pronouncement. "The age of individualism has gone, never to return."

This effort to organize the energies of the nation harmonized with a tendency in national life already partly formed in 1860 and, underneath the surface of affairs, vigorously growing; a tendency necessitated by the increase of population and other basic factors, and simply given extraordinary impetus by the war. Through this effort, as it was carried on after the war, ran a vibrant self-confidence: the exuberance of victory, the pride of a record of service. . . .

Tens of thousands of Union veterans came back from the hard lessons of war with this self-confidence born of success, and this pride born of duty done. Tens of thousands of civilians who had built machine shops, run arms factories, filled contracts for shovels, canned foods, and blankets, or managed recruiting, income tax collection, or home relief, felt the same combination of experience, confidence, and pride. Men thought in larger terms. The day of small affairs began to pass; the family firm gave way to the joint stock corporation; visions of great undertakings became common. Improvisation yielded to hardheaded planning and individualism to disciplined action. In the eight years before the postwar spent itself, the continent was spanned by the rails of the Union Pacific; Carnegie and Abram S. Hewitt respectively founded the Bessemer and open-hearth steel industries; the first big industrial pools were formed; two specially chaotic businesses, oil and tobacco, were taken in hand by Rockefeller and Duke. Labor organized the National Union; farmers organized the National Grange. Research and invention began to be organized.

Of all the changes effected by the war, this replacement of an amorphous, spineless society by a national life organized for efficient action—organized first to win the conflict, and after that for peace—was one of the greatest. The first two years of the Civil War might be called "the improvised war"; the second two years, "the organized war." The transition from one to the other was a transition from the old America to the new. It was accompanied with a corresponding alteration in the national psychology. Men's ideas were thrown into new patterns. Americans still detested regimentation; but they had learned the power—the necessity—of voluntary combination for definite objects, leaving themselves perfectly free in all other relations.

This emergence of a society organized on national lines reinforced the political nationalism generated by the conflict. It was a war for the nation as a unit; for centripetal as opposed to centrifugal impulses. We are all aware of the strength of state attachments in the prewar South. Robert E. Lee and Joseph E. Johnston, for example, fought with the Confederacy not because they approved of slavery, or endorsed secession, but because they loved Virginia. An intransigent State Rights spirit gravely crippled the Southern effort. But while we all know this, few comprehend the strength of state and regional feeling in the prewar North. General John Pope gravely proposed, early in the conflict, that all Illinois troops be used in a separate Illinois army, to be kept intact under Illinois commanders, and some Indiana officers made the same proposal for Indiana troops. The early distrust of Lincoln by such Easterners as Charles Francis Adams was founded on sectional feeling. What good leadership could come out of the raw West? Our literature before the war was not truly national; in sentiment as in the geographic distribution of authors and publishers, it was a literature of New England and New York.

Out of the furnace heat of war, in the North, came a true national passion. It would be erroneous to say that the East learned that the Westerner Grant was the Union's greatest soldier, and wept for the Westerner Lincoln as the West wept. In great degree, men simply ceased to think of themselves as Vermonters or Ohioans, Easterners or Westerners; they were Americans, and Grant and Lincoln were American leaders. I do not find the great Northern upsurge of excitement and patriotic fervor just after Fort Sumter impressive; it reflected too much cheap, frothy excitement and too little earnest, thoughtful planning. But it was at least an upsurge of national feeling, which grew stronger as the conflict went on. The long succession of disasters did as much for Northern unity as final Northern victory. It is obvious that the new spirit of nationalism profoundly reinforced the new spirit of organization.

From the world point of view, also, the replacement of a formless, amoebic America by a nation sturdily pursuing the path of organized growth was one of the most important results of the war. As we know, the abolition of slavery and the triumph of the North were telling blows for the cause of liberalism throughout the world. They constituted a vindication of democracy. The Englishman A. V. Dicey, talking with an emigrant Irishwoman in the States during the war, heard her say, "This is a blessed country, sir. I think God made it for the poor." No longer could conservative Europe respond to such statements with the jeer, "What about your slaves?" Lincoln in his Gettysburg Address placed the war in its world setting as a war to keep the hope of government of, by, and for the people alive for all mankind. John Bright, in the most famous of his many wartime defenses of America, put the conflict in the same setting. Old world privilege, he said, had a great stake in the defeat and frustration of the American democracy. . . .

Bright had been sure, even while the war was most doubtful, that the Union would succeed. He did not believe that disunion and slavery could triumph. . . .

It is impossible to deny the value to the world of the vindication of American democracy embodied in the Emancipation Proclamation and the restoration of the Union on a foundation at last built for the ages. No one would underestimate the importance of these results in contributing to the advance in British democracy shortly registered in the second Reform Act [1867], to the unification of Italy and Germany, and to the stimulation of democratic currents in France, where such haters of Napoleon III as Laboulaye had been staunch wartime defenders of the Northern cause. The victorious emergence of the nation from its trial seemed a victory for world liberalism—for the ideas of Bright and Cobden, Mazzini and Gambetta. The belief of Americans that the Civil War had given the republic that "new birth of freedom" of which Lincoln had spoken, and that America had greater lessons of liberty than ever to teach other lands, was expressed with emphasis by the most idealistic voices in our midst—by Whittier in his poem on the first autumn of peace, for example, and by Lowell in his ode for the Fourth of July, 1876, and by Emerson in his address on "The Fortunes of the Republic" in 1878, the last address he made.

Nevertheless, without underrating this impetus to liberalism, we can say that in the long run the greatest consequence of the war for the globe was the replacement of the awkward, unformed, immature nation of 1860 by the confident, purposeful, systematized nation of 1870. What had been gristle, in Burke's phrase, became bone. Once economic and social organization had gained momentum, it achieved new goals every year. We might instance a thousand men, trained in the war, who carried the change forward. One son of the Union, Francis A. Walker, would be as good an example as any. He began his career learning lessons of organization as a private in the Second Corps of the Army of the Potomac; he continued it by organizing a Federal Bureau of Statistics and a Census Bureau which became models for other lands; and he ended it by organizing the Massachusetts Institute of Technology, of which he was the true maker, a system for training engineers admired and imitated both abroad and at home. The United States strode forward, applying greater and greater system to its natural wealth, until by 1900 it was the most powerful and in many ways the best-organized industrial nation in the world.

Its great rival was Germany, which had been given a similar access of energy and self-confidence by the War of 1870, and which with its compact population and sharp economic necessities displayed an even greater bent toward organization. The two came into collision in 1917—the great exemplar of military and autocratic organization, and the great examplar of peaceful and democratic organization. Well it was that the United States had received an impulse toward disciplining and systematizing its energies as early as it did. While the first world war was still raging, the genius of technology gave birth on American soil to a great new world force—mass production, a new method of applying half a dozen components—system, speed, precision, continuous motion, uniformity, economy—to the quantity manufacture of complex engines of wealth and war. Only a highly organized nation could have brought forth this revolutionary implement called mass production, which has done so much to revolutionize the modern world, and only a nation armed with it could have won World War II.

As the United States became an organized nation, much that was ugly crept into American life. Insofar as discipline is antithetical to individual freedom, it is unpleasant, even repellent. Organization undeniably raised the standards of welfare in our society, enabling more people decade by decade to live in greater comfort and well-being. At the same time, however, it increased the strain of materialism in the United States, making people all too intent upon mere wealth and comfort. Our civilization seemed coarser, greedier, and more aggressive, than in the quiet prewar days. The country that men had died for in the 1860's seemed hardly worth the sacrifice in the 1870's and 1880's. But this was a temporary phase, which by the last decade of the century was being forgotten as new currents of radicalism and idealism made themselves felt. The nation needed the iron strength forged in the war for the great tasks that lay ahead of it. It needed the lessons of organization and association it had learned if it was to play a powerful part in world affairs, and improve its national life at home. Walt Whitman struck the right note when he called upon it to forget the errors of the past and face the challenge of the future. . . .

Even in the generation after the war, however, many remembered its truer lessons. No inconsiderable body of veterans could say what Captain Oliver Wendell Holmes, Jr.—the wounded captain whom the Autocrat of the Breakfast Table sought on the field of Antietam—said: "In our youth our hearts were touched with fire. It was given us to learn at the outset that life is a profound and passionate thing. While we are permitted to scorn nothing but indifference, and do not undervalue the wordly rewards of ambition, we have seen with our own eyes, above and beyond the gold fields, the snowy heights of honor, and it is for us to bear the report to those who come after us."

We come after, and we can hear the report; by taking it to heart our generation can redress the balance a little. Let us not cease to regard the war as proof of a breakdown of American statesmanship, and let us conceal nothing of its cruel, ignoble side. But we should make the most of its inspirations. Charles Eliot Norton said that on the whole he thought the character of Lincoln the greatest single gain of the nation from the war. Lincoln's ability to awaken the North to the moral issues bound up in the conflict; his conviction that the struggle must be fought through for the sake of man's vast future; his patience in adversity; his fortitude in defeat, his magnanimity in victory, can never be staled or lost. Beside him stands Lee; not Lee the warrior, but Lee the man—the Christian gentleman who lived a life of stainless purity, whose innate modesty never failed him, who like Grant was free from any trace of vainglory, whose consecration to duty never flagged—who, in a word, set an unsurpassable example of character. Behind these figures we have the humble soldiers from South and North alike who fought on one red field after another with unyielding courage, always ready to give up their young lives for what they deemed threatened principle and imperiled liberty.

A freshened remembrance of these inspiring elements can contribute an idealism counteractive of the materialism that accompanied the necessary work of national organization. It will justify for all the dead the statement that Carlyle made of Charles Lowell and Robert Gould Shaw, that they added each his "mite to the eternal cause of God and man."

CHAPTER 3

RECONSTRUCTION: LEGEND AND LEGACY

Until the mid-twentieth century, the Reconstruction years had traditionally been considered a bleak period in American history—a time of harshness, of violence, of corruption, and of an erroneous faith in the political maturity of the ex-slaves. "The prevailing note," wrote historian Claude G. Bowers, "was one of tragedy." According to his widely shared views, the era was one of destruction rather than reconstruction, during which neither the rebuilding of the devastated South nor a binding up of the nation's wounds occurred. These tasks had to await "redemption"—the overthrowing of the Radical governments in the South. This traditional view, somewhat modified, still prevails in many history books, although historians have long since challenged its salient points. Historical myths die hard, particularly when those myths concern a subject as complex and as varied as Reconstruction, and when they stem from deep-seated racial and sectional prejudices. Where treatment of Reconstruction has of necessity to be brief, it is unfortunate, but not surprising, that this treatment is often superficial and misleading.

In this selection Kenneth M. Stampp discusses the legend and the myths of Reconstruction. He points out the striking dissimilarity in popular legend, and in much serious history, between the treatment of the Civil War, which is seen as gallant and glorious, and that of the Reconstruction years, which are considered shameful and base. He contends that the romanticized view of the Civil War is essentially harmless, but that the unhistorical legend of Reconstruction has had a detrimental impact on the political behavior of many Americans. Professor Stampp presents a capsule summary of the "tragic legend" of Reconstruction, describes briefly the revisionists' challenges to traditional interpretations, and discusses the birth and endurance of the "tragic legend."

In reading this essay, students should seek to determine Stampp's own view of Reconstruction. Does Stampp deny that there was an element of tragedy

in Reconstruction? Does he find any heroes of the era who made positive
contributions to American history? Finally, students would do well to ponder
the fact that the revisionist challenge to the Reconstruction legend began to
emerge at about the same time that social scientists began to revise their ideas
about race. What does this say about the uses and misuses of History? What
does it say about each individual's ability to interpret maturely a past in which
a minority race played a major role?

Claude G. Bowers' *The Tragic Era* (1929), spotlights the tragic legend. C.
Vann Woodward discusses the legacy of Reconstruction in *The Burden of
Southern History* (1960), and in *Origins of the New South, 1877–1913* (1951).
Students might also read Grady McWhiney's essay on Reconstruction in
Charles G. Sellers, Jr., ed., *The Southerner As American* (1960), and other
portions of Kenneth M. Stampp, *The Era of Reconstruction, 1865–1877*
(1965). A scholarly account by a black historian is John Hope Franklin,
Reconstruction after the Civil War (1961).

*Available in a paperback edition.

THE TRAGIC LEGEND OF RECONSTRUCTION

KENNETH M. STAMPP

In much serious history, as well as in a durable popular legend, two American epochs—the Civil War and the reconstruction that followed—bear an odd relationship to one another. The Civil War, though admittedly a tragedy, is nevertheless often described as a glorious time of gallantry, noble self-sacrifice, and high idealism. Even historians who have considered the war "needless" and have condemned the politicians of the 1850's for blundering into it, once they passed the firing on Fort Sumter, have usually written with reverence about Civil War heroes—the martyred Lincoln, the Christlike Lee, the intrepid Stonewall Jackson, and many others in this galaxy of demigods.

Few, of course, are so innocent as not to know that the Civil War had its seamy side. One can hardly ignore the political opportunism, the graft and profiteering in the filling of war contracts, the military blundering and needless loss of lives, the horrors of army hospitals and prison camps, and the ugly depths as well as the nobility of human nature that the war exposed with a fine impartiality. These things cannot be ignored, but they can be, and frequently are, dismissed as something alien to the essence of the war years. What was real and fundamental was the idealism and the nobility of the two contending forces: the Yankees struggling to save the Union, dying to make men free; the Confederates fighting for great constitutional principles, defending their homes from invasion. Here, indeed, is one of the secrets of the spell the Civil War has cast: it involved high-minded Americans on both sides, and there was glory enough to go around. This, in fact, is the supreme synthesis of Civil War historiography and the great balm that has healed the nation's wounds: Yankees and Confederates alike fought bravely for what they believed to be just causes. There were few villains in the drama.

But when the historian reaches the year 1865, he must take leave of the war and turn to another epoch, reconstruction, when the task was, in Lincoln's words, "to bind up the nation's wounds" and "to do all which may achieve and cherish a just and lasting peace." How, until recently, reconstruction was

SOURCE. Kenneth M. Stampp, *The Era of Reconstruction, 1865–1877,* pp.3–15, and 23. Copyright 1965 by Kenneth M. Stampp. Reprinted by permission of Alfred A. Knopf, Inc.

portrayed in both history and legend, how sharply it was believed to contrast with the years of the Civil War, is evident in the terms that were used to identify it. Various historians have called this phase of American history "The Tragic Era," "The Dreadful Decade," "The Age of Hate," and "The Blackout of Honest Government." Reconstruction represented the ultimate shame of the American people—as one historian phrased it, "the nadir of national disgrace." It was the epoch that most Americans wanted to forget.

Claude Bowers, who divided his time between politics and history, has been the chief disseminator of the traditional picture of reconstruction, for his book, *The Tragic Era,* published in 1929, has attracted more readers than any other dealing with this period. For Bowers reconstruction was a time of almost unrelieved sordidness in public and private life; whole regiments of villains march through his pages: the corrupt politicians who dominated the administration of Ulysses S. Grant; the crafty, scheming northern carpetbaggers who invaded the South after the war for political and economic plunder; the degraded and depraved southern scalawags who betrayed their own people and collaborated with the enemy; and the ignorant, barbarous, sensual Negroes who threatened to Africanize the South and destroy its Caucasian civilization.

Most of Bowers's key generalizations can be found in his preface. The years of reconstruction, he wrote, "were years of revolutionary turmoil, with the elemental passions predominant. . . . The prevailing note was one of tragedy. . . . Never have American public men in responsible positions, directing the destiny of the nation, been so brutal, hypocritical, and corrupt. The constitution was treated as a doormat on which politicians and army officers wiped their feet after wading in the muck. . . . The southern people literally were put to the torture . . . [by] rugged conspirators . . . [who] assumed the pose of philanthropists and patriots." The popularity of Bowers's book stems in part from the simplicity of his characters. None are etched in shades of gray; none are confronted with complex moral decisions. Like characters in a Victorian romance, the Republican leaders of the reconstruction era were evil through and through, and the helpless, innocent white men of the South were totally noble and pure.

If Bowers's prose is more vivid and his anger more intense, his general interpretation of reconstruction is only a slight exaggeration of a point of view shared by most serious American historians from the late nineteenth century until very recently. Writing in the 1890's, James Ford Rhodes, author of a multi-volumed history of the United States since the Compromise of 1850, branded the Republican scheme of reconstruction as "repressive" and "uncivilized," one that "pandered to the ignorant negroes, the knavish white natives and the vulturous adventurers who flocked from the North." About the same time Professor John W. Burgess, of Columbia University, called reconstruction the "most soul-sickening spectacle that Americans had ever

been called upon to behold." Early in the twentieth century Professor William
A. Dunning, also of Columbia University, and a group of talented graduate
students wrote a series of monographs that presented a crushing indictment
of the Republican reconstruction program in the South—a series that made
a deep and lasting impression on American historians. In the 1930's, Professor
James G. Randall, of the University of Illinois, still writing in the spirit of the
Dunningites, described the reconstruction era "as a time of party abuse, of
corruption, of vindictive bigotry." "To use a modern phrase," wrote Randall,
"government under Radical Republican rule in the South had become a kind
of 'racket.' As late as 1947, Professor E. Merton Coulter, of the University
of Georgia, reminded critics of the traditional interpretation that no "amount
of revision can write away the grievous mistakes made in this abnormal period
of American history." Thus, from Rhodes and Burgess and Dunning to Randall and Coulter the central emphasis of most historical writing about reconstruction has been upon sordid motives and human depravity. Somehow,
during the summer of 1865, the nobility and idealism of the war years had died.

A synopsis of the Dunning School's version of reconstruction would run
something like this: Abraham Lincoln, while the Civil War was still in progress, turned his thoughts to the great problem of reconciliation; and, "with
malice toward none and charity for all," this gentle and compassionate man
devised a plan that would restore the South to the Union with minimum
humiliation and maximum speed. But there had already emerged in Congress
a faction of radical Republicans, sometimes called Jacobins or Vindictives,
who sought to defeat Lincoln's generous program. Motivated by hatred of the
South, by selfish political ambitions, and by crass economic interests, the
radicals tried to make the process of reconstruction as humiliating, as difficult,
and as prolonged as they possibly could. Until Lincoln's tragic death, they
poured their scorn upon him—and then used his coffin as a political stump to
arouse the passions of the northern electorate.

The second chapter of the Dunning version begins with Andrew Johnson's
succession to the presidency. Johnson, the old Jacksonian Unionist from
Tennessee, took advantage of the adjournment of Congress to put Lincoln's
mild plan of reconstruction into operation, and it was a striking success. In
the summer and fall of 1865, Southerners organized loyal state governments,
showed a willingness to deal fairly with their former slaves, and in general
accepted the outcome of the Civil War in good faith. In December, when
Congress assembled, President Johnson reported that the process of reconstruction was nearly completed and that the old Union had been restored. But
the radicals unfortunately had their own sinister purposes; they repudiated the
governments Johnson had established in the South, refused to seat southern
Senators and Representatives, and then directed their fury against the new
President. After a year of bitter controversy and political stalemate, the radi-

cals, resorting to shamefully demagogic tactics, won an overwhelming victory in the congressional elections of 1866.

Now, the third chapter and the final tragedy. Riding roughshod over presidential vetoes and federal courts, the radicals put the South under military occupation, gave the ballot to Negroes, and formed new southern state governments dominated by base and corrupt men, black and white. Not satisfied with reducing the South to political slavery and financial bankruptcy, the radicals even laid their obscene hands on the pure fabric of the federal Constitution. They impeached President Johnson and came within one vote of removing him from office, though they had no legal grounds for such action. Next, they elected Ulysses S. Grant President, and during his two administrations they indulged in such an orgy of corruption and so prostituted the civil service as to make Grantism an enduring symbol of political immorality.

The last chapter is the story of ultimate redemption. Decent southern white Democrats, their patience exhausted, organized to drive the Negroes, carpetbaggers, and scalawags from power, peacefully if possible, forcefully if necessary. One by one the southern states were redeemed, honesty and virtue triumphed, and the South's natural leaders returned to power. In the spring of 1877, the Tragic Era finally came to an end when President Hayes withdrew the federal troops from the South and restored home rule. But the legacy of radical reconstruction remained in the form of a solidly Democratic South and embittered relations between the races.

This point of view was rarely challenged until the 1930's, when a small group of revisionist historians began to give new life and a new direction to the study of reconstruction. The revisionists are a curious lot who sometimes quarrel with each other as much as they quarrel with the disciples of Dunning. At various times they have counted in their ranks Marxists of various degrees of orthodoxy, Negroes seeking historical vindication, skeptical white Southerners, and latter-day northern abolitionists. But among them are numerous scholars who have the wisdom to know that the history of an age is seldom simple and clear-cut, seldom without its tragic aspects, seldom without its redeeming virtues.

Few revisionists would claim that the Dunning interpretation of reconstruction is a pure fabrication. They recognize the shabby aspects of this era: the corruption was real, the failures obvious, the tragedy undeniable. Grant is not their idea of a model President, nor were the southern carpetbag governments worthy of their unqualified praise. They understand that the radical Republicans were not all selfless patriots, and that southern white men were not all Negro-hating rebels. In short, they have not turned history on its head, but rather, they recognize that much of what Dunning's disciples have said about reconstruction is true.

Revisionists, however, have discovered that the Dunningites overlooked a great deal, and they doubt that nobility and idealism suddenly died in 1865. They are neither surprised nor disillusioned to find that the Civil War, for all its nobility, revealed some of the ugliness of human nature as well. And they approach reconstruction with the confident expectation that here, too, every facet of human nature will be exposed. They are not satisfied with the two-dimensional characters that Dunning's disciples have painted.

What is perhaps most puzzling in the legend of reconstruction is the notion that the white people of the South were treated with unprecedented burtality, that their conquerors, in Bowers's colorful phrase, literally put them to the torture. How, in fact, *were* they treated after the failure of their rebellion against the authority of the federal government? The great mass of ordinary Southerners who voluntarily took up arms, or in other ways supported the Confederacy, were required simply to take an oath of allegiance to obtain pardon and to regain their right to vote and hold public office. But what of the Confederate leaders—the men who held high civil offices, often after resigning similar federal offices; the military leaders who had graduated from West Point and had resigned commissions in the United States Army to take commissions to the Confederate Army? Were there mass arrests, indictments for treason or conspiracy, trials and convictions, executions or imprisonments? Nothing of the sort. Officers of the Confederate Army were paroled and sent home with their men. After surrendering at Appomattox, General Lee bid farewell to his troops and rode home to live his remaining years undisturbed. Only one officer, a Captain Henry Wirtz, was arrested; and he was tried, convicted, and executed, not for treason or conspiracy, but for "war crimes." Wirtz's alleged offense, for which the evidence was rather flimsy, was the mistreatment of prisoners of war in the military prison at Andersonville, Georgia.

Of the Confederate civil officers, a handful were arrested at the close of the war, and there was talk for a time of trying a few for treason. But none, actually, was ever brought to trial, and all but Jefferson Davis were released within a few months. The former Confederate President was held in prison for nearly two years, but in 1867 he too was released. With a few exceptions, even the property of Confederate leaders was untouched, save, of course, for the emancipation of their slaves. Indeed, the only penalty imposed on most Confederate leaders was a temporary political disability provided in the Fourteenth Amendment. But in 1872 Congress pardoned all but a handful of Southerners; and soon former Confederate civil and military leaders were serving as state governors, as members of Congress, and even as Cabinet advisers of Presidents.

What, then, constituted the alleged brutality that white Southerners endured? First, the freeing of their slaves; second, the brief incarceration of a few Confederate leaders; third, a political disability imposed for a few years on most Confederate leaders; fourth, a relatively weak military occupation terminated in 1877; and, last, an attempt to extend the rights and privileges of citizenship to southern Negroes. Mistakes there were in the implementation of these measures—some of them serious—but brutality almost none. In fact, it can be said that rarely in history have the participants in an unsuccessful rebellion endured penalties as mild as those Congress imposed upon the people of the South, and particularly upon their leaders. After four years of bitter struggle costing hundreds of thousands of lives, the generosity of the federal government's terms was quite remarkable.

If northern brutality is a myth, the scandals of the Grant administration and the peculations of some of the southern reconstruction governments are sordid facts. Yet even here the Dunningites are guilty of distortion by exaggeration, by a lack of perspective, by superficial analysis, and by overemphasis. They make corruption a central theme of their narratives, but they overlook constructive accomplishments. They give insufficient attention to the men who transcended the greed of an age when, to be sure, self-serving politicians and irresponsible entrepreneurs were all too plentiful. Among these men were the humanitarians who organized Freedmen's Aid Societies to help four million southern Negroes make the difficult transition from slavery to freedom, and the missionaries and teachers who went into the South on slender budgets to build churches and schools for the freedmen. Under their auspices the Negroes first began to learn the responsibilities and obligations of freedom. Thus the training of Negroes for citizenship had its successful beginnings in the years of reconstruction.

In the nineteenth century most white Americans, North and South, had reservations about the Negro's potentialities—doubted that he had the innate intellectual capacity and moral fiber of the white man and assumed that after emancipation he would be relegated to an inferior caste. But some of the radical Republicans refused to believe that the Negroes were innately inferior and hoped passionately that they would confound their critics. The radicals then had little empirical evidence and no scientific evidence to support their belief—nothing, in fact, but faith. Their faith was derived mostly from their religion: all men, they said, are the sons of Adam and equal in the sight of God. And if Negroes are equal to white men in the sight of God, it is morally wrong for white men to withhold from Negroes the liberties and rights that white men enjoy. Here, surely, was a projection into the reconstruction era of the idealism of the abolitionist crusade and of the Civil War.

Radical idealism was in part responsible for two of the most momentous enactments of the reconstruction years: the Fourteenth Amendment to the federal Constitution which gave Negroes citizenship and promised them equal protection of the laws, and the Fifteenth Amendment which gave them the right to vote. The fact that these amendments could not have been adopted under any other circumstances, or at any other time, before or since, may suggest the crucial importance of the reconstruction era in American history. Indeed, without radical reconstruction, it would be impossible to this day for the federal government to protect Negroes from legal and political discrimination.

If all of this is true, or even part of it, why was the Dunning legend born, and why has it been so durable? Southerners, of course, have contributed much to the legend of reconstruction, but most Northerners have found the legend quite acceptable. Many of the historians who helped to create it were Northerners, among them James Ford Rhodes, William A. Dunning, Claude Bowers, and James G. Randall. Thus the legend cannot be explained simply in terms of a southern literary or historiographical conspiracy, satisfying as the legend has been to most white Southerners. What we need to know is why it also satisfies Northerners—how it became part of the intellectual paggage of so many northern historians. Why, in short, was there for so many years a kind of national, or inter-sectional, consensus that the Civil War was America's glory and reconstruction her disgrace?!

The Civil War won its place in the hearts of the American people because, by the end of the nineteenth century, Northerners were willing to concede that Southerners had fought bravely for a cause that they believed to be just; whereas Southerners, with a few exceptions, were willing to concede that the outcome of the war was probably best for all concerned. In an era of intense nationalism, both Northerners and Southerners agreed that the preservation of the federal Union was essential to the future power of the American people. Southerners could even say now that the abolition of slavery was one of the war's great blessings—not so much, they insisted, because slavery was an injustice to the Negroes but because it was a grievous burden upon the whites. By 1886, Henry W. Grady, the great Georgia editor and spokesman for a New South, could confess to a New York audience: "I am glad that the omniscient God held the balance of battle in His Almighty hand, and that human slavery was swept forever from American soil—the American Union saved from the wreck of war." Soon Union and Confederate veterans were holding joint reunions, exchanging anecdotes, and sharing their sentimental memories of those glorious war years. The Civil War thus took its position in the center of American folk mythology.

That the reconstruction era elicits neither pride nor sentimentality is due only in part to its moral delinquencies—remember, those in the Civil War years can be overlooked. It is also due to the white American's ambivalent attitude toward race and toward the steps that radical Republicans took to protect the Negroes. Southern white men accepted the Thirteenth Amendment to the Constitution, which abolished slavery, with a minimum of complaint, but they expected federal intervention to proceed no further than that. They assumed that the regulation of the freedmen would be left to the individual states; and clearly most of them intended to replace slavery with a caste system that would keep the Negroes perpetually subordinate to the whites. Negroes were to remain a dependent laboring class; they were to be governed by a separate code of laws; they were to play no active part in the South's political life; and they were to be segregated socially. When radical Republicans used federal power to interfere in these matters, the majority of southern white men formed a resistance movement to fight the radical-dominated state governments until they were overthrown, after which southern whites established a caste system in defiance of federal statutes and constitutional amendments. For many decades thereafter the federal government simply admitted defeat and acquiesced; but the South refused to forget or forgive those years of humiliation when Negroes came close to winning equality. In southern mythology, then, reconstruction was a horrid nightmare.

As for the majority of northern white men, it is hard to tell how deeply they were concerned about the welfare of the American Negro after the abolition of slavery. If one were to judge from the way they treated the small number of free Negroes who resided in the northern states, one might conclude that they were, at best, indifferent to the problem—and that a considerable number of them shared the racial attitudes of the South and preferred to keep Negroes in a subordinate caste. For a time after the Civil War the radical Republicans, who were always a minority group, persuaded the northern electorate that the ultimate purpose of southern white men was to rob the North of the fruits of victory and to re-establish slavery and that federal intervention was therefore essential. In this manner radicals won approval of, or acquiescence in, their program to give civil rights and the ballot to southern Negroes. Popular support for the radical program waned rapidly, however, and by the middle of the 1870's it had all but vanished. In 1875 a Republican politician confessed that northern voters were tired of the "worn-out cry of 'southern outrages,'" and they wished that "the 'nigger' the 'everlasting nigger' were in—Africa." As Northerners ceased to worry about the possibility of another southern rebellion, they became increasingly receptive to criticism of radical reconstruction. . . .

In the course of time . . . social scientists [have] drastically revised their notions about race, and in recent years most of them have been striving to destroy the errors in whose creation their predecessors played so crucial a part. As ideas about race have changed, historians have become increasingly critical of the Dunning interpretation of reconstruction. These changes, together with a great deal of painstaking research, have produced the revisionist writing of the past generation. It is dangerous, of course, for a historian to label himself as a revisionist, for his ultimate and inevitable fate is one day to have his own revisions revised.

But that has never discouraged revisionists, and we may hope that it never will, especially those who have been rewriting the history of the reconstruction era. One need not be disturbed about the romantic nonsense that still fills the minds of many Americans about their Civil War. This folklore is essentially harmless. But the legend of reconstruction is another matter. It has had serious consequences, because it has exerted a powerful influence upon the political behavior of many white men, North and South.

CHAPTER 4

THE INDIANS' LAST STAND: THE RESISTANCE OF CHIEF JOSEPH AND THE NEZ PERCÉS

To a very large degree, United States history, as presented in the school-books and classrooms of this nation, has been marked by a pervasive ethnocentrism. Traditionally, American history has been the experience in this country of the transplanted Western Europeans—not the Afro-Americans, the Mexican-Americans, or even the white but non-English-speaking immigrants of the post-Civil War period—and their descendants. Nor have the original inhabitants of this country, the Indians, been accorded an integral role in the American story. In standard historical treatment, the Indian has been ignored and stereotyped and thus has been robbed of human individuality and worthiness. Generally, Indians have been presented in negative terms as obstacles in the path of American progress rather than as people who made their own contribution to the American heritage.

In *The Patriot Chiefs,* a study of the long history of Indian resistance, Alvin M. Josephy, Jr. presents the Indians on their own terms, as people who had to face grave threats and crises and who acted and reacted, fought and struggled, and counseled and bargained in desperate attempts to preserve their lives and their way of life. The Indians were, of course, merely human beings; they were not all brave or heroic or noble. But Josephy recognizes that they were historical agents who actively sought to shape their own destiny. And some of the great Indian leaders—the patriot chiefs—were men of heroic stature. They are a part of our American heritage and they belong, Josephy maintains, not just to Indians but to all Americans. In the following selection, Josephy describes the resistance of Chief Joseph and the Nez Percés and their ultimate conquest by the whites. In the essay Chief Joseph emerges as a realistic historical figure. A strong and extraordinarily articulate leader, he was nevertheless doomed to end his life as an exile from the beautiful valley homeland of his people; as a consequence Chief Joseph is a fitting symbol of the tragic confrontation between white men and red men that has characterized the history of this nation.

In reading this selection, students should concentrate on the human aspects of the story and try to picture themselves in the place of Chief Joseph and his besieged people. Students would be well advised to consider the following questions. Was the conflict between the whites and the Nez Percés inevitable? Why? If this confrontation was typical of those between whites and Indians, what does this say about American claims that this nation was founded on principles of justice and concern for human rights? Finally, how much is the "Indian problem" still with us, and what does Josephy suggest is the best approach for its solution?

The student who wishes to read further on the subject of Chief Joseph and the Nez Percés should consult Alvin M. Josephy, Jr., *The Nez Percé Indians and the Opening of the Northwest** (1965). Ralph K. Andrist, *The Long Death: The Last Days of the Plains Indians** (1964), is an excellent treatment of the conquest of the Plains Indians, and in *Bury My Heart at Wounded Knee,** Dee Brown provides an entralling pro-Indian version of the events leading to the infamous massacre in 1890 that signaled the end of overt Indian resistance. Helen Hunt Jackson, *A Century of Dishonor** (1887), is a contemporary account of Indian problems in the late nineteenth century. For excellent general treatments of American Indians, see Ruth M. Underhill, *Red Man's America** (1953), Clark Wissler, *Indians of the United States** (1940), and Alvin M. Josephy, Jr., *The Indian Heritage of America** (1971).

*Available in a paperback edition.

THE LAST STAND OF CHIEF JOSEPH

ALVIN M. JOSEPHY, JR.

In June 1877, just one year after the Custer debacle, an unexpected Indian outbreak flared in the West. To an American public wearied and disgusted with a governmental policy, or lack of policy, that seemed to breed Indian wars, this one, an uprising by formerly peaceful Nez Percés of Oregon and Idaho, was dramatized by what appeared to be superb Indian generalship. One army detachment after another, officered by veterans of the Civil War, floundered in battle with the hostiles. Western correspondents telegraphed the progress of a great thirteen-hundred-mile fighting retreat by the Indians, swaying popular imagination in behalf of the valiant Nez Percés and their leader, Chief Joseph, who, as handsome and noble in appearance as a Fenimore Cooper Indian, became something of a combined national hero and military genius.

The government received no laurels, either, as the long trail of bitter injustices that had originally driven the Nez Percés to hostility became known. The war, like most Indian troubles, had stemmed from a conflict over land. For centuries the Nez Percés had occupied the high, grassy hills and canyon-scarred plateau land where Washington, Oregon, and Idaho come together. A strong and intelligent people, they had lived in peace with the whites since the coming of Lewis and Clark in 1805, and it was their proud boast that no member of the tribe had ever killed a white man.

Joseph was the leader of only one of the Nez Percé bands, a group of some sixty males and perhaps twice that number of women and children, who lived in the Wallowa Valley in the northeastern corner of Oregon. Isolated on all sides by natural barriers of high mountain ranges and some of the deepest gorges on the continent, the valley's lush grasslands provided some of the best grazing ground in the Northwest, and settlers were particularly anxious to possess it. But Joseph's band of Nez Percés had lived there in security and peace for generations, and just before he died in 1871 Joseph's father, a prominent chief named Wellamotkin, known familiarly to the whites as Old Joseph, had fearfully counseled his son: "When I am gone, think of your country. You are the chief of these people. They look to you to guide them.

SOURCE. Alvin M. Josephy, Jr., *The Patriot Chiefs: A Chronicle of American Indian Resistance*, pp. 313–315, 321–325, and 335–346. Copyright 1958 by Alvin M. Josephy, Jr. Reprinted by permission of The Viking Press, Inc.

Always remember that your father never sold the country. You must stop your ears whenever you are asked to sign a treaty selling your home. A few years more, and the white man will be all around you. They have their eyes on this land. My son, never forget my dying words. This country holds your father's body. Never sell the bones of your father and your mother."

The crisis came for Joseph almost immediately after his father's death. He was thirty-one years old, a tall and powerfully built man with the philosophical bent and strong and logical mind of a civil, rather than a war, chief. Like most members of his band he had had many friendly contacts with white men, and he did not fit the typical picture of a hostile Indian who had grown to manhood hating the Americans. Though he had come to believe that the Indians and whites did not mix well, he had a humanitarianism that transcended national loyalty and an understanding of conflicting forces that was rare in either Indians or whites.

He had been born in the spring of 1840, probably near the juncture of Joseph Creek and the Grande Ronde River in the deep, sheltered warmth of the Joseph Canyon, where his father's people and their herds waited out the winter till chinook winds told them that they could ascend to the high, greening meadows and fast-running streams of the nearby Wallowa Valley. At the time there were some four to six thousand Nez Percés; most of them lived in small fishing villages that dotted the banks of the Clearwater and Salmon Rivers and the middle stretches of the Snake and its tributaries, and were wisely spread over a vast expanse of territory. Each village or small concentration of them lived under the leadership of its own chief, and during his youth Joseph visited most of the settlements with his father, learning the tribal lore that held them all together as a single nation. It was a colorful past, filled with dramatic events that spoke of many lands and tribes other than their own. . . .

In 1871 young Joseph buried his father in the beloved Wallowa and assumed leadership of the band. Almost at once the emergency arrived. Settlers from Oregon's Grande Ronde found a pass into the valley and moved in, claiming the Indians' land. The new chieftain protested to the Indian agent on the reservation, and an investigation was undertaken by the Bureau of Indian Affairs to determine whether the Treaty of 1863 affected Joseph's band, which had not agreed to it. The inquiry resulted in a decision that the Wallowa still belonged legally to the Indians, and on June 16, 1873, President Grant formally set aside the Wallowa "as a reservation for the roaming Nez Percé Indians" and ordered the white intruders to withdraw.

Recognition of their rights brought satisfaction and relief to the Indians, but it was short-lived. The settlers, refusing to move, threatened to exterminate Joseph's people if they did not leave the valley. In defiance of the presidential order, more whites rolled in by the wagonload. As friction increased, Oregon's governor, Lafayette P. Grover, attacked Washington officials for having abandoned the government's position of 1863 and forced the Administration to reverse itself. In 1875 a new and confusing presidential edict reopened the Wallowa to white homesteaders.

The Nez Percés were dismayed. Young Joseph, called by the Indians Heinmot Tooyalakekt, meaning "thunder traveling to loftier mountain heights," counseled patience. He moved the Indian camps from the neighborhood of the settlers and again appealed to the federal authorities. The assistant adjutant general of the Military Department of the Columbia, Major H. Clay Wood, was assigned to make a survey of the conflicting claims, and in his report, forwarded to Washington by his commanding officer, O. O. Howard, the one-armed "Christian" general of the Civil War, stated, "In my opinion, the non-treaty Nez Percés cannot in law be regarded as bound by the treaty of 1863, and insofar as it attempts to deprive them of a right to occupancy of any land, its provisions are null and void. The extinguishment of their title of occupancy contemplated by this treaty is imperfect and incomplete."

At first the government took no action, but as harassment of the Indians continued and the threat increased that they might retaliate with violence, a new commission of five members was appointed to meet with the Nez Percés in November 1876 with authority to make a final settlement of the matter for "the welfare of both whites and Indians."

The commissioners—Howard, Wood, and three eastern civilians—found Joseph a disquieting figure. Thirty-six years old now, straight and towering, he seemed strongly amicable and gentle; yet he bore himself with the quiet strength and dignity of one who stood in awe of no man. And when he spoke, it was with an eloquent logic that nettled the whites, who found themselves resenting their inability to dominate him.

Why, they asked him, did he refuse to give up the Wallowa? He answered by referring to the land as the Mother of the Indians, something that could not be sold or given away. "We love the land," he said. "It is our home."

But, they insisted, [Chief] Lawyer had signed it away in 1863.

Joseph had a ready reply that embarrassed them. "I believe the old treaty has never been correctly reported," he said. "If we ever owned the land we own it still, for we never sold it. In the treaty councils the commissioners have claimed that our country has been sold to the government. Suppose a white man should come to me and say, 'Joseph, I like your horses, and I want to buy them.' I say to him, 'No, my horses suit me, I will not sell them.' Then he goes to my neighbor, and says to him, 'Joseph has some good horses. I want to buy them but he refuses to sell.' My neighbor answers, 'Pay me the money, and I will sell you Joseph's horses.' The white man returns to me and says, 'Joseph, I have bought your horses and you must let me have them.' If we sold our lands to the government, this is the way they were bought."

To all their arguments, Joseph replied with an uncompromising "No" and the exasperated commissioners made no progress with him. But events were moving against the Indians. The situation in the Wallowa had grown perilous, and the commission was under political pressure. Two excited white men had killed an Indian youth after mistakenly accusing him of stealing their horses. Joseph had had all he could do to keep his people calm, and the settlers, fearing an uprising, were arming and calling for military protection.

To the commissioners, despite the fact that it was unjust and there was no legal basis for it, there could be only one decision, and before they left the reservation headquarters at Lapwai they rendered it: Unless, within a reasonable time, all the non-treaty Nez Percés (the other bands that had not signed in 1863, as well as Joseph's people in the Wallowa) voluntarily came onto the reservation, they should be placed there by force. General Howard, symbolizing the force that would be used, signed the report along with the three easterners. Only Major Wood's name was absent; it is believed that he submitted a minority report, though it has never been found.

Immediately after the decision the Indian Bureau defined the "reasonable time" and ordered the Indians to come onto the reservation by April 1, 1877. It was almost an exact repetition of the order of a year before that had started the hostilities with the Sioux. Unable to move their herds and villages across the rugged canyons in the dead of winter, the Nez Percés appealed for another conference, and as April 1 came and went General Howard agreed to one last meeting with all the non-treaty chiefs at Lapwai. It did no good. The die had been cast, and Howard adamantly refused to discuss the commission's decision. As the Indians pleaded in proud but pitiable terms to be allowed to remain in the lands where their fathers were buried, the general finally lost patience and threw one of the most respected old chiefs, a deeply religious war leader and tribal orator named Toohoolhoolzote, into the guardhouse. It broke the spirit of the others. To gain Toohoolhoolzote's release they capitulated with bitterness and agreed to have their bands on the reservation in thirty days.

All Joseph's skill as a diplomat had to be called into play when he returned to his people. He had abandoned his father's counsel and trust, and there were cries to ignore him and go to war rather than to move to the reservation. When Joseph argued that the white man's power was too great for them to resist and that it was "better to live at peace than to begin a war and lie dead," they called him a coward. But he received strong assistance from his younger brother, Ollokot, a daring and courageous buffalo hunter and warrior who had won many tribal honors and held the respect of the more belligerent younger element. Eventually the the two brothers won agreement to the capitulation from the band's council, and the Indians prepared to round up their stock and move.

A half year's work was crowded into less than thirty days as the people combed the mountains and forests for their animals and drove them down the steep draws to the Snake. The river was in flood, and hundreds of head of stock were swept away and drowned during the tumultuous crossing. Other portions of the herds, left behind on the bluffs and plateau, were driven away by whites, who attacked the guards and harassed the withdrawing Indians. By June 2, with twelve days of grace remaining, the people reached an ancient tribal rendezvous area just outside the border of the reservation. Here they joined the other non-treaty bands and lingered for a last bit of freedom.

It was a fatal pause. On June 12 the Indians staged a parade through the camp, and one of the young men named Wahlitits, whose father had been murdered by a white man two years before, was taunted by an old warrior for having allowed the slaying to go unavenged. The next morning, his honor as a man impugned, Wahlitits stole away with two companions. By nightfall, in an outpouring of long-suppressed hatred, the youths had killed four white men along the Salmon River and wounded another one, all notorious for their hostility to the Nez Percés. The young men returned to the camp, announced what they had done, and raised a bigger party that continued the raids during the next two days, killing fourteen or fifteen additional whites and striking terror among the settlers and miners of central Idaho.

Both Joseph and Ollokot had been absent from the camp during the first raid, butchering cattle on the opposite side of the Salmon River, They returned to find the camp in confusion and the older people crying with fear and striking their tipis, intending to scatter to hiding places. Most of the Indians were certain that there would now be war, but Joseph still hoped to avert it. He tried to calm his people, assuring them that General Howard would not blame the whole tribe for the irresponsible actions of a few of its young hotheads, and urged them to remain where they were and await the troops, with whom he would make a settlement. The situation, however, had gone too far. The warriors rode around the camp, crying out that they would now give General Howard the fight that he had wanted, and the people would not listen to Joseph. One by one the bands departed to a hiding place farther south, in White Bird Canyon, leaving behind only Joseph, Ollokot, and a few of the Wallowa Indians.

Joseph's wife had given birth to a daughter while he had been across the Salmon, and he lingered with her now in their tipi. Several warriors were detailed to watch him and Ollokot, lest these leaders who had so often pleaded for peace would desert the non-treaties and move onto the reservation. But though he had vigorously opposed war Joseph would not abandon his people; two days later he and Ollokot, resolved to fight now that hostilities seemed unavoidable, joined the non-treaties in the new camp at White Bird. . . .

* * * * *

[Editors' Note: After a battle at White Bird on June 17, the Nez Percés traveled across northern Idaho into Montana. During their retreat, they engaged federal troops in pitched battles at Clearwater (July 11) and Big Hole (August 9). Army casualties at the Big Hole were heavy.]

The Indians' losses at the Big Hole had also been high. Between sixty and ninety Nez Percés had lost their lives, including Rainbow, Five Wounds, and some of the tribe's ablest warriors. Many of the casualties had been women and children, slain during the initial attack on the tipis. Joseph's wife had been among the seriously wounded, and Joseph had been seen fighting his way through the early part of the battle sheltering his new baby in his arms.

The Nez Percés now quickened their retreat across southwestern Montana. Gone were illusions that the whites would let them be. In their desperation to escape, only one haven seemed left to them. Like Sitting Bull, they would go to Canada and seek refuge among the tribes in the country of Queen Victoria. Canada was hundreds of miles away, but they would get there somehow. Looking Glass, blamed for the false sense of security that had led to so many deaths at the Big Hole, was relieved of command, and a tough fighter named Lean Elk, whom the whites had known as Poker Joe, was elevated to supreme war chief. The column headed eastward toward Targhee Pass, which would lead the refugees over the Continental Divide to the Yellowstone, where they could turn north to Canada. West of the pass, rear-guard scouts brought word that Howard was catching up and pressing close behind them again. In a bold night attack, twenty-eight warriors led by Ollokot and three other chiefs stole back to Howard's camp and ran off the general's entire pack string. Howard came to a dead halt, forced to scour the settlements for more animals, and the Indians hurried on, unhampered, across the Divide and into the area which five years before had become Yellowstone National Park.

A sight-seeing party, of which General William Tecumseh Sherman was a member, had just left the area, but the Nez Percés swooped up two other groups of campers and took them along. The chiefs insisted on humane treatment for the frightened tourists, who included a number of women. In time as the Indians continued across the park, past geysers and bubbling mudpots, the sight-seers were allowed to escape. On the eastern side of the park the Indians found themselves harassed by new bodies of troops, coming at them from posts on the Montana plains. One force of the 7th Cavalry under Colonel Samuel Sturgis tried to set a trap for the Indians in the upper Yellowstone Valley, but the Nez Percés fought their way skillfully through a mountain wilderness where the whites thought passage would be impossible and emerged on the Clark's Fork River in Sturgis's rear. Realizing he had been tricked, Sturgis gave chase with three hundred men, following the Indians across the Yellowstone River and down its northern bank past present-day Billings, Montana.

On and on the Indians hurried. Near Canyon Creek they passed a stage station and captured a stage coach. The warriors let its occupants escape into some nearby willows and had a day of great fun, driving the incongruous-looking coach along in the rear of the column. The sport ended abruptly. At Canyon Creek the bands turned north, and here, on September 13, Sturgis's hard-riding cavalry overtook them. There was a furious fight. A rear guard of Indians, hiding behind rocks and in gullies, held off the troopers while the Nez Percé women and children drove the pack strings and herds to the protection of a narrow canyon that cut north through rimrock country. Sturgis ordered his men to dismount, an error that allowed the Indians to escape into the canyon. Later the cavalry tried to follow the Nez Percés in a running fight up the canyon, but the Indians succeeded in making pursuit difficult by blocking the canyon floor behind them with boulders and brush. At darkness, weary and running out of ammunition and rations, Sturgis gave up the chase. Three of his men had been killed and eleven wounded. The Indians counted three wounded, but the long pursuit was beginning to tell heavily on them. They too were becoming tired and dispirited, and they were losing horses. Many of the animals were going lame from the difficult trek and had to be abandoned. Others were being lost in the hurry to keep moving.

Beyond Canyon Creek their old allies the Crows, now in service as scouts for the army, began to attack them. The Nez Percés fought them off in running engagements and continued across the Musselshell to the Missouri River, helping themselves to army stores at a military depot on Cow Island while a frightened sergeant and twelve men looked on helplessly from behind an earthwork. Just across the Missouri the Indians fought off a halfhearted attack by a small force from Fort Benton and hastened on across badlands and open, rolling plains to the Bear Paw Mountains. About thirty miles short of the Canadian line, exhausted by the long flight, they paused to rest, confident that they had outdistanced all pursuers.

Once more they were wrong, outflanked again by the telegraph, and this time the pause would end in their last stand. From Fort Keogh in the east, Colonel Nelson Miles, with nearly six hundred men that included the 2nd and 7th Cavalry, the mounted 5th Infantry, and a body of Cheyenne warriors, was hastening obliquely across Montana, hoping to intercept the hostiles before they crossed the border. On the cold, blustery morning of September 30, Miles' Cheyenne scouts sighted the Nez Percé tipis in a deep hollow on the plains close to Snake Creek on the northern edge of the Bear Paw Mountains. Miles ordered an immediate attack, and the Cheyennes and 7th Cavalry, supported by the 5th Infantry, charged across the open ground toward the village.

The assault caught the Nez Percés in three groups. Some, including women and children, were on the distant side of the camp and were able to mount and flee to the north, where they scattered on the broken plains to die from hunger and exposure or eventually to reach Canada in small, pitiful groups. Others, including Joseph, were trapped with the horses at some distance from the camp. A third group, at the village, found protection behind a low-lying ridge. These warriors, hidden behind rocks, opened a deadly fire on the attackers, inflicting heavy casualties and sending the troopers reeling back short of the camp. Two officers and twenty-two soldiers were killed in the assault and four officers and thirty-eight enlisted men wounded.

The 2nd Cavalry, meanwhile, had been sent around the camp to capture the Nez Percé horse herd and try to cut off escape. This unit had better luck. The troopers charged into the herd, stampeding the horses and splitting the Indians into small groups that fought back hand-to-hand or sought cover in gullies or behind rocks. A few of the Indians got away on ponies and disappeared to the north. Others, among them Joseph, crawled or fought their way back to the main body of Nez Percés and reached the camp under cover of darkness. The troopers drove off at least a third of the horses, however, and killed most of the Nez Percés' remaining war leaders, including the brave Ollokot and Too-hoolhoolzote.

The heavy casualties Miles had sustained deterred him from ordering another charge, and he decided to lay siege to the camp. He made one attempt to cut off the Indians from their water supply by establishing a line between the village and the river, but the troops detailed to the task were driven back by fierce Indian resistance. As the siege settled down, both sides dug in, continuing a desultory sharpshooting fire between the lines. The weather turned bitterly cold, and the next morning five inches of snow covered the unretrieved bodies of the dead. The Indians, wounded, hungry, and cold, suffered intensely. Using hooks, knives, and pans, the people tried to dig crude shelters in the sides of the hollows. One dugout was caved in by a hit from Miles' howitzer that had been tilted back for use as a mortar, and a woman and child were buried alive.

As the siege continued, Miles grew concerned. There were rumors that Sitting Bull, with a band of Sioux, was coming to the Nez Percés' rescue from Canada. And, even if they did not show up, Howard was getting closer, and Miles wanted the glory of Joseph's end for himself. Hoping to hurry the surrender, he hoisted a white flag over his trenches and, after negotiations with a Nez Percé who could speak English, lured Joseph across the lines. The two men parleyed amicably for a few moments, but when Joseph began to detail terms for an honorable surrender, Miles had him seized and made prisoner. The same day, however, the Nez Percés captured one of Miles' officers. The next morning an exchange was agreed to, and Joseph was returned to his camp.

The siege went on amid cold and snow flurries, and on October 4 Howard reached the battlefield with a small advance party that included two treaty Nez Percés. The appearance of their old enemy, heralding the arrival of reinforcements for Miles, finally took the heart out of the suffering Nez Percés. The next morning the two treaty Nez Percés crossed the lines and told the chiefs that if they surrendered they would be honorably treated and sent back to Lapwai. The chiefs held a final council. White Bird and Looking Glass still opposed surrender. Joseph pointed to the starving women and children in the shelter pits and to the babies that were crying around them. "For myself I do not care," he said. "It is for them I am going to surrender."

As the council broke up, Looking Glass was suddenly struck in the forehead by a stray bullet and killed. As the surviving warriors gathered around the slain chief, Joseph mounted a horse and, followed by several men on foot, rode slowly up the hill from the camp and across to the army lines where Howard and Miles awaited him. As he reached the officers, he dismounted and handed Miles his rifle. Then he stepped back and adjusted his blanket to leave his right arm free; addressing Miles, he began one of the most touching and beautiful speeches of surrender ever made.

"Tell General Howard I know his heart," he said. "What he told me before I have in my heart. I am tired of fighting. Our chiefs are killed. Looking Glass is dead. Toohoolhoolzote is dead. The old men are all dead. It is the young men who say yes or no. He who led the young men is dead. It is cold and we have no blankets. The little children are freezing to death. My people, some of them, have run away to the hills, and have no blankets, no food; no one knows where they are—perhaps freezing to death. I want to have time to look for my children and see how many I can find. Maybe I shall find them among the dead. Hear me, my chiefs. I am tired; my heart is sick and sad. From where the sun now stands, I will fight no more forever."

The fact that neither Joseph nor any other individual chief had been responsible for the outstanding strategy and masterful success of the campaign is irrelevant. The surrender speech, taken down by Howard's adjutant and published soon afterward, confirmed Joseph in the public's mind as the symbol of the Nez Percés' heroic, fighting retreat. Although the government failed to honor Miles' promise to send the Indians back to Lapwai, sympathy was aroused throughout the nation for Joseph's people. At first the Indians were shipped by flatboats and boxcars to unfamiliar, hot country in the Indian Territory, where many of them sickened and died. But friendly whites and sympathetic societies in the East continued to work for them, and public sentiment finally forced approval of their return to the Northwest. In 1885 Joseph and most of his band were sent to the Colville Reservation in Washington. Joseph made many attempts to be allowed to resettle in the Wallowa but each time was rebuffed. In 1904 he died, broken-hearted, an exile from the beautiful valley he still considered home.

EPILOGUE

The surrender of Joseph's Nez Percés in 1877 almost completed the military conquest of the American Indian. What remained was pacification rather than conquest, and it dragged on for thirteen more years as the government penned western natives on reservations and showed them with the grim use of arms that it meant to keep them there.

The wild spirits of tribesmen who would be free refused to stay penned; these men died and starved by hundreds as they broke away, again and again, trying like hunted animals to find safety from their tormentors. In 1878 elusive Bannocks were chased through the wilds of the Idaho mountains. The same year the northern Cheyennes, who had been exiled to a barren, malarial reservation in Oklahoma, burst out in an epic attempt to return to Montana's Powder River. Under Dull Knife and Little Wolf a starving, bedraggled column of men, women, and children plodded north through the central plains, pushing almost blindly over what had become the white man's country, across rivers, railroads, highways, cattle ranches, and settlers' farms, fighting off armies that tried to halt them. When some of them were finally captured and herded into another agency, the government withheld food and water from them and put some of their leaders in irons. Still they refused to give up. They broke out again, and hurried stubbornly on once more toward their old hunting grounds; this time, when overtaken by troops, they were mowed down and all but annihilated.

The next year rebellious Ute warriors were pacified in Colorado, and in the 1880s it was the turn of the fierce Apaches in New Mexico and Arizona. It took several expeditions and years of pursuit, hard fighting, and protracted councils in the mountain fastnesses of the Southwest, including Mexico, to convince Geronimo and a handful of his followers that they could no longer roam in freedom. By 1886 they too were in hand and on their way to exile in Florida.

As Indian resistance finally withered, dreams took the place of guns. History, harking back to the days of the visionary prophets of Pontiac, Tecumseh, and Black Hawk, was repeated. The crushed and demoralized western tribesmen sat in their blankets on the reservations, wondering what to do next, and in time word came to them from the distant Nevada desert of a new Indian prophet, a humble Paiute Indian named Wovoka who had received revelations from the Great Spirit. Again, Christianity and Indian aspirations came together in a new form. At his home on the Walker River reservation, Wovoka, a portly and peaceable man who had been raised in the home of a devoutly religious white family, began to work "miracles." They were the tricks of a charlatan, but he soon began to believe in his powers and the messages he received in trances. As his reputation spread among the tribes, pilgrims came to see him from all the defeated nations of the West.

His advice to them was to perform a special dance, accompanied by a chant, which eventually would restore the Indians' world as it had been before the white men had come. The soldiers, the agents, the settlers—all the conquerors —would disappear, the dead Indian heroes would come back to life, and the plains once more would be filled with buffalo. To the dispirited warriors it was an exciting prospect, and Wovoka's message traveled from tribe to tribe, igniting new hopes and dreams. Within months, Arapaho in Wyoming, Bannocks and Shoshonis in Idaho, and Sioux in the Dakotas were all shuffling in weird circles, chanting and stiffening in frenzied trances, calling back the olden days and waiting with outstretched arms for the disappearance of the whites and the return of the buffalo.

It was bound to end in tragedy, and it did in 1890. Wovoka's movement was a peaceful one, but its mystery and hold on the minds of the desperate natives unnerved the reservation agents and military leaders, who termed it "the Ghost Dance." At the Sioux' Standing Rock Agency in the Dakotas, Sitting Bull, who had returned from Canadian exile in 1881, was narrowly watched. When his people began to dance, and even to wear sacred "ghost shirts" which they believed would protect them from white men's guns and bullets, the old medicine man was ordered arrested. Like Crazy Horse, the great Hunkpapa resisted his captors and was killed in a scuffle. Other Sioux broke out at once, racing wildly for freedom. They were pursued in the snow, and at the so-called massacre of Wounded Knee in December 1890 some three hundred Indian men, women, and children were slaughtered by the raking fire of Hotchkiss guns.

The long conquest of the American Indian was ended. With the failure of Wovoka's dance and the sacred protection of the "ghost shirts," the movement collapsed. There was no more fighting. The army became garrison troops, and the problem of the surviving tribesmen settled into the hands of the civil agencies of the government.

The history of the Indians did not end in 1890, and it is not ended today. As the natives ceased to become a menace, and were herded out of sight and mind on remote and unwanted reservations, non-Indian Americans tended to forget about them. Only those who lived near the reservations knew anything about the Indians, and in general they looked down upon them, and treated them as inferior people. They had little patience with the defeated ones, and from generation to generation very little, if anything, changed in the relations between whites and Indians.

Today, seventy years after Wounded Knee, the United States government still has a perplexing "Indian problem," and the American people generally still know almost nothing about their Indian population. The image of the "vanishing American" is no more. The Indian population is fast increasing, and it is estimated that there are now more than half a million persons who can be called Indians (of full or part blood) in the United States. Over three hundred and fifty thousand of them were found to be living on reservations in 1960. But there are still Indians and Indians. They speak more than a hundred different languages. They are in all states of economic condition (from pauperism and near-starvation to affluence), range across many levels of culture (some have accepted none of the white men's culture and some are completely assimilated and undistinguishable from white men), and present a bewildering mass of local and regional problems that cannot be discussed or dismissed with brief generalizations (in handling the Indian problem the government must still cope with thousands of treaties, statutes, and individual legal decisions of the past).

On the whole, the Indians are still a proud and dignified people. But they are still a conquered people, who continue to stand in confusion and helplessness between two worlds. Their old standards and ways of life are smashed and gone, but it is not easy—even in a hundred years—for a once independent people entirely to abandon and forget what was. After Wounded Knee and until 1924 the Indians were denied freedom of religion. Now, with that freedom restored, many of them reveal that, like Popé's Pueblos in the seventeenth century, they remain true to the practices and beliefs of their fathers.

They need—and most of them welcome—the material benefits of modern American civilization, its education, medicine, technical training, and planning and development of Indian resources. The lack of interest of most of the United States in the Indians since 1890 has been partly to blame for the continuance of the "Indian problem." The Congress has been generous with funds, but policies have been erratic and confusing, and government administration of Indian affairs has too often been stupid or criminal. Agents have cheated and stolen from Indians, and have left a black record in their failure to protect whole tribes from exploitation, robbery, and other injustices by elements of neighboring white populations.

In the course of years some Indians have become educated, some wealthy, and some a productive part of American society. But many are still poorly educated, impoverished, and discriminated against as Indians. It is unthinking to characterize them in contemptuous generalizations as "drunks," "people who won't work" or "idlers who sit at railroad stations selling blankets to tourists." These are the images of a people who do not yet have a productive place in American life; who drink, like the Indians of Tecumseh's day in the Old Northwest, to forget their fate and achieve an escape; who, like King Philip's Indians in New England, do not work because the conditions of work for them are colored by humiliations and problems of the soul; and who sell blankets at stations because it is one way of remaining alive honorably and without regimentation.

Many of the Indians still have their reservations, which are not concentration camps but the only property that has been left to them. A reservation is their land base, their place of security, a home from which a young man can journey to a city in search of a job, and to which he can return if he becomes frightened, dispirited, or unemployed. Many reservations are so barren and useless that they cannot possibly support their populations. Others inevitably catch the eye of white men (for minerals, natural gas, timber, grazing lands, reservoir sites), and there is constant pressure to separate the Indians from their lands. Deceptive arguments ("free the Indians") and un-American policies (the arbitrary ending, or "termination" of federal-Indian relations without the agreement of the Indians, leading inevitably to the unprotected exploitation of the natives by neighboring whites and the dissolution of the reservation) are headline material today, and reflect the fact that the "Indian problem" is still far from solved.

Its solution requires the interest and knowledge of non-Indians who up to now have known nothing about Indians. Since 1890 the Indians have been almost exclusively the "possession" of government agents, certain sympathetic church and charitable groups, museum keepers, and students of anthropology, ethnology, and sociology. In a way they dehumanized the Indian, but it did not matter, because the rest of the population was too busy to care. What is left now is the dusty and almost meaningless arrowhead in a museum display box, the television image of what Indians were never like, and assorted prejudices and impatient demands for the Indians to "hurry up and get assimilated, damn it."

So the issue is still joined. The forces in American life that want Indians to get off the reservations and be like all other Americans may have their way. But the Indians will resist patiently for decades still to come, and it will not happen easily or soon. When it does occur, much of the greatness and majesty and wonder of the United States will have disappeared. Indian culture and Indian thinking, untreasured by the unknowing, will be gone, and only the history books will be able to tell us of it and make us wonder why we did not enfold it and make a place for it in our national life.

CHAPTER 5

THE GREAT WEST
AND THE TRADITION
OF AMERICAN VIOLENCE

Americans have always been exceptionally romantic in their views of the Great American West. The West—that expansive land of vast rolling plains, of gigantic mountain ranges, of fertile valleys, and at once of fantastic beauty and brutal harshness—presented a great challenge to Americans. The West has been a symbol of the pioneer spirit, of American energy and drive, and of rugged individualism and self-reliance. The conquest of the Plains Indians, the initial exploitation of Western resources, and the ultimate settling and peopling of the region have generally been viewed as simply steps in the inexorable march of American progress. Scholars have extolled the contributions of the Western frontier to American character and institutions, and the appeal of the West to modern Americans is apparent from the long-standing popularity of Western movies, television shows, and clothing styles.

In this selection, Professor Joe B. Frantz spotlights another aspect of our Western heritage. While affirming the positive contributions of the frontier heritage to American life, Frantz argues that the Western experience also left a negative legacy of more than fleeting significance. A long-time student of the West, Frantz points out that violence—ranging from relatively minor incidents of fighting or exploitation to brutal lynchings and large-scale massacres—was commonplace on, perhaps even endemic to, the American frontier. The author describes, in some detail, the violence that was spawned on the frontier; he discusses the basic causes of violence, the various types (individual, mob, the racially or ethnically motivated), and the end results. Finally, Professor Frantz notes that the frontier heritage has tended to promote the American penchant for violence right down to the present. He deplores the romanticism that colors the American perspective of the past and suggests that the violence that characterized the frontier has no place in a "nation whose problems are corporate, community, and complex."

In reading this selection, the student would do well to focus on the general problem of violence in this nation. To what extent has the United States been a violent country? To what extent are we still a violent society? How does Professor Frantz explain the prevalence of violence on the Western frontier? Does the evidence that the author presents justify his conclusion that the frontier legacy of violence continues to exert an unfortunate influence on American society? What does Professor Frantz suggest as the best way to lessen or reduce the negative impact of the frontier heritage on the American people?

In addition to the excellent study from which this selection is taken (H. D. Graham and T. R. Gurr, eds., *Violence in America,** (1969), the student can gain insights into the subject of violence in America from such works as Richard Wade, *Urban Violence* (1969), Truman Capote, *In Cold Blood** (1966), and Dan T. Carter, *The Scotsboro Case** (1969). Violence against Indians is documented in works cited in the introduction to Chapter 4, against blacks in the twentieth-century South in George B. Tindall, *The Emergence of the New South, 1913–1945** (1967), and against the labor organization, the Industrial Workers of the World (I.W.W.), in Bernard A. Weisberger, "Here Come the Wobblies!", *American Heritage*, June 1967. The *Report of the National Advisory Commission on Civil Disorders** (The Kerner Report, 1968), and The Final Report of the National Commission on the Causes and Prevention of Violence, *To Establish Justice, To Insure Domestic Tranquility* (1969), are also pertinent.

*Available in a paperback edition.

THE FRONTIER TRADITION: AN INVITATION TO VIOLENCE

JOE B. FRANTZ

On September 26, 1872, three mounted men rode up to the gate of the Kansas City fair, which was enjoying a huge crowd of perhaps 10,000 people. The bandits shot at the ticket seller, hit a small girl in the leg, and made off for the woods with something less than a thousand dollars. It was highhanded, and it endangered the lives of a whole host of holiday-minded people for comparatively little reward.

What makes the robbery and the violence notable is not the crime itself but the way it was reported in the Kansas City *Times* by one John N. Edwards. In his front-page story he branded the robbery "so diabolically daring and so utterly in contempt of fear that we are bound to admire it and revere its perpetrators."

Two days later the outlaws were being compared by the *Times* with the knights of King Arthur's Round Table:

It was as though three bandits had come to us from storied Odenwald, with the halo of medieval chivalry upon their garments and shown us how the things were done that poets sing of. Nowhere else in the United States or in the civilized world, probably, could this thing have been done.

Quite likely this deed was perpetrated by the James brothers: Jesse and Frank, and a confederate. The details really do not matter. What pertains is the attitude of the innocent toward the uncertainly identified guilty. The act had been perpetrated by violent, lawless men. If the *Times* is any indication, a respectable section of the people approved of their action. No one, of course, thought to ask the little girl with the shattered leg how she felt about such courage. Nearly 17 months later, Edwards was quoted in the St. Louis *Dispatch* as preferring the Western highwayman to the Eastern, for "he has more qualities that attract admiration and win respect; . . . This comes from locality . . . which breeds strong, hardy men—men who risk much, who have friends

SOURCE. Joe B. Frantz, "The Frontier Tradition: An Invitation to Violence," in H. D. Graham and T. R. Gurr, eds., *Violence in America,* New York, Signet Books, 1969, pp. 119–142. Copyright 1969 by Joe B. Frantz. Reprinted by permission of the publisher.

in high places, and who go riding over the land, taking all chances that come in the way." The purpose here is not to belabor one reasonably anonymous newspaperman of nearly a century ago, but merely to point up a fact—and problem—of the American frontier.

The frontier placed a premium on independent action and individual reliance. The whole history of the American frontier is a narrative of taking what was there to be taken. The timid never gathered the riches, the polite nearly never. The men who first carved the wilderness into land claims and town lots were the men who moved in the face of dangers, gathering as they progressed. The emphasis naturally came to be placed on gathering and not on procedures. Great tales of gigantic attainments abound in this frontier story; equally adventurous tales of creative plundering mark the march from Jamestown to the Pacific. It was a period peopled by giants, towers of audacity with insatiable appetites. The heroes are not the men of moderate attitudes, not the town planners and commercial builders, not the farmers nor the ministers nor the teachers. The heroes of the period, handed along to us with all the luster of a golden baton, are the mighty runners from Mt. Olympus who ran without looking back, without concern about social values or anywhere they might be going except onward.

We revere these heroes because they were men of vast imagination and daring. We also have inherited their blindness and their excesses.

Just by being here, the frontier promised the spice of danger. And danger, to paraphrase Samuel Johnson, carries its own dignity. Danger therefore was the negotiable coin of the American frontier, and the man who captured his share of danger was a man of riches, beholden only to himself.

To live with danger means to be dependent to a considerable degree on one's own resources, and those resources in turn must be many and varied. Courage and self-reliance, while not exclusive with the frontiersman, take on an enlarged dimension because so many instances of their use can be recalled. Whereas the town neighbor or the corporate manager may need a type of moral courage that exceeds the physical in its wear and tear on the human soul, such downtown courage is hardly recountable and seldom even identifiable. But when the frontiersman has faced down an adversary, he usually has a fixed moment in his life when he can regale an audience or when others can recall admiringly his dauntlessness. Even a foolhardy adventure brings applause. To the human actor no reward is more desirable.

The fact that back East, which meant from ten miles behind the cutting edge of civilization all the way to the more sophisticated capitals of Europe, men were daily facing monumental problems of planning, and sometimes even of surviving, meant nothing to the frontiersman. Nothing in the frontiersman's way of life gave him any sympathy for the man who made his decision on paper or in the vacuum of an office or stall. Decision was made on the spot, face to face. The questions were simple; the solutions, equally simple. Today that heritage of the frontier continues in more remote areas. The subtleties of law and order escape the isolated mountain man, for instance, whether he be in Wyoming or in eastern Kentucky. If a man does wrong, you chastise him. Chastisement can take any form that you think is necessary to hold him in line. One of the acceptable forms is murder, which means that lesser violence visited upon the offending person is even more acceptable. Such behavior has the advantage of being swift and certain, without the agony of deciding what is comparatively just and without the expense of trials and jails and sociologists and welfare workers.

Of course, one reason that this simplistic attitude toward settlement of problems prevailed on the frontier was a physical one of lack of jails. Where do you put a man when you possibly have no place to put yourself? To be neat and economical, you must put him away. This may mean tying him to a tree and leaving him to starve or be stung to death; if he has been real mean, you might like to wrap him in rawhide and then let the sun shrink the rawhide slowly around him until he is gradually strangled. Or you might find it more economical to find a convenient tree with a branch a sufficient height off the ground. The scarcity of jails then, either nonexistent or inadequate, often left the frontiersman with little choice, insofar as he was concerned, except to hang, lynch, or ignore the offender.

What do you do with a man whose crime may not really warrant execution? Either you execute him anyway, stifling your doubts, or you let him go. If you let him go, as happened frequently, then you may have set a killer at large to roam. In Arkansas in the generation during which Judge Isaac C. Parker ran his notorious Federal court, more than 13,000 cases were docketed, of which 9,500 were either convicted by jury trial or entered pleas of guilty. During a 25-year period at Fort Smith, 344 persons were tried for offenses punishable by death, 174 were convicted, and 168 were sentenced to hang. Actually 88 of these were hanged, and six others died either in prison or while attempting to escape.

By current standards the hangings themselves would have been invitations to violence. One contemporary of the judge tells of the hanging of John Childers, a halfblood Cherokee Indian charged with killing a peddler for his horse. A thunderstorm had come up, and a bolt of lightning struck nearby just as the death trap was sprung. "A moment later the ghastly work was done, the cloud had vanished and all that was mortal of John Childers hung limp and quivering," the reporter writes. "The entire proceeding, the grim service of the law, . . . filled the spectators with awe."

Standing next to Judge Parker in local fame was George Maledon, a smallish Bavarian celebrated as "the prince of hangmen" for having executed more than 60 criminals and shooting two to death during 22 years prior to 1894. Twice he executed six men at one time and on three other occasions he hanged five together. People discussed his record with all the enthusiastic calm of a present-day discussion of Willie Mays' possibilities for overtaking the homerun record of Babe Ruth. As for Maledon, when he was once asked by a lady whether he had qualms of conscience, he replied in his soft way, "No, I have never hanged a man who came back to have the job done over." This same reporter describes Judge Parker as "gentle, kind, familiar and easily approached."

The truth is, the lawman was as closely associated with violence as the outlaw. The greatest gunfighters frequently played both sides of the law, shooting equally well. Bill Hickok comes down as a great lawmen in Kansas. He also shared a good many of the qualities of a mad dog. Hickok first came to public notoriety near Rock Creek, Nebraska, where from behind a curtain in the Russell, Majors, and Waddell station he put a single rifle bullet through the heart of one David McCanles, who had come with a hired hand and his 12-year-old son to protest nonpayment of a debt. Hickok was acquitted on a plea of self-defense. For this dubious bit of law tending, Hickok became a national hero, although it took a half-dozen years for his notoriety to become nationwide. He filled in that time by doing creditable work for the Union Army, and pursuing a postwar career as a gambler in Missouri and Kansas. This stretch of social service was punctuated by a town square gun duel which left Hickok standing and his adversary forever departed.

In his long hair and deerskin suit, Hickok could have joined any police confrontation in Chicago or Berkeley a century later. Nonetheless he became a deputy U.S. marshal out of Fort Riley, and helped rescue 34 men besieged by redskins 50 miles south of Denver. With this background he was elected sheriff of Ellis County, Kansas, in August 1869. He killed only two men, which is not meant as an apologia, for he was credited with many more. His fame as a stanchion of the law brought him to Abilene as city marshal in the spring of 1871. Whereas his successor, the revered Tom Smith, had operated from the mayor's office, Hickok utilized the Alamo Saloon, where he could fill in his time playing poker and drinking the whiskey for which he also had a storied appetite. He ran a tight, two-fisted town, especially aimed at keeping undisciplined Texas cowboys in hand. When 6 months later he killed Phil Coe, as well as (by mistake) his own policeman, he was soon sent packing by the town. Naturally enough, he left this life as the result of a shot in the back while playing poker in a Black Hills gambling joint. This violent man is the hero who is supposed to have quelled violence on the frontier and to have brought the blessings of organized law and order to our Western civilization. But he was ever ready to kill, on either side of the law.

One writer, detailing the lives of the bad men of the West, has put together an appendix consisting of the bad men and another one of the peace officers.

Among the bad men he lists are Judge Roy Bean, who dispensed the "Law West of the Pecos." Hickok is also listed with the bad men. Ben Thompson shot up Kansas and almost crossed with Hickok, and wound up as a city marshal of Austin, Texas. Bill Longley was a deputy sheriff and one of the more notorious killers in the business. Doc Holliday was a lawman in both Kansas and Arizona under Wyatt Earp. And Arizona remains split to this day whether Earp belongs with the bad men or the good. Certainly the frontier story is replete with men of peace who were equally men of violence.

Undoubtedly a lot of violence spawned on the frontier emanated from the restlessness engendered by successive wars. The American Revolution, the war of 1812, the Mexican War, and the Civil War all disgorged some men who had tasted action and could not return to the discipline of the settled world. Consequently they stayed on the frontier, where their training and penchant for direct action held some value. Undoubtedly this was more true of the survivors of Civil War action than of any of the other major wars. The men who fought in the Western areas of the Civil War, both North and South, enjoyed more than a little activity as guerrillas. But what does a guerilla do when he has no more excuse for hit-and-run tactics? Either he settles down on a Missouri farm or he continues to hit and run against targets of his own devising. The most notorious of such men would have to be the James brothers, though their company is entirely too large. The Jameses could rob and kill almost with impunity if they selected their targets well. Since the James boys had been on the Southern side, they were cheered by their Southern fellows, embittered by the outcome of the war, who felt a bit of reflected glory in the harassment of the cold-blooded Yankees. Reputedly, Ben Thompson tried to get John Wesley Hardin to kill Wild Bill Hickok because Hickok shot only Southern boys. For once Hardin, the most prolific killer of them all, turned down an opportunity to notch his gun again. Had he shot the Yankee Hickok, he might have become a true Southern hero instead of just another killer— well, not just another killer—who needed to be put away. All across the West the antagonisms of the late conflict continued, and were justified really in the name of the war. It did not matter that you killed, so much as whom you killed.

Running parallel with this tendency for a strong individual to range himself actively on one side or the other of the law is the tendency throughout history of men and groups to take the law into their own hands, sometimes with reasonably lofty motives. As John Walton Caughey has written, "to gang up and discipline an alleged wrongdoer is an ancient and deep-seated impulse." Whether such impulses run counter to a belief in the orderly pursuit of government is not debatable here. The fact is that throughout history societies, both frontier and long fixed, have moved through phases of private settlement of what should be public disputes. The operation of the Ku Klux Klan in a settled South with its centuries-old civilization is a case in point. Vigilantism is a disease or a manifestation of a society that feels a portion of its people are out of joint and must be put back in place whether the niceties of legal procedure are observed or not. That the end justifies the means is the authorizing cliché.

Not unmixed with vigilantism is frequently a fair share of racism, which has its own curious history on the American frontier. In some ways the frontier was the freest of places, in which a man was judged on the quality of his work and his possession of such abstractions as honesty, bravery, and shrewdness. The Chinese merchant, the Negro cowboy, the Indian rider—all were admired because of what they could do within the frontier community and not because of their pigmentation. On the other hand, the only good Indian was a dead Indian, "shines" could seldom rise above the worker level, and "coolies" were something to take potshots at without fear of retribution, either civil or conscience. Just as lynching a Negro in parts of the South was no crime, so shooting an Indian or beating an Oriental or a Mexican was equally acceptable. Like all societies, the frontier had its built-in contradictions.

In Kansas cowtowns, shooting Texas cowboys were a defensible act per se; popular agreement in that area was that although there might here and there be a decent cowboy, nonetheless most cowboys were sinister characters who were likely to ruin your daughter or your town. In other words, cowboys and Texans were in the same class as snakes—the garter snake can be a friendly reptile in your garden, but stomp him anyway in case he grows into a dangerous rattler.

But then, cowboys, whether Texan or Montanan, had a notoriously brazen unconcern toward nesters and grangers as Wyoming's Johnson County war will attest. How could the cattleman believe in legal law enforcement if, as one stockman put it, no jury of "Methodist, Grangers and Anti-Stock" would convict the most blatant cattle thief? A. S. Mercer, who felt that cattlemen were a menace to his Wyoming, nonetheless concluded that "as a matter of fact, less stealing and less lawlessness [occur] on the plains of the West than in any other part of the world." Backing himself, Mercer quotes the Federal census report of 1890, which points out that the Northeastern states, "which are supposed to be most civilized," had 1,600 criminals to the million people while Wyoming ran 25 per cent less, or 1,200 to the million. However, the real cattleman dislike was for the sheepherder, who was lower than a nester, rustler, or even a cowboy who had married a squaw. As one Scotsman who emigrated opined, when he brought his flock down from the hills in Scotland, people would exclaim, "here comes the noble shepherd and his flock." Out west, however, they said "here comes that damned sheepherder and his bunch of woolies!"

Certainly the cowboy treatment of the sheepman showed something less than the normal extension of dignity due a fellowman. Cattlemen tried intimidation, and if that failed, they tried violence. If mere violence were not enough, next came murder, either for the sheepman or his flocks. As public sympathy was generally with the cattlemen, the sheepman had no recourse at law if his herder were killed or his sheep driven off the range. As a general rule, as in most vigilante situations, the cowboy always tried to outnumber his sheepherding adversary by five or ten to one, preferably all on horseback to the one herder on foot.

Nowhere was the sense of vigilante violence more noticeable than in the cattleman-sheepman feud. It was vigilantism, for cowman looked on the sheepman's mere presence as immoral and illegal, an intrusion on his frontier life as he knew it. Along the upper reaches of Wyoming's Green River, for instances, a masked group, organized by the cattlemen, attacked four sheep camps simultaneously. The group blindfolded the herders, tied them to trees, and spent the remainder of the night clubbing to death 8,000 head of sheep. From wholesale dispatch of sheep to wholesale dispatch of men is really but a short, sanguine jump.

The Graham-Tewksbury quarrel furnishes another example. The Grahams and the Tewksburys had hated each other in Texas, and when both families moved to Arizona, the hatred moved in the wagons with them. Originally both Grahams and Tewksburys ran cattle, but in Arizona the Tewksburys turned to sheep after awhile. The usual charges of range violation, and the natural animosity for Tewksburys by Grahams, and vice versa, led to occasional potshotting that was looked upon by all but the participants as good clean fun.

Open conflict erupted when eight cowboys rode into the Tonto Basin of central Arizona, not really suspecting danger. But the Tewksbury brothers with five cronies were holed up in the basin, and in 10 seconds three cowboys were dead and two others wounded. Within a month, the cowboys had besieged the Tewksbury ranch headquarters, killing John Tewksbury. Retaliation followed retaliation. Within 5 years, all peaceable ranchers had been driven from the country, and 26 cattlemen and six sheepmen had been killed. None of this was considered murder, but simply an intermittent pitched battle to see who would prevail. And not at all incidentally, the Graham-Tewksbury feud provided the plot of one of Zane Grey's most widely accepted eye-popping novels, *To The Last Man,* read by youth and adult, western housewife and New York dentist alike.

The coming of barbed wire into the cattle-country led to another outburst of vigilantism. Violence alone was insufficient against barbed wire because it was an inanimate object that did not directly pit man against man. Like the men it fenced in and fenced out, barbed wire was savage, unrefined, cruel, and hard. And in a sense, like the men whose ranges it controlled, it helped make the Great Plains finally fit for settlement.

As fence-cutting skirmishes broke out from Texas all the way north to Montana, people were killed, property destroyed, business crippled, and otherwise peaceful citizens alienated from one another. Men cut fences because their cattle were thirsty and their tanks were enclosed, or because they desired the good grass now out of bounds, or because the large ranching syndicates had fenced in whole counties. The XIT Ranch in Texas enclosed within wire grasslands approximately the size of the State of Connecticut. To fence in the XIT required 6,000 miles of single-strand wire. The Spur Ranch, also in Texas, erected a drift fence in 1884–85 that strung out for 57 miles, while an old Two Circle Bar cowboy told of seeing 10 wagonloads of barbed wire in the middle 1880's in transit from Colorado City, Texas to the Matador Ranch. Again, men gunned down fence builders, violated enclosed land, and otherwise took the law into their own hands in resisting the coming of a new order. But legality eventually prevailed, and many men who had fought the new orderliness came to embrace it.

In effect, vigilantism was nothing more than lynching. Despite the fact that the South has been internationally damned for its lynching proclivities, it must share some of the tradition with other parts of the world, most notably with the frontier. Nowhere was lynch justice more swift, certain, or flourishing than on the frontier. Human life simply was not as valuable on the frontier as property. Taking a human life was almost as casual as our killing 50,000 people a year now by automobile murder. The fact that Colt's revolver and the repeating rifle were present and the courtroom was frequently absent undoubtedly aided such an attitude. Mitigating or extenuating circumstances for the transgressor were virtually unknown. Either he done it or he didn't.

Granville Stuart, the leading Montana vigilante, tells the story of a Billy Downs who was suspected of selling whiskey to Indians, stealing horses, and killing cattle. One July 4 the vigilantes ordered Downs and another man, an unsavory character known as California Ed, from Downs' house. Both men pleaded guilty to stealing horses from Indians, which was hardly a crime, but denied ever stealing from white men. On the other hand investigation showed their pen with 26 horses with white men's brands, none of the brands their own. A fresh bale of hides bore the brand of the Fergus Stock Co. The two men were carried out to a nearby grove and hanged.

Cattle Kate, otherwise known as Ella Watson and mentioned in Owen Wister's *The Virginian,* and her companion Jim Averill were accused of branding mavericks. In the summer of 1889 they swung from a pine.

In Las Vegas, New Mexico, the following warning was posted in 1880:

To murderers, confidence men, thieves:

The citizens of Las Vegas are tired of robbery, murder, and other crimes that have made this town a byword in every civilized community. They have resolved to put a stop to crime even if in obtaining that end they have to forget the law, and resort to a speedier justice than it will afford. All such characters are, therefore, notified that they must either leave this town or conform themselves to the requirement of law, or they will be summarily dealt with. The flow of blood MUST and SHALL be stopped in this community, and good citizens of both the old and new towns have determined to stop it if they have to HANG by the strong arm of FORCE every violator of law in this country.

Vigilantes

Not too far away, in Sorocco, New Mexico, the vigilantes hanged a Mexican monte dealer because they were incensed at his two employers, despite the fact that those employers were paying the vigilantes $12 a day to keep their monte tables open.

In effect, the Western frontier developed too swiftly for the courts of justice to keep up with the progression of people. Therefore the six-gun or rope seemed superior to judicial procedure. In 1877, for instance, Texas alone had 5,000 men on its wanted list. And Theodore Roosevelt pointed out, "the fact of such scoundrels being able to ply their trade with impunity for any length of time can only be understood if the absolute wildness of our land is taken into account." Roosevelt tells how in 1888 "notorious bullies and murderers have been taken out and hung, while the bands of horse thieves have been regularly hunted down and destroyed in pitched fights by parties of armed cowboys." Small wonder that foppish Bat Masterson was once fined $8 for shooting a citizen through the lung. After all, the man had deserved it.

In Denver, according to one visitor from England, "murder is a comparatively slight offense," a sign of being fashionable.

Until two or three years ago, assassination—incidental not deliberate assassination—was a crime of every day. . . . Unless a ruffian is known to have killed half-a-dozen people, and to have got, as it were, murder on the brain, he is almost safe from trouble in these western plains. A notorious murderer lived near Central City; it was known that he had shot six or seven men; but no one thought of interfering with him on account of his crimes. . . .

The truth is that vigilantism, or "group action in lieu of regular justice," as Caughey calls it, reflects the thinking of a substantial body of local sentiment. The community sits in judgment. It condones because it believes. However, a vital difference exists between vigilantism of the frontier and the vigilantism of the latter 20th century. The pioneer was beyond the reach of regular justice; he had to fill the vacuum. Sometimes he filled it with grave concern for the decencies of human relations. More often he moved in a state of emotion, even as modern society would like to have done following the deaths of the two Kennedys when the identities of the assassins were suspected. . . .

The difficulty with frontier vigilantism is that it has no stopping place. Men accustomed to taking law into their hands continue to take law into their hands even after regular judicial processes are constituted. They continue to take the law into their hands right into these days of the 1960's. They do not approve of a man or a situation, and they cannot wait for the regular processes to assist their realizations. They might not know a frontier if they saw one and they certainly are not aware of the extension of the frontier spirit down to themselves. But they do know that they must get rid of the offending member or section of civilization. So they burn down a ghetto, they loot and pillage, they bury three civil rights workers beneath a dam, or they shoot a man in a caravan in Dallas or on a motel balcony in Memphis. True, to them the law and the other civilized processes may be available, but like the frontiersman they cannot wait. But whereas some frontiersmen had an excuse, these people merely operate in a spirit which does violence even to the memory of the frontier. . . .

Actually the idea of the vigilance committee goes back to Puritan forefathers, whether it is their pointing out witches at Salem or their branding an "A" on a young girl's flesh. Back in 1830 in Illinois a mining rush wrapped around the unexciting metal of lead, ran the town of Galena, Illinois, into the usual welter of saloons, gambling halls, and disregard for law and order. Local citizens formed a vigilance committee. In effect the good moral people who violated the rights of the Mormons at Nauvoo were a self-constituted vigilance group. Iowa, never prominently associated with violence, had its own lead and land rush in the 1840's, and again the law-respecting farmers formed vigilance committees to rid Dubuque of its raffish lead-mining element and Keokuk of its "coarse and ferocious water men." . . .

The truth is, every frontier State went through its period of lawlessness and its corresponding period of mobocracy designed to bring the lawless element under control. Further, the reformers did not cease imposing their personal ideas of reform with the coming of judicial processes. The truth is also that a century later, with or without our frontier background as justification, groups of citizens still make charges outside the law, and some even insist on enforcing those charges. A proper frontier tradition is great and effective, a true heritage for a people who must have heroes to point directions. But a frontier heritage misstated and misapplied is a disservice to the true cause of heritage and a negation of the freedom for which many frontiersmen gave their lives.

Invariably we return to a continuing, fundamental problem of race hatred. Nowadays it is dramatized as between black and white. Once it was between red and white. The hatred may not have been endemic, but the incursions of the white men on the Indian land drove the red man again and again to desperate, savage, and invariably futile war. The missionary loved the red man, from the days of the Spaniard clustered around the Texas and California missions down to the Quakers preaching brotherly love during the Indian massacres of President Grant's days. The fur trader also found the Indian a friend, and particularly found great comfort in the Indian woman. The Indian accepted both occupational groups.

But the one man who could neither assimilate the Indian nor be accepted by his red brother was the farmer. As the farmer moved westward, cutting back the forests, muddying up the streams, and beating back the game, the Indian's enmity toward him grew deadly. As for the frontiersmen, the Indian ranked somewhere below the dog. Certainly the Indian was well below the Negro slave, for the latter had function and utility. How do you handle an element for which there is no positive use? You exterminate it, especially if in your eyes it has murderous propensities. And so the inevitable, as virtually all the world knows, happened. The conflict between the two races, in the words of Ralph Gabriel, "like a forest fire, burned its way westward across the continent." The noble savage was not noble at all in the sight of his adversary but a beast who bashed babies' heads up against trees and tore skin bit by bit from women's bodies. Each atrocity on either side evoked an equal retaliation. The list is long and painful, and no credit to either side.

From the standpoint of 20th century society, however, the white-Indian conflict for 300 years has important implications. For one thing, during the periodic lapses into peace which the young American nation enjoyed, these vacations from war did not by any means allow only for dull consolidation of the nation's politics and economics; instead they offered prime time for violent internal action. Almost always an Indian war was going on somewhere. On some wing of the frontier the white man was being menaced by the Indian, or he was menacing the Indian. He was running the Indian out of the woods, he was running him off the grasslands, he was running him across the desert and over the mountains to the west. With an insatiable earth hunger he was destroying the Indians' hunting grounds, until eventually he destroyed the game itself. This is not to discount those sincere Americans who had an interest in Indian culture and a desire for the two races to live side by side, but merely to point out that if any young man, full of the rising sap of the springtime of life, wanted to flex his muscles and pick a fight, he could find some Indian to fight against. The fact that the frontier also attracted the rootless and the drifters, and that these were often desperate men, added to the conflict and the inability to maintain peaceful Indian relations.

A mere listing of the battles with Indians would cover hundreds of pages in 6-point type. . . .

And if you get home from a war or a skirmish, you have instant hero status if you have halfway behaved yourself. There is a premium on killing Indians, a premium whose dividends continue through life. Men who came in after the end of Indian wars falsely delegated themselves as Indian fighters as they grew older and no one could prove them wrong. Often, criminal acts against other white men could be forgiven because a man had distinguished himself in combat against the Indians. Thus the retreating Indians constituted a kind of omnipresent safety salve for those people who liked to dance with danger, vitalize themselves with violence, and renew themselves with revenge.

Actually, although the only good Indian might be a dead one, there were two types of Indian. There were the peaceful ones, like California's 150,000 "Digger" Indians, a tranquil people, who lived off the product of the land. There were also the warrior Indians, like the Sioux and the Apache. The white frontiersman generally looked on both with suspicion and distaste. California's miners murdered the Diggers as though they were endangered by them. On the other hand, murdering the warrior Indian was often a question of killing before you got killed, which simplified the problem. Skilled horsemen, these Indians, largely from the Great Plains, hit and ran with tactics that would have brought admiration from such mounted generals as Phil Sheridan, Jeb Stuart, or Erwin Rommel. Theirs was lightning warfare, and at full run they could loose twenty arrows while their longer-shooting foes were trying to reload. The wars themselves are reasonably straightforward, and could perhaps be condoned as inexorable conflicts. But the individual atrocities have no justification, even though at the time the perpetrators were often saluted as heroes. This latter statement holds true for both sides.

Nowhere has a lust for blood been more deeply etched than in the infamous Sand Creek massacre. Shortly after sundown on November 28, 1864, Col. J. M. Chivington and his men left Fort Lyon, Colo., to surround the followers of Chief Black Kettle. At dawn Chivington's militia charged through the camp of 500 peaceful Indians, despite Black Kettle's raising an American and then a white flag. Not just warriors were killed. Women and children were dragged out, shot, knifed, scalped, clubbed, mutilated, their brains knocked out, bosoms ripped open. Four hundred and fifty Indians in varying stages of insensate slaughter lay about the campground. There is no defense whatsoever for the action. It was bloodier than Chicago or Detroit or Harlem ever thought of being. Chivington and his cohorts were widely hailed as heroes by many of their fellow Americans.

Perfidy was not all on one side. During the summer of 1866, troops working on the Powder River road were constantly harassed by Indian attack. In a complete, efficient, and economical performance the Sioux killed every straggler, raided every wagon train bringing in supplies, and attacked every wood-cutting party. Finally in December, when a wood train was assaulted, Capt. W. J. Fetterman led a party to its relief. The Indians ambushed him, and left all 82 members of his party to rot on the field of battle. What Sitting Bull's detachment did to reckless and feckless Colonel George A. Custer at the Little Big Horn is known to everyone who ever looked at the Old Anheuser-Busch calendar or a Remington painting. Two hundred and sixty-five men were completely wiped out by 2,500 Sioux. . . .

Sometimes it was not racial arrogance at all, but a simple antagonism to people with different outlooks. Thus Joseph Smith, Brigham Young, and other Mormons ran into the inflammatory and adamant opposition of local people, whether they lived in northeastern Ohio, Missouri, Illinois, or Utah. The Gentiles, believing presumably in all the Christian precepts, including love thy neighbor, did not love anyone whose faith was so far from theirs. It was difficult enough for a Campbellite on the frontier to accept a Baptist or one of John Knox's followers; Catholics and Jews were barely tolerable; the Mormon, a latecomer to the world of organized religion, was downright intolerable. His position was made less tenable by the fact that he tended to prosper, which induced Gentile grumbling that Mormons must be in league with the devil. And then one night at Carthage, Missouri, a properly organized area, a mob broke into the jail where Joseph Smith and his brother had been lodged for protection, and slaughtered the two Mormon leaders. Back east across the river, angry Gentiles served notice that the Mormons could leave or else. . . .

The war with Mexico undoubtedly has some roots in racial arrogance on both sides. In fact, the whole severance of Texas from Mexico was brought about by men from the United States lately come to that vast area, and impatient with Mexican law and administration. Because the Mexicans felt that the Anglos represented a materialistic and restless culture, they were equally intolerant of their Anglo neighbors. . . .

The ensuing overwhelming defeat of the Mexican forces and the wholesale dissection of Mexican territory into the giant maw of the North Americans only exacerbated distrust between the two nations. For the next 40 years Mexicans raided north of the Rio Grande. The Texans called them bandits. In pursuit of the Mexicans, Texans ranged south of the Rio Grande, where the Mexicans called them bandits. Both sides were right, and both were equally wrong. Again, as with the Indians, the killing of one race by another was perfectly justified back home. The Texas Rangers, a law enforcement group, raided Mexicans along with Indians as natural enemies, and seldom gave any Mexican, whether a national of the United States or of Mexico, the benefit of the doubt. . . .

If during this essay it seems as if the frontier heritage is predominantly negative and directed toward violence, such a conclusion is misleading. The purpose here has been to examine a facet of frontier heritage, that surface which not only condoned but actually encouraged the idea and practice of violence but which undoubtedly plays a role in shaping 20th-century American attitudes. The examination could go into as much detail as the danger, the frontier heritage established the idea of the individual's arming himself. This activity is almost unique with the United States frontier. Instead of a central armory to which men could go to gather their arms, each man bore his own. He thus had it always at the ready. When danger arose, he could get together with another man, and another and another, until an armed mob was on its way. It might be a mob in the best posse sense, or it might be an extra legal group which felt that its private preserves and attitudes were threatened. But it was always a mob.

The prevalence of arms over the fireplace of every frontier cabin or stacked by the sodhouse door endures in the defense which groups like the National Rifle Association membership carry on today against attempts to register arms and control the sale of guns and ammunition. A man had to have a gun, not solely for game to feed his family but because he had to be ready to defend. This heritage continues. As of this writing, it still prevails in most parts of the Nation. Almost no other country permits such widespread individual owner- ship, but the United States through its frontier experience has historical justifi- cation. In pioneer days a frontier boy came of age when his father presented him his own gun as surely as a town boy came of age by putting on long pants or his sister became a woman by putting up her hair. In many areas of the United States in A.D. 1969 a boy still becomes a man, usually on his birthday or at Christmas, when his father gives him a gun. A generally accepted age is twelve, although it may come even a half-dozen years sooner. The gun may be nothing more than a target weapon, but the boy is shown how to use it and how to take care of it, and he is a gun owner and user, probably for the next 60 years of his expected life on this earth. Whether he shoots sparrows out of the eaves of the house, quail and deer in season, or his fellowman with or without provocation remains for his personal history to unfold. The fact is that in his gun ownership he is following a tradition that goes back to John Smith and Jamestown and has persisted ever since.

And yet, as every schoolboy knows, the frontier has given us other traits which also mark us and often improve us. The frontier made us materialistic, because we needed things to survive. The frontier, by the very act of its being there for the taking and taming, gave us an optimistic belief in progress which again has marked the nation for greatness. The frontier fostered individualism as in no other region of the world. It gave us mobility; a man could move up and down the social, economic, and political scale without regard to what he had been before. The frontiersman could remold institutions to make them work. The frontiersman did not necessarily believe in individual freedom, except for himself, for he turned to his constituted government for every kind of help, particularly economic. The frontier also made him physically mobile long before the mechanics of transportation made such mobility easy. The frontier made him generous, even prodigal and extravagant, particularly where national resources were concerned. The frontier undoubtedly made the American nationalistic.

Thus we see a blending of a man's qualities that is both good and bad. If the good could somehow be retained, while those qualities which have outlived their usefulness could be eschewed or dismissed forever, the human material which constitutes this nation could develop in the direction of an improved society. To argue which facets of the frontier experience have outlived their utility can be argued interminably, but certainly the wistful look backwards which Americans, informed and uninformed, cast toward the violence associated with the frontier has no place in a nation whose frontier has worn away. The time for everyone, from scenario writers to political breast beaters to economic and social individualists, to proclaim the virtues of the frontiersman and his reliance on simple solutions and direct action does not befit a nation whose problems are corporate, community, and complex.

CHAPTER 6

RACE RELATIONS IN THE NEW SOUTH: 1870-1900

The Supreme Court desegregation decision in 1954 *(Brown* v. *Board of Education of the City of Topeka)* touched off a vigorous defense of segregation by white Americans, particularly Southerners. Segregation, it was argued, had traditionally served as the basis for an entire "way of life." According to this version of history, physical separation of blacks from whites had characterized race relations both in antebellum days and in the years after Southerners had redeemed their section from Radical control. Only briefly, during the bitter Reconstruction period, had the pattern of segregation been tampered with, and then with ill results. Hence, the argument went, neither the Supreme Court nor any other body could effectively "legislate" race relations, which were governed by mores and customs rooted deep in the American and Southern past.

But the *Brown* decision and the increasingly important role of race relations in contemporary national affairs also prompted professional academic concentration on black history and race relations. One of the most significant and influential products of the new research is C. Vann Woodward's classic study of *The Strange Career of Jim Crow,* originally delivered in the fall of 1954 in a lecture series at the University of Virginia. In this selection from that work, Professor Woodward concentrates on race relations in the South in the 1870s, the 1880s, and the 1890s. He is concerned particularly with the general treatment of blacks by whites, with the degree of association and contact between the races, and with the amount of segregation in political and civil life, in social and religious institutions, and in public conveyances and other places of public accommodation.

The student should carefully avoid reading into this essay meanings that are not supported by what Woodward actually says. Pertinent to this suggestion, for example, is this question: What does Professor Woodward say about the 1870s, the 1880s, and the 1890s as a golden age of race relations? Most important, what is the author's primary purpose, explicitly stated, in this selection? Do you think he achieves this purpose? Finally, what was the nature of race relations during this period? Was there any fairly consistent pattern in Southern race relations in the post-Reconstruction years? What does this reading suggest about the immutability of folkways? Do you find Professor Woodward's thesis and findings surprising?

In addition to exploring other portions of the Woodward volume* (1955) and Woodward's brilliant essay, "The Strange Career of a Historical Controversy" in his recent book, *American Counterpoint: Slavery and Racism in the North-South Dialogue** (1971), students can read with profit two monographs in the specific area: Charles E. Wynes, *Race Relations in Virginia, 1870–1902* (1961), and Frenise A. Logan, *The Negro in North Carolina, 1876–1894* (1964). Robert R. Jones and Henry C. Dethloff, "Race Relations in Louisiana, 1877–1898," *Louisiana History,* IX (Fall 1968), is a specific application of the Woodward thesis to Louisiana. Woodward's own *Origins of the New South** (1951) has much useful material. For the influence of legislation on folkways, see "Ought There To Be a Law?" in Gordon W. Allport, *The Nature of Prejudice** (1954).

*Available in a paperback edition.

FORGOTTEN ALTERNATIVES

C. VANN WOODWARD

The Redeemers who overthrew Reconstruction and established "Home Rule" in the Southern states conducted their campaign in the name of white supremacy. The new rulers did not, however, inaugurate any revolution in the customs and laws governing racial relations. They retained such segregation practices as had grown up during Reconstruction, but showed no disposition to expand or universalize the system. Separation of the races continued to be the rule in churches and schools, in military life and public institutions as it had been before. And as the new governments added what few new public services they built—schools, hospitals, asylums, and the like—they applied existing practices of segregation, sometimes by law and sometimes without. But the new order represented no striking departures in this respect.

After Redemption the old and the new in race relations continued to overlap as they had during Reconstruction. The old heritage of slavery and the new and insecure heritage of legal equality were wholly incompatible as ideas, but each in its own way assured a degree of human contact and association that would pass with the fading of the old heritage and the eventual destruction of the new. Race relations after Redemption were an unstable interlude before the passing of these old and new traditions and the arrival of the Jim Crow code and disfranchisement.

One heritage of the old order that persisted far into the new was the pattern of residential mixture in the older cities and towns. A Northern reporter remarked with puzzlement in 1880 upon "the proximity and confusion, so to speak, of white and negro houses" in both the countryside and cities of South Carolina. This pattern of "proximity and confusion" continued for decades in the older parts of the South. Another heritage of the old order that kept physical contact between the races from becoming an issue and an irritant was both psychological and economic. The Negro bred to slavery was typically ignorant and poor and was not given to pressing his rights to such luxuries as hotels, restaurants, and theaters even when he could afford them or was aware of them. So far as his status was concerned, there was little need for Jim Crow

SOURCE. C. Vann Woodward, *The Strange Career of Jim Crow,* second revised edition, pp. 31–36, 41–45, and 64–65. Copyright 1966 by Oxford University Press, Inc. Reprinted by permission of Oxford University Press.

laws to establish what the lingering stigma of slavery—in bearing, speech, and manner—made so apparent.

At the same time the more confident, assertive, and ambitious members of the race had not forgotten the vision of civil rights and equality that Reconstruction had inspired. Still fresh in their memories was an exhilarating if precarious taste of recognition and power. The hopes and expectations aroused by these experiences had been dimmed but not extinguished by the Compromise of 1877. The laws were still on the books, and the whites had learned some measure of accommodation. Negroes still voted in large numbers, held numerous elective and appointive offices, and appealed to the courts with hope for redress of grievances. Under these circumstances a great deal of variety and inconsistency prevailed in race relations from state to state and within a state. It was a time of experiment, testing, and uncertainty—quite different from the time of repression and rigid uniformity that was to come toward the end of the century. Alternatives were still open and real choices had to be made.

A thorough study by Charles E. Wynes, *Race Relations in Virginia,* finds that in this state "the most distinguishing factor in the complexity of social relations between the races was that of inconsistency. From 1870 to 1900, there was no generally accepted code of racial mores." During those three decades, according to this study, "at no time was it the general demand of the white populace that the Negro be disfranchised and white supremacy be made the law of the land." Until 1900, when a law requiring the separation of the races on railroad cars was adopted by a majority of one vote, "the Negro sat where he pleased and among the white passengers on perhaps a majority of the state's railroads." There were exceptions, but "they became fewer and fewer" toward the end of the period. The same was true of the street cars. In other public accommodations and places of entertainment the black patron often met with rebuff and sometimes eviction, but not always, for "occasionally the Negro met no segregation when he entered restaurants, bars, waiting rooms, theatres, and other public places of amusement." There were risks, but no firm policy of exclusion, and this "led many Negroes to keep trying for acceptance, just as it led at least some whites to accept them." There were crosscurrents and uncertainties on both sides, but in spite of this there remained a considerable range of flexibility and tolerance in relations between the races in Virginia between 1870 and 1900.

More than a decade was to pass after Redemption before the first Jim Crow law was to appear upon the law books of a Southern state, and more than two decades before the older states of the seaboard were to adopt such laws. There was much segregation and discrimination of an extra-legal sort before the laws were adopted in all states, but the amount of it differed from one place to another and one time to another, just as it did in Virginia.

The individual experiences and the testimony regarding them presented below are not offered as conclusive evidence or as proof of a prevailing pattern. They are the observations of intelligent men with contrasting backgrounds and origins about a fluid, continually changing, and controversial situation. It would be perfectly possible to cite contemporary experiences and testimony of a contrasting character. To appreciate the significance of the following episodes and experiences one has only to attempt to imagine any of them occurring in any of the states concerned at any time during the first half of the twentieth century. The contrast will be less immediately apparent, and perhaps even lost, to those whose personal experience and memory does not extend quite so remotely as the 1940's, but they might ask confirmation from their elders.

I

Suspicions of the South's intentions toward the freedmen after the withdrawal of federal troops were naturally rife in the North. In 1878 Colonel Thomas Wentworth Higginson went south to investigate for himself. The report of his findings, published in the *Atlantic Monthly,* is of particular interest in view of the Colonel's background. One of the most militant abolitionists, Higginson had lost some of his zeal, but he had been one of the "Secret Six" who conspired with John Brown before the Harpers Ferry raid, and during the war he had organized and led a combat regiment of Negro troops. In Virginia, South Carolina, and Florida, the states he visited in 1878, he found "a condition of outward peace" and wondered immediately if there did not lurk beneath it "some covert plan for crushing or reënslaving the colored race." If so, he decided, it would "show itself in some personal ill usage of the blacks, in the withdrawal of privileges, in legislation endangering their rights." But, he reported, "I can assert that, carrying with me the eyes of a tolerably suspicious abolitionist, I saw none of these indications." He had expected to be affronted by contemptuous or abusive treatment of Negroes. "During this trip," however, he wrote, "I had absolutely no occasion for any such attitude." Nor was this due to "any cringing demeanor on the part of the blacks, for they show much more manhood than they once did." He compared the tolerance and acceptance of the Negro in the South on trains and street cars, at the polls, in the courts and legislatures, in the police force and militia, with attitudes in his native New England and decided that the South came off rather better in the comparison. "How can we ask more of the States formerly in rebellion," he demanded, "than that they should be abreast of New England in granting rights and privileges to the colored race? Yet this is now the case in the three states I name; or at least if they fall behind in some points, they lead at some points." Six years later, in a review of the situation in the South, Higginson found no reason to change his estimate of 1878.

The year 1879 provides testimony to the point from a foreign observer. Sir George Campbell, a member of Parliament, traveled over a large part of the South, with race relations as the focus of his interest. He was impressed with the freedom of association between whites and blacks, with the frequency and intimacy of personal contact, and with the extent of Negro participation in political affairs. He commented with particular surprise on the equality with which Negroes shared public facilities. He reported some discrimination but remarked that "the humblest black rides with the proudest white on terms of perfect equality, and without the smallest symptom of malice or dislike on either side. I was, I confess, surprised to see how completely this is the case; even an English Radical is a little taken aback at first."

In the first year of Redemption a writer who signed himself "A South Carolinian" in the *Atlantic Monthly* corroborated the observations of the Englishman regarding the Negro's equality of treatment on common carriers, trains, and street cars. "The Negroes are freely admitted to the theatre in Columbia and to other exhibitions, lectures, etc.," though the whites avoided sitting with them "if the hall be not crowded," he added. "In Columbia they are also served at the bars, soda water fountains, and ice-cream saloons, but not generally elsewhere." They were not accepted in hotels and numerous other accommodations.

Twenty years later, in 1897, even though many concessions had by that time been made to racism, a Charleston editor referring to a proposed Jim Crow law for trains could still write: "We care nothing whatever about Northern or outside opinion in this matter. It is a question for our own decision according to our own ideas of what is right and expedient. And our opinion is that we have no more need for a Jim Crow system this year than we had last year, and a great deal less than we had twenty and thirty years ago." In his view such a law was "unnecessary and uncalled for," and furthermore it would be "a needless affront to our respectable and well behaved colored people."

Southern white testimony on the subject has naturally been discounted as propaganda. If only by way of contrast with later views, however, the following editorial from the Richmond *Dispatch,* 13 October 1886, is worth quoting: "Our State Constitution requires all State officers in their oath of office to declare that they 'recognize and accept the civil and political equality of all men.' We repeat that nobody here objects to sitting in political conventions with negroes. Nobody here objects to serving on juries with negroes. No lawyer objects to practicing law in court where negro lawyers practice. . . . Colored men are allowed to introduce bills into the Virginia Legislature, and in both branches of this body negroes are allowed to sit, as they have a right to sit." George Washington Cable, the aggressive agitator for the rights of Negroes, protested strongly against discrimination elsewhere, but is authority for the statement made in 1885, that "In Virginia they may ride exactly as white people do and in the same cars."

More pertinent, whether typical or not, is the experience of a Negro. In April, 1885, T. McCants Stewart set forth from Boston to visit his native state of South Carolina after an absence of ten years. A Negro newspaperman, corresponding editor of the New York *Freeman*, Stewart was conscious of his role as a spokesman and radical champion of his race. "On leaving Washington, D.C." he reported to his paper, "I put a chip on my shoulder, and inwardly dared any man to knock it off." He found a seat in a car which became so crowded that several white passengers had to sit on their baggage. "I fairly foamed at the mouth," he wrote, "imagining that the conductor would order me into a seat occupied by a colored lady so as to make room for a white passenger." Nothing of the sort happened, however, nor was there any unpleasantness when Stewart complained of a request from a white Virginian that he shift his baggage so that the white man could sit beside him. At a stop twenty-one miles below Petersburg he entered a station dining room, "bold as a lion," he wrote, took a seat at a table with white people, and was courteously served. "The whites at the table appeared not to note my presence," he reported. "Thus far I had found travelling more pleasant . . . than in some parts of New England." Abroad a steamboat in North Carolina he complained of a colored waiter who seated him at a separate table, though in the same dining room with whites. At Wilmington, however, he suffered from no discrimination in dining arrangements. His treatment in Virginia and North Carolina, he declared, "contrasted strongly with much that I have experienced in dining rooms in the North." Another contrast that impressed him was the ease and frequency with which white people entered into conversation with him for no other purpose than to pass the time of day. "I think the whites of the South," he observed, "are really less afraid to [have] contact with colored people than the whites of the North."

Stewart continued his journey southward, rejoicing that "Along the Atlantic seaboard . . . [in] all the old slave States with enormous Negro populations . . . a first-class ticket is good in a first-class coach. . . ." From Columbia, South Carolina, he wrote: "I feel about as safe here as in Providence, R.I. I can ride in first-class cars on the railroads and in the streets. I can go into saloons and get refreshments even as in New York. I can stop in and drink a glass of soda and be more politely waited upon than in some parts of New England." He also found that "Negroes dine with whites in a railroad saloon" in his native state. He watched a Negro policeman arrest a white man "under circumstances requiring coolness, prompt decision, and courage"; and in Charleston he witnessed the review of hundreds of Negro troops. "Indeed," wrote Stewart, "the Palmetto State leads the South in some things. . . ."

One significant aspect of Stewart's newspaper reports should be noted. They were written a month after the inauguration of Grover Cleveland and the return of the Democrats to power for the first time in twenty-four years. His paper had opposed Cleveland, and propaganda had been spread among Negro voters that the return of the Democrats would mean the end of freedmen's rights, if not their liberty. Stewart failed to find what he was looking for, and after a few weeks cut his communications short with the comment that he could find "nothing spicy or exciting to write." "For the life of [me]," he confessed, "I can't 'raise a row' in these letters. Things seem (remember I write seem) to move along as smoothly as in New York or Boston. . . . If you should ask me 'watchman, tell us of the night' . . . I would say, 'the morning light is breaking.' "

So far nearly all the evidence presented has come from the older states of the eastern seabord. In writing of slavery under the old regime it is common for historians to draw distinctions between the treatment of slaves in the upper and older South and their lot in the lower South and the newer states. In the former their condition is generally said to have been better than it was in the latter. It is worth remarking an analogous distinction in the treatment of the race in the era of segregation. It is clear at least that the newer states were inclined to resort to Jim Crow laws earlier than the older commonwealths of the seaboard, and there is evidence that segregation and discrimination became more generally practiced before they became law. Even so, there are a number of indications that segregation and ostracism were not so harsh and rigid in the early years as they became later.

In his study of conditions in Mississippi, Vernon Wharton reveals that for some years "most of the saloons served whites and Negroes at the same bar. Many of the restaurants, using separate tables, served both races in the same room. . . . On May 21, 1879, the Negroes of Jackson, after a parade of their fire company, gave a picnic in Hamilton Park. On the night of May 29, 'the ladies of the [white] Episcopal Church' used Hamilton Park for a *fete*. After their picnic the Negroes went to Angelo's Hall for a dance. This same hall was used for white dances and parties, and was frequently the gathering place of Democratic conventions. . . . Throughout the state common cemeteries, usually in separate portions, held the graves of both whites and Negroes." Wharton points out, however, that as early as 1890 segregation had closed in and the Negroes were by that date excluded from saloons, restaurants, parks, public halls, and white cemeteries.

At the International Exposition in New Orleans in 1885 Charles Dudley Warner watched with some astonishment as "white and colored people mingled freely, talking and looking at what was of common interest. . . . On 'Louisiana Day' in the Exposition the colored citizens," he reported, "took their full share of the parade and the honors. Their societies marched with the others, and the races mingled in the grounds in unconscious equality of privileges." While he was in the city he also saw "a colored clergyman in his surplice seated in the chancel of the most important white Episcopal church in New Orleans, assisting the service."

A frequent topic of comment by Northern visitors during the period was the intimacy of contact between the races in the South, an intimacy sometimes admitted to be distasteful to the visitor. Standard topics were the sight of white babies suckled at black breasts, white and colored children playing together, the casual proximity of white and Negro homes in the cities, the camaraderie of maidservant and mistress, employer and employee, customer and clerk, and the usual stories of cohabitation of white men and Negro women. The same sights and stories had once been favorite topics of comment for the carpetbaggers and before them of the abolitionists, both of whom also expressed puzzlement and sometimes revulsion. What the Northern traveler of the 'eighties sometimes took for signs of a new era of race relations was really a heritage of slavery times, or, more elementally, the result of two peoples having lived together intimately for a long time—whatever their formal relations were, whether those of master and slave, exploiter and exploited, or superior and inferior.

It would certainly be preposterous to leave the impression that any evidence I have submitted indicates a golden age of race relations in the period between Redemption and complete segregation. On the contrary, the evidence is overwhelming. It was, after all, in the 'eighties and early 'nineties that lynching attained the most staggering proportions ever reached in the history of that crime. Moreover, the fanatical advocates of racism, whose doctrines of total segregation, disfranchisement, and ostracism eventually triumphed over all opposition and became universal practice in the South, were already at work and already beginning to establish dominance over some phases of Southern life. Before their triumph was complete, however, there transpired a period of history whose significance has been neglected. Exploitation there was in that period, as in other periods and in other regions, but it did not follow then that the exploited had to be ostracized. Subordination there was also, unmistakable subordination; but it was not yet an accepted corollary that the subordinates had to be totally segregated and needlessly humiliated by a thousand daily reminders of their subordination. Conflict there was, too, violent conflict in which the advantage lay with the strong and the dominant, as always, but conflict of some kind was unavoidable so long as there remained any contact between the races whatever.

The era of stiff conformity and fanatical rigidity that was to come had not yet closed in and shut off all contact between the races, driven the Negroes from all public forums, silenced all white dissenters, put a stop to all rational discussion and exchange of views, and precluded all variety and experiment in types of interracial association. There were still real choices to be made, and alternatives to the course eventually pursued with such single-minded unanimity and unquestioning conformity were still available.

Before the South capitulated completely to the doctrines of the extreme racists, three alternative philosophies of race relations were put forward to compete for the region's adherence and support. One of these, the conservative philosophy, attracted wide support and was tried out in practice over a considerable period of time. The second approach to the problem, that of the Southern radicals, received able expression and won numerous adherents, but the lack of political success on the part of the radical party of Populism limited the trial by practice of that philosophy to rather inconclusive experiments. The liberal philosophy of race relations, the third approach, received able and forceful expression, but was promptly and almost totally rejected and never put to practice in that period. All three of these alternative philosophies rejected the doctrines of extreme racism and all three were indigenously and thoroughly Southern in origin. . . .

My only purpose has been to indicate that things have not always been the same in the South. In a time when the Negroes formed a much larger proportion of the population than they did later, when slavery was a live memory in the minds of both races, and when the memory of the hardships and bitterness of Reconstruction was still fresh, the race policies accepted and pursued in the South were sometimes milder than they became later. The policies of proscription, segregation, and disfranchisement that are often described as the immutable "folkways" of the South, impervious alike to legislative reform and armed intervention, are of a more recent origin. The effort to justify them as a consequence of Reconstruction and a necessity of the times is embarrassed by the fact that they did not originate in those times. And the belief that they are immutable and unchangeable is not supported by history.

CHAPTER 7

THE AMERICAN PEOPLE IN THE LATE NINETEENTH CENTURY

As noted in several previous chapters, the Civil War period marked a major turning point in United States history. A more strongly united nation emerged as the period of sectional conflict drew to a close in the 1870s, and the reunification helped pave the way for the momentous changes that the nation experienced in the late nineteenth century. As Carl Degler suggests, the industrialization of the country in the postwar period constituted nothing less than an economic revolution of massive proportions. A necessary concurrent change of equal importance was the growth of American cities. Urbanization proceeded at such a pace that by 1920 a majority of Americans lived in cities. Industrialization, urbanization, and the changes produced by the Civil War and reconstruction brought deep-seated social, economic, and political adjustments and, in the process, altered the composition, the values, and the lifestyles—the very face—of the American people.

It is with these profound and irrevocable changes in the American population that Professor Bernard A. Weisberger is concerned in this selection. Prior to 1865, the United States had been primarily a rural nation with a relatively stable and cohesive population that shared common goals and beliefs. After the Civil War, waves of immigrants came into the country, and they and former residents of rural America flocked in ever-increasing numbers to the cities. Whatever their dreams for the future and their hopes of carving out for themselves positions of economic independence, most of the newcomers to the cities settled into a class of permanent wage earners. The new economic order profoundly affected the mass of industrial laborers—both those of immigrant and those of native stock—as well as the continuing large group of American farmers. Another group of Americans, the blacks, most of whom had been recently liberated from slavery, saw their dreams frustrated as they faced unexpectedly strong discrimination in education, politics, and economic life. In this selection Professor Weisberger focuses on the immigrant, the industrial laborer, the black man, and the embattled farmer; these were the people who composed the new American population of the late nineteenth century, and Weisberger describes their conditions, their aspirations, their problems, and their attempts to deal with the difficulties they faced.

While reading this selection, the student should keep in mind the following questions. Was there a common, fundamental problem faced by the immigrant, the black, the laborer, and the yeoman farmer? If so, what was it? What were the particular problems faced by the various groups of "newcomers," how did they seek to solve them, and what degree of success did they have? Was there any similarity in the way the "newcomer" groups attacked their problems? Finally, what is the nature of the American population of the 1980s, and do we still have some of the same problems that faced "old" and "new" Americans in the late nineteenth century?

For an excellent discussion of the new American population of the late nineteenth century, see the appropriate sections of Carl N. Degler, *Out of Our Past: The Forces That Shaped Modern America** (1970). Degler has a particularly insightful treatment of labor. Oscar Handlin deals sensitively with the problems of immigrants in *The Uprooted: The Epic Story of the Great Migrations That Made the American People** (1951). August Meier, *Negro Thought in America, 1880–1915** (1963), and W. E. B. DuBois, *The Souls of Black Folk** (1903), provide useful insights into black life and thought in this period. For the problems and responses of agrarian America, see Chapter 10 in this volume.

*Available in a paperback edition.

A NEW AMERICAN POPULATION (1870–1910)

BERNARD A. WEISBERGER

In one sense, the Civil War was a struggle to determine whether there was a single American people instead of "the people of the several states." The affirmative answer was registered at Appomattox Courthouse on April 9, 1865. Yet this national populace, whose political existence was guaranteed by the war, began to change irrevocably after 1865. Before then, it was a relatively stable group of people much alike in wealth, calling and beliefs, who lived primarily in rural areas. As postwar years went by, the populace changed into an interdependent mass of men and women of varied backgrounds—largely city dwellers and industrial workers. New occupational and social groups came into being, and had to find fresh ways of dealing with each other. Moreoever, the Jacksonian ideals of equality and individualism were hard to apply in such an enlarged and altered nation. The social struggles of the period from 1870 to 1914 partly reflected the difficulty of the task.

OUTSIDERS AND OLD VALUES

We have already seen evidence of the tidal pull of the city on rural folk. The economic changes associated with this migration from the farm are clearly shown by census statistics. In 1860, out of a gainfully employed population of about ten and a half million, approximately six and one quarter million were involved in farm occupations as opposed to trade, industry, transportation, and the professions. By 1880, a work force of seventeen million was almost equally divided—eight and one half million in farming, and a similar number otherwise employed. By 1890, however, persons who worked in agriculture numbered ten out of twenty-three million, and in 1910 fewer than thirty percent of about twenty-six million working Americans were on farms. More than half the nonfarm workers in 1910 were engaged in mining, manufacturing, construction, transportation, and public utilities. In less than a lifetime, we had become a nation of industrial workers instead of a nation of farmers.

We became also a nation of noticeable newcomers. The word "noticeable" is important to bear in mind. Total annual immigration to the United States

SOURCE. Bernard A. Weisberger, *The New Industrial Society,* pp. 70–95. Copyright 1969 by John Wiley & Sons, Inc. Reprinted by permission of John Wiley & Sons, Inc.

after the Civil War rose from a quarter of a million in 1865 to peaks of nearly 800,000 in 1882 and a million in 1905, with occasional declines, especially in depression years. . . . A high point was established with 1,285,349 immigrants in 1907 and, by 1910, the total number of foreign-born in the country was fourteen million—with another nineteen million of "foreign or mixed parentage." These fourteen million foreign-born were 14.5 percent of the total American population. But in 1860 the country's four million "nonnative" residents constituted about 13.2 percent of the total population. Thus, despite popular assumptions to the contrary then and since, there was no striking change in the total proportion of the foreign-born. There was, however, a dramatic change in the visibility of the "alien" because of a change in the sources of immigration and the occupations available to recent arrivals. Until the 1890s, immigrants from the British Isles, Germany, Scandinavia, Switzerland, and Holland made up more than 8.5 percent of the total. But the great surge of immigration, from 1896 to 1914, consisted mainly of newcomers from Austria, Hungary, Italy, Russia, Greece, Rumania, and Turkey. A large proportion of them, moreover, found their way into mines, mills, and factories. In twenty-one industries studied by a Congressional commission in 1910, nearly 60 percent of all employees were foreign-born, and two-thirds of these were from the countries of Southern and Eastern Europe. What a native American was apt to see when he confronted the "foreigner," in that year, was an urban lower-class wage earner from a cultural background entirely different from that of his own parents and grandparents. The incoming German, Norwegian, or Irishman found communities where his own kind had been known for a generation or more: the Sicilian, the Greek, the Pole, or the Magyar was doubly a stranger.

In a sense, too, the four million freedmen of 1865, whose numbers had increased to just under ten million by 1910, were also newcomers. True, the first Negroes had landed in Virginia in 1619, the year before the *Mayflower* arrived off Cape Cod but, as independent members of society, the ex-slaves and their children were as inexperienced and even more handicapped than immigrants just down the gangplank.

These sweeping changes in the composition and activity of the populace were creating a new social order. Yet it was one still officially guided by the expectations of an earlier era. In a youthful America, social thought dealt with a few basic figures: the yeoman, the artisan, the merchant, the professional man. Their self-sufficiency and ambition were the cornerstones of American democracy. Their freely chosen government spared them burdensome regulations and taxations, educated them, and encouraged them to pursue their self-interest. As the nation grew, so did their opportunities. Proof of success was in the ownership or enlargement of productive property. This was the goal of all laudable effort and the proof of respectability. Abraham Lincoln explained it to a Wisconsin agricultural-fair audience on the eve of the Civil War as he defined and glorified "free labor." The "prudent, penniless beginner," he said, worked for another for a time, accumulated a competency, then became an owner who toiled on his own account, and perhaps employed others on the way up. "If any continue in the condition of a hired laborer for life," Lincoln continued, "it is because of a dependent nature which prefers it, or singular folly or improvidence or misfortune."

The vision was keyed to the old Puritan virtues of hard work, hard study, and advancement. Yet, in deifying growth, the vision also encouraged speculative investment and capital risk. In the quest for economically fruitful ventures, many respectable nineteenth century Americans (who would not have borrowed a dime for personal expenditures) did not hesitate to go deeply into debt in order to invest in lands, banks, canals, and business ventures of every kind. Their hopes of success glowed brightly, no matter how far-fetched the project. This was not considered as gambling but as contributing to progress. Faith in progress legitimized the crapshooter lurking in the heart of every respectable citizen who laid out a spare dollar in land or stock purchases.

Such was the dream that formed the substance of a confident young nation's outlook on life. It was one of the forces that energized people who, for the most part, had access (or legitimate hope of access to the means of genuine economic independence—land, professional learning, and income-generating property. But the new America of the 1880s and 1890s was full of people for whom the old promises did not hold true. The industrial worker could not hope to own the vast machinery that employed him, no matter how much he shunned improvidence and folly. The newly arrived immigrant could scarcely enter the race of life advantageously with nothing available to him but an unskilled job and a tenement flat. Self-improvement was equally difficult for the ultimate outsider—the Negro—whom Reconstruction's philanthropy left jobless and landless, twice cursed with blackness and poverty. Even the land-owning, staple-crop farmer found success to be elusive. He was caught in an impersonal market system; he was made dependent on others who furnished him with machinery and transportation; and he was reduced from a "noble yeoman" to a self-employed laborer on a heavily mortgaged farm with no prospect of change in sight.

These new personages of social reality wanted to live by the code of diligent advancement which, by 1880, was national orthodoxy. Yet they could not, and consequently were condemned by the already-arrived as if they *would* not.

THE IMMIGRANT: PROBLEM OR PROMISE?

In the half century that followed the Civil War, nearly twenty-five million people moved to the United States, a number equal to the entire population

of the trans-Mississippi west in 1910. They came as a part of a general migration of Europeans to all corners of the world, set on their way by powerful and
fateful forces of industrialism and nationalism. These forces had arisen first in
Northern and Western Europe, and the first flow of migration, begun long
before the war, brought Germans, Scandinavians, and people of the British
Isles. The same railroads and steamships which brought competing products
that drove the foreigner from his tiny farm or his workbench stood ready to
carry him cheaply to a new life in the seaboard cities or in the midwestern
valleys. For many years, the Germans continued to settle along the Great
Lakes and the Ohio and Mississippi rivers, and especially in the fast-growing
centers of commerce and industry—Cincinnati, St. Louis, Milwaukee, and
Chicago. Swedes and Norwegians settled heavily in the northern Great Plains
and engaged largely in farming. Finnish, Welsh, Irish, and Scottish laborers
felled trees, mined copper, and laid track in both the old and the new Northwest.

The Greek, Italian, Hungarian, Polish, Serbian, and Rumanian immigrants
arrived at the end of the century, when the economic and national readjust-
ments of the modern age began to exert their uprooting energies in Italy,
Austria-Hungary, Russia, and the Balkans. These immigrants found a new
kind of America. Choice farmland was less available for the taking. The bulk
of labor demand was in low-paying city jobs in domestic service or in unskilled
occupations in factories or on construction gangs. Inevitably, the most recent
newcomers clustered at the foot of the social ladder.

They arrived at precisely the time when thinking Americans were profoundly disturbed by the very existence of urban poverty and were tempted to
find scapegoats on whom to blame its unavoidable problems. For some Americans, the recent immigrant was this kind of scapegoat. A still-living legend
began to take shape, (1) of an "old" immigration of substantial families who
brought with them savings, skills, willingness to work, and a desire to share
in community responsibilities; and (2) of a "new" immigration of families,
predominantly illiterate and untrained, willing to work for a pittance and live
in animal squalor, complaisantly delivering votes to the "boss," crowding the
jails and almshouses, and clinging tenaciously to alien communities and folkways, in indifference (if not hostility) to national institutions. Since the "new"
immigrants were overwhelmingly from unfamiliar ethnic stocks, it was possible to reinforce them with the testimony of a misinterpreted Darwinism, which
held that these characteristics were not the stigmata of poverty but were bred
in the cells by the unalterable machinery of genetics. They were, in short,
"beaten races."

Like all stereotypes, this molding of the immigrants cruelly ignored exceptions. The Italian fruit peddler and the Polish coal heaver were flaunted as
evidence that these groups were attracted by the basest callings, but the Italians

who grew vines in California, or the Poles who bought abandoned Connecticut farms and became truck gardeners were overlooked. The Czech glassblower who could read two languages—German and his own—was denounced as an "illiterate" along with the genuinely unlettered Croatian steel puddler. The successfully Americanized Jewish clothing-store owner was forgotten by opponents of immigration who worried about the assimilation of the Lithuanian sweatshop garment maker, in flight from Russian anti-Semitism, who slept on rags in a basement. The millions of immigrants whose hopes for themselves and their children were to achieve middle-class style were branded as dangerous when a foreign-born anarchist or Socialist hit the headlines. Critics muted the whole contribution of foreign-born intellectuals to national arts, letters, and scientific endeavor, and the contribution of immigrant workers to building the economy.

The post-1890 immigrants did behave in ways that were novel to American experience but that were clearly dictated by their environment. They clustered in ethnic neighborhoods of pronounced "foreign" flavor, partly to ease the shock of transplantation. If some of these neighborhoods were slums, it was a natural result of the fact that the newcomers could afford only the lowest rents. The alliance between the immigrant and the boss rested on the machine's forthright offer of direct help to the new voter with his bread-and-butter problems. If anything was needed to prove that the "alien's" life style was a matter of response to his needs rather than his heredity, it was the speed with which the new immigrants and their children, once they achieved an improvement in status and income, tended to abandon their "old-country" clubs, newspapers, neighborhoods, churches, and political leaders.

This kind of defense of the immigrant's supposed strangeness would not have impressed a growing group of advocates of immigration restriction, who gathered strength in the 1890s. They were drawn from several sources. A traditional rural anti-Catholicism motivated the American Protective Association, which was founded at Clinton, Iowa, in 1887. Although the Association faded after reaching a peak membership of half a million in 1894, its task was taken up in 1915 by a revived Ku Klux Klan. A second restrictionist element was furnished by old-stock Americans of good family, who resented the vulgarity and corruption that they saw as characteristic of the new America, and blamed the immigrant for much of it. An Immigration Restriction League, founded in the depression year of 1894, included such distinguished New Englanders as the historian John Fiske, the economist Francis A. Walker, and Senator Henry Cabot Lodge. Their sense of loss and fear was expressed by Henry Adams when he wrote of himself that his world was dead, and "Not a Polish Jew fresh from Warsaw or Cracow . . . but had a keener instinct, and intenser energy [to survive in a competitive, acquisitive society] and a freer hand than he." Fear was also the strongest motive behind a third group favoring restriction: organized labor. Unionists considered the immigrant as a competitor for jobs and a threat to wage standards, even though immigrants themselves joined locals when opportunity offered, and formed a significant part of the membership of unions such as those of the cigarmakers, the garment workers, and the coal miners. The charge that the immigrant was a "pauper laborer" was aimed particularly at Asian immigrants, and an early outburst of working-class restrictionism took place in 1878 in California, where a Workingmen's Party won a number of offices on a platform including an end to the admission of Chinese to the United States. (It seems ironic that education-hungry Chinese and Japanese, who conformed to the canons of thrifty, hardworking, clean, and the Calvinistic ethic better than most "old immigrants" and native Americans, should have been hardest hit, but bigotry knows no logic.)

The federal government responded to pressures of restrictionism with a series of acts. Chinese immigrants were excluded from the United States in 1882. Laborers, imported under contract, were banned in 1885. Various bills before Congress, prior to 1915, proposed the exclusion of paupers, victims of particular diseases, known criminals, prostitutes, "undesirables," and illiterates. Some of these provisions became law, but literacy tests were defeated by Taft and Wilson with presidential vetoes. Nevertheless the trend was toward the closed door. A diplomatic "gentlemen's agreement" of 1907 barred almost all further Japanese immigration while, in 1910, the congressionally appointed Dillingham Commission embodied the theory of the "unassimilable new immigration" in a lengthy report. Fourteen years later, Congress approved a National Origins Act limiting total immigration and setting rigid quotas on the admission of Southern and Eastern Europeans.

However, even as the restrictionists gained momentum, millions of the new immigrants were actually becoming assimilated, and were replacing their native traditions and outlooks with American ideas of what constituted success and good citizenship. This was most evident among the immigrant youngsters in the schoolyards, who enthusiastically embraced all things American from Plymouth Rock to baseball. "Go to the public school," a reporter counseled the fearful immigrants, "and hear the children speak the tongue that is sweet to your ear; hear their young voices as they salute the flag that is *theirs.*" In fact the Americanizing process was so thorough that some social critics later lamented that it destroyed the possibilities of a rich multinational culture. It is likely, however, that the average immigrant of 1910 was quite willing to be entirely loyal to the American way in all things, if given permission.

The resistance to granting this permission was a part of the difficulty in stretching the ideal of opportunity for all to fit new circumstances. The inconsistency of nativism was wryly caricatured by "Mr. Dooley," Finley Peter Dunne's make-believe Irish bartender:

. . . As a pilgrim father that missed the first boats, I must raise me claryon voice again' th' invasion iv this fair land and be the paupers an' arnychists iv effete Europe. Ye bet I must—because I'm here first. . . . Me frind Shaughnessy says . . . "Tis time we done something to make th' immigration laws sthronger" says he. . . . "But what ar-re th' immygrants doin' that's roonous to us?" I says. "Well," says he . . . "they don't assymilate with th' counthry," he says. "Maybe th' counthry's digestion has gone wrong fr'm too much rich food," says I, "perhaps now if we'd lave off thryin' to digest Rockyfellar an' thry a simple diet like Schwartzmeister, we wudden't feel th' effects iv our vittels," I says. "Maybe if we'd season th' immygrants a little or cook thim thurly, they'd go down better," I says.

THE YEOMAN IN TROUBLE

To call the farmer an "outsider" in American life appears, on the surface, to be a misnomer. He had been praised by generations of orators as the backbone of society, and the Republican party had won in 1860 with the promise that the public domain should be free soil, reserved for him against the competition of slavery. The Homestead Act of 1862, bestowing a free 160 acres on any citizen who would cultivate them, seemed to fulfill that promise, and to many farming Americans this, rather than the freeing of the Negro, was the Republicans' finest achievement.

But the wholly independent farmer, dwelling on his own soil, afraid of no man, was a figure of a fading past. New farm machines and the railroad enabled him to grow and sell far more produce with the same investment of labor. These blessings enabled him to specialize in the production of market crops without diverting his energies (as his grandfather did) to hunting for his food and to making his own clothes and furniture. But, simultaneously, these blessings of progress reduced the number of farmers and involved him tightly in the web of large-scale capitalistic production and exchange, at great cost to his autonomy. . . .

. . . [Although the Eastern farmer faced serious problems in the late nineteenth century, he] was fortunate compared to the Southern farmer and, in some ways, he was better off than the farmer in the Mississppi Valley and the states immediately to the west of it. This happened for several reasons. The Homestead Act, for one thing, had not built the "New Jerusalem." Much of the best land in the West was included in grants to the railroads or to the states for educational and other purposes, and had to be bought. Many prime areas were preempted by ranchers, lumbermen, and mining companies, often in violation of the Homestead Act. The "free farm" was, by no means, readily available. . . . In short, only half (or less) of the public domain, and probably not the best half, was being given away. Capital was still needed to buy a farm, and was usually secured by going into debt. . . .

Indignation against arbitrary and unjust railroad rates ran high in agricultural regions. . . .

The farmer also resented what he considered as sharp practices by the merchants who graded and bought his grain, and the bankers who lent him money for his operations. Nature also seemed at times to conspire with [the] yeoman's enemies, as droughts, hail, and locusts wiped out crops in a few weeks or hours that represented a year's heavy labor . . . Essentially the farmer suffered from the fact that he was one of an army of small, competing producers, unable to control very easily the cost, quantity, or time of sale of what he grew. . . .

The bitter isolation of prairie life sank the iron deeper into the soul of the farmer who lived there. He was unable to see anything but debt and drudgery in his own and his children's future, and the injustice stung more deeply because he believed, as an article of faith, that he alone produced "natural" wealth, while those who transported, processed, and sold his crops were parasitic middlemen. . . .

. . . Civilization had enabled . . . [the American farmer] to produce more, with less brute effort, and to live more comfortably than most of the world's other "agriculturists." Yet business and professional men seemed to be succeeding more spectacularly in the new America, and the rush of progress left the farmer behind the middle-class urbanite in status as well as income. It was not enough to survive. American values demanded success. A farm populace without prospects of success was a new and disturbing element in society.

THE BLACK BOTTOM RAIL: THE NEGRO

The depression-stricken farmer was a fallen hero of the myth that blended agriculture and virtue into one. The post-Reconstruction Negro was in a different situation. He supposedly had no way to go but upwards from slavery. Yet he, too, was doomed to disappoint the expectations of his "friends," the molders of Radical Reconstruction. They believed that, since the ninety percent of the nation's Negroes who lived in the South in 1877 had been given freedom, the ballot, and access to public education, the keys to self-improvement were in their hands. By that year, therefore, even most Republicans believed that the nation might withdraw the protection it had extended the freedmen since the war's end.

Unfortunately, these genial assumptions were untrue. To begin with, Negroes were left without the primary foundation of self-help: economic security. The Radicalism of the late 1860s stopped short of legislating Thaddeus Stevens' suggestion that land expropriated from "rebel" planters be given to the freedmen. Few Negroes, moreover, possessed the means to occupy federal public lands in the South reserved for homesteaders between 1866 and

1876. Nor were most Negroes able to bid for lands that went under the auctioneer's hammer for tax delinquency. The result was that of all Negroes living on farms in 1900, three out of four were tenants—and only 192,993 of the country's eight million Negroes at that date owned farm homes. As a sharecropper or cash renter, the Negro farmer was even more vulnerable to exploitation by merchants and lenders than his white counterparts. Attempts to stimulate Negro migration from the South, like the efforts that sent about 40,000 people to Kansas in 1879, failed because money donated for land purchases, tools, seed, and stock was too scarce.

As a worker the Negro found that both industry and organized labor tended to bar the door to him. Negroes worked at many skilled trades in the South. They were carpenters, bricklayers, plasterers, plumbers, barbers, painters, and other things. Attempts to unionize them, however, fell afoul of racial prejudice. The national labor organizations of the period (see pp. 97–101) generally considered the Negroes as competitors for jobs instead of additions to the ranks. A National Labor Union, founded in 1866, successfully urged Negroes to form an all-Negro counterpart organization. The Knights of Labor, dating from 1869, more aggressively recruited and integrated Negroes. In 1886, when its membership had reached a peak of 700,000, perhaps 60,000 were Negroes. But in the 1890s, the American Federation of Labor began to dominate the organized labor movement in America, and it allowed constitutent unions to set their own racial policies. Many of them (such as the machinists, boilermakers, plumbers, steamfitters, and shipbuilders) exluded Negroes altogether or kept them in segregated and ineffectual locals.

In 1900, Negro workers belonged to only five out of sixty unions covering the skilled trades. Eighty percent of all unionized Negroes belonged to the miners' and longshoremen's unions, which were essentially organizations of the unskilled. Negroes found only a few unskilled jobs in the burgeoning factories of the new South. They represented less than four percent of the labor force in manufacturing. The black man might swing a pick or a shovel, or fetch, lift, and scrub, but he was not likely to rise to dignity and self-support by the exercise of professional and craft skills. And when this "lowest paid, least appreciated and least organized" of all American laborers failed to feed his family, his womenfolk went to work as domestics. In the first year of the new century, 40.7 percent of Negro women were gainfully employed, in contrast to 16 percent of white women.

Improvement through education was almost impossible. Southern state governments skimped badly on education in general, and the Negro got the leftovers of an offering that was meager to begin with. New Hampshire's Senator Henry Blair tried, in the 1880s, to have Congress provide financial assistance to Southern education from surplus federal revenues, but failed. The few Negroes who managed somehow to prepare themselves for higher education found only a handful of Negro colleges open to them in the South. These were weakly supported by philanthropy and received small amounts of state assistance. Some, like Fisk University in Tennessee, were academically ambitious. Others, like Hampton Institute in Virginia, or Tuskegee Institute in Alabama, were concerned primarily with vocational education and character building. The earnestness of their founders, faculties, and students could not entirely compensate for their serious limitations as nurseries of intellect and professional knowledge.

Nor could the Negro exert political influence in order to remedy his condition. The Fifteenth Amendment was largely unenforced, as Southern whites drove the ex-slaves from the ballot box by means ranging from fraud to violence. Mississippi furnishes an illustration of the gradual but inexorable decline in Negro participation in politics after 1876. In that year, twenty-one Negroes served in the state legislature; in 1890 there were five, and a few Negroes in minor county posts. Thereafter, even such token officeholding fell before an onslaught of white supremacy. Southern states modified their constitutions to allow for election laws with devices such as literacy, taxpaying, and property tests, which could be manipulated to exclude Negroes and admit whites. . . . Mississippi led the way with this kind of constitutional revision in 1890, followed by South Carolina, Louisiana, and eventually the other formerly Confederate states. Senator Henry Cabot Lodge of Massachusetts sponsored a measure in 1890 to permit federal supervision of elections where deliberate exclusion of voters was charged. Congress did not pass the bill, however. The nation was still seventy-five years short of once more guaranteeing the Negro a free ballot.

The handicaps of the Negro were compounded by the humiliations of segregation, in which the nation acquiesced. In the Civil Rights cases of 1883, the Supreme Court held that while Negroes were United States citizens entitled to the equal protection of the laws, they were not guaranteed thereby against discrimination by owners of hotels, theaters, and restaurants. In *Plessy v. Ferguson,* in 1895, the highest court affirmed the validity of a Louisiana law requiring "separate but equal" accommodations on railroads. In effect, the two decisions legalized the Jim Crow laws, and nullified most of the Fourteenth Amendment, just as the South was perfecting methods of evading the Fifteenth Amendment.

The Negro was thus hobbled legally, socially, economically, politically, and educationally, yet somehow was supposed to prove his worth by bettering his condition in life, as national expectations dictated. Astonishingly, many Negroes did exactly that. In commenting on the restraints imposed upon Negroes, the historian is in danger of overlooking the race's achievements under difficulty. Negro literacy rose from 20.1 percent in 1870 to 55.5 percent in 1900. Negro churches and religious bodies struck lasting roots in the black community. A small but significant number of Negro businessmen flourished in the soil of oppression, for a paradox of segregation was that it forced Negroes to turn to other Negroes for services, thus encouraging black entrepreneurship. Negro professionals also found opportunities among their own race, as about 1700 Negro physicians, 21,000 teachers, 15,000 clergymen, and 730 lawyers of 1900 proved. Although successful, professional, black men numbered only a few in every hundred, they were a living refutation of the stereotyped belief that the American descendants of Africans were naturally inferior and, in the words of a Southern writer, had "not yet exhibited the qualities of any race which has advanced civilization."

Nevertheless, the overall prospects of the Negro in the United States in the 1890s were thoroughly unpromising. Midway through the decade, a remarkable black leader appeared with a plan for improving them. This was Booker T. Washington. He was born in slavery in Virginia in 1856. As a boy he toiled in a coal mine while acquiring the rudiments of education, and doggedly worked his way through Hampton Institute in the very best tradition of self-made Americans. He was appointed superintendent of Tuskegee Institute in 1881, and was remarkably successful. He became convinced at Tuskegee that the Negro's first need was for economic self-sufficiency, and that the white South, also struggling to escape from regional poverty's grip, might help Negroes to achieve that goal in return for the surrender of claims to immediate political and social rights. In 1895, an invitation to open an exhibit of Negro business achievements at the Cotton States Exposition in Atlanta gave Washington a chance to publicly propose this exchange.

Washington's speech outlined what was soon called "the Atlanta Compromise." To Negroes, he announced that their best hopes lay in cultivating the friendship of their inevitable neighbors, the Southern whites, who were willing to give black men "a man's chance" in the world of commerce. Efforts to prosper in agriculture, industry, and business would bring more certain rewards than agitation for political and social rights which could come only in the wake of economic progress. "The wisest of my race," he said, "understand that the agitation of questions of social equality is the extremest folly and that progress in the enjoyment of all the privileges that will come to us must be the result of severe constant struggle rather than of artificial forcing." To whites, he recommended a reliance upon the potential labor contribution of the Negroes, the "most patient, faithful, law-abiding and unresentful people that the world has seen." Together, white and black Southerners could realize Henry Grady's flourishing, visionary new South—"in all things . . . purely social . . . as separate as the fingers, yet one as the hand in all things essential to mutual progress."

The address was a sensation. . . . Washington was launched on a career as "official spokesman" for the Negro. He was pictured on the covers of northern magazines, awarded honorary degrees, invited to lunch at the White House by Theodore Roosevelt and, above all, consulted in any project for funneling money into the training of Southern Negroes. He also underwent severe criticism from others of his race, who claimed that he abandoned the Negro's just claim to full citizenship in return for donations to an inherently debasing segregated educational system. Opponents also asserted that his plan for turning more Negroes into small tradesmen and artisans offered no real future to them in a business system dominated by large and powerful organizations. W. E. B. DuBois, a Harvard-educated Negro sociologist, charged that Washington's glorification of hard work and accumulation overlooked the problems and needs of talented and intellectual Negroes, denied the particularly poetic and imaginative qualities of Negro life, and merely aped middle-class white materialism. Washington's defenders claimed, in response, that he only disputed priorities, not goals, with other Negro "liberators," believing that economic opportunity must precede acceptance. This debate is not yet dead in Negro life. . . .

. . . [In any event, Washington's] belief that the chance to earn a dollar in a factory was more valuable in 1895 than the right to spend it in an opera house never was tested because factory doors and opera houses alike remained closed, for the most part, to black wage earners. Yet the enthusiasm with which whites embraced Washington's formula for preserving discrimination and simultaneously reaffirming economic improvement as the highest of goals showed how shrewdly he read the national mind.

THE PERMANENT WAGE EARNER

The political orators who outlined the glories of "free labor" in 1860 assumed that the hired laborer was only temporarily at work for someone else. When the "prudent, penniless beginner," as Lincoln called him, had accumulated a stake, he would emerge from his cocoonlike hireling stage in the butterfly colors of self-employment. Twenty-five years later, however, the scope and speed of large-scale industrialization made it clear that the 1860 script would not be followed. A permanent class of wage earners would be as much a feature of modern life as the factory or the corporation itself, and to this class most Americans who earned their bread would eventually belong. This change in the social expectations of the laborer was in itself a profound source of anxiety and discontent in the "new" post-1877 nation.

Workingmen had more to complain of, however, than the dwindling prospects of their becoming independent capitalists. During the concluding quarter of the century, wage levels as a whole were low. True, evidence shows that they did not usually fall far behind living costs, and occasionally exceeded them. But figures based on overall averages do not adequately reflect the problems of individual workers in depressed areas, or in particular industries at different times. The persistence of demands for wage increases in industrial disputes shows that the laborers themselves in great number placed inadequate pay high on their list of grievances. In an advancing and success-minded country, adequacy meant more than bare subsistence.

However, there were other complaints that are easier to define precisely. The average work day was a long one and, despite all the labor-saving machinery of the age, it shrank only from eleven to ten hours between 1860 and 1890. The replacement of hand skills with machine techniques made it possible for veteran craftsmen to be replaced with lower-paid unskilled workers, including women and children. The physical conditions of industrial labor were repulsive. Employers, involved in fierce competition, were not of a mind to increase their costs by providing sanitary facilities for their factory hands or safety devices on their machines. Above all, the sharp upswings and downturns of the business cycle in an unregulated economy brought to life the worse threat of all: insecurity. Samuel Gompers, as a boy in London, heard idle workmen on the streets crying: "God strike me dead. My wife, my kids want bread and I've no work to do." He was to hear the same lament many times in the America to which he migrated in 1863.

As early as 1866 there were some men who realized that workers in large-scale industry would have to organize (precisely as corporations themselves were organizing in combinations) if they hoped to exert pressure on managers to meet their demands. Leaders of about a dozen national unions of skilled workers—men like William H. Sylvis of the iron molders, John Siney of the anthracite miners, and Richard Trevellick of the ship carpenters—joined that year in calling a convention, which established the National Labor Union (NLU). This, presumably, was a first step in the mobilization of the laboring hosts. The composition and fate of the NLU, however, illustrated basic difficulties in the way of creating a strong and united movement. The term "labor" not only described the work of individuals as diverse in skill as ditch-diggers and diamond-polishers, but was also the word used for any effort resulting in the production of wealth. Under that generous definition (widely accepted in the 1860s), farmers, professional men, and manufacturers were entitled to participate in the task of improving "labor's" rewards by whatever means seemed to them appropriate.

The working classes showed little interest in . . . [the middle-class program of the NLU]. Attendance at NLU conventions, especially by delegates from unions, shrank irretrievably until the organization died in 1872. . . .

In 1869 an imaginative organizer named Uriah Stephens created, with a group of fellow garment-cutters, a secret society that was to be the nucleus of another nationwide labor organization. Stephens called his clandestine fraternity the Noble and Holy Order of the Knights of Labor, and endowed it with a set of mystical rites, symbols, and titles. In doing this, he showed a shrewd sense of the workingman's psychic needs, for to be a Venerable Sage or a Worthy Foreman created a more exhilarating self-image than to work merely as the secretary or the president of Local Sixteen. Although the members were aware of the strife between capital and labor, and worked in secrecy to protect themselves against employer reprisals, they nonetheless subscribed to a set of principles which, like those of the National Labor Union, exalted uninterrupted production and cooperation. Stephens' florid constitution for the Knights actually excluded from the circle of social harmony, and from membership, only the drones of society—bankers, lawyers, and liquor dealers. The demands of the Order included national ownership of railroads, telegraphs, and telephones but, otherwise, were substantially like those of the NLU.

Organizationally, however, the Knights differed from the NLU in a significant respect. The unions that sent delegates to NLU conventions were national bodies of workers in the same calling. But as the knights grew, their local assemblies (usually drawn from a single craft or shop) were grouped *regionally* into district assemblies, which consequently included laborers of various occupations. Representatives of these mixed assemblies came to dominate policy-making in the Order. To an even greater extent than the NLU, therefore, the Knights pursued general reform objectives, on which workingmen of widely different skills and needs could agree.

In 1881, Terence V. Powderly became the General Master Workman, the grandiloquent name for the leader of the Knights. Although trained as a machinist, he was more of a middle-class reformer than a representative of labor. He entered politics as a Greenback candidate for the mayoralty of Scranton, Pennsylvania in 1878 and won three successive terms and, despite the distrust of lawyers expressed by the founder of the Knights, Powderly studied law independently and was admitted to the bar in 1894. He was an advocate of industrial arbitration and cooperatively owned factories. But he was an enemy to alcohol, land speculation, and monopoly. The "reformist" orientation of the Knights' constitution made a man of Powderly's outlook a natural choice as chieftain. He was effective as an educator and debater, and persuaded the Order to abandon secrecy and seek alliances and support among the general public. Partly as a result of this decision, membership grew to a peak of 700,000 in 1886. Part of the increase, however, resulted from the militancy of certain local assemblies which in effect, functioned as trade unions by presenting demands to employers, and organizing boycotts and strikes (over Powderly's objections). Thousands of restless workingmen were seeking for labor organizations that would operate in precisely this way.

The heirs of labor's urge for collective power, however, were not the Knights but the founders of the American Federation of Labor (AFL), which began its existence in 1881 as the Federation of Organized Trade and Labor Unions.

Five years later it reorganized and adopted the name by which it is still known. The genesis of the AFL was in the tribulation of the national unions in the depression years of 1873 to 1877. Many of these unions were seriously weakened by the loss of members, dues, and battles. In the reorganization and housecleaning that often follows institutional crisis, a new breed of leaders began to take over.

The spokesmen for the trade-union movement in the 1880s were well typified by men like Peter J. McGuire, of the carpenters, or Adolph Strasser and Samuel Gompers of the cigarmakers. They were distrustful of utopianism, either as preached by socialists or by white-collar reformers with whom the unions had made an unfruitful alliance in the NLU. Gompers and Strasser were also wary of a militancy that led workmen into premature and poorly financed strikes. As officers in the Cigarmakers International, they provided a system of dues and benefits that made their union a model of financial stability. They also centralized control of the union in such a way as to discourage locals from independent action.

In a sense, these architects of the new unionism were simply applying to the union movement the principles of coordination and advance planning, which were used by the successful giants of the business world. The purpose behind the moves of Strasser and Gompers was to allow the Cigarmakers International executive committee to select a given segment of the industry where a strong demand might succeed, and then permit a local to strike, backed by the full resources of the union, precisely as a business firm might focus on a campaign against a single competitor.

Although they sought economic warfare with the employer, unionists like Gompers and Strasser were willing to confine their efforts to the sphere of wages and working conditions. They were impatient with the pitfalls, compromises, frets, and delays of political involvement, and were especially cool to proposals for sweeping changes such as the abolition of the wage system itself. They accepted its existence, sought to improve cigarmakers' conditions within it, and left it to others to build the New Jerusalem. "We are all practical men," Strasser told a Senate Committee in 1885. "We fight only for immediate objects —objects that can be realized from day to day."

These were the operating principles of the various trade unionists who organized the AFL. They were determined that the basis of a national labor movement should be a set of strong organizations of skilled specialists, each supreme in its own jurisdiction. They wrote a constitution that rigidly preserved that craft autonomy. They were reluctant to embark on broad-gauge social crusades, and they created a structure that guaranteed almost permanently the emergence of leaders who would confine themselves to restricted objectives. The first of these was Gompers, who became the first AFL president and held the office with only one year's interruption until his death in 1924.

Fiercely energetic, combative, persuasive and shrewd, Gompers was a magnificent captain. The AFL passed the Knights in membership a few years before 1886 and, by 1904, had nearly a million and three-quarter members enrolled in its ranks while the older organization had virtually ceased to exist.

The triumph of the AFL over the Knights was of lasting impact. The "pure and simple trade unionism" of a Gompers, devoted to the securing of "bread and butter" for workers, superseded the search for social perfection that seemed to characterize the AFL's rival organizations, whether middle-class or Socialist. Although Gompers did not permanently renounce political action by unionists, and although he was certainly idealistic in his own fashion, he won more than the support of pragmatic unionists. He also secured the toleration of a large element of the American population which had looked upon the very idea of a powerful labor movement with uneasiness.

This was perhaps the most crucial of his victories. Widely publicized acts of violence marked labor's emergence to self-consciousness. In 1877 striking railway workers burned depots and freight cars in Baltimore, Pittsburgh, and St. Louis. In 1886 an unknown hand threw a bomb into a mass meeting in Chicago's Haymarket Square, killing and wounding a number of policemen and bystanders. Three anarchists died on the gallows wrongfully convicted of that crime. Strikers at the Homestead Plant of the Carnegie Steel Company exchanged murderous gunfire with private detectives and strike-breakers in 1892 and, in 1894, a national railroad strike threatened to paralyze the economy and led to rioting and the occupation by federal troops of Chicago. These and similar episodes deeply touched the anxieties of editors, ministers, legislators, and other social observers who feared that a conflict between capital and labor had begun which could only end in social revolution.

It is ironic that the American urban middle class came to accept Gompers, a firm believer in the strike, rather than Powderly, the spokesman of "harmony" and "cooperation," as the leader to save the country from class war. Yet they did: "bread-and-butter" unionism seemed more in the American grain that a political crusade to universalize justice and progress—a sign of how far the country had come from the days of the founding of the Republican party. This does not mean that the country embraced the AFL with enthusiasm. Labor strife continued into the 1930s with lockouts, court injunctions, and "scabs" freely employed against strikers, amid general national approval. But Gompers, like Booker T. Washington, became an officially recognized spokesman for his "minority" group. In 1903 he was invited to join the National Civic Federation, an organization of "progressive-minded" big businessmen seeking a reconciliation between labor and the corporation, and recognizing in the AFL a practically operated, sound corporation like their own. He was courted by both parties in 1908, endorsed the Democrats in

1912, and played an important part in getting labor behind the war effort in 1917. . . .

Like Booker T. Washington, in fact, he was accused of betraying the idealists in his following. The AFL pattern of autonomy for constituent unions of skilled workers left the unskilled at the mercy of the employers. Similarly, the draining away of radical idealism in the union movement contributed greatly to an apathetic rank and file that tolerated corruption on the part of union presidents, as long as the bacon was brought home in the form of benefits. The AFL turned its back on the needs of the Negro and the new immigrant except for token statements of good will and high future hopes.

But Gompers (like Washington) may have made the best bargain attainable at the time. There can be no final answer. By leading a new kind of labor movement that matched the expectations of those who molded twentieth century American public opinion, he had given at least some workers a place in the sun. Moreover, progressive politicians between 1900 and 1916 proved willing to develop an alliance with labor, which bore fruit in laws aimed against some of the more glaring abuses in the industrial system.

CHAPTER 8

THE POPULAR CULTURE
OF THE GILDED AGE

The term, "the Gilded Age," the title of a novel by Mark Twain and Charles Dudley Warner, was meant to apply particularly to the popular culture of the late nineteenth century. Historians, in treating the public taste of the period, have generally accepted the view implied in this term—that of bright, imitation gold concealing inferior material underneath. They have pictured the age as vulgar, gaudy, and brassy—as, in fact, the most tasteless age in American history. Vernon Louis Parrington, whose work was instrumental in creating the stereotyped picture of the Gilded Age, observed that good taste reached its lowest ebb in the 1870s, and few historians have chosen to disagree with him. The widespread acceptance of the Parrington stereotype has discouraged responsible examination of the culture of this era.

In this selection, Robert R. Roberts suggests that the popular culture of the Gilded Age requires not so much a reappraisal as a careful and serious initial appraisal. This he seeks to provide, albeit within the limits of an article-length essay. Professor Roberts carefully constructs a working definition of popular culture, discusses the relationship between popular and classical culture in the Gilded Age, and attempts to place the popular culture of that age in the context of nineteenth-century cultural development. Roberts covers the various aspects of popular culture from popular novels, humor literature, journalism, religious revivals, the Chautauqua movement, and entertainment, to the success of figures such as P. T. Barnum and Robert Ingersoll.

The student should focus on a number of important questions while reading this selection. First, was the Gilded Age a particularly distinct period in the history of popular culture, as is often suggested? If not, does that age seem to have any characteristic quality of its own? Second, what constituted the style or "flavor" of the age? What were the common characteristics of the public attitudes on such matters as success, work, leisure, the family, and art? Finally, do you believe it possible, and productive, to compare the popular culture of the Gilded Age and that of today? Such a comparison would necessitate the consideration of our popular heroes, modes of dress, means of entertainment, and goals in life.

An outstanding collection of documents on this subject with a brief, but excellent introduction is Henry Nash Smith, editor, *Popular Culture and Industrialism, 1865–1890** (1967). For the traditional point of view, see Vernon Louis Parrington, *The Beginnings of Critical Realism in America, 1860–1920** (1930). Lewis Mumford, *The Brown Decades: A Study of the Arts in America, 1865–1895** (1931), is a valuable study of one aspect of Gilded Age cultural development, and Foster Rhea Dulles, *A History of Recreation: America Learns to Play** (1940), contains much interesting material. Also consult pertinent biographies and studies of religion, education, journalism, the graphic arts, and literature during this period.

*Available in a paperback edition.

GILT, GINGERBREAD, AND REALISM: THE PUBLIC AND ITS TASTE

ROBERT R. ROBERTS

The popular culture of the Gilded Age does not need a reappraisal so much as a serious appraisal. Earlier and later eras have had their historians of manners and mores, and several special phases of the popular culture of the Gilded Age have been treated—in the fields of books, magazines, literature, and the theater, for example—but the record is spotty and unfocused.

The scene is generally set by repeating with dramatic and telling enunciation of the vulgarity and crassness of the era, pointing with scorn at the usual objects of contempt—the gingerbread French chateaus on Fifth Avenue, iron deer on front lawns, and bric-a-brac in the cluttered middle-class living room, or "parlor." This opinion divested, the historian leaves the impression that no other age would be guilty of such crass and patent bad taste, and then shies by saying "yet," indicating the vitality and strength of a nation bursting with economic growth, population increase, and even attention to things of the mind. This usually leads to a discussion of certain seminal and exceptional minds—the artists, scientists, writers—who save the age from total disgrace. Somewhere in the discussions of Mark Twain, the Darwinists, Josiah Willard Gibbs, William James, and C. S. Peirce, the whole notion of popular taste or culture disappears and is never touched upon. . . .

The general pattern for evaluations of the culture of the Gilded Age goes back to V. L. Parrington, who, in his colorful section on the thought of this era, so tellingly characterizes the corruption, the brassiness, the hypocrisy of the dominant figures from Jim Fisk to Dwight L. Moody—perhaps not always justly, but always entertainingly. And, of course, there is substantial justice in this approach; there was corruption, it was a gaudy age, and the contrasts between public professions of morality and actual behavior were frequently glaring. The unfortunate results of this approach are twofold: first, the fundamental nature of the popular culture of the age is lost in these generalizations; and second, the results of a closer examination tend to be prejudged by these

SOURCE. Robert R. Roberts, "Gilt, Gingerbread, and Realism: The Public and Its Taste," in H. Wayne Morgan, ed., *The Gilded Age, A Reappraisal.* Syracuse, N.Y., Syracuse University Press, 1963, pp. 169–195. Copyright 1963 by Syracuse University Press. Reprinted by permission of the publisher.

popular views. Let us eschew some of these preconceptions, if possible, and direct attention to some of the basic factors which ought to be a part of a serious study of the popular culture of the Gilded Age.

There is always the preliminary question of definition. It is quite obvious that the enduring works of art and the far-ranging works of the mind are likely to attract more attention from historians than the more ephemeral products of popular appeal. It may even be that the artist has insights and understanding which the purveyor of popular entertainment cannot afford, even if he were capable of them. But such rules are not invariably true and the works of Mark Twain might be cited as evidence that art and popularity are not necessarily incompatible. Nevertheless, in attempting to define what is meant by popular culture the historian must first respect the adjective in that phrase. As Carl Bode said in introducing his study of popular culture: "Popularity has been my touchstone. . . . This is a book on the people's choice.". . .

Obviously popular culture can cover a vast number of activities, from the daily newspaper to the mass revival meeting, from the Chautauqua lecture platform to the touring Shakesperian troupe. A useful beginning here is once again that of Carl Bode. He indicates that his definition of the scope of the term lies between that of the cultural anthropologist, with his interest in all aspects of a culture, and that of the literary historian with his restricted field of interest. To Bode, the definition would include the popular forms of painting and sculpture, literary productions, music, and the theater. This flexible approach can be broadened or restricted to cover the typical popular activities of any given period. Together these areas make up the means of expression of the ideas and beliefs accepted by the majority and the institutions to which the people turned most frequently to hear the various expressions of their ideals and aspirations. Whether it was to hear Dwight Moody in the pulpit, Russell Conwell on the lecture platform, or Joseph Jefferson behind the proscenium arch, the American people of this era assembled in large numbers, paid admission fees or took up great collections, and listened patiently as these culture-heroes declaimed on what seemed to the audiences to be the eternal verities.

Another phase of popular culture rarely dealt with, especially in this period, is the extent to which the traditional classical culture of western Europe belonged to the people and flourished on a popular level. In the novels of this era there remained a fundamental stratum of the great tradition of the eighteenth-century English novel, though heavily covered by Victorian ideas of morality and propriety. Dickens had not yet become a "classic," but was simply a popular writer, very likely the "world's most popular author." Dickens belonged to the world of art and also to the popular culture of the America of the middle and late nineteenth century.

The arts also permeated American life. Russell Lynes begins *The Tastemakers* with some quotations from one George Makepeace Towle, a traveler returned to America from England, who wrote that he heard "boys in the street singing and whistling Mozart and Rossini, and hand organs grinding out the arias from *Faust* and *Lucrezia Borgia,*" as well as the usual ballads, minstrel songs, and patriotic hymns. Towle was also impressed by the liveliness of the American theater, including "more performances of Shakespeare in America . . . than . . . in England" and "tragedy, fine old comedy and the 'free and easy' burlesque." This is certainly a notable commentary on the state of the arts in America in the Gilded Age. . . .

Such examples testify to the extent to which the traditional culture of the Western World, albeit sometimes in debased forms, continued to hold sway in America. There was a healthy mingling of popular and classical culture in the years of the Gilded Age. It is quite unfair to dismiss the culture of these years without noting this important fact. It may well be that one opera house in a middle-sized American town in the 1880's offered more of the classic tradition in music and drama in one year than the combined television networks of the United States do in the same period of time in our own age.

This was hardly an idyllic society of popular acclaim of great art and happy and wholesome popular arts without exception; the general trend was actually in the opposite direction. These years saw the rise of magazines and newspapers of mass appeal and of transformation in the theater and other forms of entertainment that produced an increasingly wide gap between popular culture and higher standards of art. And, of course, there were exceptions all through the years of the Gilded Age. There was the difference between the public image of Mark Twain and the skepticism and bitterness of his private world; there were the lonely paths of such artists as Albert Ryder and George Inness and the anti-philistinism of James M. Whistler. There were also the remnants of the world of the Boston Brahmins in the persons of the Adams brothers or Francis Parkman, who believed that the American people were patronizing shoddy lectures and buying tasteless magazines. And there were such pre-Civil War monuments as Longfellow and Emerson who lived on into the postwar decades and did not find them good. Still, in none of these instances nor in the era itself was there any extensive spirit of *épater le bourgeois.* The coterie artist and the self-conscious rebel against middle-class values were not in evidence in any major way. This familiar schism, so characteristic of the twentieth century, had yet to appear significantly in America in the Gilded Age.

On the mingling of traditional and popular culture in the Gilded Age, it is pertinent to point out that the description of this culture as "derivative" is quite true. England, naturally, contributed most heavily to American popular culture. The common name for the prevailing moral view of the universe has come to be "Victorian," obviously not a native American product. The most popular style of middle-class domestic architecture was called the "Queen Anne". . . .

The years of the Gilded Age do not constitute a convenient, closed unit in the area of popular culture. In almost every activity in this era a considerable change was taking place, usually at a different rate. The press, for example, remained from the 1850's (having emerged from the stage in which newspapers were purely party organs) to the 1880's in the phase of personal journalism in which a few great editors such as Bowles, Dana, and Greeley dominated. In the early 1880's the American theater entered a new stage which came to be called the "Golden Age of the Road." Equally significant changes were taking place in the field of minstrelsy and in the Chautauqua movement. American popular culture in this period defies exact classification or precise chronological limitations. Generally, the American popular culture of the 1870's resembled that of the 1850's more closely than it did that of the 1890's, and the 1880's probably entailed the greatest changes. The transitions were often still ahead or were in beginning stages.

An excellent example is the area of popular arts. There was a continuity and unity from the 1850's through the 1880's, which period has been called the "hey-day of cheap and popular art for everyone." But this began before the Civil War. The much praised "simple arts," whether hooked rugs or clipper ships, had gone into decline in the 1850's. Lewis Mumford in his *Brown Decades* delivers this judgement: "When the Civil War broke, architecture in America had been sinking steadily for a generation. Order, fitness, comeliness, proportion, were words that could no longer be applied to it: construction was submerged in that morass of jerry-building, tedious archaism, and spurious romanticism that made up the architectural achievements of the nineteenth century." In the decades after the Civil War there was tastelessness in art and architecture; showiness and gaudiness appeared alongside of the factory and the tenement house in unhappy juxtaposition, and there was a flowering of exotic styles and excess ornamentation. But it is patently unfair to charge the men of this era with sole responsibility for casting off a valuable tradition and replacing it with shoddy vulgarity. The Gilded Age was to a great degree, particularly in the popular arts, a product of the techniques and tastes of pre-Civil War Ameria.

Two notable examples of this general point would be the continued popularity of Currier and Ives prints and Rogers sculpture groups. Currier began his print business in 1835, the partnership with Ives was formed in 1857, and they published and sold their prints with tremendous success until 1907. Today these prints have become collector's items; what was then produced to meet the broadest possible tastes is today valued as art. Another popular phenomenon of the world of art was John Rogers the sculptor. His first popular work was "The Checker Players" in 1859, and he went on to become "not only a household name but a household ornament." In both cases talent and honest craftmanship gained a deserved popularity from the American public and serve as an index to public tastes as well as to the continuity of the period from before the Civil War well into the late nineteenth century. . . .

No popular literature is so well remembered as the famous "dime novels" [of the Gilded Age]. The history of this genre—its beginnings in the fertile mind of Erastus Beadle, its noblest examples, such as Edward Ellis' *Seth Jones; or The Captives of the Frontier,* and its degeneration into cheap hackwork for children, as the famed Nick Carter series—has been told before. The usual story in these books, of heroic deeds on the wild frontier, maintained the prevalent celebration of the individual and the persistent moralism of the popular literature of the Gilded Age.

The religious novel was still another genre which had its seedtime before the Civil War and blossomed luxuriantly in the immediate postwar years. The persistent interest in such novels in these years is not difficult to understand. These were years of challenge and trial for American churches, particularly for the traditional Protestant denominations. Orthodox theologies which had been subject to liberalizing influences in the pre-Civil War decades were now abruptly challenged by currents of scientific thought, notably, of course, the Darwinian hypothesis of the evolution of species. Probably no other topic occupied so much time in pulpit discourse or space in the religious press, and this interest was bound to carry over to the general public. Furthermore, the ethical ideal and social programs of the churches were being severely tested by the social and economic problems of an urban-industrial growth of nearly frightening proportions. When the faith of the fathers and the traditional values are being sorely tried, people often eagerly grasp for reassurance in most guises, and perhaps most eagerly in a happy fictional world where an omnipotent author can manipulate the plot to produce the triumph of those same ideals and beliefs. . . .

In the 1880's there appeared one of the major popular novels in American history. In the pages of *Ben Hur,* General Lew Wallace successfully combined the powerful appeal of religion, the glamor of an historical setting in the Roman Empire, and the sheer excitement of plain old melodrama. It should not be difficult for those of us who have recently witnessed a vast and costly version of this story in motion picture form to understand its tremendous vogue. Professor Hart has said, "If every American did not read the novel, almost everyone was aware of it." This novel was the precursor of a rage for historical fiction in the 1890's and, of course, continuing into our own time. . . .

Perhaps the theme most often used for critical treatment by the historians of the Gilded Age is that which may be described as the self-help and success theme, with a strong admixture of inspiration. Here is the most undisguised worship of success and, outside the pages of Herbert Spencer or William Graham Sumner, the most unalloyed celebration of individualism. The theme was begun early in childhood with the widespread use of the McGuffey readers; there was an edition in 1857, to which a High School Reader was added in 1863, and further editions in 1879 and on into the twentieth century. These readers conveyed the well-known lessons of honesty, industry, obedience, thrift, piety, punctuality, and many other such virtues. Fame and fortune were likely to result from the strict adherence to these rules of living. This was reinforced by the popular Horatio Alger books in which the young hero would find that a life of virtue and a chance to save the daughter of a rich man from drowning could lead to an opportunity and ultimate success. The role of chance in these success stories and the hackwork literary quality seem to escape the memory of those who recall the books with great fondness. . . .

The American public did not, however, patronize only historical or religious fiction or self-help literature; it was also eager to read and to listen to the boisterous company of humorists that flourished in these years. The techniques of these humorists were not new in American life—the grotesque exaggerations of the Davy Crockett type of story, the rural parody of the style and manners of "city folk," and the artful mishandling of the English language were all inherited from an earlier America. After the Civil War, there was an increasing consciousness of the peculiar traits of regions and localities. The fact that the economic forces of the time were driving the nation toward a greater degree of nationalism and a diminution of the differences between the sections and regions produced an audience for those writers and lecturers who specialized in the portrayal of the unique and disappearing types in American life. The Yankee, the middle western "hayseed," the rough and ready westerner, and various southern types all found a public for their brands of humor.

The leaders of this school of humorists included such men as David Ross Locke (Petroleum V. Nasby), Charles Farrar Browne (Artemus Ward), and Henry Wheeler Shaw (Josh Billings). From their poses as "hayseeds" or other types, these humorists poked fun at the customs and conventions of the Gilded Age. Josh Billings wrote in his *Farmer's Allminax,* "Most people repent ov their sins bi thanking God they aint so wicked as their nabors." Artemus Ward got off his share of quotable remarks, such as: "I tell you, feller citizens, it would have been ten dollars in Jeff Davis' pockets if he had never been born," or "Old George Washington's fort was not to hev eny public man of the present day ressemble him to eny alarmin extent.". . .

From the ranks of these regional humorists came two men who deserve special attention. Bret Harte and Mark Twain. Harte's sentimental tales of rough and ready characters with hearts of gold do not belong to the annals of great literature, but in him the frontier produced a writer who could give life to its experiences. This vein must have run out for Harte, however, for after his great success with *The Luck of Roaring Camp and Other Stories* he seems to have lost his artistic touch and his popularity. Samuel Clemens belongs to the realm of great literature; suffice it to say that in him the local colorists, the parodists, and the rough humorists of the West produced a genius, and his genius transmuted this raw material, just entertainment in other hands, into the closest thing to an epic of the Gilded Age.

In the field of magazine publishing there is a certain unity in the years of the Gilded Age, though the major innovations in this field came in the 1890's. On the other hand, in newspaper publishing there took place in the 1880's a major change, the fall of great editors and personal journalism to powerful owners and syndicates. The difference in response appears to be more a matter of difference in rate of change than anything else. Actually only a few years separated the "new Journalism" from such magazine innovators as *Forum, Arena, Cosmopolitan,* and others. In both cases new business methods, decreased costs, lower prices, the demands of advertising, and the need for mass distribution, diminished the personal note and encouraged the rise of the merchant of news.

The content of the newspapers of the Gilded Age resembled that of the pre-Civil War years. The changes that would be called "yellow journalism" had not occurred; the sensationalism, the comics, and other attributes of modern newspapers were not yet noticeable in the newspapers of the 1870's and just beginning in the 1880's. An upstate New York farmer continued, after Greeley's death, to subscribe to the *Tribune* in belief that Horace was still responsible for its contents, and, if he missed the news of the death of the great editor, this mistake was understandable. Technical changes took place; the telegraph and the cable, the press associations, expensive new machinery, labor unions, and advertising revenue were transforming the newspaper from a personal organ to a big business. By the time Pulitzer and Hearst had emerged as major owners in the 1890's, the style and content of the newspaper would be transformed to accord with this technical revolution. . . .

The content of . . . [the cheap weekly story-papers] reflects the tastes and beliefs of the period, as it seems safe to assume that the publishers of these competitive enterprises tried to give the American middle class what it wanted. The moral tone was smugly proper. In works reeking with self-righteousness, the publishers assured their readers that their particular publication was a family paper and the innocent daughters of the household could be permitted to read it in complete confidence.

The bulk of the material in these papers was fiction, largely serialized versions of the romantic or historical novels of such authors as Mrs. [E. D. E. N.] Southworth or Sylvanus Cobb, Jr., if the publisher was fortunate enough to have one of these popular writers under contract; if not, of course, there were always imitators who could produce remarkably similar tales. . . .

Though not so widely read as the story-papers with their popular appeal, the actual leaders of the magazine world in these years were the genteel, learned, and massive aristocrats such as *Harper's Weekly* or *Monthly, Atlantic, Galaxy,* or *Scribner's.* Some of these, notably the Harper publications, can be called popular; all of them reflect the tastes and ideas of the middle class and could be found on parlor tables whether they were read or not. They were badges of serious intellectual interests and sound opinions. They were part of popular culture, since their contents reflected what the dominant class believed and what they thought they should know and talk about.

It is more difficult to know what to do with a periodical such as the *Nation* and its small circulation of some 8,000 as compared for example, with 100,000 for the Harper magazines or 200,000 in 1885 for *Scribner's* (known by then as *Century Magazine*). Certainly the *Nation* seems to have been the journal of the intellectual classes; yet it usually demanded improvements and reforms of certain types. The mild liberalism of the Cobden or Manchester school of economics, the moral rectitude, and the authoritative tone that Edwin Lawrence Godkin instilled in the *Nation* were not suited to a popular magazine but were eminently suitable for a successful class which believed that things were going well on the whole and that certain improvements could be made by men of good will and upright character, but that no fundamental changes were required. . . .

One might suppose that the American people of the post-Civil War years spent all of their leisure time reading novels, story-papers, newspapers, and magazines. Considering the lower percentage of educated persons in those years, those who did have high school or college educations must have read a great deal for the publishing industries of the era to have flourished so and to have produced such a variety. In many cases, the readers were seeking a familiar goal—escape to a world of danger and high adventure, exotic settings, and occasionally, sex and violence. The urban world of factories and offices must have made such escape ever more necessary since the vogue for this kind of fiction, beginning in the 1850's, constantly increased through the years of the Gilded Age. But the readers also sought reaffirmation of the traditional values, the beliefs and ideals of an earlier America of town and countryside, and these they found especially in the novels and story-papers. The educated minority found the same reassurance in the firm moral tone and the determined factuality and seriousness of the journals of opinion.

In the United States in these same years, industry was going through a time of revolutionary change and growth, and the nation was undergoing a social transformation as industry and urbanism grew with awe-inspiring rapidity; depressions, immigration, labor disputes, all competed for space in the press. Yet the fiction, essays, poems, and editorial advice of the popular publications were all redolent of a rural and village land. The revolution in values lagged behind the revolution in the social structure, and this was most clearly evident in the popular literature of the age.

But Americans then, as now, did not spend their evenings and Sundays solely in reading. They heard lectures, attended the theater, went to curiosity museums and circuses, and participated in self-improvement classes at Chautauqua institutes. In all of these they sought something similar to what they sought in their reading—the escape from reality of Barnum's collection of curiosities or the artificial world of the theater, the confident proclamation of the "old truths" in a Moody revival meeting, or the self-help and inspiration at a Chautauqua. They may have attended that new phenomenon, organized, big-league baseball. In any case, there were many varied activities available to the public, and most of them flourished in these years.

Religious revival meetings were a national favorite to many, and no revival team compared in popularity to Dwight L. Moody and Ira D. Sankey. Moody in 1875 was "the rising young tycoon of the revival trade as Andrew Carnegie was of the steel trade or John D. Rockefeller of oil." He was the revivalist who coupled businesslike methods with the "old fashioned gospel," and his success was enormous. In this he was substantially aided by Ira D. Sankey, who took charge of the music and contributed stirring solo renditions of popular gospel hymns. But Moody was the driving force in this revival movement of the 1870's and 1880's. . . . He was a remarkably persuasive example of the peculiar combination of the revolution in techniques and the cultural lag in values which characterized so much of the popular culture of the Gilded Age. His methods were modern but his message consisted of forceful repetitions of the "old truths." This combination made him the most popular and significant revival preacher of the Gilded Age.

There were many famous preachers in this age, some conservative in theology, a few, liberal; some who argued that Christianity should be applied to the social problems of the day, others who preached on sin and salvation alone. But one man stood out as somewhat of a symbol of the middle-class pulpit and created one of the great sensations of the time—Henry Ward Beecher. He was not a typical preacher. The typical minister was more conservative, not nearly so successful, and certainly not as controversial. Yet Beecher spoke with tremendous authority from his Plymouth Congregational Church in Brooklyn, New York, and from his editorial position on the *Independent*. His message had wide popular appeal. . . .

As with Moody, the traditional values, without the complex theology and harsh punishments of the old faith, were restated and combined with considerable dramatic ability and commercial skill to gain tremendous popularity. . . .

Another fascinating episode in the history of popular culture in the Gilded Age is the early history of the Chautauqua movement. Most accounts of this movement dwell upon the later phase, known as the circuit or tent Chautauqua. This latter development was the commercialization and standardization of Chautauqua for purposes of taking Chautauqua on the road, and it led to some degradation of the content of Chautauqua as pure entertainment attractions gradually supplanted most of the educational programs (students of educational television may find some historical precedents here). . . . But this was a development of the turn of the century and not part of the Gilded Age. . . .

The self-improvement drive and the success-through-knowledge theme demonstrated again that the American people of the Gilded Age eagerly sought the learning that was available in their time. If this phenomenon is linked with the free library movement, which had tremendous growth in the years 1878 to 1898, the already noted prosperity of the book publishing industry (climaxed by the spectacular royalty check paid by Samuel Clemens for his publishing house to former President Grant for the sum of $200,000), and the magazine boom, it is obvious that the thirst for knowledge and the desire for culture were prominent characteristics of the public attitude of the Gilded Age. To be sure, this search customarily led simply to the reaffirmation of the values rooted in the experiences of that age. The benefits of private property, the beauties of the law of competition, and the stewardship of men of wealth were main themes of Chautauqua lectures on social and economic subjects. But it would be strange indeed if the popular institutions of a society purveyed ideas contrary to the accepted values of that society. We may expect that the lonely prophet or perceptive intellectual or sensitive artist will confront a society with its failures and injustices, but surely the culture-heroes will not, and the purpose of studying the latter is to identify the popular ideas, not the unconventional ones.

Again the impression may linger that the public of this time devoted itself entirely to reading and listening to sermons and lectures; such was plainly not the case. The Gilded Age was the time of the rise of spectator sports, of the birth of the modern circus; it was a great era in the history of minstrelsy and a "golden age" of the theater. As the people gathered in cities and worked in factories, it became necessary to substitute organized recreation and spectator events for the games and entertainments of rural society. For these spectacles, on the playing field or on the stage, the audiences were large and enthusiastic. This period witnessed the first mammoth three-ring circus under "three acres" of circus tent and the opening of the nation's foremost opera house, the historic Metropolitan, in New York City in 1883.

In the realm of theater, there were three developments which any student of the popular culture must consider: the dominance of the "road"; the vogue for light musicals and scenic splendors, including the spectacle of the scantily attired female form; and, finally, the popularity and decline of minstrelsy. . . .

The third of these trends in show business is the role of the minstrel show.

The minstrel show dates back to the between-acts specialty numbers of blackface performers in the pre-Civil War era, especially one Thomas Rice, famed for his "Jump Jim Crow" number. In this period the stock Negro character of the stage evolved, bearing little or no resemblance to any actual Negroes. From this came the authentic minstrel company with end men, jokes, and songs. This form of entertainment had its heyday in the period from 1850 to 1870. Thereafter, the competition to form even bigger and more elaborate shows caused a loss in the quality of the performances. This loss, plus increasing expenses and competition with vaudeville, burlesque, and musical comedy caused minstrels to go into a long decline which ended the form in the 1920's.

The success of the minstrel show does cast some light on the public attitude toward racial minorities in the Gilded Age. Such stereotypes were a commonplace of that era. In particular, the Negro was portrayed on stage, in dialect stories, and in illustrations as a comic fellow, "ludicrously inept," often putting on "airs . . . above his true station in life," but withal a happy, good-natured type, perhaps gifted at singing or dancing, but never as a "person of consequence or dignity." This was an age when racial distinctions were taken as obvious and inescapable. Those who were concerned about the conditions of minority groups acted from paternalistic motives, not from a sense of the legitimate dignity and worth of all men. . . .

The popular culture of the Gilded Age cannot be encompassed in an essay. There is too much to consider. Nothing has yet been said about the giant figure of P.T. Barnum, for example, whose promotions were of more than passing importance in the field of entertainment. Though it was not so much Barnum himself as it was his partners—W. C. Coup, in particular—who created the modern circus, the "greatest show on earth," Barnum remains the symbol of this achievement. Obviously the growth of the circus was tied to the growth of railroads and centers of population adequate to support such an enterprise. In the field of entertainment the gigantic circus was related to the spirit of the age, an age of great enterprises of all kinds, from spanning a continent with iron rails to building a multimillion-dollar business empire. P. T. Barnum belongs among the empire-builders of this era.

Still another fascinating episode in the popular culture of the Gilded Age was the drawing power of the famed agnostic, Robert Ingersoll. It was not just Moody or Beecher or Barnum who could attract crowds with ideas and attractions that were plainly acceptable to most people, but a brilliant orator could bring large crowds into the lecture halls to hear their own religion criticized and challenged. . . .

Several general propositions can be ventured about the popular culture of this period, all of which deserve consideration in any lengthy study. There was a revolution in the technical phases; because of improved transportation, large cities, and improved business methods, as well as a changing society, all of the institutions that purveyed popular culture were being transformed. The newspapers and magazines had to revise their methods and their appeal; the Chautauqua was commercialized and standardized; revivalism took on business methods; minstrelsy could not survive the competition of this new age in entertainment. The changes that grew out of this revolution in methods, however, were felt in later years with more force than in the Gilded Age itself. But the need for greater sales was surely evident in the popularity of the sentimental-romantic stories in magazines in serial form and then in book form, both of which were major features of the post-Civil War decades.

The degree of continuity between the Gilded Age and the pre-Civil War years deserves notice. The years before the Civil War have been called the "Sentimental Years," but this characterization with its implication of sentimentalization of human relationships could with equal accuracy be applied to the Gilded Age. The death of loved ones, the idealization of the family, and the celebration of romantic love were all powerful themes through the Civil War and into the postwar years.

Closely related to this continuity is the degree to which the popular works of the Gilded Age clung to the values and beliefs of an earlier time. Indeed, the insistent celebration of these virtues of an earlier America leads to the conclusion that there was an awareness of the forces that were transforming the nation and a fierce resistance to them.

But in spite of these continuities and the characteristics shared with American popular tastes of any period, there was something of a characteristic quality to the Gilded Age. The period came to an end as the 1880's drew to a close. The transformation of the publishing industry, the rise of theatrical syndicates, the passing of the "golden age of the road," the decline of minstrelsy, the disappearance of the cheap story-papers, all marked the change. Something would be lost, perhaps best described as the folk element, that which had endured into an industrial age from an earlier America. Another casualty of the more highly organized society was the uninhibited individualism, which for all its unfortunate results, lent a colorful and fascinating quality to this era. And, finally, there was a loss of that sense of assurance and abundant optimism which, though a substantial part of the American character in all periods, was assuredly at a high point in the Gilded Age.

These losses were bound to occur as the technology of an industrial society advanced, and mass markets for art and entertainment were made possible, even necessary. It is probably well that artists and entertainers or, at least, their promoters and business managers should have organized for this new age, but it is also permissable to feel a twinge of nostalgia for an age when the individual seemed a bit more significant. The Gilded Age was still a time when a bold editor could display his personality in his paper, a colorful preacher could become a national figure almost in the manner of a motion picture star, and every housewife could hope to become a famous writer with her latest romantic tale. And all of this they could do with a firm belief in the triumph of their cause and surpassing faith in the imperviousness of their moral armor.

CHAPTER 9

THE IMMIGRANT
IN AMERICA

As we saw in a previous selection, immigrants flocked to the United States in such numbers (nearly 25,000,000) in the 50 years after the Civil War that they brought profound change to the composition of the American population. By the late nineteenth century the great stream of "new immigration" had reached flood tide; Russians, Poles, Serbs, Greeks, Hungarians, Rumanians, and Italians now comprised the bulk of the incoming flow of immigration. Most of the new immigrants were Catholics or Jews, and their ideas and customs differed markedly from those of old-stock Protestant Americans. The immigrants were primarily from rural peasant backgrounds, but circumstances forced them to crowd into the industrial cities and towns and to accept employment as low-paid, unskilled laborers. The conditions under which the immigrants lived and worked made them the natural targets of criticism and pejorative stereotyping by more fortunate Americans. These Americans talked much about the "immigrant problem." They wondered if the new immigrants could be assimilated into American life, and they ultimately turned to immigration restriction to moot that question.

Immigration history has not been ignored by American scholars. Historians have long recognized that the United States is a country of immigrants, and they have called attention to the profound and pervasive influence of immigration in the development of the nation. But scholars have generally concentrated on the impact of immigration on American development rather than on the history of the immigrants themselves. Like the stories of other masses of people in American history—Indians, Afro-Americans, laborers, and the poor—the actual experience of the immigrants has been largely neglected until fairly recent times. An exception to this pattern is Oscar Handlin's classic study, *The Uprooted* (1951), which tells the story of the late nineteenth and early twentieth century migrations to the United States from the perspective of the immigrants themselves. Handlin picks up the story in the Old World, follows the immigrants on their journeys to America, and describes their lives in their new homeland. This technique allows Handlin to give careful consideration to the profound cultural and psychological adjustments that the immigrants were called on to make in their transition from a traditional peasant environment to a thoroughly strange, modern, and complex world. Some of the varied and difficult problems faced by the immigrants are apparent in Professor Handlin's sensitive portrait of family life, which follows as the selection for this chapter.

The student should read this selection not so much for information but for the purpose of acquiring a sense of what the immigrant experience was all about. Try to put yourself in the places of various members of an immigrant family. Try to imagine the problems you would face and the anguish you would experience if you were to emigrate from the United States and settle in a country with a radically different environment and culture. Does Handlin's approach give you a better understanding of the immigrant experience than a less subjective and more traditional treatment might? Does the subjectivity of Handlin's essay have a place in good historical study and writing?

In addition to Handlin's *The Uprooted: The Epic Story of the Great Migrations That Made the American People** (1951), the student who is interested in the immigrant experience will find useful Mary Antin, *The Promised Land** (1911), and Theodore C. Blegen, ed., *Land of Their Choice; the Immigrants Write Home* (1955). Maldwyn Allen Jones, *American Immigration** (1960), is a good survey of American immigration, and John Higham, *Strangers in the Land** (1955), is an excellent treatment of the movement for immigration restriction.

*Available in a paperback edition.

THE IMMIGRANT FAMILY IN TRANSITION

OSCAR HANDLIN

Sometimes at night she'd wake and turn to feel if he were there. She'd reach the space across to where he lay, sense the reassuring bulk of him. She'd hug the thought. *All else has passed away with our passing from that place. But this will never change. By holy matrimony he has made me wife and mother to his family. That* (fiercely) *we can hold intact.*

In morning's light the certainty was gone. Through the day the fear came that this most intimate part of life would not remain the same. At the stove later she paused while the long spoon in her hand continued its mechanical stirring; she looked in bewilderment at the gathering table. Would the strangeness of the setting make strangers also of these her dear ones? Resolve came back, but confidence not altogether. It would be a desperate battle to hold firm in these relationships, outside the context that had nurtured them.

The difficulty was that formerly the family had not been a thing in itself, but an integral element of the village community. It had been fixed in a framework of numerous links and knots that held each individual within it in his place. As the functioning unit within the economy it was the means through which bread was produced and consumed. No one could live except as the member of a family.

As the medium for holding and transmitting land, its stability had been vital to social order. Every change in its structure affected the whole community. On the quality of a single marriage depended the welfare of all the brothers and sisters and less directly a widening circle of other persons. The connection with the soil had also been an element in extending these affiliations beyond the single household to a broad range of other kin tied together by inheritance, of blood and of possible claims to a common patrimony.

The family had therefore never been isolated. Its concerns were those of the entire village. While each home was expected to be the source of its own discipline, the community stood ready with sanctions of its own to make sure that children were obedient, that parents were good, and that relatives were

SOURCE. Oscar Handlin, *The Uprooted: The Epic Story of the Great Migrations That Made the American People.* Copyright © 1951 by Oscar Handlin. Reprinted by permission of Little, Brown and Company.

helpful to each other. The network of mutual rights and obligations had thus the support of both an inner and an outer control.

Emigration took the family out of the village. The mere going was disruptive. The struggles of departure and resettlement subjected the household to a severe strain under most trying and most unusual conditions and at the same time deprived it of the counsel and assistance upon which it had traditionally depended. When so many new decisions were to be made, they had to be made alone. That alone distinguished the new family from the old.

In America also the economic unity of the common household enterprise disappeared. The minority who found their way to the farms or who, by their labors, maintained little businesses where wife and children could work along with the father, held on to the former ways. Vestiges of the old order also remained in the sweating homework system; as the father brought back the bundles that would be sewn into shirts or twisted into artificial flowers, the gathered group in the tenement room recaptured the sense of common effort familiar in recollection from the Other Side.

These were, however, but byways in the economy. In the characteristic immigrant employment, the individual was hired as an integer. He was one line in the ledger, one pair of hands on the floor, one pay envelope at the window, with no reference to who was there at home. Ultimately this pattern supplanted all others. Would they continue to take his bidding, to toil in the dim room with him, the one to pocket all, when they could go out to be their own wage earners? There was no point to it. Of what inheritance could he deprive them?

Properly speaking the family no longer had an income; there were only the combined incomes of its members. The larger unit was now a source of weakness rather than of strength. Those who could, broke away; it was madness for a man who was capable of supporting himself to maintain the ties of uncle or cousin when those ties would only draw off a share of his earnings. Those who remembered the old obligations, alas, were generally those more likely to consume than to produce—the aged, the weak, the ill. With these the circumstances, and with no outside force to assign the blame, the extensive family of the Old World disintegrated. *So it is now, a brother stabs his brother, a sister drowns her sister, for profit's sake.*

Steadily the relatives dropped away; the husband, wife, and children were left alone. Where need compelled additions to the income of this narrower household, it was better to take in boarders, tenants, on an impersonal, cash-down basis. The more compelling duties of the old extended family were treacherous here; it was safer by avoiding them to transform the relationship into one of mere occasional sociability.

The bonds to those left at home also disintegrated. There was a piece of land, and if he had not gone away it would have been his; but having gone away he ought not ask that it be sold and money sent to him in America. Endless quarreling followed. Or the old folks, staying, bitterly resented the departed son who should have been the staff on which they might lean in age. *You went to make money and you forgot that you left parents; may God and your own children care for you as you for us.*

Is it the loss of income they minded, or the sadness of being abandoned? *We cannot know whether we shall yet speak with you, embrace you, at least once before our death.* It does not matter. The demands are too heavy on both emotions and purse. The old ties gradually are loosened. The family steadily tapers down to the conjugal unit, a father, a mother, and their immediate offspring. The New World has separated them from all the others who would have been one with them in the Old.

Perhaps for that reason she wished so intensely to hold together what was left. From mistress in an extensive household she had become mother of a more intimate group; that hard core she would labor to keep intact.

The early experiences of the new family entity fed her hopes. That they were cut off from all else that was familiar led the members to value each other the more. With whom else could they discuss the memories of the past and the problems of the present? Depending upon each other because there was no one else upon whom they could depend, they drew steadily together.

The very process of migration had been shared. Mostly they had come together, together faced the open road and the closed quarters of the steerage. In the long lapse of time between departure and arrival, they were deprived of the busying occupations of the farm, of the comradeship of neighbors, and had for company only one another. The occasion was one for deeper understanding; and long after the final settlement, recollections would come back of the joys and tribulations of the way, come back to unite those who had made the journey together.

The warmth of participation in the enterprise of crossing cheered even those later immigrants who divided for the critical steps, husband first to make a start, wife and children after. Such a separation created problems of its own, but it did not of itself lessen the attachment of the partners to it. Though the ocean lay between, they were joined by the gravity of the common effort.

That is why, as the years passed and they thought back to the first exploratory days in America, it seemed to them that the family had been strongest and purest before its exposure to the new life. As strangers they had known no one. Evening brought them always back together. Excited with discoveries or downcast with disappointments, they communicated to one another the freshness of occurrence. They knew then they were one like the meager loaf from which they would begin each to slice the sustenance of all. It was a tenement room or a sod hut. But it was home; and those who came to it worn out with wandering acquired for home an enduring devotion.

Only soon, the conditions of their being in the United States would break in upon them. The narrow family would not remain alone together. Individually, its members in going out would make each their own adjustments to the society about them, and coming back would be less alike. Man and woman, boy and girl, they would find for themselves new roles and establish for themselves new relationships. It would happen more quickly in the cities than on the farms where a rural environment extended the family's isolation. But ultimately it would happen everywhere. The woman meditating by the stove would resist it. But already as they took their places her heart chilled to the fear of failure.

Across the long table they confronted each other, the two who were now central to all. It was as if daily they felt the need of a fresh view of the familiar features in the light of the new experiences. In the anxious regards were mingled two questions. Is this the same being united to me those many years ago and now still unchanged? How adequate will this union be to the present demands upon it?

Indeed these were no longer the man and woman joined in wedlock at that distant date; they had never then imagined that such questions might ever arise. Their marriage had not been the product of an individual passion, but a social arrangement under the oversight of the community. She had accepted the obligations of her situation, to be obedient and faithful, to further his health and comfort, to be a good and kindly wife, the crown of her husband's life. He had taken on the responsibilities of the efficient provider who would safeguard her from degrading work, keep want away, and mildly satisfy her will. The union upon which fortune smiled was one blessed with the dignified respect of the partners for their rights and duties.

The day they turned their backs upon the old home, the relationship began to change. At the very outset, the course of the crossing led to troubles. In the long suspended period between departure and arrival, neither he nor she had duties or could expect fixed dues. They were then thrown more together than ever before, but as never before found it difficult to judge one another. The intimacy of shared miseries brought them together, but, as it were, only to be the more conscious of each other's deficiencies. A sorry figure he made, lounging about from day to day with nothing to do; while her derelictions of housewifely obligations were served up in the stale biscuits of every meal.

If migration involved a temporary separation as, after 1880, it often did, the results were more disruptive still. He went away to the sound of the children's crying; and heard it echo through the months apart. In his unaccustomed singleness, he came to miss what before he had taken for granted, the warmth of the woman's presence. *As the fish thirst for water, so I long for you.*

It is hard to know what may happen across that far dividing distance. *Only I beg you write more often.* As the letters fail to appear, for she is not familiar to the pen, worries take their place, and suspicions. Resentful, he asks a friend in the village to inform him of her doings. Does she hold to the home? At the same time the fear will rise lest she be unable to manage. The stock of grain may be too small, the labor in the field too hard. Cautionary advice covers the pages he sends home.

She has the advantage of waiting in a known place in the company of the children. But her double role is burdensome; she cannot be as he was, head of the household. The boys are unruly and, though she gives them some of the broomstick, they are slow to obey. She hires a hand to help in the field, but he is negligent; he has not for her the fear as for a master. Often she thinks of her husband and what a life he must lead there among strangers, his work heavier than a stone, his strength being drained away into a foreign soil. *The day passes in labor but in the evening I long very much and at night I cannot sleep. We can be united in heart and thought but that satisfies me not. Take us or come back; let it be so or so; as it is I exist neither upon ice nor upon water.*

Sometimes the months stretch out and the separateness widens. He sets himself a goal: I will have a thousand rubles and then send for them. But the goal is never attained. Meanwhile he is hardened in his bachelor life and puts off indefinitely the day of reunion. Or she at home grows reluctant. The dread of the new place mounts up in her and feeds off the complaints in his letters. She wishes him back—enough of this America—and when the call comes, procrastinates.

Whatever division, long or short, appeared in the transplantation was not mended in the resettlement. On the farms, the man could resume his place as head of the household enterprise; but the millions who stayed in the cities found their positions drastically altered. She could not think that he was here satisfying his obligations toward the family. No longer the sole or even the main provider, he seemed to her wanting in the most critical duty of all. Why, there were times when she herself or the children earned more than he, times when he sat home idle while they went out to bring home his bread. When he was taken on, it was not at work she understood or could respect. Away at some menial task, she could not regard him as she had that husbandman who had once managed their tiny plot and had brought up her sons to follow in his steps.

Nor could he be satisfied as to her adequacy for the life of the New World. Deprived of the usual household chores of the garden, the needle, and the loom, she appeared often lethargic; the blood hardly ran in her veins. On the other hand management of the domestic economy under American conditions was frequently beyond her comprehension. When the results were unhappy—disorderly quarters, poor food—it was hard to draw the line between the effects of negligence and the effects of poverty and ignorance. The necessity that drove her to labor for others was the source of resentment, both because it reflected upon his own abilities and because it took her away from her proper job in the home.

Roles once thoroughly defined were now altogether confounded. The two got on under the continual strain of uncertainty as to their place in the family, as to their relationships to each other. And their experience, no longer one for the two, added constantly to that underlying uncertainty.

Sometimes it was he went out to the wide world, learned the language of the country, and grew sophisticated in the ways of the place, while she was confined to the flat and remained ignorant of the rudiments of English. *I at least know where there's an Eighth Street, and a One Hundred and Thirtieth Street with tin works, and an Eighty-fourth Street with a match factory. I know every block around the World Building and the place where the car line stops. But you know no more than if you had just landed.* Sometimes it was she, in service in some other's home, who earlier learned the ways—what food they ate and clothes they wore and how they sat of an evening in the polished sitting room. It was bitter hard to be the satisfying helpmate when one could hardly guess what wants the other had.

As the situation clarified, aspects at first hidden emerged with oppressive distinctness. In the Old World her status had been fixed by a variety of elements—whose daughter she was, what dowry she brought, into what family she married. Let her husband be unfortunate or unskillful or unthrifty, she had still a set place in the village. Here her fate was completely tied up in his success. What she was or had been mattered nothing, only what he could do. Well, it was galling to see what other, lesser women had, to watch their men push their way ahead. The utter dependence on his efforts put an acrimonious tone in her greetings as he came nightly home no better than before.

Nagging demands he could not meet confirmed his own inner doubts about himself. Was not the whole migration the story of his succession of failures? He had been unable to hold on to the land, to direct the family comfortably across the ocean or to establish it securely on this side. He felt respect ebb away and carried about a gnawing shame at his own lack of capacity. Most of all, he resented his loss of authority. Indeed he became accustomed to request, not to order, but knew it was not right it should be so; and he resented his wife's growing dominance over the household. It was a poor state of affairs when the cow showed the way to the ox.

In the secret night when her stirring waked him he did not move. Fatigue pinned him down. Yet sleep would not return. Instead an angry tension crept into his heart. Her body's presence intruded on his consciousness. Limbs rigid, he pushed the thought away; to this demand too he would not respond, by so much had he now lost his manhood.

Clenched eyelids would not keep the moonlight out. Not a beam came down the narrow airshaft; still his sight tingled to the streaks reflected from a distant meadow where they had walked amidst the long grasses, and had been young, eager for the enjoyment of each other to which marriage had opened the way. There had been no strain then; what the community had to that day forbidden, it now welcomed; and these two had been carried along by confidence in the rightness of their acts, by certainty they would each be gratified.

It was coming away that had first added wormwood to the taste. They had lost the benevolent oversight of the village which by its insistence on traditional propriety had answered every how and when. Now the deed required ever a decision; it raised ever some question; and it involved some clash of wills, his or hers. By leaving they had created doubts they knew not how to resolve.

He remembered the darkness of successive borrowed beds. In the enforced closeness of boardinghouses and shipboard he had stifled the groping desires. Years later, the confined warmth of many bodies would come back to assault his senses, would bring the painful recollection of urges never satisfied. And in this place that was their own it was rare that wish and opportunity coincided. In the cramped quarters they had been never alone and therefore never really together. Often there was the startling chill of interruption—the uneasy stirring of a child, the banging progress of a neighbor through the ill-lit hall. Always there was the uncertainty of when and how. Even the times when, flushed with the cheap certitude of liquor or with the passing exuberance of some new job, he had asserted his passion, there had followed inevitably an aftermath of regret and doubt. What had really been given and what received in these exchanges?

Perhaps he should not have expected more. He himself knew the dull indifference that came with being often tired. He knew too her deep fear of recurrent childbirth. Not that this was a subject of conversation between them; but it took no words to convey her dismay at each discovery of her condition. But the terms must be accepted, the price paid. Worse would follow the attempt to void it; often enough she had heard the stories of such a one, desperate at the approach of an eighth or ninth, who had sought the relief of self-abortion and had found only the painful death of blood poisoning.

Vaguely also they suspected that there were ways of forestalling pregnancy. But the old wives' knowledge did not extend that far; in this matter the midwife was not helpful; and, as for doctors—why, if a woman had thought of them, she would have found it difficult even to frame the terms of her inquiry. The husband had once cautiously sounded out an apothecary, but got only a jocular response: *Better sleep out on the fire escape, Joe.* Besides it all smacked of the illicit and the shameful. The law frowned on it; the priest cautioned against it; and deep inner forebodings conjured up the visions of nature's reprisals for interference with her processes.

There was, therefore, not much joy to their desiring; the shadow of the reckoning was too close. There was no blame. Only, sometimes, as she nursed her discontent, the thought came to her that, if only he had managed better, all would be otherwise. And he, reading the accusations in her eyes, felt the pangs of a sudden guilt, the acknowledgement of his own inadequacies. At such times, a sullen anger entered the household, lingered unexpressed for days. The mornings when he went to work, he carried off a pained exasperation. Suspicions might come; the scandal of that other's wife, who with the boarder shamed her home, might cross his mind. The memory galled his wounds and, returned that night, edged his answers with acerbity. Peace then departed in an exchange of taunting words, then blows, and sad conciliation.

Some men surrendered. Confronted by intolerable burdens they deserted their families, lost themselves alone somewhere and put thus an end to this striving. Then the fatherless home, adrift, was not long from its foundering.

Mostly however they held together, the man and woman. Yes, partly it was the thought of the children that kept the family whole and partly it was the consciousness that in abandoning each other they would sever every last tie with their own past, diminish thereby their own human identity. Yes, often as they lay there, longing for escape to an undefined freedom, there was no move simply because the effort seemed too great, the means far out of reach.

But it was more than that that curbed the passing wish to flee. But it was more than that that drew them at last to each other. The old fixed order of respect between husband and wife had disappeared as the obligations on which it rested became irrelevant in the New World. Without the protective cover of well-defined roles they faced each other as individuals under the most trying conditions. That was difficult. But then as he looked upon this person who shared his bed and recalled the long way she had come, the sufferings she had borne, his heart went out to her. And then as she sensed the turning of his eyes upon her and thought of the little pleasures all his efforts brought, her heart went out to him.

It was not pity that sealed them in this attachment, but the brief glimmers of comprehension that they shared a life as they shared a bed. They were individuals, separate, two, and had been so since they left the village. But they had been two together. In those moments of recognition they knew they had been partners in a common experience and were now involved in a common situation. Only in each other could these beings find the complete understanding that would alone bring what they so desperately wanted, some reaffirmation of their own human dignity. For warmth they moved toward each other, for the warmth that came from the knowledge that here was consolation. Another knew and understood. That was a precious certainty, where all else was insecure.

About the children they can feel no certainty whatever.

This country is full of children. In the morning their clatter down the staircase fills the house. In the afternoon they occupy the streets. In the evening they pour back into the waiting flat which they quickly distend with the clamor of their ceaseless activity.

The immigrants were by no means strange to the idea of full families. The little ones had always made up a sizable part of the village population. But the spot had not been so taken up with their presence. They had had each their places, where they ought to be and where they ought not to be. They had had each their functions, what they ought to do and what they ought not to do. They had not been, therefore, so prominent in the sight of their elders. . . .

They might suppose it was the same as they strolled to worship on a holiday, Papa, Mama, and the boys and girls, covering the paved walk in a pair of uneven rows. They were wrong. Even then they knew the momentary solidarity would disintegrate before the day was over. They no longer cohered as a family and, as individuals, could scarcely say how they stood one to another.

The divisions created by differences of experience were too great. The older ones, sedately in the rear, had been eight or nine or in their teens in the year of the crossing. They had vivid memories of the Old Country, of the troubles that drove them off, and of the hardships of the journey. They spoke their mother's language and their unaccustomed English bore a heavy accent that united them with their past. Trained under the discipline of the household that had been, they were still ready to accept obligations. Necessity had long since heaped responsibilities upon them; no doubt they had been wage earners since soon after their arrival.

There was impatience in their scrutiny of the younger ones. Before them were two to be watched, scrabbling along without regard for appearances. These had been infants or little more when the migration came; their early childhood had passed under the unsettled conditions of the transition. They had never learned the proper ways at home, and a brief attendance at the public school had confused them so they knew not where they stood. They were clumsy in the speech of both the old land and the new; their names came from abroad but had already been corrupted into nicknames here. They were neither one thing nor the other.

At the head of the procession toddled the citizens. These more fortunate ones had been born into their environment. They had never known the Old World; they had not shared the experience of coming. They were Americans from the start, had lisped the words in English, and often received names appropriated from the older inhabitants.

It was at such times the parents were fullest of their responsibilities. As they led the way on these occasions they became gravely conscious of a disturbing uncertainty. What if the children should cease to follow, should take it into their heads to march off in some altogether strange direction! It was difficult enough to show them the right ways around the corners of the city blocks; it was infinitely more difficult to show them the right ways around the twisting curves of the new way of life.

As they consider the heaviness of their tasks, the mother and father grow somber. They remember the failures. Their minds go to that one who came to them as if on a visit, then sickened and went away. It occurs to them that they cannot possibly meet their obligations to the children. Not only that the food will hardly go around to nurture all, not only that the mended garments pass from one to another, but that by the act of migration, they, the parents, have destroyed the birthright of their sons and daughters. These boys who should be picking berries or hunting nuts, these girls who should be approaching mastery of the stove, have all been robbed and must endure the present, enter the future without their proper due. To each other, the parents acknowledge the guilt: *Yes, dear, and therefore let us sacrifice ourselves and live only for them. If there is any hope in this world, it is not for us but for them.*

It was easier to bend the neck in readiness than to be certain that the yoke would fit. With bewilderment the immigrants learned that to be willing to sacrifice was not enough, that their children must be also willing to accept the sacrifice; and of that there could be no confidence. The initial dissimilarities of experience widened with time as youngsters ventured out from the home and subjected themselves to influences foreign to their elders. The life of school and the life of street completed the separation between the generations.

If it did nothing else to the child, the school introduced into his life a rival source of authority. The day the little boy hesitantly made his way into the classroom, the image of the teacher began to compete with that of the father. The one like the other laid down a rigid code of behavior, demanded absolute obedience, and stood ready to punish infractions with swift severity. The day the youngster came back to criticize his home (*They say in school that . . .*) his parents knew they would have to struggle for his loyalty.

That was an additional reason why the immigrants loved to create educational institutions of their own; they hoped thereby to minimize the contest. But the parochial schools were expensive and spread very slowly; they accommodated at best only a small fraction of the children. The strong-minded and well-to-do could hold out against the pleas of their offspring who wished to go where everyone else went; mostly the newcomers were compelled by circumstances and by the law to depend on public instruction.

The building itself was familiar enough; this was one of the known landmarks of the neighborhood. The idea of attendance was also familiar; this had happened already to older brothers and friends. And as the lad entered the yard, even sight of the fellows playing or waiting in line had the appearance of familiarity; he recognized some from around his own block, the others were much like himself. The public school was universal, but each nevertheless reflected the quality of the homogeneous residential district within which it was situated. In effect it was Irish or Jewish or German or Polish; the first impression it made on the new scholar was that of the altogether familiar and the altogether expected.

The ringing bell broke the continuity of his life; as he walked up the cast-iron staircase he left the narrow orbit of his home and moved into the limitless world. He stood in the stiff lines and sat motionless in the formal rows of seats. He learned silence and passivity who had never before felt restraints on his actions. He came to conform to rules; there were ways of rising and of sitting, ways to come dressed, ways to leave the room on certain occasions, and ways without words to signal the need. This order would now be his life.

Mostly the boys accede, and the girls too. At least the youngest do. There are truancies, some from their stubborn will, some from their shame at the poverty of clothing, some from necessity that keeps them home or sends them out to work. But mostly they give in and come. There is vaguely an understanding that the school will help them get on; and everyone else goes, so they go along. Besides they fear the law, want no trouble.

Only often, as they sat in the torpid classrooms, their attention wandered from the drone of recitations. Through the windows, gray filmed-over, they could see the bustle of purposeful men. By contrast, the school seemed empty of achievements, empty of the possibility of achievement. For what reason were they thus confined? What could they hope to gain from all this?

They did not ask those questions. They had long ago heard the trite answers. They came in order to grow up good and useful citizens. How would the school help them? By teaching them what was in these books.

Idly the boys fingered the battered volumes from which wisdom was to flow. There was no need to open them; the bold type of their pages was familiar enough from constant drilling.

THIS IS JACK. THIS IS JACK'S HOUSE. THIS IS JACK'S DADDY. JACK GOES SHOPPING. JACK GOES TO SCHOOL. ON THE WAY HE MEETS A COW. ON THE WAY HE MEETS A SHEEP. JACK COMES HOME. JACK FALLS ASLEEP.

And surely enough, across the top from page to page the brightly colored pictures show it all. Blue-eyed and blond, Jack himself stares out over the nice white collar and the neatly buttoned jacket. Across the green lawn, from the porch of the pretty yellow house, a miraculously slim mother waves. By the side of a road that dips through the fields of corn, the animals wait, each in turn to extend its greeting. There it all is, real as life.

Except that it is all a lie. There is no Jack, no house, no brightly smiling

"Mummy." In the whole room there is not a boy with such a name, with such an appearance. One can walk streets without end and there will be never a glimpse of the yellow clapboards, of the close-cropped grass. Who sleeps like Jack alone in the prim room by the window to be wakened by singing birds? *Good morning, Mr. Robin.* The whole book is false because nothing in it touches on the experience of its readers and no element in their experience creeps into its pages.

Falsity runs through all their books, which were all written to be used by other pupils in other schools; even the arithmetic sets its problems in terms of the rural countryside. Falsity runs through all their education. They learn the songs their mothers never sang. They mouth the words of precepts with no meaning: *A rolling stone gathers no moss. Make hay while the sun shines.* But what stone, what moss, what hay? The time that man appeared to speak from the platform and roused them, he shook them with his talk until they cheered the thin line at Bunker Hill, at Plymouth through the snow. *Our fathers' God, to Thee* . . . Then later they thought, *Whose fathers?* Again a deception!

They themselves compounded the enormity of the untruth by the inability to give it the lie. From the desk the teacher looked down, a challenge they dared not meet. It was foolhardy of course to question her rightness. What an arsenal was at her command to destroy them! The steel-edged ruler across the knuckles was the least of her weapons. Casually she could twist the knife of ridicule in the soreness of their sensibilities; there was so much in their accent, appearance, and manners that was open to mockery. Without effort she could make them doubt themselves; the contrast of positions was too great. As she snapped shut the closet upon the symbols of her ladyhood within—the white gloves, the rolled-up umbrella, and the sedate hat—she indicated at once the superiority of her own status. There was visible evidence of her correctness in her speech and in her bearing, in her dress, and in the frequent intimations of the quality of her upbringing.

Perhaps a few were touched with sympathy at the condition of their charges. But what these offered was pity, nobler than contempt, but to the children no more acceptable. It was rare indeed to find the dedicated woman whose understanding of her students brought a touch of love into her work. . . .

It took no uncommon sagacity to learn it was better not to question the teacher's world. The wise fellow kept his mouth shut and accepted it; he came to believe in a universe, divided as it were into two realms, one for school and one for home, and each with rules and modes of behavior of its own.

Acquiescence was no solution, however. Their lives could not be so divided. As the children of the immigrants grew up, they felt increasingly the compulsion to choose between the one way and the other. For some, the vision of the yellow house was peremptory. The kindness of a teacher, taken with the earnestness of the exceptional good student, may have opened the prospect of attaining it. Or the intense will of the ambitious youngster may have done so. Or the desperate dislike of a repressive home may have made this the only tolerable alternative. In any case, this way involved the complete identification with Jack, and that meant the total rejection of the origins and the background Jack could not have had.

Only a few, however, had the ability or the desire to make the radical break. The much greater number recognized the existence of the world they saw through school, were even willing to acknowledge its superiority, but they were not willing or, perhaps, not able to enter it themselves; their ties with their families were still binding. They developed perforce a kind of life of their own, an intermediary ground from which they could enter when necessary both the life of the school and the life of the home.

The setting generally was the street, where the young were free of oversight and masters of themselves. The boys and girls of an age who played together fell spontaneously into little coteries, for the very acts of play depended upon a sense of community and upon some degree of organization. There could be no games without rules and without subjection to the sanctions that enforced them. The interests of these groups changed as their members matured, from childhood to youth to adolescence to adulthood. But with notable persistence the members held together at least until marriage made them heads of families in their own rights or until they moved out of the neighborhood.

But the boys in the gang had also learned something from the school and from the world it represented. The teacher had told them, and the books, that the end was to get ahead, to make good, to strive so that success might come. They must not repeat the errors of their fathers who had not made good, had not gotten ahead. The consequences of failure were everywhere apparent about them. . . .

In the face of this whole development the immigrants were helpless. They had neither the will nor the ability to turn their offspring into other directions. The nominal authority of the fathers was only halfheartedly used; they were cruelly torn by the conflicting wishes that their sons be like themselves and yet lead better lives than they. Sensing that the school and street would tear the next generation away, the parents knew not how to counteract those forces without injuring their own flesh and blood. . . .

In truth, the children were more in this world than they the parents. Often it was necessary for the fathers to turn for enlightenment to their sons. *We also keep a paper, but you have read more and studied in school.* The young wore their nativity like a badge that marked their superiority over their immigrant elders. It was this superiority that gave the second generation its role as mediator between the culture of the home and the culture of the wider society in the United States.

Accepting that role, the immigrants nevertheless resented it. It reversed the proper order of things. They could remember how they themselves had feared and respected the father; and they were embittered by their own failure to evoke the same fear and respect from their children. Beyond the loose behavior at the table and in the streets, these parents sensed the tones of ridicule. In their eyes the young Americans were undisciplined and ungrateful, good only at throwing stones and snow at strangers. When the boys and girls were small, it was still possible to curb their rebelliousness; the swift punishment of the strap held them temporarily in line. But as age increased their power, they were not so amenable to authority. As they grew in knowledge and in craftiness, as their earnings rose above those of the head of the family, they ceased to bow to restraints and would no longer be ordered about.

Adolescence was therefore a time of acute crisis, and particularly for the girls. As infants they had played with their brothers, but already at seven or eight they were excluded from the society of the gang and thereafter had little to do with boys. In girlhood they stayed close to their mothers since the home was to be their place. But even they could not be shut off from the world outside. They went to school or to work, observed the American familiarity of association between men and women, and soon enough revolted against the old restrictions. The learned to dress like others, with petticoats dragging behind to shut out the air and with their waists laced up in corsets so tightly the blood could not flow; and they lost their health—or so it seemed to their elders.

The worry was that they could not be guided by the safe rules of the Old World. They knew too much, boys as well as girls. Coming down Ann Street, they could not help but notice the "jilt shops" open for the dubious satisfaction of the sailors. Sometimes they could earn pennies distributing the cards of the brothels that flourished in their neighborhoods; and it was often years before they got to understand that a hotel could be other than a house of assignation. Why, even at home, through the thin walls, through the open windows, across the narrow courts, came the revealing sights and sounds. It was all familiar enough by the time they were of an age to conduct their own exploratory operations. . . .

Here was the ultimate barrier between the generations: they would never understand each other's conception of marriage. Sure, the parents tried to explain the nature of this most crucial step, that this was a means of extending on in time the continuity of the family, that it involved the sacrifice of personality toward some larger end: *From a maiden you will become a married woman, from a free being a slave of your husband and fortune.* The children would not listen. For them, marriage was an act of liberation by which they cast off the family ties and expressed themselves as persons through the power to love.

Nor could the children make their parents understand the longing for individuality. To enter upon such a relationship without consultation with one's elders, to make such decisions on the basis of chance impressions, to undertake this partnership with a stranger of unknown antecedents, was a madness of the reason. To many a saddened father and mother it seemed that their sons and daughters had moved gross passion to the center of marriage and had thereby obscured the true end of the family, perpetuation of the succession of generations.

Often enough, then, the old couple were left alone. Looking back across the years, they realized they had been incapable of controlling the course of events. Out of the village context and without the support of the community, the family as they had known it had been doomed. Though they clung to the vestige of home and urged their children to hold together, they would never recapture the essential solidarity. . . .

Perhaps they never took the time to make a balance sheet of their lives, those two old ones left alone, never stopped to reckon up how much they had gained and how much lost by coming. But certainly they must occasionally have faced the wry irony of their relationships with their offspring. What hope the early seasons of their years had held was hope of efforts for their children's sake. What dreams they had had were dreams of the family transplanted, that generation after generation would bear witness to the achievement of migration.

In the end, all was tinged with vanity, with success as cruel as failure. Whatever lot their sons had drawn in this new contentious world, the family's oneness would not survive it. It was a sad satisfaction to watch the young advance, knowing that ever step forward was a step away from home.

CHAPTER 10

THE AGRARIAN RESPONSE TO INDUSTRIAL AMERICA

The Populists have long been a source of disagreement among historians, who have viewed them variously as the liberal descendants of the Jeffersonian and Jacksonian champions of agrarian democracy, as reactionary opponents of industrial and urban development, as the precursors of Progressive and New Deal reform, as "calamity howlers" and malcontents actually uncommitted to principles, and as narrow, bigoted, conspiracy-minded nativists and early-day fascists. Any realistic broad interpretation of the Populists must deal with the major issues raised by these various views. It must present the Populists' philosophy and their attitudes on government and the economy, particularly on the economic changes of the late-nineteenth century; it must evaluate the Populists as reformers and as practical politicians; it must determine whether the Populists were narrowly and aggressively nativist and racist. In short, it must tell us who the Populists were and must pinpoint their significance in history by focusing on what they ssought to do and on what they actually achieved.

Walter T. K. Nugent attempts to do just this in the concluding remarks from his study of Kansas Populism. Because it is a study of the Populists in only one state, Nugent's work must be used carefully. Kansas was an important Populist state, and Nugent's interpretation of Kansas Populism contains valuable suggestions for a more generalized view of the Populists, but the student must consider carefully the limits of the historical analogy suggested by Professor Nugent in the concluding paragraph of this selection. Although Nugent is concerned particularly with the relation of Kansas Populism to nativism, he necessarily comes to grips with the basic considerations about the Populists, raised in the paragraph above. There emerges in this essay, then, a clear and persuasive view of who the Populists were and the nature of their movement in Kansas.

In reading this selection, the student should first consider the historical utility of Professor Nugent's study. How useful is this study for an understanding of the Populists by the general American history student? Do you agree with the limits of analogy suggested by Nugent? Second, what is Nugent's view of the Kansas Populists? What were they trying to do, and how did they go about it? What did they achieve? Finally, does the liberal nationalism of the Kansas Populists have any lessons for modern America?

The literature on this topic is enormous. John D. Hicks, *The Populist Revolt; A History of the Farmers' Alliance and the People's Party** (1931), and Robert F. Durden, *The Climax of Populism: The Election of 1896** (1966), present Populism as a rational and pragmatic response to economic hardships. Richard Hofstadter, in *The Age of Reform: From Bryan to F. D. R.** (1955), is highly critical of various aspects of the Populist movement. Norman Pollack, in *The Populist Response to Industrial America: Midwestern Populist Thought** (1962), views the embattled People's Party as the vanguard of serious radical challenge to the corruptions of modern America. Lawrence Goodwyn, *Democratic Promise: The Populist Movement in America,* (1976), represents a major revision of Hicks; should be read by anyone interested in the subject or period.

*Available in a paperback edition.

THE TOLERANT POPULISTS

WALTER T. K. NUGENT

The foregoing chapters have narrated the story of the Populist movement in Kansas, with special reference to the relations between the Populists and non-American ideas, groups, and persons. Although a sizable body of literature appeared during the 1950's that asserted that the Populists were deeply hostile to things non-American, the Kansas story does not support those assertions. In fact, it supports something more like the opposite of each of the outstanding points of criticism.

The Populists have been accused of nativism, both of a personal kind and of an ideological kind; instead, they were friendlier and more receptive to foreign persons and foreign institutions than the average of their contemporary political opponents. They have been accused of "conspiracy-mindedness"; for them, however, tangible fact quite eclipsed neurotic fiction. They have been accused of anti-Semitism, both personal and ideological; instead they consistently got along well with their Jewish neighbors and consistently refrained from extending their dislike of certain financiers, who happened to be Jews, to Jews in general. They have been accused of chauvinism and jingoism, especially with reference to the Spanish-American War; instead, such lukewarm support as they gave collectively to Cuban intervention was based on quite different grounds, and as a group they strongly opposed the imperialism that the war engendered. Finally, they have been accused of selling out their vaunted reform principles by seeking political fusion with the Democratic party, especially in 1896, and thus of revealing a neurotic instability; but instead, fusion was for them a legitimate means to the accomplishment of real, if limited, reform. In the case of Kansas, the largest of the wheat-belt Populist states, the five principal criticisms of Populism voiced by recent writers not only do not square with the facts, but should be replaced with a viewpoint so much in contrast as to be practically the opposite. Briefly put, this viewpoint is as follows.

Populism in Kansas was a political response to economic distress. From the early days of the Farmers' Alliance, the progenitor of the People's party, to

SOURCE. Walter T. K. Nugent, *The Tolerant Populists: Kansas Populism and Nativism,* pp. 231–243. Copyright © 1963 by The University of Chicago Press. Reprinted by permission of The University of Chicago Press.

about 1892, relief of economic difficulty was virtually the sole reason for the party's existence; after 1892 this purpose was alloyed to some degree with the desire of the party to perpetuate itself as a political organism. In both periods, however, economic difficulties remained the party's chief reason for being, and relief of them its main objective. Populism called for the enactment of a set of legislative reforms by state and federal governments and accepted the extension of governmental power involved in such enactment. In its most complete and ideal form, the Populist program appeared in the national party platform of 1892, the "Omaha Platform," but this platform bore no more nor less relation to the practical operations of the party than platforms usually do. In Kansas the People's party placed its emphasis consistently on the three questions of land, money, and transportation, which were the issues causing greatest distress in that particular state. Since monetary reform seemed to have the broadest political appeal of all the reforms called for in the Populist program, it received more stress than the rest of the program at the time (1894–97) when the party seemed to have its best chance of succeeding.

As Populism followed the ways of practical party politics in the program that it offered and in the issues it chose to stress, it took a practical approach to its sources of support as well. Economic distress cut across lines of religion, of nationality origins, of race, of previous political affiliation, even of occupation and of wealth and status. To so great an extent was this the case that it is not even accurate to say that the Populists accepted or sought the support of third-party men, Republicans, Democrats, immigrants of many kinds, organized labor, city dwellers, and others, to broaden their agriculturalist base. For these groups were in and of Populism from the beginning. The job of the party leaders was therefore not so much to attract new groups but to be sure that the party program appealed to each of those groups already there and to spread the Populist message to further individual members of the existing coalition, of which the lowest common denominator was a desire for one or more specific economic reforms.

As a result, large numbers of every politically consequential foreign-born group then in Kansas, with the exception of the Mennonites, became active Populists. Party leaders received this support warmly and eagerly, except for one or two occasions: the 1894 state convention and probably the one of 1890. At those times, certain influential leaders supported the non-economic issues of women's suffrage and prohibition so vocally that they led the party to take positions unacceptable to many foreign-born groups. Even here, however, the attitude of these leaders to the foreign-born was one of indifference not of hostility. The fact of the matter seems to be, to judge by statements made by the delegates on the floor of the 1894 convention, that many Populists were simply unconcerned with ethnic groups or foreign matters; they were neither favorable nor hostile, except when they thought they might justifiably appeal to ethnic bloc votes or when they cited examples of enlightened foreign institutions to document their own reform program. To the great majority of Populists, in 1894 and at other times, foreignness and certainly Jewishness were simply not affective categories. For practical political reasons, among others, the Populists expressed themselves favorably toward foreign groups, either abroad or close at hand. This was certainly true of the fusionists; it was true of the non-fusionists except when women's suffrage and prohibition got in the way; it was even true, at times, of the Middle-of-the-Road group, which combined antibanker (including English, Anglo-Jewish, and Wall Street banker) rhetoric with some benevolence toward immigrants as individuals.

Many leading Populists were in fact first or second generation immigrants. In the 1890's the Populists surpassed the Republicans in the proportion of their state legislators who were foreign-born. Foreign-born Populists abounded among county-level officeholders, county committeemen, precinct workers, and delegates to county, district, and state political conventions. Wherever an ethnic group existed, there existed as well its Populist voters and Populist leaders, with the exception of the Mennonites, who were undeviatingly Republican. The Populists, however, had immigrant blocs of their own, especially on the frequent occasions of county and state-level fusion with the Democrats. The party organization appealed to foreign-language groups with pamphlets, newspapers, and campaign speakers. They presented much the same arguments to their polyglot audience as the party was making to the English-speaking voters. The only difference was in window dressing, such as testimonials from Prince Bismarck and from German political economists in support of silver coinage. At their 1894 state convention, and prior and subsequently in their newspapers, the Populists forthrightly condemned the American Protective Association, the most influential and widespread nativist organization since the Know-Nothings.

On three contemporaneous issues relating directly to immigrants, the Populists took positions that might seem at first glance to have been nativistic, but in each case their attitude to the immigrant was neutral or favorable. When they attacked "alien" landholding, they were attacking landlordism, not the immigrant small landholder. When they called for an end to contract or "pauper labor" immigration, they clearly excepted "worthwhile" or "sturdy" immigrants and based their position on labor competition, not on racism. When their congressmen supported the Lodge-McCall literacy test to restrict immigration, they apparently did so as the only practical way to enact the bill's riders, which would have lessened labor competition, and almost never expressed approval of the philosophy of superior and inferior, desirable or undesirable, races put forward by Lodge and the Immigration Restriction League. In each of these three instances the Populists based their actions on reasonable economic grounds, if not especially perceptive or laudable ones.

Their aim was to attract the political support of organized labor, of tenant farmers, and very likely of Irish-Americans.

The rhetoric of Populism was highly charged with nationalism, but it was a nineteenth-century kind of nationalism that did not include the nativistic or anti-Semitic characteristics of some twentieth-century right-wing nationalists. Only two foreign groups fell under the censure of any considerable number of Populists. This censure was a consequence of two issues firmly rooted in economic realities and in neither case did they grow out of or were they extended to racial or nativistic antagonism. The two groups were English or Anglo-Jewish financiers and English or Anglo-Irish landlords, respectively responsible in part for money stringency and for large landholding. Many Populists feared that the trend toward tighter money and tighter land would continue unchecked unless these two groups, *and their American or Gentile associates,* were stopped. In both cases the antipathy of the Populists clearly extended to all malevolent financiers, monopolists, and land barons, whether English or American, whether Jew or Gentile, whether native or alien. For the Populists, or many of them, to have laid their troubles at the door of a mixed group of English, Anglo-Jewish, and American capitalists may have been naive and simplistic, but the point is that the common denominator of their hostility was not nativism or anti-Semitism but distrust and dislike of a truly unsympathetic economic class. In some cases their anti-English attitude transcended this economic base, since the economic problem meshed so well with the rather widespread anti-English attitude shared by many nineteenth-century Americans as part of the American Revolutionary tradition. But the English people escaped the censure placed upon certain financially powerful Englishmen, and Jewish financiers escaped any blame whatever as Jews, although a few of them, as investment bankers, shared the criticisms heaped by the Populists, or rather, some of their more outspoken rhetoricians, upon the wickedness of powerful financial interests in general. This was certainly the case with the terms "Shylock" and "Rothschild," which appeared with some frequency in Populist literature but which were cachets not of Jewish conspiracy but of oppressive finance.

So far did Populist expressions of friendliness to Jews as individuals, in Kansas and elsewhere, to Jews as a group, to English immigrants, to English institutions such as co-operatives and public ownership of utilities, outweigh the expressions that might be construed with effort as Anglophobic or anti-Semitic, and so specious are the grounds upon which the Populists have been accused of Anglophobia, anti-Semitism, or nativism, that these accusations must simply fall without support. There is an exception that proves the rule. A handful of Populists sometimes let their antipathies include "racial characteristics" of these two groups, especially the English, and thereby they evidenced irrationality and prejudice. They were atypical. Many, in fact nearly all, of these Populists were attached to the Middle-of-the-Road Populist splinter group in 1894 and 1896. This group attempted to overthrow the recognized state leadership, whose reform credentials were at least as old and respectable as the dissidents'; it was in all probability subsidized by the Republican state organization; and it received the support of less than 1 per cent of the rank and file at the polls in 1896 and of the Populist press.

In what, then, did their nationalism consist? It is difficult to answer such a question, because to accuse such a pragmatic, anti-intellectual people as these agrarians of having possessed "concepts" or "ideas", much more a "system," is itself a distortion. They did, however, possess felt attitudes that were forced into words to form the rhetoric of their speeches and editorials. Needless to say, the scribes and leaders of Populism came closer than anyone else to expressing these views in logical form, subject, of course, to political exigencies. But it can be assumed that their rhetoric must have been congenial to the rank and file—otherwise they would have been unable to attract and to hold that rank and file. Nonetheless, the rhetoric is undoubtedly more radical, more logically organized, and much more explicit than the views of the mass of the party. In their rhetoric, Populist nationalism consisted of a feeling that the United States was a different *kind* of political society from any that had ever existed before and therefore more worth preserving than any previous one. America was not just another nation-state but an embodiment of certain ideals. It was the embodiment of democratic republicanism: a society where the people rule, where the governed consent to their governors, where the rights of life, liberty, and property are protected because this very protection is the object of their own self-goverment. It was the embodiment, too, of economic democracy: where resources wanted only honest labor to be translated into the reality of abundance, where opportunity was equal, where the distribution of the nation's wealth was equitable. It was the antithesis of Europe and Europe's corruption, decadence, parasitical upper classes, stagnation, and economic and political oppression. It was a place, in short, where the people rule for themselves and for the protection of their natural rights. Or, at least, so it should have been.

Yet who were the people? The answer is already implied. The people were those who believed in the ideals of democratic republicanism, of economic democracy, and of freedom from European conditions of life. The people were those who actively sought the preservation of those ideals. They were those who labored by their own hands, who had equal opportunities to labor and to accumulate, who used the resources of the United States to produce their own and the nation's wealth. They were those who created wealth rather than those who manipulated wealth already produced. Very often this legitimate wealth-producing activity was defined by the Populists as agricultural and laboring activity; those who farmed or labored were by definition the real people. This corresponded conveniently both to what might roughly be called the Jeffersonian-Jacksonian tradition and to the actual political bases of the People's party's support. Translated into the rhetoric of a political campaign, it often meant emphasizing "the producing classes" or the common bonds of "the farming and laboring people."

The conscious derivation for all of this was the American Revolution, and secondarily, the War of 1812. These struggles successfully created a nation embodying this set of ideals. Such conscious roots made it easy, of course, for some Populists to look upon the machinations of English financiers as a third and final attempt by England to subjugate America. It was primarily through the American Revolution that a nation of, by, and for the people was created and through it that all that was wrong with Europe and Britain was left behind.

Consequently, it was up to the people—often implying the farmers and laborers—to see to it that this nation, this unique society, did not perish from the earth. Who threatened its extinction? Certainly not the refugee from European misery, at least so long as he, too, believed in American republicanism and opportunity. In this unique kind of nation the doors were open to those who wished legitimately to share its benefits. The goods of this nation were not to be shut up inside for the exclusive use of those already there but rather to beckon as to a flourishing haven those who wished to escape the oppression of a decadent Europe. The nation was, in Lincoln's words, a last, best hope of earth. The immigrant was to show his good faith in these ideals by becoming a citizen and remaining permanently (as the Populists' alien land law provided) and by not attempting to destroy the opportunity of individuals already possessing it (as Populist demands for an end to "pauper labor" immigration showed). For an immigrant to take away the job of an American laborer was unnecessary anyway, since opportunity and America were virtually synonymous.

The "worthwhile" or "sturdy" immigrant was not, then, the enemy of American nationality. In fact, he seemed to justify the Populist approach to American nationality—certainly he did in the case of immigrant agricultural colonies in Kansas, which had been very successful—and he was therefore quite welcome. But who then *was* the enemy? To most Populists who thought about the matter beyond their immediate economic distress—and by no means all of them thought through their views of American nationalism with anything like the completeness that this sketch might imply—the enemy lay in certain recently emergent opportunities for malevolence. America was shifting from a predominantly rural and agricultural nation to one predominantly urban and industrial. This shift was in no way evil in itself. Populist spokesmen such as Senators Peffer and Harris had expressly denied any hope of turning back the clock, and if they were not absolutely delighted with a process that seemed to be toppling the farmers and their allies from political and economic predominance (if indeed they had ever possessed it), they were determined to live with such a trend. What is more, they were determined to see that these changes should benefit all the people and not just a few; that they should take place in such ways as to guarantee democratic republicanism and economic democracy. The majority of them therefore accepted industrialization but condemned monopoly, accepted banking and finance but condemned usury and financial sleight of hand, welcomed accumulation but condemned economic feudalism, welcomed enterprise but condemned speculation. It was not industry and urbanism that oppressed them, they thought, but their abuse.

For most Populists these considerations identified the enemy well enough. An appealing program, aimed conveniently at the relief of immediate distress as well as at the placing of new trends within the old ideals, could be constructed without further ado. A rhetoric quickly emerged that concerned itself with attacking landlordism, transportation monopoly, and money shortages, and this rhetoric remained the basic vehicle of Populist ideas from start to finish. In a minority of cases, however, it seemed convenient to personalize the enemy, and in doing so, some Populists passed the bounds of precise statement. At times, American financiers and monopolists such as the Belmonts, Morgans, and Vanderbilts, English financiers such as the Rothschilds, American and English land and mortgage loan companies, and prominent American statesmen such as Sherman, McKinley, and Cleveland, together seemed to form a common and inimical class dedicated to the people's overthrow. Ever since the Civil War this group seemed to have conspired to bring about the economic destruction of the farmers and their allies. This minority of Populists thereby dealt with the money question in terms of a "money power." Yet even they nearly all used the term "conspiracy" in a general sense to mean the common attitudes of an entrenched and powerful minority, and only a tiny proportion meant by the term an explicit conspiratorial agreement, as when they referred to Ernest Seyd and the "Hazzard Circular" of the sixties and seventies. But most Populists did not voice this line, a fact more remarkable if one grants that rhetoric tends to be more radical than the general feeling of its political following. This "conspiracy" was, in addition, a financial one and not a Jewish or English one. To look at a close-knit community of interest and to see in the mind's eye a conspiracy is not necessarily great irrationality but rather a lack of factual knowledge about the competitive methods of late nineteenth-century capitalism. If antibanker, antimonopoly, or anticapitalist statements formed fairly frequent themes in Populist rhetoric, Populists of every hue made it clear that it was usury, irresponsible economic power, and minority rule that they were opposing and not the industrial revolution, urbanism, or capitalism and banking as such. The abuse of new trends, not the trends themselves, had driven them, they felt, from their once uncontested eminence. Now they wanted to regain that eminence and accepted the fact that it could never again be theirs alone. If agrarian class predominance was over and done with, plutocratic class predominance should be scuttled before it progressed any further. Then economic democracy would be reborn.

The Populist view of American nationality, with its stress on democratic republicanism and economic democracy, was therefore intended to be at once majoritarian, individualistic, and humanitarian. That it was a nationalism naïvely humanitarian rather than aggressive appeared very clearly in the Populists' approach to the Cuban insurrection and the Spanish-American War. They sympathized deeply with the insurgent Cubans and viewed their uprising as a struggle for freedom and democracy much like the American uprising of the 1770's. In Kansas this sympathy expressed itself in a moral support for the insurrectionists that sprang from a confident view of their own moral righteousness. Nonetheless, the Populist press and Populist congressmen held back from armed intervention, took a cautious attitude to the blowing up of the *Maine,* restrained themselves from anything more vigorous than sympathetic gestures toward the Cubans in spite of the Spanish "despotism" and "Weylerism" they believed the Cubans to be suffering, and in unison with their Democratic neighbors hoped that war could be avoided. This was very close to the Republican position also. When war came, they supported it as everyone else did, but until then their humanitarian sympathy for the Cubans was checked by the fear that a war beginning with Cuban intervention could only benefit large financial interests. The Kansas Republicans' coolness toward Cuban intervention resulted mainly from the caution that McKinley maintained into April, 1898, and the desire of the Kansas Republicans' to support their own administration. The Populists avoided the Republicans' scornful references to Cuban or Spanish racial inferiority and far more frequently then the Republicans took a humanitarian view of the matter. In Kansas the Populists were not violent jingoes. Furthermore, unlike the Republicans in their area, and other people elsewhere, the official Populist position on the question of American imperial expansion for commercial or military purposes, which arose after Dewey's victory in Manila Bay, was to join the Democrats in opposing expansion and in demanding that the United States leave the Philippines and other potential colonies alone. They were interested in the spread of American democratic ideals, in the overthrow of Spanish oppression of Cuba, if this could be done without the commitment of American armed forces, but not at all in American conquest or colonization. Populism in Kansas apparently lost many adherents because of this stand but it remained the official party position nevertheless.

It is worth noting that Populist opposition to imperialism was much more firmly expressed than Populist sympathy to the Cuban insurrectionists, because the Democratic party was also much less firm on the latter question than on the former. As a matter of fact, official Populist rhetoric was tailored to fit the political exigencies involved in getting along with the Democrats not only on the war and imperialism issues but on most other questions as well. Political fusion with the Democrats on all levels marked Kansas Populism very strongly, and to some writers, fusion has meant that the Populists lacked any real dedication to the principles they so vigorously espoused. But the Populist movement chose political means to accomplish its program of economic reform; it was a political party, not a pressure group or an ideological front; for better or worse it therefore bound itself to use partisan methods. If one looks no further than the Omaha platform of 1892 to find out what Populism stood for and then observes that many planks in the platform were soft-pedaled in 1892 and later for the sake of fusion and political success, one might assume that Populist devotion to reform principles was a sham. But this is a superficial view. Fusion was the only apparent way to achieve any reforms, any accomplishment of any principles at all, and the degree to which the People's party was willing to fuse with the Democrats in Kansas was the degree to which it possessed political common sense. The identification of fusion with dedication to principle, rather than with a sellout, comes into even greater relief as soon as one recalls the shabby story of the Middle-of-the-Road Populists, those self-styled simon-pure reformers who almost certainly connived at the defeat of the reform party with the local Republican organization. The prevalence of fusion sentiment indicates as well the willingness of the Populists to seek out and accept the support of the foreign-born blocks that ordinarily made their political home in the Democratic party. It also indicates their pragmatic approach to political action, their willingness to use an obvious means at hand to achieve legitimate political ends, and their flexibility, which stood in such contrast to the rigidity of the Middle-of-the-Road Populists.

The political horse sense that provided them with their receptivity to fusion was a natural outgrowth of the immediacy of the distress from which their movement sprang. It accounted, too, for the apparent anomaly of a radical program based on conservative ideals. For the Populists of Kansas were not a collection of rag-tag calamity howlers, ne'er-do-wells, and third-party malcontents, as William Allen White and others have suggested, but a large body of people of diverse occupational, wealth-holding, and status levels. As a group they were hardly distinguishable from their Republican neighbors, except for a probably higher mortgage indebtedness, and their greater degree of political and economic awareness. The great majority could be called "middle-class," and they were interested in preserving what they considered to be their middle-class American ideals and substance. These were being threatened, they felt, not by the facts of industrialism and urbanism but by their existing *shape*. To change that shape, they settled upon the device of a political party.

Their view of the future was one in which many wrongs would have to be righted, many present trends would have to be redirected to conform to old ideals, for that future to become acceptable. Yet they were confident that this would happen. In several ways they were confused, ill-informed, and behind the times. They were unaware of urban problems, for example, and they never understood that money reform was basically a solution only to agricultural problems, if indeed to them, and not a solution for growing monopoly or for inequities of wealth distribution. Yet if this is ture, it is true as well to acquit them of nativism, anti-Semitism, conspiracy-mindedness, jingoism, lack of principle, and of living in some neurotic agrarian dream world. They were bound together not by common neuroses but by common indebtedness, common price squeezes, common democratic and humanitarian ideals, and common wrath at the infringement of them. From this wrath rose the Farmers' Alliance, and from the Alliance their ultimate instrument of protest, the People's party. The Populists were far too concerned with land, money, and transportation; and also, later on, with the mechanics of winning and keeping public office, to have much time to worry about whether their ideals were mythical or their anxieties neurotic. Tight money and foreclosure sales were the products of nobody's imagination. Even in their rhetoric they were too busy preaching positive reforms in a depression to be concerned with racism or anti-Semitism or agrarian Arcadias; and in their practical political activities, they took all the help they could get.

The Populists were liberal nationalists bringing to radical social changes a radical response. By such means they meant to re-assert what they considered to be the fundamental ideals upon which their society had previously depended —in their view of history—and must continue to depend—in their view of political philosophy. They undertook this task in the Kansas of the 1890's, with its particular kind of social structure, its particular distribution of wealth and income, its specific economic conditions, and its peculiar laws and traditions. These particularities form the limits of historical analogy, and they give no grounds for making the Populists the gawky ancestors of Father Coughlin or of Senator Joseph R. McCarthy. They make it very difficult to call the Populists the descendants of the Jeffersonians and Jacksonians or the precursors of Progressivism or the New Deal, although with these movements the Populists shared a considerable body of ideals. They make it unrealistic even to equate the Kansas Populists with Populists of other regions or other states.

This particular set of facts, however, allows the Populists of Kansas to be judged on their own grounds. The verdict is very simple. They were people who were seeking the solution of concrete economic distress through the instrumentality of a political party. By this means they would not only help themselves but they would redirect, not reverse, the unsatisfactory trends of their time to correspond with the ideas of the past. This involved profoundly the political co-operation of the foreign born, and it involved a deep respect and receptivity for non-American institutions and ideas.

CHAPTER 11

WAR AND EMPIRE

The Spanish-American War was not much of a contest, and Americans could well look on it, in Secretary of State John Hay's words, as a "splendid little war." After only 10 weeks of fighting, Spain was badly beaten and the American victory was assured. Although losses from disease were high, only 379 Americans died as a result of combat wounds. But the war was more than a lark. Its results constituted a major turning point in American history. They signaled the abandonment of the policy of limited expansion to contiguous territory, and marked the first time that the United States had acquired possession of territory not ultimately intended for statehood. As a result, the nation gained a new status in international affairs, although it had long been an important factor in world diplomatic calculations. Some historians suggest, however, that the real significance of the events of 1898 is not in the immediate results listed above, but in the very process by which they came to pass, and in the long-range influence that this process and its products had on American foreign relations.

In this selection, Richard Hofstadter seeks to determine how and why the United States became involved in the Spanish-American War and the subsequent "imperialistic" venture in the Philippines. Significantly, Professor Hofstadter treats American involvement in war and imperialism as separate questions, although in both cases he finds his answers primarily in domestic developments in the United States. The war with Spain, Hofstadter suggests, was the result of popular reaction to the major social crises (or convulsions) of the 1890s. Things looked bad to many Americans in the late 1890s and, as a result, there was a significant intensification of two tendencies in popular thought and behavior: humanitarian reform and national self-assertion. The expression of these moods accounted for the crusade to "free Cuba from the Spanish yoke." On the other hand, Hofstadter suggests that the American entrance into the Philippines was essentially the result of the activities of a small group of imperialists who became concerned with the broad aspects of national power because of their dissatisfaction with their own roles in the domestic life of late nineteenth-century America. In short, the popular base

149

of the imperial adventure was narrower than that of the war that preceded it.

These are the basic questions on which the student must focus in this selection: How do we explain America's entry on the paths of imperialism in the 1890s? What differences and similarities marked our involvement in the war and our involvement in imperialism? What was "the psychic crisis of the 1890s" and what were the important factors involved in its development? What does Hofstadter say of the roles played by economic motivations, the yellow press, and the American political process in involving America in war and imperialism? Finally, do you believe that Hofstadter's foray "onto the high and dangerous ground of social psychology" contributes to a better understanding of this subject?

From a plethora of studies on the War and American imperialism, the student might best consult the provocative essay by Norman A. Graebner, "American Imperialism," in *Main Problems in American History,** Vol. 2 (1968), edited by Howard H. Quint, Dean Albertson, and Milton Cantor, and the appropriate chapters of Arthur A. Ekirch, Jr., *Ideas, Ideals, and American Diplomacy** (1966), George F. Kennan, *American Diplomacy, 1900–1950** (1951), and Foster Rhea Dulles, *America's Rise to World Power, 1898–1954** (1954). Ernest R. May, *Imperial Democracy: The Emergence of America as a Great Power* (1961), focuses on the Spanish-American War, and H. Wayne Morgan, *America's Road to Empire: The War with Spain and Overseas Expansion** (1965), is also useful and up to date. Walter LaFeber, in *The New Empire: An Interpretation of American Expansion, 1860–1898* (1963), makes a strong and provocative case for the role of American agrarian and business spokesmen in supporting imperialism.

*Available in a paperback edition.

MANIFEST DESTINY AND THE PHILIPPINES

RICHARD HOFSTADTER

The taking of the Philippine Islands from Spain in 1899 marked a major historical departure for the American people. It was a breach in their traditions and a shock to their established values. To be sure, from their national beginnings they had constantly engaged in expansion, but almost entirely into contiguous territory. Now they were extending themselves to distant extra-hemispheric colonies; they were abandoning a strategy of defense hitherto limited to the continent and its appurtenances, in favor of a major strategic commitment in the Far East; and they were now supplementing the spread of a relatively homogeneous population into territories destined from the beginning for self-government with a far different procedure in which control was imposed by force on millions of ethnic aliens. The acquisition of the islands, therefore, was understood by contemporaries on both sides of the debate, as it is readily understood today, to be a turning-point in our history.

To discuss the debate in isolation from other events, however, would be to deprive it of its full significance. American entrance into the Philippine Islands was a by-product of the Spanish-American War. The Philippine crisis is inseparable from the war crisis, and the war crisis itself is inseparable from a larger constellation that might be called "the psychic crisis of the 1890's."

Central in the background of the psychic crisis was the great depression that broke in 1893 and was still very acute when the agitation over the war in Cuba began. Severe depression, by itself, does not always generate an emotional crisis as intense as that of the nineties. In the 1870's the country had been swept by a depression of comparable acuteness and duration which, however, did not give rise to all the phenomena that appeared in the 1890's or to very many of them with comparable intensity and impact. It is often said that the 1890's, unlike the 1870's, form some kind of a "watershed" in American history. The difference between the emotional and intellectual impact of these two depressions can be measured, I believe, not by any difference in severity, but rather

SOURCE. Richard Hofstadter, "Manifest Destiny and the Philippines," in Daniel Aaron, ed., *America in Crisis,* New York: Alfred A. Knopf, Inc., pp. 173–177, 179–191, and 197–199. Copyright © 1952 by Alfred A. Knopf, Inc. Reprinted by permission of Alfred A. Knopf, Inc.

by reference to a number of singular events that in the 1890's converged with the depression to heighten its impact upon the public mind.

First in importance was the Populist movement, the free-silver agitation, the heated campaign of 1896. For the first time in our history a depression had created an allegedly "radical" movement strong enough to capture a major party and raise the specter, however unreal, of drastic social convulsion. Second was the maturation and bureaucratization of American business, the completion of its essential industrial plant, and the development of trusts on a scale sufficient to stir the anxiety that the old order of competitive opportunities was approaching an eclipse. Third, and of immense symbolic importance, was the apparent filling up of the continent and disappearance of the frontier line. We now know how much land had not yet been taken up and how great were the remaining possibilities of internal expansion both in business and on the land; but to the mind of the 1890's it seemed that the resource that had engaged the energies of the people for three centuries had been used up; the frightening possibility suggested itself that a serious juncture in the nation's history had come. As Frederick Jackson Turner expressed it in his famous paper of 1893: "Now, four centuries from the discovery of America, at the end of one hundred years of life under the Constitution, the frontier has gone, and with its going has closed the first period of American history."

To middle-class citizens who had been brought up to think in terms of the nineteenth-century order, things looked bad. Farmers in the staple-growing region seemed to have gone mad over silver and Bryan; workers were stirring in bloody struggles like the Homestead and Pullman strikes; the supply of new land seemed at an end; the trust threatened the spirit of business enterprise; civil corruption was at a high point in the large cities; great waves of seemingly unassimilable immigrants arrived yearly and settled in hideous slums. To many historically conscious writers, the nation seemed overripe, like an empire ready for collapse through a stroke from outside or through internal upheaval. Acute as the situation was for all those who lived by the symbols of national power—for the governing and thinking classes—it was especially poignant for young people, who would have to make their careers in the dark world that seemed to be emerging.

The symptomatology of the crisis might record several tendencies in popular thought and behavior that had not been observable before or had existed only in pale and tenuous form. These symptoms fell into two basic moods. The key to one of them is an intensification of protest and humanitarian reform. Populism, Utopianism, the rise of the Christian Social gospel, the growing intellectual interest in Socialism, the social settlement movement that appealed so strongly to the college generation of the nineties, the quickening of protest in the realistic novel—all these are expressions of this mood. The other is one of national self-assertion, aggression, expansion. The tone of the first was sympathy, of the second, power. During the 1890's far more patriotic groups were founded than in any other decade of our history; the naval theories of Captain Mahan were gaining in influence; naval construction was booming; there was an immense quickening of the American cult of Napoleon and a vogue of the virile and martial writings of Rudyard Kipling; young Theodore Roosevelt became the exemplar of the vigorous, masterful, out-of-doors man; the revival of European imperialism stirred speculation over what America's place would be in the world of renewed colonial rivalries. But most significant was the rising tide of jingoism, a matter of constant comment among observers of American life during the decade.

Jingoism, of course, was not new in American history. But during the 1870's and '80's, the American public had been notably quiescent about foreign relations. There had been expansionist statesmen, but they had been blocked by popular apathy and statecraft had been restrained. Grant had failed dismally in his attempt to acquire Santo Domingo; our policy toward troubled Hawaii had been cautious; in 1877 an offer of two Haitian naval harbors had been spurned. In responding to Haiti, Secretary of State Frelinghuysen had remarked that "the policy of this Government . . . had tended toward avoidance of possessions disconnected from the main continent." Henry Cabot Lodge, in his life of George Washington published in 1889, observed that foreign relations then filled "but a slight place in American politics, and excite generally only a languid interest." Within a few years this comment would have seemed absurd; the history of the 1890's is the history of public agitation over expansionist issues and of quarrels with other nations.

II

Three primary incidents fired American jingoism between the spring of 1891 and the close of 1895. First came Secretary of State Blaine's tart and provocative reply to the Italian minister's protest over the lynching of eleven Italians in New Orleans. Then there was friction with Chile over a riot in Valparaiso in which two American sailors were killed and several injured by a Chilean mob. In 1895 occurred the more famous Venezuela boundary dispute with Britain. Discussion of these incidents would take us too far afield, but note that they all had these characteristics in common: in none of them was national security or the national interest vitally involved; in all three American diplomacy was extraordinarily and disproportionately aggressive; in all three the possibility of war was contemplated; and in each case the American public and press response was enthusiastically nationalist. . . .

When President McKinley took office he was well aware that nationalist enthusiasm had reached a pitch that made war very likely. . . . At the time . . . [he] sent his war message to Congress he knew quite well, and indeed made a passing reference to the fact, that Spain had already capitulated to the demands the United States had made upon her. . . . Evidently McKinley had concluded that what was wanted in the United States was not so much the freedom of Cuba as a *war* for the freedom of Cuba.

Historians say that the war was brought on by sensational newspapers. The press, spurred by the rivalry between Pulitzer and Hearst, aroused sympathy with the Cubans and hatred of Spain and catered to the bellicosity of the public. No one seems to have asked: *Why was the public so fatally receptive to war propaganda?* I believe the answer must be sought in the causes of the jingoism that had raged for seven years before the war actually broke out. The events of the nineties had brought frustration and anxiety to civically conscious Americans. On one hand, as Mark Sullivan has commented, the American during this period was disposed "to see himself as an underdog in economic situations and controversies in his own country"; but the civic frustrations of the era created also a restless aggressiveness, a desire to be assured that the power and vitality of the nation were not waning. The capacity for sympathy and the need for power existed side by side. That highly typical and symptomatic American, William Allen White, recalls in his *Autobiography* how during the nineties he was "bound to my idols—Whitman, the great democrat, and Kipling, the imperialist." In varying stages of solution the democrat and imperialist existed in the hearts of White's countrymen—the democrat disposed to free Cuba, the imperialist to vent his civic spleen on Spain.

I suspect that the readiness of the public to over-react to the Cuban situation can be understood in part through the displacement of feelings of sympathy or social protest generated in domestic affairs; these impulses found a safe and satisfactory discharge in foreign conflict. Spain was portrayed in the press as waging a heartless and inhuman war; the Cubans were portrayed as noble victims of Spanish tyranny, their situation as analogous to that of Americans in 1776. When one examines the sectional and political elements that were most enthusiastic about the war, one finds them not primarily among the wealthy Eastern big-business Republicans who supported McKinley and read the conservative dignified newspapers, but in the Bryan sections of the country, in the Democratic party, and among the patrons of the yellow journals. During the controversy significant charges were hurled back and forth; conservative peace-advocates claimed that many jingoists were hoping for a costly war over Cuba that could be made the occasion of a return to free silver; in return, the inflammatory press often fell into the pattern of Populist rhetoric, declaiming, for example, about "the eminently respectable porcine citizens who—for dollars in the money-grubbing sty, support 'conservative' newspapers and consider the starvation of . . . inoffensive men, women and children, and the murder of 250 American sailors . . . of less importance than a fall of two points in a price of stocks." Although imputations of base economic motives were made by both sides, it is also significant that the current of sympathy and agitation ran strong where a discontented constituency, politically frustrated by Bryan's defeat, was most numerous. An opportunity to discharge aggressions against "Wall Street interests" coolly indifferent to the fate of both Cuban *insurrectos* and staple farmers may have been more important than the more rationalized and abstract linkage between a war and free silver. The primary significance of the war for the psychic economy of the nineties was that it served as an outlet for aggressive impulses while presenting itself, quite truthfully, as an idealistic and humanitarian crusade. The American public was not interested in the material gains of an intervention in Cuba. It never dreamed that the war would lead to the taking of the Philippines. Starting a war for a high-minded and altruistic purpose and then transmuting it into a war for annexation was unthinkable; it would be, as McKinley put it in a phrase that later came back to haunt him, "criminal aggression."

III

There is one odd paradox in the evolution of sentiment from a war over freeing Cuba to a peace treaty acquiring the Philippines by conquest. The big-business-conservative-Republican-McKinley element, overwhelmingly hostile to this romantic and sentimental war, quickly became interested in the imperialism that grew out of it. The popular Populist-Democratic-Byranite element, which had been so keen for the war, became the stronghold—although by no means resolute or unbroken—of opposition to the fruits of war. This much, however, must be said of both the populace and the business community: if the matter had been left either to public clamor or to business interests, there would have been no American entrance into the Philippines in 1898.

The dynamic element in the movement for imperialism was a small group of politicians, intellectuals, and publicists, including Senator Henry Cabot Lodge, Theodore Roosevelt, John Hay, Senator Albert J. Beveridge, Whitelaw Reid, editor of *The New York Herald Tribune,* Albert Shaw, editor of the *Review of Reviews,* Walter Hines Page, editor of the *Atlantic Monthly,* and Henry and Brooks Adams.

Most of these men came from what are known as good families. They were well educated, cultivated, patrician in outlook. Anglo-Saxon in background, noncommercial in personal goals and standards, and conservative reformers in politics. Although living in a commercial world, they could not accept business standards for their own careers nor absorb themselves into the business community. Although they lived in a vulgar democracy, they were not democratic by instinct. They could not and did not care to succeed in politics of the corrupt sort that had become so common in America. They had tried their hands at civic reform, had found it futile, and had become bored with it. When they did not, like Henry Adams, turn away from American life in bitterness, they became interested in some large and statesmanlike theater of action, broader than American domestic policy. Although there were men of this sort in the Democratic ranks, like Walter Hines Page, they were most influential within the Republican Party, which during the mid-nineties had become committed to a policy of expansion.

In general, this group of imperialists was inspired by the navalist theories of Mahan and by the practical example of what they sometimes referred to as Mother England. They saw that a new phase of imperialism had opened in the Western world at large, and they were fearful that if the United States did not adopt a policy of expansion and preparation for military and naval struggle, it would be left behind in what they referred to as the struggle for life or, at other times, as the march of the nations. They were much concerned that the United States expand its army and particularly its navy; that it dig an isthmian canal: that it acquire the naval bases and colonies in the Caribbean and the Pacific necessary to protect such a canal; that it annex Hawaii and Samoa. At their most aggressive, they also called for the annexation of Canada, and the expulsion of European powers from the Western hemisphere. They were much interested in the Far East as a new theater of political conflict and investment possibilities. They were, indeed, more interested than business itself in the Pacific area, particularly in China, as a potential market. As Professor Pratt has observed: "The need of American business for colonial markets and fields for investment was discovered not by businessmen but by historians and other intellectuals, by journalists and politicians."

The central figure in this group was Theodore Roosevelt, who more than any other single man was responsible for our entry into the Philippines. Throughout the 1890's Roosevelt had been eager for a war, whether it be with Chile, Spain, or England. A war with Spain, he felt, would get us "a proper navy and a good system of coast defenses," would free Cuba from Spain, and would help to free Ameria from European domination, would give "our people . . . something to think of that isn't material gain," and would try "both the army and navy in actual practice." Roosevelt feared that the United States would grow heedless of its defense, take insufficient care to develop its power, and become "an easy prey for any people which still retained those most valuable of all qualities, the soldierly virtues." "All the great masterful races have been fighting races," he argued. There were higher virtues than those of peace and material comfort. "No triumph of peace is quite so great as the supreme triumphs of war." Such was the philosophy of the man who secured Commodore Dewey's appointment to the Far Eastern Squadron and alerted him before the actual outbreak of hostilities to be prepared to engage the Spanish fleet at Manila.

Our first step into the Philippines presented itself to us as a "defensive" measure. Dewey's attack on the Spanish fleet in Manila Bay was made on the assumption that the Spanish fleet, if unmolested, might cross the Pacific and bombard the west coast cities of the United States. I do not know whether American officialdom was aware that this fleet was so decrepit that it could hardly have gasped its way across the ocean. Next, Dewey's fleet seemed in danger unless its security were underwritten by the dispatch of American troops to Manila. To be sure, having accomplished his mission, Dewey could have removed this "danger" simply by leaving Manila Bay. However, in war one is always tempted to hold whatever gains have been made, and at Dewey's request American troops were dispatched very promptly after the victory and arrived at Manila in July 1898. Thus our second step into the Philippines was again a "defensive" measure. The third step was the so-called "capture" of Manila, which was actually carried out in co-operation with the Spaniards, who were allowed to make a token resistance, and in exclusion of the Filipino patriots under Aguinaldo. The fourth step was an agreement, incorporated in the protocol suspending hostilities between the United States and Spain, that the United States would occupy the city, bay, and harbor of Manila pending a final settlement in the peace treaty. The fifth step came much later, on December 21, 1898, when McKinley instructed the War Department to extend the military goverment already in force at Manila to the entire archipelago. This began a fierce revolt by the Filipino patriots, who felt that they had been led to expect a much different policy from the American government. Two days before the vote was taken in the Senate on the ratification of the peace treaty, the patriots and the American forces fought their first battle and American soldiers were killed, a fact that seems to have had an important influence on public discussion. Once again, administrative action had given a sharp bias to the whole process of political decision. Tyler Dennett goes so far as to say that by authorizing a campaign of conquest while the Senate was still discussing the situation, McKinley "created a situation . . . which had the effect of coercing the Senate." This is a doubtful conclusion, but there is some reason to believe that the hand of expansionists was strengthened by the feeling that opposition to the administration's policy would be unpatriotic.

This much can certainly be said: by the time our policy could be affected by public discussion a great deal had already been accomplished by the annexationists. The tone of the argument was already weighted towards staying in simply because we were there. As McKinley put it: "It is not a question of keeping the islands of the East, but of leaving them." It is not an easy thing to persuade a people or a government during the pitch of war enthusiasm to abandon a potential gain already in hand. Moreover, a great social interest hitherto indifferent to the Philippines, the business community, quickly swung around to an expansionist position. The Protestant clergy, seeing a potential enlargement of missionary enterprise, also threw in its weight. For the first time the group of imperialists and navalists had powerful allies. Business began to talk about the Philippines as a possible gateway to the markets of eastern Asia, the potentialities of which were thought to be very large. The imperialist group itself was much heartened and, with the help of Navy officers, put increasing pressure upon a rather hesitant administration to follow through.

There seemed four possible ways of disposing of the Philippine problem. The first, returning the islands to Spain, found favor nowhere. The second, selling or otherwise alienating the Philippines to some other power, seemed to invite a possible general European war; and it would hardly be more justified morally than remaining in possession outselves. Moreover, we were being encouraged by England to remain in the Philippines, for American possession of those islands was much more palatable to England than possession by any other power. The third possibility, leaving the Philippines to themselves and giving them the independence Aguinaldo's men had been fighting for, was equivalent in most American minds to leaving them to anarchy. It also seemed to be another way of encouraging a scramble among other powers interested in the Far East. The final possibility was some form of American possession, in the form of a protectorate or otherwise. In the beginning there was much sentiment for merely retaining a naval base and coaling station on the island of Luzon, or perhaps the island of Luzon itself. Second thought suggested, however, that such a base would be endangered if the rest of the islands were left open to possible occupation by other nations. The dynamics of the situation suggested an all-or-none policy, and the administration drifted rapidly towards annexation of the entire archipelago.

IV

The American public had not previously been either informed about or interested in the Philippines. In the entire eighty-year period from 1818 through May 1898, only thirty-five articles about the islands had appeared in American magazines. At the moment of Dewey's victory the press, although given over to encouraging the public jubilation, did not show an immediate interest in taking the islands. However, sentiment grew with considerable rapidity. As early as July 1898, the *Literary Digest* noted that the leading Republican papers were pro-expansion. A sample of 65 newspapers taken by the magazine *Public Opinion* in August showed that 43 per cent were for permanent retention of the Philippines, 24.6 per cent were opposed, and 32.4 per cent were wavering. In this case, "wavering" usually meant formerly opposed to expansion but apparently changing views. By December 1898, when the crucial debate in the Senate was beginning, the *New York Herald* polled 498 newspapers on the subject of expansion and found that 305, or 61.3

per cent, were favorable. New England and the Middle States showed clear margins in favor of expansion, the West an overwhelming margin; the South alone, by a thin margin, was opposed. The state of press opinion does not *measure* public feeling, but probably does indicate the direction in which public opinion was moving.

To President McKinley, a benign and far from aggressive man, public sentiment was of great importance. He was not a man to lead the American people in a direction in which their sympathies were not already clearly bent. There was a current joke: "Why is McKinley's mind like a bed? Because it has to be made up for him every time he wants to use it." However unjust to the President, this does characterize his response to public opinion. He was not by temperament an expansionist, but if his immediate advisers and the public at large were preponderantly for annexation, he was willing to go along, and was thoroughly capable of finding good reasons for doing so. During the fall of 1898 he left Washington for a tour of the West, and made a great many brief speeches sounding out public opinion on annexation of the Philippines, on which he seems to have tentatively been determined in his own mind. He found a warm reception for himself and an enthusiastic response to the idea of expansion. Evidently his intent was confirmed by this exposure to public opinion and also by advices concerning the state of the public mind from correspondents and advisers, and when he returned to Washington those who were opposed to expansion found him unmovable. The Peace Commission negotiating the treaty in Paris was instructed to ask for all the Philippine Islands, and this provision was included in the peace treaty signed on December 10, 1898.

The debate over the retention of the Philippines then went through two phases. During the first, which lasted from December 1898 to the second week in February 1899, the question was argued both in the Senate and in the forums of public opinion. This phase neared its end when, on February 6, the Senate narrowly voted to ratify the peace treaty; it was definitively closed on February 14, when a resolution sponsored by Senator Bacon of Georgia, calling for early Philippine independence, was rejected by the preciously narrow margin of one vote—the casting vote of the Vice President, which resolved a 29–29 tie. The second phase of the debate extended throughout 1899 and 1900, when American policy toward the Philippines was a matter of general public discussion and a partisan issue in the Presidential campaign of 1900.

Who was for and who against annexation? In large measure it was a party issue. The *New York Herald* poll showed that of 241 Republican papers 84.2 per cent were *for* expansion, and of 174 Democratic papers 71.3 per cent were *against* expansion. In some degree it was also a young man's movement. Geographically it extended throughout all sections of the country, and seems to have been favored everywhere but in the South, although even there it was strong. We do not have a clear index of public opinion for the period, but the practical politicians, whose business it was to gauge public sentiment in the best way they knew, concluded that the preponderant feeling was overwhelmingly for annexation.

The debate over the acquisition of the Philippines was perhaps no more than a ceremonial assertion of the values of both sides. The real decisions were made in the office of Theodore Roosevelt, in the Senate cloakroom, in the sanctums of those naval officers from whom the McKinley administration got its primary information about the Philippines during its period of doubt over annexation, and by McKinley's own testimony, in the privacy of his chambers late at night. The public was, by and large, faced with a *fait accompli* that, although theoretically reversible, had the initial impetus of its very existence to carry it along. The intensity of the public discussion, at any rate, showed that the American conscience had really been shocked. No type of argument was neglected on either side. Those who wanted to take the Philippines pointed to the potential markets of the East, the White Man's Burden, the struggle for existence, "racial" destiny, American traditions of expansion, the dangers of a general war if the Philippines were left open to a European scramble, the almost parental duty of assuming responsibility for the allegedly child-like Filipinos, the incapacity of the Filipinos for self-goverment, and so on. The anti-imperialists based their essential appeal on political principle. They pointed out that the United States had come into existence pledged to the idea that man should not be governed without his consent. They suggested that the violation of these political traditions (under which the nation had prospered) was not only a gross injustice to others, of which we should feel deeply ashamed, but also a way of tempting Providence and risking degeneration and disintegration as a sort of punishment for the atrophy of one's own principles. They pointed also to the expense of overseas dominions, standing armies and navalism, and the danger of being embroiled in imperialist wars.

Many leading anti-imperialists were men of great distinction; their ranks included by far the greater part of the eminent figures of the literary and intellectual world. Most of them were, however, in the unfortunate position of opposing the fruits of a war that they had either favored or failed to oppose. Unlike the expansionists, they did not have complete control of a major party (there were more expansionists among the Democrats than there were anti-expansionists among the Republicans). They were hopelessly heterogeneous: Gold Democrats, Bryan Democrats, New-England-conscience Republicans, and a scattering of reformers and intellectuals.

They organized late—the Anti-Imperialist League grew up in the months after November 1898—and their political leadership, however ardent in sentiment, pursued a hesitant and uncertain course. Their most eminent political leaders were chiefly old men, and the strongest appeal of the anti-imperialist movement seems to have been to the old high-principled elements in the country, while the imagination of the young was fired far more by the rhetoric of expansionism. It seems clear that the main chance of this minority was to use its position in the Senate to deny the necessary two-thirds approval to the peace treaty acquiring the islands from Spain. Here the opponents of annexation might have delayed it long enough to give themselves a chance to reach the public. But William Jennings Bryan, for reasons that are not altogether clear, persuaded enough members of his party to vote for the treaty to lose the case. Bryan hoped to continue the fight, of course, and grant independence later, but over his conduct and his explanations there hangs a heavy sense of inevitable defeat, stemming from his recognition that the voice of the majority demanded the bold and aggressive policy. . . .

VI

Since Julius W. Pratt published his *Expansionists of 1898* fifteen years ago it has been obvious that any interpretation of America's entry upon the paths of imperialism in the nineties in terms of rational economic motives would not fit the facts, and that a historian who approached the event with preconceptions no more supple than those, say, of Lenin's *Imperialism* would be helpless. This is not to say that markets and investments have no bearing; they do, but there are innumerable features of the situation that they do not explain at all. In so far as the economic factor was important, it can be better studied in terms of the relation between the depression and the public mood.

The alternative explanation has been the equally simple idea that the war was a newspapers' war. This notion, once again, has some point, but it certainly does not explain the war itself, much less its expansionist result. The New Deal period showed that the press is not powerful enough to impose upon the public mind a totally uncongenial view of public events. It must operate roughly within the framework of public predispositions. Moreover, not all the papers of the nineties were yellow journals. We must inquire into the structure of journalistic power and also into the personnel of its ownership and editorship to find out what differentiated the sensational editors and publishers from those of the conservative press, and what it was about their readership that led the former to the (correct) conclusion that they could expand their circulations by resorting to jingo sensationalism.

There is still another qualification that must be placed upon the role of the press: the press itself, whatever it can do with opinion, does not have the power to precipitate opinion into action. That is something that takes place within the *political* process, and we cannot tell that part of the story without examining the state of party rivalries, the derivation and goals of the political elites, and indeed the entire political context. We must, then, supplement our story

about the role of the newspapers with at least two other factors: the state of
the public temper upon which the newspapers worked, and the manner in
which party rivalries deflected domestic clashes into foreign aggression.

When we examine the public temper, we will find that the depression,
together with such other events as the approaching completion of continental
settlement, the growth of trusts, and the intensification of internal social
conflict, had brought to large numbers of people intense frustrations in their
economic lives and their careers. To others they had brought anxiety that a
period of stagnation in national wealth and power had set in. The restlessness
of the frustrated classes had been heightened by the defeat of Bryan in 1896.
The anxieties about the national position had been increased among statesmen
and publicists by the revival of world imperialism, in particular by the feeling
that the nation was threated by the aims of Germany, Russian, and Japan. The
expansionist statesmen themselves were largely drawn from a restless upper-
middle-class elite that had been fighting an unrewarding battle for conservative
reform in domestic politics and that looked with some eagerness toward a more
spacious field of action.

It is a psychological commonplace that we tend to respond to frustration
with acts of aggression, and to allay anxieties by threatening acts against
others. It seems suggestive that the underdog elements in American society
showed a considerably higher responsiveness to the idea of war with Spain than
the groups that were more satisfied with their economic or political positions.
Our entry into the Philippines then aroued the interest of conservative groups
that had been indifferent to the quixotism of freeing Cuba but were alert to
the idea of capturing new markets. Imperialism appealed to members of both
the business and political elites as an enlargement of the sphere of American
power and profits. Many of the underdog elements also responded to this new
note of national self-assertion; others, however, looked upon our conduct in
the Philippines as a betrayal of national principles. Anti-expansionists attempted to stir a sense of guilt and foreboding in the nation at large. But the
circumstances of the period 1898–1900—the return of prosperity and the quick
spectacular victories in war—made it difficult for them to impress this feeling
upon the majority. The rhetoric of Duty and Destiny carried the day. The
anti-expansionists had neither the numbers nor the morale of their opponents.
The most conspicuous result of their lack of drive and confidence can be seen
in the lamentable strategy of Bryan over the ratification of the treaty.

Clearly this attempt to see the war and expansion in the light of social
history has led us onto the high and dangerous ground of social psychology.
On this terrain we historians are at a great disadvantage; we are inexpert
psychologists, and in any event we cannot get the kind of data for this period
which would satisfactorily substantiate any psychological hypotheses. However, we have little other choice than to move into this terrain wherever simple

rationalistic explanations of national behavior leave us dissatisfied. What I have attempted here is merely a preliminary sketch of a possible explanatory model that would enlarge our conception of our task. It needs further inquiry —which might make it seem more plausible at some points, more questionable at others.

CHAPTER 12

PROGRESSIVISM

The period from 1890 to 1917 is unique in the history of American reform. As Mr. Dooley, the fictional Irish mouthpiece of the social critic, Finley Peter Dunne, observed with customary sarcasm, Americans are generally great reformers only "f'r a short distance." Hence, American reform movements usually have been of short duration and have not been followed closely by other periods of reform. But only a few years after the decisive defeat of Bryan and Populism in 1896, the United States experienced another pervasive reform movement. Because the Progressive movement followed so closely on the heels of Populism, scholars have long been concerned about the relationships between the two movements. The traditional view that Progressivism was basically a continuation of Populism has been challenged in recent decades as inadequate and misleading.

In this selection, Eric F. Goldman examines the Progressive movement within the framework of modern American reform. In particular, Professor Goldman relates Progressivism to two of its nineteenth-century antecedents—agrarian-dominated Populism and the liberalism of patrician reformers. Indeed, the author suggests that the new movement was based on a "least common denominator" that was emerging out of the union of the two older reform movements. Goldman discusses the circumstances of the early 1900s that led to the decline of Populism, the existence of other worrisome conditions that prompted further reform, and the nature of the "fresh movement of dissidence."

In reading this essay, the student should consider the following questions. First, how does Professor Goldman explain the seeming paradox of the decline of Populism and the almost simultaneous rise of Progressivism during the "good times" of the early 1900s? Second, what specific differences, and what similarities, does the author see between these two reform movements? More fundamentally, what subtle and less precisely measurable difference does he perceive? Finally, what was the essential nature of Progressivism, as analyzed by Goldman? What was the "least common denominator" of liberalism and Populism on which Progressivism was based?

To attempt to pinpoint the three or four most outstanding works on Progressivism is almost foolhardy. Indispensable, however, to the serious student are the works of Richard Hofstadter, particularly *The Age of Reform: From Bryan to F.D.R.** (1955), and those of George E. Mowry, particularly *The Era of Theodore Roosevelt** (1958). Two other important studies are Robert H. Wiebe, *Businessmen and Reform: A Study of the Progressive Movement** (1962), and Gabriel Kolko, *The Triumph of Conservatism: A Reinterpretation of American History, 1900–1916** (1963). Both are more or less critical of the earlier historical works that pit reformers against conscienceless businessmen and bosses. For a good statement from another perspective, students should see Louis Filler, *Crusaders for American Liberalism** (new edition, 1950).

*Available in a paperback edition.

A LEAST COMMON DENOMINATOR

ERIC GOLDMAN

Less than two years after the election of 1896, bands were blaring Sousa's "Stars and Stripes Forever" and Colonel William Jennings Bryan, astride a glistening black horse, was using the famous voice to command a regiment of Nebraska Volunteers. The Spanish-American War was on, a war that proved much more personal for most Americans than either World War I or II. Except for a handful of dissenters, the fight to free Cuba from Spanish rule was a national hoopla against fetid Old World tyranny. The brief ten months of fighting even provided a hero to suit every taste—the laconic Admiral Dewey ("You may fire when ready, Gridley"), the pious Captain Philip, of the *Texas* ("Don't cheer, boys, the poor fellows are dying"), blaspheming Bob Evans, of the *Iowa,* General Joe Wheeler, the gallant old Confederate cavalryman who "laid away a suit of gray to wear the Union blue," and, of course, Teddy Roosevelt, Harvard '80, leading cowboys, bricklayers, and farm hands in a pell-mell charge up Kettle Hill. When it was all over, a thousand commentators noted that the nation seemed united as it had not been for years. "The Spanish War finished us," Tom Watson added. "The blare of the bugle drowned the voice of the Reformer."

It was not quite that simple. The Spanish-American War came in the midst of a number of circumstances that were blunting class strife and decreasing the pressure from the bottom of society. The election of 1896 was scarcely over when the depression ended and the whole nation was bathed in the soothing sun of prosperity. Unlike the prosperity years of the Eighties, this period's good times did not leave the farmers feeling outrageously cheated of their share. During the first decade of the twentieth century the prices of agricultural products increased almost fifty per cent while the money value of rural property doubled. The real wages of urban workers were not rising, or at least were not rising appreciably. Yet the philanthropies of the new millionaires— whatever the ethics of the way the fortunes had been made—were bringing benefits to urban lower-income groups that ranged from increased library facilities to better medical care, and tax-supported facilites from which the

SOURCE. Eric F. Goldman, *Rendezvous with Destiny: A History of Modern American Reform*, pp. 54–65. Copyright © 1952, 1956 by Alfred A. Knopf, Inc. Reprinted by permission of Alfred A. Knopf, Inc.

whole community benefited were rapidly developing. Public education, that traditional avenue of opportunity, was going through a phenomenal expansion that made any previous stage of development seem slow. By 1910 the coveted high-school diploma was accessible to all except the poorest or those living in the least-settled areas. West of the Appalachians, the land-grant colleges were making even a college degree nothing spectacular for the child of a moderately succesful farmer.

City and countryside were both receiving balms for their special irritations, largely as a result of long-running developments that were now showing pronounced effects. The factory hand had less of a feeling that he was considered an animal, to be herded at the demand of the front office. Out of expediency, a sense of decency, or a combination of both, some of the older leaders in industrial circles, most notably Mark Hanna, were suggesting that capitalists could act too imperially. ("A man who won't meet his men half-way," said Hanna, "is a God-damn fool.") Contrary to popular legend, the rising generation of business leaders did not consist largely of self-made men. Most of the executives were the sons of successes, and, while no less interested in profits, they were often less crass in their attitude toward their employees.

In the agricultural areas, loneliness was being relieved by increasing settlement, the rural free delivery system established in 1896, the growth of lodges and church organizations, and the products of onrushing technology. The farm woman who was such a goad to discontent in the Eighties was often, twenty years later, the contented housewife, preening over the frame house that replaced her sod home, using a shiny new mechanical cleaner to get time for an Eastern Star meeting, even, if the farm was not too far from a city, making a place in the budget for one of Mr. Bell's deliciously clanging boxes. Early in the new century Mary Ellen Lease forsook agitation for Brooklyn, and she had no successor on the prairies.

In the more genial atmosphere of the early 1900's, low-status groups and occupations were finding a greater acceptance. When Samuel Gompers turned to labor organizing in the Seventies, his activities brought virtual ostracism to his family; thirty years later, vaudevillians were genially patting their bellies as they referred to "my Sam Gompers." The farmer, more than ever, was the "hayseed," but he was no longer the "anarchistic Populist." Middle-class America was dropping its frightened snarling for unworried, almost kindly condescension toward the back country. The new immigrant might still be the "wop" or the "hunky," but a happier nation was less concerned with pushing the newcomer down, and the recent immigrant could more confidently feel, as the Hungarians were saying, that "The President is Mister and I am Mister too."

"In the United States of today," a Boston newspaper greeted the New Year in 1904, "everyone is middle class. The resort to force, the wild talk of the nineties are over. Everyone is busily, happily getting ahead." If the picture was hardly so idyllic, class and regional tensions were certainly relaxing and a good deal of the old bounce, the old faith in America as opportunity, was coming back. Once more most of the nation's families confidently laid plans for the next step up in the world. Once more most of the country could, without feeling foolish, believe in an always better tomorrow.

Yet the early 1900's were not to be a repetition of the late Sixties. The basic economic and social facts had changed, and changed so drastically that few could fail to note the differences. The frontier, so invitingly open in 1870, so worrisomely closing in the Eighties and Nineties, was now definitely a part of history, and the questions Henry George had raised as early as 1879 were real beyond any sneers at radical Jeremiahs. The decades of agrarian distress had left their mark. By 1900, more than one third of the American farmers did not work their own acres. The big factory dominated the industrial scene to such an extent that only the most optimistic employee still dreamed of owning his own plant. The concentration of the whole nation's wealth was reaching a state where one per cent of the population owned more than the remaining ninety-nine per cent put together. Most obvious of all, most arrestingly obvious, the trustification of industry was still racing ahead, and taking on a form that made it especially menacing to the ambitious small entrepreneur.

As the century turned, J. P. Morgan and Andrew Carnegie engaged in a few swift maneuvers and the nation's first billion-dollar trust had been created. Here was a United States Steel Corporation substantially controlling the production of steel products from hairpins to cranes; here was a spectacular step forward in the process of transferring the control of industry to bankers or banking syndicates. "It was bad enough to have million-dollar trusts run by a few men," the *Chicago Evening Post* expressed the widespread feeling, "but what is going to happen to the farmer, the worker, and the small businessman when we have billion-dollar combines maneuvered by a handful of men who have never been in a plant and who think of a factory as just another chip in a gigantic financial poker game?"

What was going to happen, scores of other commentators answered, was that the United States would find itself under socialist rule. "Grasping and unrelenting monopoly," conservative newspapers were saying, meant inevitable government ownership or governmental controls so stringent that no significant vestige of free enterprise would be left. The fear that the country was careening toward socialism was accentuated by the rapid growth of the party itself. The year after Bryan's defeat, one wing of the socialist movement broke away from the domination of Daniel De Leon and adopted a moderate, flexible program. In a short time this group had captured most of the people who considered themselves socialists and was developing a national following far larger than any previous socialist strength in the United States. The new socialism had a characteristic that made it especially worrisome to a nation of anti-socialists. Its leader, Eugene Debs, was no easily dismissed outcast. He was Indiana-born, a crony of James Whitcomb Riley, a heretic who challenged the gods with a homey Hoosier twang. The crucial convention that established the new socialism in 1901 was made up of delegates who were eighty per cent native-born, a percentage higher than the national ratio. Across the country, doctors, professors, pharmacists, and the Chairman of the Committee on Community Problems of the Terre Haute Ladies' Cultural Group were helping to elect an estimated three hundred socialists to local political offices. Socialism, one of the party executives could boast, was no longer "an exotic plant in this country."

Under the circumstances, if all America was becoming more middle-class in outlook, the middle-class outlook was increasingly friendly to reform. For the first time considerable numbers of small businessmen and white-collar workers were joining factory hands and farmers in a restless questioning. At the top of the society, among the Best People, more men and women were talking reform and more of those interested in change were linking demands for clean government with an advocacy of governmental moves to help the lower-income groups. The breakaway from old-style liberalism among upper-class reformers was most marked in patrician circles. A business-minded reformer might be quite happy with a cleaner, more efficient government that operated in behalf of the corporations; patrician reformers were hardly satisfied with liberal triumphs that left intact their long-time target, the parvenu plutocracy. Patrician reformers also evidenced an especially strong concern over the growth of socialism, in part because their extensive contacts with Europe provided a goading reminder of how discontent could swiftly build up movements for government ownership.

Once again a revealing example was provided by the Maryland aristocrat, Charles Bonaparte. In the war on Grantism, Bonaparte had thought politically of the impediments to his ideal of rule by an elite. The "one great issue," Bonaparte believed in those days, was "fair or fraudulent elections." By the early 1900's Bonaparte was thinking politically and economically of the obstacles in the way of his system, and he attacked both political bosses and those "big, strong, greedy, over-prosperous animals of the . . . pig order," the trust magnates. Within a decade after the defeat of Bryan, a patrician President named the patrician Bonaparte his Attorney General, and the intonation of the appointment was caught by a journalist who wrote that Bonaparte, "with his natural hatred of vulgar and greedy rich men," would prove "a terror to every trust magnate in the country who comes under that head." One of Bonaparte's "infirmities," a friend added, was his "hostility to certain forms of economic progress." If this hostility seemed an infirmity to the friend, who was associated with corporation America, it also represented the bridge by which the

patrician reformer moved beyond liberalism and brought his wealth and prestige to a fresh movement of dissidence.

At first the new reformers had no special name for themselves. "Liberal"
was too closely associated with Clevelandism. "Populist" called up the dour
radicalism of the Nineties. Gradually the term "progressivism" took its place
after "liberalism" and "Populism" as the label for another, quite different
attempt to reform post-Civil War America.

In many fundamentals progressivism continued Populism. For both movements, the central problem was opportunity and they aimed to "restore"
opportunity by quite similar programs. Government was to be democratized
in order to make it more amenable to reform. Reform meant primarily the
ending of governmental interventions that benefited large-scale capital and a
rapid increase in the interventions that favored men of little or no capital.
Many of progressivism's specific proposals came straight from Populism, including the direct election of United States senators, the initiative and the
referendum, anti-trust action, a federal income tax, the encouragement of
trade-unions, and an eight-hour day. In the spirit of Populism, progressives
took up new proposals for direct democracy or the advancement of lower-
income groups, most notably popular primaries, the recall of elected officials,
workmen's compensation legislation, and minimum-wage and maximum-hour
laws. The new reform also continued Populism's political recognition of
women. The cities were producing their own female activists, and these women,
for the most part talented and well educated, made effective advocates of
feminism in the eyes of progressives.

Yet progressivism was not simply the Populist buggy rolled out for a new
century. More urban in its base, progressivism was much more genuinely
concerned with the problems of labor and was far more inclined to include
small businessmen and white-collar workers in the groups it wanted to help.
Equally important, progressivism was developing its own special attitude toward the immigrant.

The progressives did not entirely drop Populism's anti-immigrant feeling.
One of the country's best-known progressive spokesmen, the sociologist Edward Ross, provided the era's most effective formula for fear of immigration
by arguing that the "squalid" newcomers bred rapidly while the old stock,
"struggling to uphold a decent standard of living," stopped at two or three
children. Many progressives also carred over the Populist fear that unlimited
immigration kept wage scales down and consequently they continued the
Populist demand for restriction of the influx. But progressivism as a movement
was far more friendly than Populism to the immigrants who had already
arrived. It was tending toward a genuine acceptance of the newcomers, even
toward espousal of an important role for him.

Progressives made up the dominant element in the settlement houses that were undertaking the first systematic "Americanization" work, and the Americanization they advocated was no one-way street. The immigrant was not only to learn, settlement workers emphasized; he was to teach. While assimilating, he was to preserve the parts of his heritage which did not conflict with adjustment to the United States and he was to enrich American culture by bringing to it desirable ideas or customs from his old-country background. This type of Americanization was enthusiastically approved by Israel Zangwill, a British Jew who had become familiar with American settlement work by serving as head of an organization that helped Russian Jews flee the pogroms to the United States. In 1908 Zangwill wrote his enthusiasm into *The Melting Pot,* one of those occasional literary works that both express and further a social movement.

The chief characters of Zangwill's play were all immigrants in New York City—an Irish Catholic, a Jew-hating nobleman who had personally conducted pogroms in Russia, his daughter, and a young Russian Jew whose parents had been murdered at the order of the nobleman. The theme was the general benefit to be derived from what Zangwill called an "all-around give-and-take," between the various groups of immigrants and between all the newcomers and the old stock. At the end of the play, as the Jew and the Jew-killer's daughter prepared to marry, the young man looked out to a sunset and proclaimed it, "the fires of God round His crucible."

DAVID: There she lies, the great Melting Pot—listen! Can't you hear the roaring and the bubbling? (*he points east*). There gapes her mouth —the harbour where a thousand mammoth feeders come from the ends of the world to pour in their human freight. . . . Celt and Latin, Slav and Teuton, Greek and Syrian,—black and yellow—

VERA: Jew and Gentile—

DAVID: Yes, East and West, and North and South, the palm and the pine, the pole and the equator, the crescent and the cross—how the great alchemist melts and fuses them with his purging flame! . . . Ah, Vera, what is the glory of Rome and Jerusalem where all nations and races come to worship and look back, compared with the glory of America, where all races and nations come to labour and look forward!

"Romantic claptrap," *The New York Times* critic snorted, and Zangwill's gushing prose is certainly hard to read today without wincing. But in a more sentimental era, the play provided for thousands of progressives an exciting expression of their desire for an attitude toward the immigrant that was more generous and hopeful than Populist snarling.

In the political field, progressivism was altering Populism by the greater degree to which it sought centralization. The Populists may not have been afraid of pyramided power, and the progressives certainly did not ignore reform possibilities on the municipal and state levels. But the increasing urge to centralize was showing itself in a number of ways, of which the two most important were greater dependence on federal rather than state action and on executives rather than legislatures.

The progressives were men in a hurry, and even at their best legislatures must always seem slow and cumbersome. The legislatures of the turn of the century, reformers constantly learned in additional ways, were hardly legislatures at their best. At the same time, able individuals were showing the prodigies that could be performed by one skillful reformer in an executive position. Under the circumstances, progressives relied increasingly on the "good man" who would bring to reform the decisiveness of a Carnegie and would maneuver, drive, or skirt around a legislature. The desire to provide efficient by-passes heightened progressive enthusiasm for the administrative commission, the device which gave long-time, quasi-legislative powers to a few men appointed by the executive.

Simultaneously progressives were becoming discouraged about the potentialities of action by the states. The problem with which the reformers were most concerned, the large corporation, did not yield readily to state action. No one of the huge businesses operated in only one state, and state regulations usually ended up in creating a maze of conflicting statutes that hindered the efficiency of corporations without exacting from them any real social responsibility. Worse yet, state social legislation was being thrown out by state courts almost as fast as it was passed. Quite obviously, Washington was no perfect base for reform. But the federal Constitution did explicitly empower Congress to regulate interstate commerce and national action did seem the logical way to regulate corporations operating on a national scale. In the early 1900's, much more than in the Populist era, reform eyes were focusing on Washington.

If progressivism was going beyond Populism in its attitude toward centralization, it was pulling back in another important respect. Progressivism virtually gave up the Populist attempt to make the Southern Negro an equal citizen. It paid little attention to the Negro problem as a whole and, to the extent that it worried over the black man at all, gave its support to the program of a Negro whose life had been a preparation for compromise.

Born to slavery and to poverty so great that his bed was a bundle of rags, Booker T. Washington had been helped to his education by a series of kindly whites. The Negro school he was invited to run, Tuskegee Institute, was founded on the initiative of Southern whites, and continued white aid permitted Washington to build Tuskegee from a dilapidated shanty for thirty students to forty-six substantial buildings offering thirty trades to fourteen hundred pupils. It is possible to exaggerate the amount of faith in the white man which this background gave Booker Washington. His was a practical, canny mind, operating in a situation that suggested bargaining Negro equality for some Negro advances. ("Actually," W. E. B. Du Bois once remarked, "Washington had no more faith in the white man than I do," which was saying that he had little faith indeed). But whatever was going on behind that calm, pleasant face of Booker Washington, he spoke no belligerence toward the white man and no call for immediate equality.

When he was asked to address the Atlanta Cotton Exposition in 1895, Washington put his philosophy into sentences that immediately became famous as the "Atlanta Compromise." The Negro should accept political inequality, Washington said, provided he was given the opportunity to advance economically and educationally; in time, having prepared himself for the wise use of the vote, he would be granted the privilege. Washington bluntly repudiated any drive for social equality. "In all things that are purely social," he declared in his most widely quoted sentence, "we can be as separate as the fingers, yet one as the hand in all things essential to mutual progress."

In the early 1900's Washington's argument had the force of apparent success. His program was the first to promise any substantial advance for the Negro which the nation as a whole seemed willing to accept. Tuskegee Institute and similar schools were rapidly turning out trained Negroes who could train others and, by supporting themselves in decency, win respect for the whole race. In the decade between 1900 and 1910, Negro illiteracy throughout the country declined from forty-four to thirty per cent, while the number of farms owned by Southern Negroes increased at a rate four times more swiftly than the growth of the Negro population. Progressives interested in the Negro observed all this and remembered the violence and quick failure that had come with Populist attempts at equality. They were inclined to become enthusiastic, to help make Booker T. Washington the first Negro national hero—and to let well enough alone.

In other, less important details, progressivism also moved away from Populism, but the core of the differences between the movements lay in a consideration that no discussion of specific variations would adequately reveal. Agrarian-dominated Populism, with its desperate sense of being left behind, its doubts whether anyone could be both a businessman and a decent citizen, its inclination to suspect the man with well-fitted clothes or polished grammar, was not the only base of progressivism. The new reform was a product of the cities as much as of the farms, an amalgam of the Best People's liberalism and of the nobody's Populism, a middle doctrine for a nation rapidly committing itself to middle-class ways of thinking.

Progressivism accepted business America, even was enthusiastic about it, and aimed merely to correct abuses. It prized cultivation, manner, and efficiency; quite characteristically, progressivism restored liberalism's emphasis on civil-service reform. Above all, progressivism replaced Populist grimness with a gusty, dawn-world confidence, worrying about America but not worrying about it enough to turn to extremes. The ominous Populist distinction between "producing" and "nonproducing" classes fast disappeared from reform terminology. To the progressive, America was never farmers or industrial workers locked in a class struggle with big capital. America was always "the people," some of whom were richer and more powerful than others, but all of whom could be given back their birthright of opportunity by moderate, practical moves.

The restoration of opportunity by giving stronger powers to more democratized governments, a businesslike restoration with no disreputable caterwauling—such was the least common denominator of the thinking that was rising out of the union of liberalism and Populism. It was a denominator to which each progressive added his own integers; it had its confusions, its vagaries, and its dodges. But it was a sweepingly appealing program, the most national one since the Republican platform that rode Lincoln into the White House, and for most progressives it carried the kind of emotional intensity that whirls political movements ahead.

"In fact," the progressive journalist Ray Stannard Baker has remembered his mood in the early 1900's, "I used to be sure reform would sweep the country, that is, I always used to be sure until I talked to the man next to me on the street car." Throughout progressive America a growing confidence in the program was accompanied by a growing awareness that the program alone was not enough. Progressivism was face to face with a potent set of hostile ideas, ideas that had been tangled up with the middle-class rejection of Populism and that did not quickly wither as the middle-class attitude moved toward dissent. Somehow the progressives had to dissolve away the argument that their whole program was unscientific, contrary to human nature, antidemocratic, unconstitutional, and immoral.

CHAPTER 13

THE UNITED STATES AND WORLD WAR I

American involvement in World War I was undoubtedly one of the most important developments in modern American history, and scholars have long been concerned with precisely how and why the United States was drawn into this conflict. As they are apt to do, historians have disagreed strongly, and sometimes pettily, concerning this matter. Was the dominant factor in American intervention the effectiveness of British propaganda? Was it the influence of prointerventionist American business interests? Or the unneutrality, from the outset, of the Wilson administration? Was the American entry a realistic action to safeguard American national interest, or was it the beginning of an ill-conceived moralistic crusade to reform the world? And what was the role of President Woodrow Wilson in leading the United States into war?

In this selection, David Trask considers American involvement from the broad perspective of viewing World War I as the initial phase of the Twentieth Century War—a cycle of warfare that began in 1914, continued until 1945, and whose aftermath still lingers. The early decades of the twentieth century, Trask suggests, were particularly demanding on American leaders. They were years of unprecedented and profound change, and therefore it is unfair to make invidious comparisons between the wisdom of early American statesmen and the follies of their twentieth-century successors. Trask believes that the response of the United States to World War I was determined by the American past, and he views Wilsonian internationalism as a direct reflection of the historical national progressive-liberal tradition. In treating the details of American intervention, Professor Trask identifies precisely the two sets of events that ultimately brought about American entry, deals with Wilson's aggressive but unsuccessful diplomacy, and points up the President's primary motives in finally making the decision for war.

This provocative essay raises important questions. First, what does Trask suggest about the likelihood of consistent American diplomatic success in the future? In the author's belief, what lesson should Americans learn about the applicability of American traditions and ideas in the world of today and tomorrow? Does Trask think that Wilson exercised considerable discretion in the process of American intervention, or that the President was significantly limited by a national consensus, as well as the course of events? Finally, do you believe that American intervention was actually in the national interest?

Out of the voluminous bibliography on this topic, the student might begin with Herbert J. Bass' collection of readings, *America's Entry Into World War I: Submarines, Sentiment, or Security?* (1964). There are excellent chapters on the subject in Donald Brandon, *American Foreign Policy: Beyond Utopianism and Realism* (1966), and Arthur A. Ekrich, Jr., *Ideas, Ideals, and American Diplomacy: A History of Their Growth and Interaction* (1966). The pertinent section of George F. Kennan, *American Diplomacy, 1900–1950* (1951), is interesting and useful. Arthur S. Link treats Wilson's role in depth in *Wilson the Diplomatist* (1957). Ernest R. May's *The World War and American Isolation, 1914–1917* (1959), is highly valuable. Walter Millis' *The Road to War* (1935), is an example of the anti-Wilson view, popular in the 1930s, which influenced American neutrality legislation on the eve of World War II.

*Available in a paperback edition.

THE TWENTIETH CENTURY WAR: THE FIRST PHASE

DAVID TRASK

If the imperial interlude launched America on its voyage into world history, the events of 1914–1918 and after completed the passage. At just the moment when the Americans prepared to reap the benefits of their nineteenth-century accomplishments, they found themselves inextricably tangled in that pattern of plenary violence which has become the most significant hallmark of world history in our time—the Twentieth Century War. The hostilities of 1914 began a cycle of warfare which continued until 1945, and its aftermath still lingers. The collapse of the European balance after a hundred years of stability inaugurated patterns of world-historical change still far from complete. Historians still argue endlessly about the origins and causes of that breakdown, giving particular stress to factors like nationalism, militarism, imperialism, and industrialization. The century turned into one of those terrible eras of violence which usually mark the disruption of the established order and herald the beginning of new departures.

The jumbled history of our times often seems impossible to organize and interpret; the confusion of so much that was new and different constantly defeats efforts to unravel the labyrinth of recent events. And yet, our limited perspective permits at least a few broad generalizations. Certainly the great conflict of 1914–1918 which began the Twentieth Century War so shattered Europe, and indeed the entire western world, that it made unlikely an early escape from vast instability. The very intensity of World War I sowed the seeds of further conflict. And then, again, the very debility of the West—immensely weakened by nothing less than an international civil war, if the western world is considered a quasi-political entity—encouraged aggression by nonwestern powers in Asia, particularly Japan until 1945 and China in more recent years. Finally, the destruction of all the great European imperial powers allowed nationalist movements in the old colonial world of Africa and Asia to acquire commanding strength. For almost five hundred years, the West had dominated

SOURCE. David Trask, *Victory Without Peace*, pp. 51–67. Copyright © 1968 by John Wiley and Sons, Inc. Reprinted by permission of John Wiley & Sons, Inc.

the rest of the globe. That dominance came to a fiery end in the flames of the Twentieth Century War.

Each principal phase of the Twentieth Century War—the First Conflict of 1914–1918, the Long Armistice from 1919 to 1939, the Second Conflict of 1939–1945, and the troubled Aftermath of recent years—made more apparent the consequence of these developments. Europe was less and less the center of world affairs. If the locus of power shifted for the time being to the great outlying powers of the western world, the United States and Soviet Russia, the recovery of independence in ancient Asian societies such as China, India, and Araby confirmed the redemption of power in regions long victimized by western imperial exploitation. It seemed entirely possible that the revivified eastern societies might ultimately surpass the greatest countries of the western world.

What engendered the pervasive violence of the age? Was it, perhaps, the superannuation of that system of nation-states which had emerged at the dawn of modern history? There were new things under the sun in the twentieth century. Novel complexities wrought by profound intellectual and technological innovations were increasingly difficult to accommodate within the conventional order of power. If this reality was difficult to comprehend, it was because of the prior beatitudes of nation-state organization. That grand tradition seemed too effective to question. Most people thought that the complexities of the new age could be accommodated by adjustment of the international *status quo* rather than its displacement. They all too easily assumed that the nation-state was the final stage of world-political evolution, an ultimate expression of political genius.

From time immemorial, humanity has condemned itself to pandemic violence because it refused to recognize the imperatives of change. The city-state organization of the ancient Mediterranean world had seemed entirely sufficient for all time to those who benefited from its accomplishment, but a long season of warfare ensued when it became obsolescent. The universal empire of the Romans, which replaced the older city-state system, seemed to be an ultimate political accomplishment, but it also succumbed to time, the destroyer of all human pretension, and another term of violence was visited upon civilization. Only the invention of the nation-state system brought Europe out of a thousand years of political stagnation. The achievements of the national idea were so imposing that it is easy to understand why our present commitment to it is so overwhelming. Nevertheless, even before the twentieth century, forces were in motion comparable in their disruptive effect to those which had undermined the ancient Greek and Roman orders of things. As in the past, those who benefited from the ongoing system tended either to defend it *in toto* or to urge reform from within. It was almost impossible to believe that the nation was as replaceable as the cave, the village, or the city as the prime center of political organization and loyalty.

More sensitive spirits thought they discovered a necessity to adopt supranational political organization—sovereign authority beyond the nation—in order to resolve modern international tensions by means short of violence. Of course, supranational polity by no means required the destruction of nations. It meant simply that they must recede in importance. National loyalties would have to be subordinated to a more comprehensive faith, as fealty to the city-state had been subordinated to the imperial idea of Rome two thousand years before. All too often, prophets of a new political order were dismissed as Utopians. The scoffers failed to weigh the odds against survival within the established order of things. Admittedly, it was one thing to recognize the necessity for change but another to determine effective means of accomplishing it.

The United States was suddenly exposed to a world of change which slowly repudiated the political order within which the newest of the powers had come to maturity. If the foreign policy of the United States before 1914 matured successfully in the congenial atmosphere of the long peace following the Congress of Vienna, the crowning accomplishment of the nation-state system, it ran its later course in the highly inhospitable context of the Twentieth Century War. That war presaged the passing of the old accustomed statecraft. All too often historians extol the wisdom of early American statesmen, particularly the generation of the Founders, and condemn the follies of their successors. This invidious comparison scouts the difficulties of the revolutionary changes which took place during the earlier decades of the twentieth century. It was the fortune of American statesmen from the time of Woodrow Wilson to cope with truly unprecedented waves of profound change. Latter-day change was far more complex than that of the late eighteenth century and certainly far less favorable to American security.

It is easy enough to detail the failings of modern American statecraft, but they were human failings which proceeded from kinder intentions and greater dedication than some of their critics seem to realize. Intellectual integrity commands a detailed criticism of American foreign policy during the Twentieth Century War, but not because those who presided over the destiny of the Republic were always stupid or selfish. They were as confused as everyone else by the arcane outcomes of an unexampled era of change. In the circumstances, the story of American leadership during the half-century just past is a tale of courage and fortitude as well as a catalog of error.

As the Twentieth Century War began its grisly course, the Republic found itself in a fundamentally satiate condition. America had attained its growth; it was comparable in its development to Rome at the time of Caesar Augustus. This condition did not mean that no worlds to conquer remained to the American people, but it did mean that as of about this time they became more concerned with exploiting the national territorial legacy than in expanding it. Few desired further national adventurism in the pattern of 1898. Those who have are naturally inclined to the preservation of the going order. Those in want or concerned about want favor reform or revolution according to the degree of their alienation from the established condition. The burden of affluence dictated a pervasive American tendency to act in support of the international *status quo*—to adopt conserving policy with respect to world affairs.

The imperatives of the age required at least a tremendous alteration within the established order; they probably demanded even more. Many men and women of this century elsewhere in the world believed that the established order was totally inadequate to contend with the complexities of the new age. They argued that only a complete retooling would permit the survival of the race. In America, few radicals raised their voices effectively. Basic debate on questions of American foreign policy during this century has taken place largely between reformers who hoped to purify the ongoing international system and those who preferred to support it without change.

Those Americans who urged reform drew inspiration from the historic national tradition of faith in progress. If the United States was sated by success as of 1914, it continued to respond to a markedly progressive ideology—an ideology born during its earliest years and nurtured into principles of democratic society and polity which in its essentials went generally unquestioned by practically all meaningful factions within the relatively narrow range of domestic political controversy. Those clear distinctions which differentiated European radicals and reactionaries, or even liberals and conservatives, were largely absent from the American scene. If the United States possessed a viable conservative tradition, it differed vastly from that of Europe. America was born free, and the great national bounty insured plenty to all those with sufficient energy and imagination to draw upon it, given the felicitous state of international affairs. The domestic political outcome was a pervasive consensus, a liberal or progressive commitment shot through almost the entire polity. With some notable exceptions like Hamilton and Calhoun, those in the American past who called themselves conservatives were usually pale reflections of their liberal enemies.

So it was that despite their affluence—their undeniable presence in the House of Have—the Americans embodied political sympathies and ideas which made them peculiarly sensitive to those who continued in the House of Want. If those who possess never fully understand the meaning of poverty, they can mitigate the eternal conflict of have and have not by embracing a reformist ideology and maintaining a reform temper. Recognition of these requirements inspired that internationalist departure in American foreign policy which found its inception in the mind and heart of Woodrow Wilson during the initial phases of the Twentieth Century War. Wilsonian internationalism has survived into our own time, considerably altered as well as chastened by the tribulations of a violent age. It remains to be seen whether that tradition, however noble, is sufficient unto the day.

The United States entered into the maelstrom of the Twentieth Century War as a satiate-progressive nation, its citizens basically desiring the maintenance of the international *status quo* but receptive to reforms within the going order to benefit peoples less fortunate than themselves. At times, of course, especially when it seemed that all their fine enterprises went unappreciated by others, they gave full rein to their satiety and relapsed into lethargy. If Wilson reflected the progressive instincts of the American people applied to global politics in perhaps their finest form, a generation of successors including the early Franklin D. Roosevelt concerned themselves with national interests to the exclusion of international responsibility. The later Franklin D. Roosevelt revived and built upon the Wilsonian tradition, and his successors generally continued the pattern, deprived of the advantageous circumstances which had allowed evasion of international obligations in the wake of the Wilsonian debacle.

If America's progressive outlook has produced much that is truly admirable, it is open to certain criticisms in its international applications. What is good for Americans is not necessarily good for others. The isolated condition of America in its formative years united with unparalleled national accomplishment during a protected childhood to inculcate in American minds a sense of perfection which was hardly legitimate. It is hard to admit that national commitments which have worked splendidly at home are less than universally applicable. It is of great significance that over time the American people have gradually learned at least parts of this lesson, although frequent backsliding sometimes seems to undo all that has been done to broaden their horizons. It remains to be seen whether the lesson can be fully absorbed in time to help in avoiding still another cataclysm far more destructive than the two violent phases of the Twentieth Century War which have gone before.

Indeed, it remains to be seen whether American ideas of international peace and justice, however noble in conception, are in fact fully applicable to the revolutionized condition of the world today and tomorrow. We see through the glass darkly, but it is the part of wisdom as well as virtue to grasp what is necessary for the well-being of others. As in that mundane world of getting and spending to which we are all eternally condemned, it is well to remember that a larger community of interest transcends all lesser dissensions.

With these considerations in mind, it is time to resume the narrative of American foreign policy, a narrative of its evolution to the present day in the context of unparalleled violence and cruelty—the Twentieth Century War.

*   *   *   *   *

The origins and causes of World War I, the first phase of the Twentieth Century War, are hidden in a quagmire of preliminaries reaching deep into the nineteenth-century past, but it is certain that the collapse of the European balance opened the door to Armageddon. By 1914 all that was needed to ignite the conflagration was a spark, and it came at Sarajevo on June 28, 1914. When a group of Bosnian patriots shot down the Austrian Archduke Francis Ferdinand and his consort, there followed a chain of events which precipitated general warfare in little over a month's time. Austria-Hungary soon issued an ultimatum to Serbia, hoping once and for all to put down the South Slav agitation behind the assassination at Sarajevo. Russia, the protector of Serbia, came to that small country's support. Germany than honored its obligations to Austria-Hungary. When France supported Russia, the fat was in the fire. Britain hesitated, hopeful of avoiding involvement, but Germany could not wait. Seeking out the best route to France, the armies of Wilhelm II violated the borders of Belgium. Britain then declared war. By August 4, 1914, all Europe was aflame.

The written history of wars is usually dominated by those who win, and World War I is no exception. The "official" version of its causes, largely French and British in origin, is that German aggression caused the outbreak of 1914. A dissenting claque of "revisionist" scholars, affronted by this simplism, have argued vehemently that Germany had to take arms against a crushing "encirclement" which threatened the very survival of the realm. More circumspect analysts usually parcel out war guilt among all the concerned parties.

Most accounts of origin and causation hardly mention the United States; it is presumed that the Republic had little or nothing to do with the prehistory of the war. This is not strictly true. The events of the imperial interlude influenced the calculations of various European chanceries in many subtle ways during the chaotic years preceding the assault on Belgium. In addition, historians often ignore the possibility that sins of omission often bulk as large as overt acts. The United States might have exercised an extraordinary influence for peace had it discerned the drift of things and entered actively into the affairs of Europe. But "ifs" cannot be taken too seriously, and the United States has largely maintained its reputation as an innocent bystander in 1914.

After the German army burst deep into France and Russia established an eastern front, the war settled down to a long and exhausting struggle. The western battle stalemated along a tremendous line reaching from the North Sea to Switzerland. Millions suffered and died along those dreary trenches during five interminable campaigns, but the front hardly varied at all until the final months of the war. In contrast, a war of movement took place in the East; opposing armies made great leaps forward and precipitate movements to the rear with bewildering rapidity. Unlike the campaign in France, the general trend in the East was toward German-Austrian victory. By 1917, Russia had been all but taken out of the struggle.

Other nations joined the fray from time to time. Like all general wars, the conflict of 1914–1918 had a marked tendency to expand, drawing in all manner of nations for all manner of reasons. Japan entered on the side of its British ally, and Turkey joined the Central Powers. Italy seceded from the Triple Alliance and augmented the exterior coalition in 1915. Rumania and Greece followed Italy, but Bulgaria adhered to the Germans. A series of special treaties, largely secret, interlocked each of the coalitions in a network of diplomatic engagements which vastly complicated the diplomacy of the war and its aftermath.

The horrendous battles waged at either end of the continent soon began to have their effect; they insensibly sapped away the vitality of European civilization. Americans still do not fully appreciate the enormous shock of World War I. As time ran on, the struggle became not only more global but also more total. It turned into what the German military analyst, Colmar Von Der Goltz, called a war of the nation in arms—a conflict to the death for all the stakes —engaging not only the last energies of fighting men but whole civilian populations as well. The bitterness of the struggle produced a tendency toward political extremes. The leaders of contending nations often moved to the right, casting their lot with a past that was daily being extinguished on the bloody battlefields of the continent. Other desperate men, out of power, became convinced that the old order was totally bankrupt. They contemplated social revolution to do away with all that was ancient and to replace it with an entirely new order. A massive upheaval finally occurred in Tsarist Russia, where the seeds of rebellion had sprouted for many years. If most of Europe fought for traditional objectives, the Russian revolution of 1917 posed a truly radical alternative to established politics.

*   *   *   *   *

The United States surveyed these developments at first with a certain detachment but later with growing alarm. As soon as war began, Woodrow Wilson issued a conventional proclamation of neutrality but coupled with it an unconventional appeal to the people to remain neutral in thought as well as deed. Wilson acted in the spirit of a hundred years and more of national aversion to Europe and Europe's ways. He could hardly guess that the drift of events precluded a permanent neutrality. The United States became the last of the great powers to enter the European war, taking this step in April 1917, but not before its President had conceived an impressive scheme to assure a just and lasting peace during years to come. Wilson's grand design posed a middleground liberal alternative to the European tendencies toward reaction and revolution.

America's intervention was in one dimension a culmination of those historic friendships and antagonisms which had matured during the imperial interlude. The events of 1914–1917 brought into sharp relief the hard realities behind the Anglo-American association and the German-American tension of prewar years. Of greatest import, of course, was the fact that Germany constituted a new threat to the "liberties of Europe," whatever its original intent. This fact was by itself sufficient to induce an anti-German sentiment among Americans. The security of the United States rested on a divided Europe. Ironically, this "realistic" motive for belligerency was not in fact the fundamental inspiration of Woodrow Wilson, although he could not have failed to consider it. What, then, ultimately brought on the American entry—historians like to call it the "reinforcement"—of 1917? The answer resides in two interrelated stories. One deals with the events set in motion by Germany's use of a novel engine of war, the submarine. The other is the unsuccessful effort of Wilson to mediate the war.

If Americans from the first favored the cause of the Allies, they were principally concerned with avoiding involvement, and the President shared this feeling. A near pacifist, Wilson had an outspoken advocate of peace as his secretary of state, the redoubtable William Jennings Bryan, who spent much of his time in the State Department negotiating a series of "cooling off" treaties with no less than thirty nations providing a year's moratorium in disputes while joint commissions inquired into the facts of the situation. Despite his inclination, the President was carried along by forces over which he could exercise only minimal control, chief among which was the question of neutral rights.

The European war rapidly dislocated international trade; in America the consequence was a sharp economic downturn. At the same time, belligerent powers sought credits in the United States to finance the purchase of materials and foodstuffs, required for the war. Bryan quickly imposed restrictions on foreign loans by American bankers, hoping by this device to safeguard American neutrality, but European powers used their own resources to make needed purchases in the United States. International law clearly specified that neutral nations could trade with belligerents in time of war if they avoided traffic in contraband items. It soon became obvious that the war had opened a wide range of markets previously closed to American traders, and it was equally evident that a thriving commerce with the belligerent powers would relieve the recession at home and stimulate a considerable boom.

The fly in the ointment was that the new trade would benefit only the Allies. British sea power controlled the surface seas sufficiently to insure that only a trickle of trade with neutrals would reach the Central Powers across oceans.

As in the past, Britain imposed a strict blockade on shipments to its enemies. The chief neutral trader affected by the blockade was the United States. Faced with a difficult decision, Wilson permitted legitimate neutral trading, although it was bound to discriminate against the Central Powers. The new commerce revived the American economy but precipitated dangerous encounters with Germany.

To combat the British blockade, Germany turned to the submarine. In February 1915, Berlin announced a blockade in the waters adjacent to the British Isles and warned neutrals that their vessels were subject to undersea attack without warning if they entered the proscribed zones. The United States objected immediately, standing on traditional interpretations of neutral rights. The law of war on the high seas provided that belligerents could interdict neutral commerce with enemies only after visiting and searching neutral vessels and uncovering contraband materials. The President sent a note to Germany stating that it would be held to a "strict accountability" if any American ships were attacked without the formality of visit and search. The British blockade of the Central Powers hardly met the strict requirements of accepted procedure under international law, but it did not endanger lives or preclude profits. If German policy went unchallenged, these things might occur.

On May 7, 1915, a German submarine torpedoed the British liner *Lusitania,* a noncombatant vessel carrying contraband munitions as well as passengers. Some 1200 people died, including over 120 Americans. This horrible disaster inaugurated a long and dangerous controversy between the United States and Germany. Wilson remained calm, utilizing diplomacy to obtain redress. He demanded that Germany repudiate the practice of unrestricted submarine warfare. A number of notes went to Berlin, insisting on proper observance of established neutral rights. At first Chancellor Bethmann-Hollweg attempted obfuscation and delay. He could advance some interesting arguments in behalf of German policy. The submarine was not like conventional vessels of war. It was extremely vulnerable to gunfire from very small weapons which could easily be mounted on merchantmen. It was also vulnerable to the so-called British "mystery ships," well-armed ships disguised as merchantmen sent out to hunt down submarines. Despite the force of these arguments, Bethmann-Hollweg finally accepted the American demands, fearful of a declaration of war implicitly threatened by Wilson. After a German submarine sank another British liner, the *Arabic,* causing the deaths of two more Americans, Germany notified Washington that it would observe traditional rules in dealing with liners. The *Arabic* pledge temporarily cleared the air, but in March 1916, another submarine attacked a French channel steamer, the *Sussex,* and sank it without warning. Wilson then threatened to break diplomatic relations, an act eliciting the *Sussex* pledge, in which Germany promised more forthrightly than before to respect international law concerning neutral and noncombatant ships on the high seas.

Wilson had won a great diplomatic contest, but the cost was high. He was now more or less committed to war on Germany if the *Sussex* pledge should be repudiated. The price of settlement was a sacrifice of diplomatic flexibility. America's national honor was now at stake. As long as Germany sustained its commitment, all would be well, but resumption of unrestricted submarine war would almost certainly force an American declaration of war. For the moment, Germany stood by its pledge, but the tide of battle ultimately led to a change of policy.

If the submarine controversy greatly frightened pacifists and other opponents of war who feared it might ultimately draw the United States into the European struggle, it also alarmed sturdy nationalists like the vigorous ex-President Theodore Roosevelt. He and others participated in an untiring campaign to impose "preparedness" on the country. William Jennings Bryan had opposed the *Lusitania* notes, propounding more cautious initiatives. When the controversy passed he determined to resign, convinced that the President had erred seriously in not accepting his counsel of restraint. Robert Lansing succeeded him at the State Department. He was an experienced international lawyer who entertained advanced pro-Allied sentiments. Soon after, the State Department lifted the ban on private American loans to belligerents, and trade with Britain and its allies expanded at a profitable pace. To deal with the advocates of preparedness, Wilson authorized a limited armaments program. Both the army and the navy benefited by legislation passed in 1916, quieting the clamor of T. R. and his minions.

As these events ran their course, the President had matured a strategy for bringing about a European peace. He and his most intimate counselor, Colonel Edward M. House, recognized that continuance of the war could only cause further tragedy for the growing list of belligerents and that it would increasingly jeopardize American neutrality. The submarine controversy confirmed this latter judgement. Appalled by the destructive nature of the war and determined to safeguard the interest of the United States, the President's initial effort to find ways and means of intervening constructively in behalf of peace was to send House to Europe as an unofficial emissary in February 1915 in order to make inquiries about the basis of potential negotiations. House soon ascertained that American mediation at the time was out of the question. Neither coalition would entertain thoughts of discussions as long as victory seemed attainable, and high hopes for the campaign of 1915 existed on both sides of the war.

This setback failed to deter Wilson and House; they became more and more interested in American mediation as the terrible casualties of 1915 mounted in the several theaters of war. Wilson was convinced that the causes of the war derived from inveterate European practices conductive to instability. Among these vices he gave special weight to militarism and imperialism, to his mind natural attributes of European error. Like so many of his countrymen, Wilson instinctively partook of that age-old national distinction between decadent Europe and pristine America. Despite his pronounced sympathy for the cause of the Allies, he was early assured that all of Europe had been seriously implicated in the processes leading to the Great War. It might be said that the President founded the "revisionist" interpretation of its origins and causes. If his desperate desire to mediate stemmed partially from considerations of national interest, reflecting his response to the sated condition of the nation, he also responded to the national sense of mission. He believed that the United States was called to a unique role in world history as propagator of those grand principles which had been so beneficial to the homeland. This sense of mission was a special corollary of America's pervasive progressive tradition, of which Wilson was a prime exponent. He hoped not only to uphold the national interest but to insure the well-being of all other peoples as well.

At some point in his contemplation of the European war, Wilson began to weigh a second general objective to accompany mediation. For many years a good number of Americans had agitated for a general association of nations to preserve world peace. The President became increasingly interested in this concept, and particularly in what he came to call a league of nations. In this potential organization, he espied a way of policing the world in order to frustrate international wrongdoers and also a means of organizing social and economic activities to enhance the general well-being and progress of humanity. The league of nations concept ingeniously reconciled America's satiate condition and its progressive aspirations. If a league would stabilize the going order, it would also encourage constructive reform, giving scope to the interests and aspirations of nations less fortunate than the United States. The project held out special attraction to a man like Wilson, filled as he was with a compulsive desire to accomplish great humanitarian deeds as well as to shield the Republic from danger.

Obviously no league could be created until the recovery of peace. To this end the President once again dispatched Colonel House to Europe late in 1915. As before, he was to determine whether a basis existed for mediation. Also, he was empowered to arrange a deal with Great Britain in order to force German cooperation. This tactic was a legacy of the late discontents over the submarine; at this time Wilson believed that Germany was the chief obstacle to a negotiated peace. The House-Grey memorandum of February 1916, signed by the British foreign secretary and the President's servant, provided that on notification from the Allies, the United States would call for negotiations. If Germany refused, the United States would probably enter the war. Here was a bold plan indeed. Had it been publicized at the time, those of isolationist sentiment would have raised an unprecedented outcry. The exigencies of the great European war had already moved Wilson to diplomatic enterprises far beyond any previously contemplated by an American President —far more advanced than the projects of the energetic Theodore Roosevelt, whose intervention at Algeciras paled by comparison.

As it happened, the House-Grey memorandum was not implemented. The same realities precluding mediation earlier in the war insured against success in 1916. The Allies remained confident of victory. No nation engaged in a conflict as desperate as World War I could voluntarily accept a negotiated peace short of its ultimate war aims as long as total victory still seemed feasible. Growing desire in Britain for a more vigorous prosecution of the war resulted in the replacement of the Asquith ministry by a coalition government headed by the aggressive David Lloyd George. Because Britain never asked the United States to appeal publicly for peace negotiations, the House-Grey machinery never went into operation.

During the summer and fall of 1916, Wilson campaigned for re-election. His victory of 1912 had stemmed from a split in the Republican Party between its Regular and Progressive wings. No such advantage aided him in 1916, but he managed a close victory over Charles Evans Hughes of New York. Wilson had guided a remarkable legislative program through the Congress, one source of his popularity, but the principal slogan of the campaign, "He kept us out of war," also had marked appeal. The result of the election strengthened the President's determination to seek a negotiated peace, despite the bleak prospect. In December 1916, he began his final attempt, sending a note to the belligerent powers requesting them to state their war aims. Wilson would then determine whether they provided an opening for negotiations. This departure greatly annoyed the Allies, but Britain's failure to utilize the House-Grey memorandum, coupled with a relative period of calm in German-American relations, had turned Wilson's feelings temporarily against the western coalition. Early in January 1917, Wilson told House that the United States would not enter the war; it would constitute a "crime against civilization."

Once again Wilson encountered frustration, although his effort culminated in one of the great political orations in American history. None of the replies to the appeal of December were really helpful, but the President decided to make a dramatic public call for a negotiated settlement, an outcome he chose to call "peace without victory." On January 22, 1917 he went before the Congress and laid out his dual approach to world settlement. Asking the belligerents mutually to recede from their more advanced war aims and to accept an early peace conference, he also made an explicit appeal for a league of nations. He could not know that plans were already in motion to insure that his last and greatest attempt at mediation would fail.

On January 9, 1917 the German emperor authorized a resumption of submarine warfare at the beginning of February, a decision prompted by the assumption that Germany could end the war before the United States could bring its power to bear. When the German ambassador in Washington, Count Johann von Bernstorff, delivered notification of this decision, the world anticipated an immediate American declaration of war, but the President delayed his final decision. Profoundly opposed to military involvement, the President had been victimized by two prior developments. He had lost diplomatic flexibility by threatening Germany with dire consequences if it resumed unrestricted submarine warfare. He had also expended great energies in a noble but quixotic attempt to mediate the war, an enterprise doomed to failure as long as either of the opposing coalitions entertained hopes of final victory. Seeking alternatives to full belligerency, Wilson first contemplated armed neutrality, a distinctly pro-Allied step but short of war, although he hesitated to make even this move until word arrived late in February of the Zimmermann note from Germany to Mexico proposing an alliance with that country in return for financial assistance and recovery of territories lost to the United States after the Mexican War. When Wilson asked Congress for permission to arm merchantmen, a faction in the Senate he called "a little group of willful men" blocked the authorization. Wilson then discovered executive power sufficient to order the step.

Despite a desperate desire to remain at peace, Wilson was swept along by developments to which he ultimately had to bow. One obstacle to belligerency was that it meant cooperation with the autocratic Russian goverment, but this objection was swept away after the overthrow of the Tsar early in March and the establishment of a provisional government. Very soon, word came of German attacks on American shipping, and also of British desperation as financial conditions worsened and the submarine took a dreadful toll of merchant ships. Finally, on April 2, 1917, Wilson went to Congress and asked for war. The United States, he said, would fight for a just and lasting peace to make the world safe for democracy. "To such a task," he concluded, "we can dedicate our lives and our fortunes, everything that we are and everything that we have, with the pride of those who know that the day has come when America is privileged to spend her blood and her might for the principles that gave her birth and happiness and the peace which she has treasured. God helping her, she can do no other." The speech of April 2nd definitively abandoned the hoary traditions of isolation and neutrality. At that moment, America entered fully into world history. On April 6th, the Congress completed action on the declaration of war.

Why did Wilson opt for belligerency, despite every desire on his part and that of the American people to maintain neutrality? Certainly the cards had been stacked against neutrality from the very beginning. Always before, when Europe had become engaged in general warfare, the western hemisphere had been drawn in. The destruction of the European balance was itself a compelling reason for belligerency. The course of events long before 1914 more or less insured that the United States would ultimately act with Great Britain to restore a stable European balance. In addition, Wilson had to respond to the outcome of the submarine controversy; national honor was at stake.

But in the end, Wilson's decision stemmed most importantly from his profound desire to bring about a world settlement based upon the twin principles of peace without victory and a league of nations. These goals he believed to be not only American but also universal necessities, which must prevail. Having failed to accomplish his end by peaceful means, he finally decided to complete his project by the sword. War was the only means left to him to establish sufficient influence to dominate the postwar peace congress. Thus did Woodrow Wilson embark upon the greatest experiment in national mission undertaken by the United States to his time. The President was impaled on the horns of a truly agonizing dilemma. To turn away from war was to abandon all hope of a just and lasting peace; to accept war was to plunge the United States into what he himself said was "the most terrible and disastrous of all wars, civilization itself seeming to be in the balance." For Woodrow Wilson, "the right [was] more precious than peace," and he launched his crusade for a *pax Americana* on that somber note.

CHAPTER 14

THE MEANING OF THE 1920s

The 1920s—like the 1890s, but unlike many other decades in American history—have usually been considered a distinct period with identifiable characteristics of its own. The decade has been interpreted in a number of ways. It has been viewed as a frivolous period and identified by such labels as "the Jazz Age" and "the Roaring Twenties." Such terms bring to mind a series of images associated with the decade: flappers and the Charleston, bathtub gin and speakeasies, Babe Ruth and Jack Dempsey, the Model-T Ford, Clara Bow and Rudolph Valentino, and dozens of other equally interesting and celebrated symbols and figures. But historians and writers have not ignored the darker side of the decade. The 1920s were also a repressive period when some of the more ominous forces of modern society were on the upswing. The decade witnessed the revival of the Ku Klux Klan, the culmination of the movement for the restriction of immigration, fundamentalist attacks against Darwinian evolution and liquor, and a general upsurge of racism, bigotry, and intolerance in thought and action.

The traditional interpretations of the 1920s have a firm basis in the historical record of the period, but in some respects they appear contradictory, and they somehow seem inadequate and even superficial. In the following selection, Lawrence W. Levine attempts to arrive at a more fundamental meaning for the 1920s. Professor Levine suggests that the shaping forces of the period were a belief in change and progress and a concurrent dread of change coupled with a nostalgic longing for a golden past. Levine finds evidence for this interpretation in the self-image of the 1920s as reflected in the popular culture of the era. The author examines various aspects of popular culture, from films, comic strips, serious art, religion, the Lindbergh phenomenon, and the automobile craze, to the stances and rhetoric of the Anti-Saloon League, the antievolutionists, the immigrant restrictionists, and the Ku Klux Klan. The fundamental ambivalence that Levine finds in the period produced serious tensions but never led to total paralysis. The era was not, he argues, "primarily a backward-looking decade," but one in which change was significantly influenced and shaped by the dualism between a past and future orientation.

In reading this selection, the student should consider the following questions. First, does Professor Levine make a persuasive case that the ambivalence between the belief in progress and nostalgia for the past was the shaping force of the 1920s? Do you agree that this is a more useful interpretation of the period than the traditional views? Has a similar ambivalence characterized all of American history to some degree? Finally, what evidence do you see of such ambivalence in contemporary America?

There are a number of provocative studies of the 1920s. One of the earliest attempts to analyze the decade and one that has set the tone for many of our impressions and interpretations is Frederick Lewis Allen, *Only Yesterday**
(1931). An excellent synthesis of the 1920s is provided by William E. Leuchtenburg in *The Perils of Prosperity, 1914–1932** (1958). Other interpretive treatments of value are Paul Murphy, "The Sources and Nature of Intolerance in the 1920's," *Journal of American History,* LI (June 1964); Lawrence W. Levine, *Defender of the Faith: William Jennings Bryan, The Last Decade, 1915–1925** (1965); and Robert Moats Miller, "The Ku Klux Klan," in *Change and Continuity in Twentieth-Century America: The 1920's* (1968), edited by John Braeman, Robert H. Bremner, and David Brody.

*Available in a paperback edition.

PROGRESS AND NOSTALGIA: THE SELF-IMAGE OF THE 1920s

LAWRENCE W. LEVINE

Americans have always been comfortable with the idea of progress. The belief that inevitable change brought with it inevitable advancement and betterment fit easily with, and was reinforced by, the stress on the individual, the belief in human perfectibility, the relative rootlessness and lack of tradition, the unparalleled mobility, the indefatigable optimism, the sense of uniqueness and destiny that has characterized so much of America's history. "Democratic nations," de Tocqueville wrote, taking the United States as his model, "care but little for what has been, but they are haunted by visions of what will be; in this direction their unbounded imagination grows and dilates beyond all measure." Evidence of the validity of de Tocqueville's observation abounds everywhere, from Jefferson's assertion, "The creator has made the earth for the living, not the dead," to Senator Orville Platt's jubilant announcement in the last decade of the nineteenth century, "We live in a new creation. Literally, the old things have passed away and all things have become new. Human society is full of creators." When Emerson proclaimed that the one fundamental split in society was between the Party of the Past and the Party of the Future, the Party of Memory and the Party of Hope, and described himself as "an endless seeker, with no past at my back," he seemed to be speaking for his countrymen in general.

Only recently have scholars come to the realization that the ode to progress, no matter how eloquently composed, was not alone in the land; it was accompanied by a cry of longing for what had been. The compulsion to peer forward was paralleled by an urge to look backward to a more pristine, more comfortable, more familiar time. Nostalgia is beginning to be recognized as an historical force no less prevalent and perhaps no less important than the idea of progress. Nor were its roots dissimilar. The imagery which pictured nineteenth century Americans as latter-day Adams in an Edenic "Garden of the World," may have allowed them to visualize themselves as free to rise, favored as they were by a perfect and completely open environment and untrammeled by the taint

SOURCE. Lawrence W. Levine, "Progress and Nostalgia: The Self-Image of the 1920's," in Malcolm Bradbury, ed., *The American Novel and the 1920's,* London: Arnold, 1971. Copyright © 1971 by Arnold Press. Reprinted by permission of the publisher.

of original sin or the heritage of the past, but it also confronted them with the dilemma of whether the roads from Eden could lead anywhere but down. Richard Hofstadter has captured this dilemma perfectly in his ironic comment that "the United States was the only country in the world that began with perfection and aspired to progress." Thomas Jefferson served as a paradigm of this dilemma when he assured his country of its destined power and influence at the same time that he urged it to retain its purity and simplicity by remaining a nation of agrarians.

The central paradox of American history, then, has been a belief in progress coupled with a dread of change; an urge toward the inevitable future combined with a longing for the irretrievable past; a deeply ingrained belief in America's unfolding destiny and a haunting conviction that the nation was in a state of decline. This duality has been marked throughout most of America's history, but seldom has it been more central than during the decade after World War I. The force of nostalgia was manifest in the 1920s in three related but distinct forms: a national movement to restore to America a former purity, cohesiveness, and national purpose which had been diluted by the introduction of "alien" elements and ideologies; a cultural schism which saw a large segment of the population alienated from modernity and longing to return, at least symbolically, to a golden past; a profound ambivalence toward the future which affected the actions and rhetoric of even some of the most fervid apostles of the "New Era."

I

The 1920s were ushered in by the failure of a prophecy—specifically, Woodrow Wilson's prophetic assurance to his countrymen that he was leading "this great peaceful people into war" in order to foster the worldwide adoption of American democratic principles and forms: "for democracy, for the right of those who submit to authority to have a voice in their own Governments, for the rights and liberties of small nations, for a universal dominion of right." To enlist the American people fully in this cause, German ideology was converted into the very antithesis of everything America stood for. Prussian militarism had to be contained to ensure the principle of self-determination of all peoples; German materialism had to be defeated if the principles of Christianity which the United States represented were to have any chance of universal application. "This war," a member of the Committee of Public Information wrote to George Creel, "is being fought in the minds of great masses of people as truly as it is being fought on the battle fields of Europe."

How seriously this missionary impulse was taken is illustrated by the American reaction to the February Revolution in Russia. The United States was the first nation to extend diplomatic recognition to Kerensky's provisional government for, as Wilson put it, the overthrow of Czarist autocracy in Russia now gave America "a fit partner of a League of Honor." From the beginning the United States viewed the Russian Revolution through the prism of American ideology. "It was the American flag that has brought about the peaceable revolution in Russia," the *Des Moines Register* concluded on March 23, 1917, "And it is the American flag that will bring about the revolution in Germany, peaceable or violent, for that revolution is bound to come. It is American ideals that dominate the world." When Russian determination to fight the war faltered in the spring of 1917, the United States sent a commission headed by Elihu Root to reassure the provisional government and strengthen its will. After some time spent in travelling through Russia, Root wired Wilson: "We have found here an infant class in the art of being free containing 170 million people and they need to be supplied with kindergarten material. . . ."

The October Revolution, which established Lenin and Trotsky in power, and the Versailles Treaty, which indicated that the war aims of the Allies were not in concord with those of Wilson, left the messianic prophecies of the United States everywhere in ruins. The resulting disappointment supposedly impelled a disillusioned American people to turn inward, to abandon their former dreams, to forsake idealism for hedonism. "Feeling cheated," Lloyd Morris has written, "the war generation was cynical rather than revolutionary. It was tired of Great Causes. . . . It wanted slices of the national cake. There resulted the general decision to be amused."

In fact, the immediate aftermath of World War I exhibited the opposite tendencies. Americans did not abandon their old verities and values but reasserted them with renewed vigor. The psychologist Leon Festinger and his associates, in their study of prophetic movements, have concluded that while there are limits beyond which belief will not withstand disconfirmation, the introduction of contrary evidence often serves not to destroy the belief but rather to strengthen the conviction and enthusiasm of the believers. The dissonance resulting from the clash of a belief system and facts which tend to discredit it produces anxiety which can be reduced in one of three ways: by discarding the disconfirmed belief; by blinding oneself to the fact that the prophecy has not been fulfilled; by reconfirming the belief and increasing proselytizing in the hope that "if more and more people can be persuaded that the system of belief is corect, then clearly it must be correct."

Although Americans exhibited all three tendencies during the 1920s, the latter two, and especially the third, constituted by far the most prevalent responses. With respect to Russia, for instance, there was little disposition to recognize that Americans had misinterpreted the direction and meaning of the revolutions of 1917. At first the Bolshevik regime was seen as merely a passing phase in the Russian drive to adopt American ideals. George Kennan predicted that the new regime would fail because it violated "certain fundamental economic laws," and for two years after the October Revolution the *New York Times* repeatedly (ninety-one times in all) reported that the Bolsheviks were on the brink of defeat. While Wilson joined England and France in an abortive attempt to bring down the new government by sending troops to Siberia, his ultimate response was to deny the existence of the Bolsheviks by withholding recognition—a refusal in which the United States persisted until Franklin Roosevelt took office in 1933.

On the domestic front too, the defeat of American predictions concerning the effects of World War I resulted in a nationwide tendency to reassert the viability and meaning of the very principles and beliefs upon which the failed prophecy had been erected. The full significance of the Red Scare of 1919 cannot be grasped unless it is perceived as an attempt to restate traditional American values, to reconfirm long-standing American images, to purify the nation and call it back to its historic mission by ridding it of intruding ideologies and groups. Professor Stanley Cohen, utilizing the anthropological theories of Anthony F. C. Wallace, has likened the Red Scare to a "revitalization movement" (other examples of which were the American Indian Ghost Dance cults of the late nineteenth century and the Boxer movement in China from 1898 to 1900), which under the spur of the intensive social disruption attempts to relieve anxiety by reviving central cultural beliefs and values and eliminating alien influences.

The emphasis upon revivification was omnipresent in the early postwar years: in the national repudiation of every possible form of radicalism; in the reaction against strikes and unionization; in the race riots of 1919 which struck out against the changed image and status of black Americans; in Warren Harding's assurance to his countrymen that theirs was a time for "not heroics but healing; not nostrums but normalcy; not revolution but restoration." A substantial portion of the nation faced the new decade not in excited anticipation of what might be or in stubborn satisfaction with what was, but with a nostalgic yearning for what had been. Americans continued to have grandiose hopes for the future, but increasingly their dreams were molded upon the patterns of the past.

Nowhere was this clearer than in the national attitude toward immigration and acculturation. A heterogeneous conglomeration of peoples, Americans above all other nationalities have had to strive for a sense of national identity and speculate endlessly about the process by which the diverse national and ethnic groups emigrating to the United States became American. The most familiar concept, of course, was that of the melting pot, which Crévecoeur spoke of as early as the 1780s when he wrote, "Here individuals of all nations are melted into a new race of men," and which Frederick Jackson Turner was still celebrating at the end of the nineteenth century when he concluded that "In the crucible of the frontier the immigrants were Americanized, liberated, and fused into a mixed race, English in neither nationality nor characteristics." "America is God's crucible," the hero of the 1908 play *The Melting Pot* exclaimed. "A fig for your feuds and vendettas! Germans and Frenchmen, Irishmen, and Englishmen, Jews and Russians—into the Crucible with you all! God is making the American."

The concept of the melting pot was a unique and difficult base upon which to build a sense of identity, since it posited an ever-changing American image dependent entirely upon the ethnic components that were "melted" down. Indeed, for many Americans the concept was too difficult and, as Milton Gordon has shown, the melting pot was continually confronted by a counter-concept—in the idea of Anglo-conformity. If immigrants to the United States could not accomodate themselves to the nation's character, "moral, political and physical," John Quincy Adams wrote in 1818,

the Atlantic is always open to them to return to the land of their nativity and their fathers. To one thing they must make up their minds, or they will be disappointed in every expectation of happiness as Americans. They must cast off the European skin, never to resume it.

"Our task," an educator asserted one hundred years later, "is to . . . assimilate and amalgamate these people as a part of our American race, and to implant in their children, so far as it can be done, the Anglo-Saxon conception of righteousness, law and order, and popular government. . . ."

A number of reformers during the Progressive Era went the melting-pot idea one step further in complexity by arguing for "cultural pluralism." The United States, they maintained, should become a "democracy of nationalities," a "nation of nations," in which every ethnic group retained many of its identifying characteristics, each living in harmony with the others. While this concept may have come closer to describing the reality of the acculturation process than either of the others, it never took strong hold of the American imagination. World War I not only made it difficult for ideas like cultural pluralism to take root, it led to the rejection of the melting pot itself. Profoundly disturbed by the sight of German- and Irish-Americans openly calling for the victory of the Central Powers and immigrants from the subject peoples of the Austrian Empire along with English- and French-Americans siding with the Allies, large numbers of Americans, from the President down, reacted against what were popularly called "hyphenated Americans." "When the Klan first appeared," its Imperial Wizard Hiram Wesley Evans recalled,

the nation was in the confusion of sudden awakening from the lovely dream of the melting pot. . . . [Nordic Americans] decided that even the crossing of salt water did not dim a single spot on a leopard; that an alien usually remains an alien no matter what is done to him. . . . They decided that the melting pot was a ghastly failure. . . .

For all his hyperbole, Evans reflected the national mood. In the Americanization movement, with its emphasis upon "One country, one language, one flag," and in the immigration acts of 1921 and 1924, with their national origins formula, which reversed the tide of immigration from southern and eastern Europe and Asia in favor of the more familiar northern European countries, this mood was made explicit. Americans in the postwar era were turning away from the idea of the melting pot, with its dynamic, future-oriented concept of national identity, and embracing the notion of Anglo-conformity, which looked to the past and took as its model the early Anglo-American. If the term "melting pot" remained in use, it came to symbolize less and less a crucible which boiled *down* differences into the image of the old American. To be sure, the melting-pot concept had been attacked periodically in the nativist movements of the nineteenth century, but not until the 1920s was the reaction strong enough to legislate it out of existence. In their immigration policies, as in so much else, Americans during the 1920s exhibited a national urge to turn backward in an effort to recapture the images and meaning of their country's youth.

II

It would, of course, be an egregious misreading of the 1920s to maintain that it was *primarily* a backward-looking decade. The "New Era" deserved its title in many respects. The impact of the new technology, of the automobile, of mass production and consumption, of the radio, the movies, and other forms of mass media, of modernist religious teachings in the churches, of the enhanced political and cultural influence of large cities, of the greater emphasis upon science in the schools, which now reached far greater proportions of the population than ever before in American history, of new moral codes and standards, was very real and constituted what Walter Lippmann called the "acids of modernity" which were eating into and transforming the entire society.

Historians, in emphasizing these developments to the exclusion of all else, however, have been in danger of ignoring the tone and aspirations of a large part of the United States. As I have argued elsewhere at greater length, the tendency to see the 1920s as an age of materialism in which the American people turned their backs upon idealism and reform does not accurately describe a decade which was marked by furious struggles waged over prohibition, religion, the rights of Catholics and Jews, the very nature of the morality and ethos that would define and guide Americans in the years to come. If the term "idealism" is used to define not merely those movements of which historians approve but any movement that puts forward a set of principles about which people feel strongly enough to band together and fight for, then idealism and crusading zeal were still very much alive throughout the decade.

The millions of Americans who joined or at least sympathized with the Ku Klux Klan and fundamentalist movements and who fought for the enforcement of prohibition were an indication that a substantial part of the population greeted the new forces of the 1920s with a sense of loss, frustration, and antipathy. They were as alienated from the ethos and developments of the age as the bitterest members of the Lost Generation. They attempted to reverse the trends dominating modern America and return to the moral and ethical code of the past. They longed for the *Gemeinschaft,* the community, which they had been brought up to believe was central to America. They constituted one half of a pervasive sectional and cultural schism that disrupted the prewar progressive coalitition, prevented the resurgence of a new political and economic reform movement, rendered the Democratic Party almost impotent, and prevented the 1920s from ever becoming the materialistic, hedonistic age it has been pictured as.

The United States, with its heterogeneity, individualism, mobility, and success ethic, may never have furnished fertile soil for the growth of a true *Gemeinschaft* culture characterized by permanence, intimacy, and binding tradition. But the rural, small-town cultures of nineteenth-century America, which Robert Wiebe has called "island communities," at least approached this ideal in principle if not always in fact. The insularity of these communities was first seriously disturbed by the nationalizing tendencies of the expanding industrial economy after the Civil War. This threat to the independence and integrity of small-town America helped give rise to the reform movements of the late nineteenth and early twentieth centuries, which Richard Hofstadter has characterized as efforts "to release familiar and traditional ideals under novel circumstances." By the early decades of the twentieth century the threat had expanded inevitably to the social and cultural spheres. The further Americans were carried from their version of the *Gemeinschaft* the more ideal it seemed to become.

In 1925 a woman in Muncie, Indiana, recalled that

In the nineties we were all much more together. People brought chairs and cushions out of the house and sat on the lawn evenings. We rolled out a strip of carpet and put cushions on the porch steps to take care of the unlimited overflow of neighbors that dropped by. We'd sit out so all evening. The younger couples perhaps would wander off for half an hour to get a soda but come back to join in the informal singing or listen while somebody strummed a mandolin or guitar.

By the twenties the citizens of Muncie were besieged by newspaper and magazine advertisements uring them to buy automobiles and "Increase Your Weekend Touring Radius." "A man who works six days a week," a banker was quoted in one such ad, "and spends the seventh on his own doorstep certainly will not pick up the extra dimes in the great thoroughfares of life." On July 4, 1891, a Muncie merchant noted in his diary: "The town full of people—grand parade with representatives of different trades, an ox roasted whole, four bands, fire-works, races, greased pig, dancing all day, etc." On July 4, 1925, Robert and Helen Lynd found Muncie deserted; its inhabitants had taken to the road.

The automobile was only the most visible and dramatic symbol of the new forces that were eroding traditional standards and modes of action in religion, morality, familial patterns, life styles. The changes left large numbers of Americans bewildered and alienated. Unlike the writers and artists of the Lost Generation they could not escape to Europe or to bohemian enclaves within the United States. Instead they attempted to contain the forces reshaping America through a series of movements which, unlike the Red Scare and anti-immigration movements, were regional rather than national in character. It is important to understand that the cultural regionalism exemplified by prohibition, fundamentalism, and the Klan was psychic and not purely geographic in character. All three movements had supporters in large cities as well as in small towns and rural communities, but it would be a mistake to deduce from this that they were therefore urban as well as rural in tone and purpose. The large numbers of urban migrants from rural, smalltown America faced a difficult, often impossible, cultural adjustment which left them bereft of identity. They, perhaps even more than those who remained behind, craved a lost sense of community and longed for a reassertion of the old moral values. Though they were technically urbanites—inhabitants of the *Gesellschaft*— they were psychically attuned to the cultures from which they had emigrated. They supported prohibition, fundamentalism, and the Klan precisely because these movements promised a real or symbolic flight from the new America back to the familiar confines of the old.

The fate of the prohibition experiment provides an excellent example. Prohibition came into being as a movement during the reform ethos of Jacksonian America and retained its reformist overtones right down to the 1920s. It won the support of a large segment of the nation's progressives and was passed in the form of a constitutional amendment during the Progressive Era itself by reformers who could see nothing more reactionary in deciding that man for his own good must not drink alcoholic beverages than in ruling that he must not eat impure beef or work in dangerous and unhealthy surroundings. "Those who labor for prohibition," William Jennings Bryan declared, "are helping to create conditions which will bring the highest good to the greatest number without any injustice to any, for it is not injustice to any man to refuse him

permission to enrich himself by injuring his fellowmen." To dismiss prohibition as simply a reform that failed is to miss the importance of what occurred
to it during the Twenties. As an *institutional* reform its impact was significant.
In spite of lax and inefficient enforcement, the consumption of alcohol during
the 1920s was from thirty to fifty per cent lower than it had been during the
period 1911–1915. If this was not reflected in the image of the 1920s it was
because prohibition had the greatest impact upon the beer-drinking working
classes and was least effective among the wealthier professional classes, who
could afford bootleg liquor and who set much of the tone and style of the
decade. Nevertheless, sharply decreased rates of arrests for drunkenness, hos-
pitalization for alcoholism, and the incidence of such diseases as cirrhosis of
the liver, all attest to the relative effectiveness of the reform.

Prohibition failed in the Twenties not because it was institutionally impossible but because it was more than an institutional reform. It was in addition,
as Joseph Gusfield has argued so convincingly, a "symbolic reform" which
gave recognition and legitimacy to the norms and values of rural, Protestant
America. It existed as a national symbol of the work habits and morality of
the old America; it clearly told every immigrant and every urbanite what it
meant to be an American; it attempted to make the American Protestant ideal
of the good life national by enshrining it in law. "The hope of perpetuating our
liberties," an advocate of prohibition maintained, "is to help the foreigners
correct any demoralizing custom, and through self-restraint assimilate American ideals." This cultural imperialism, perhaps even more than the material
effects of the reform, infuriated the urban, industrial, immigrant populations
who constituted the chief opponents of prohibition. As the decade progressed,
prohibition was transformed from a complex reform movement into an essentially cultural crusade which cut through the lines of reform. Increasingly it
lost many of its reformist supporters and forged natural alliances with the
multitude of other movements which had as their aim the nostalgic reassertion
of a fading life style.

The very defensiveness of these movements in the face of the new developments of the twenties forced them into an aggressive posture. Their fears and
aspirations were evident in the rhetoric of the Klan's leader, Hiram Wesley
Evans, who lamented in 1926 that "the Nordic American today is a stranger
in large parts of the land his fathers gave him." Traditional Americans, Evans
complained, were beset by confusion and hesitancy "in sharp contrast to the
clear, straightforward purposes of our earlier years." They were plagued by
futility in religion and a general moral breakdown: "The sacredness of our
Sabbath, of our homes, of chastity, and finally even of our right to teach our
children in our schools fundamental facts and truths were torn away from us.
Those who maintained the old standards did so only in the face of constant
ridicule." Robert Moats Miller has argued that the Klan of the Twenties was

a genuine counterrevolutionary movement. Certainly, under Evans' leadership it sought to combat and defeat the entire host of evils threatening its countrymen. The Klan, Evans warned, would be satisfied with no less than "a return of power into the hands of the everyday, not highly cultured, not overly intellectualized, but entirely unspoiled and not de-Americanized average citizen of the old stock."

In the final analysis, however, the movements for which Evans spoke were less counterrevolutionary than defensive; movements on the run which were struggling vainly to stay off the erosion of their cultures and life style—but not at the price of giving up all of the advantages of modernity. It is this that explains why they were so often content with the symbols rather than the substance of power. By the middle of the decade the fundamentalists had begun to stem the tide of the modernist advance within the churches and, through local pressure and intimidation, had made serious inroads upon the teaching of evolution in the schools. But this was not enough. They demanded such statewide laws as the Tennessee Anti-Evolution Act of 1925 not because they really desired to overturn modern education in the states and the nation, but because they craved the comfort of statutory symbols which would settle the question of whose version of the good society was legitimate. The Governor of Tennessee recognized this when, after signing the bill into law, he told the legislature: "After a careful examination, I can find nothing of consequence in the books now being taught in our schools with which this bill will interfere in the slightest manner. Probably the law will never be applied." All that the framers of the bill intended, he insisted, was to lodge "a distinct protest against an irreligious tendency to exalt so-called science, and deny the Bible in some schools and quarters. . . ."

The extent to which symbols became paramount was manifest in the trauma and fear induced by Al Smith's campaign for the Presidency in 1928. It was not Smith's political program, which in many respects met the economic needs of rural, small-town America better than that of the Republican Party, nor even his Catholicism which activated these feelings, but his urban background, his appeal to the polyglot populations of the big cities, his very speech, dress, and manner. Al Smith, the Anti-Saloon League's journal observed, "is different from any candidate of either party within the knowledge of the present generation. . . . He is not in harmony with the principles of our forefathers." The southern Democratic editor George Fort Milton warned that Smith's primary appeal would be to the aliens, the Negroes, the Catholics, the Jews, "who feel that the old America, the America of the Anglo-Saxon stock, is a hateful thing which must be overturned and humiliated," and called upon "the old America, the America of Jackson and of Lincoln and Wilson" to rise up in wrath" and defeat them. Although the nationalizing and standardizing forces of large-scale industry and the mass media were more deeply entrenched in the Republican Party of Herbert Hoover, Smith's defeat was greeted with widespread rejoicing. America, the *St. Paul Pioneer Press* announced jubilantly, "is not yet dominated by its great cities. Control of its destinies still remains in the smaller communities and rural regions, with their traditional conservatism and solid virtues. . . . Main Street is still the principle thoroughfare of the nation."

III

Had nostalgia in the 1920s been confined to the national tendency to reassert traditional values and images following the failed prophecies of World War I and to the past-oriented movements of the culturally alienated, it could be treated as an important force but one still on the periphery of a decade that seemed so dedicated to and enamored of change. The most pervasive manifestation of nostalgia in the Twenties, however, took the form of the ambivalence I discussed at the outset of this essay. In 1914 Walter Lippmann wrote of Woodrow Wilson's "inner contradiction": "He knows that there is a new world demanding new methods, but he dreams of an older world. He is torn between the two. It is a very deep conflict in him between what he knows and what he feels." This inner contradiction ran like a thread throughout the decade.

No one has seen this more perceptively or illustrated it more brilliantly than John William Ward in his study of the reaction to Charles Lindbergh's flight across the Atlantic in 1927. Lindbergh had not been the first to conquer the Atlantic. Almost ten years before his flight a British dirigible had crossed the ocean and in 1919 two planes, one manned by a crew of five and the other with two aboard, repeated the feat. But Lindbergh did it *alone.* "No kingly plane for him," an American bard rhapsodized, "No endless data, comrades, moneyed chums;/No boards, no councils, no directors grim—/He plans ALONE . . . and takes luck as it comes." In a technological age of growing organization, complexity, and facelessness, Lindbergh symbolized the self-sufficient individual of the past. Compared to Robinson Crusoe, Daniel Boone, Davy Crockett, he was a reminder of America's own uncomplicated beginnings; a product not of the city but of the farm, not of schools and formal training but of individual initiative and self-contained genius.

There was, of course, something jarring in all this. Lindbergh had not been alone. He was enveloped in a plane which was the product of the city, of technology, of organization. In spite of their odes to individualism, Americans really never lost sight of this. Lindbergh himself recognized it when he paid tribute to the industries that had created his plane and entitled the volume describing his flight, *We.* President Coolidge proudly pointed out that over one hundred companies had furnished material and services in the plane's construction. Thus on the other side Lindbergh's flight was recognized as the triumph of modernity. As another American poet put it: "All day I felt the pull/Of the Steel Miracle." In these two reactions Professor Ward has documented one of the basic tensions in American life. The crucial point is that this tension was not merely present in the antithetical reactions of different groups but *within* the responses of the same groups and individuals. Americans were still torn between the past and the future, the individual and society.

It is difficult to find any aspect of American culture in the Twenties that did not exhibit this tension. Motion pictures, which came into their own as a popular art form during the decade with 100,000,000 people attending 20,000 theatres weekly by 1926, seem on the surface to have been one long celebration of the new woman, the new morality, the new youth, the new consumption patterns that marked postwar America. Films with such titles as *Forbidden Fruit, Flapper Wives, Week-end Wives, Parlor, Bedroom and Bath, Madness of Youth, Children of Divorce, Modern Maidens, Dancing Mothers, Love Mart* were advertised as featuring "Brilliant men, beautiful jazz babies, champagne baths, midnight revels, petting parties in the purple dawn, all ending in one terrific smashing climax that makes you gasp." The reality fell short of the promises. As uninhibited as they might have been, the movies of the Twenties rarely failed to conclude without a justification of the moral standards of the past. Flappers and "It" girls married at the end of the film and entered a life of middle class respectability. Faithless husbands and wives mended their ways and returned to patient, forgiving mates. The new women may have been depicted as tough but, as David Robinson has put it, their toughness was used to protect their purity, not to dispose of it. The widespread popular revulsion against the excesses of the first wave of postwar movies forced Hollywood to resort to the cliché of the happy and moral ending, a standard which never marked European movies to the same extent and which made them seem, to movie critics at least, less artificial and more realistic.

The career of Cecil B. DeMille is instructive. After attempting to make the bathroom and bedroom national shrines in his series of postwar sexual comedies, DeMille turned to the public for suggestions for new films. Impressed by the number of requests for religious themes, DeMille hit upon a new formula in his widely popular films, *The Ten Commandments* (1923) and *The King of Kings* (1927). Sex and orgies were still prominent, but they were now placed within a religious framework with a moral message. "Better than any other director of the era," Arthur Knight has written of DeMille,

he seems to have apprehended a basic duality in his audiences—on the one hand their tremendous eagerness to see what they considered sinful and taboo, and on the other, the fact that they could enjoy sin only if they were able to preserve their own sense of righteous respectability in the process.

This was the result not of hypocrisy but of the kind of tension manifest in the response to Lindberg. Just as Americans could accept the fruits of modern technology only if they could assure themselves that the potency of the individual was enhanced in the process, so they could enjoy the freedom of the new morality only by surrounding it by the verities of the past.

The continued popularity of the comedy film throughout the Twenties provided an outlet for the disquiet the decade produced in many Americans. Charlie Chaplin, Buster Keaton, Harold Lloyd, the Keystone Kops, did not celebrate the new age, they satirized it; they did not worship order and stability, they emphasized surrealistic anarchy and mayhem; they did not deify the products of a consumer society, they destroyed them with willful abandon; they did not bow down to the image and manners of the new middle classes, they parodied them with hilarious accuracy. They focused not on the strong but on the weak, not on the confident man on the make but on the bewildered man whose direction and goals were uncertain.

Even more indicative of the difficulty Americans had in embracing the new was the increased popularity of the Western film, which reached its classic stage in the Twenties. The West continued to be a place of regeneration. In *The Mollycoddle* (1920), a young man brought up amid the decadence and over-civilization of France returned now to his native West and regained the latent virility which enabled him to throw off his effete manners and emerge as a hero. Above all, the West continued to be the center of virtue and morality. The Western heroes of the 1920s—Tom Mix, Buck Jones, Hoot Gibson—were strong, clean-living, uncomplicated men who needed the help of neither institutions nor technology in defeating darkly clad villains and urban scoundrels. They were living embodiments of the innocence, freedom, and morality which Americans identified with and longed to regain if only vicariously.

The desire to escape from the complexity of their own time led American moviegoers back beyond the history of their own West. In the immensely popular films of Douglas Fairbanks—*The Mark of Zorro* 1920, *The Three Musketeers* 1921, *Robin Hood* 1922, *The Thief of Bagdad* 1923–1924, *Don Q., Son of Zorro* 1925, *The Black Pirate* 1926, *The Gaucho* 1927, *The Iron Mask* 1929—and in the desert epics of Rudolph Valentino, Americans were transported to a world in which moral issues were clearly delineated and the ability of the individual to influence his own destiny was undiluted by modernity. This search for simplicity accounts also for the surprising success of such anthropological documentary films as *Nanook of the North* 1922 and *Moana* 1926 as well as the literary vogue of Harlem and the fascination with Negro folklore throughout the decade. In these recreations of Arctic Eskimos, South Sea Islanders, urban and rural blacks, Americans of the Twenties were able simultaneously to feel superior to those who lacked the benefits of modern technology and to envy them for their sense of community, their lack of inhibitions, their closer contact with their environment and with themselves.

During the 1920s the newspaper comic strip, like the movies, became a regular feature of American popular culture, with tens of millions of readers daily by 1924. Like the movies, too, the comic strip had its anarchic side. *Mutt and Jeff, Bringing Up Father, Abie the Agent, Barney Google, Moon Mullins, Krazy Kat,* laughed at propriety, order, romantic love, the sanctity of money and position. It was through the medium of nostalgia rather than satire, however, that the strips had their greatest impact. "If historians of the next century were to rely upon the comic strip," Stephen Becker has written, "they would conclude that we were a peaceful lot of ruminant burghers from 1920–1929, with only occasional flashes of inspired insanity, and that our social conflicts and national crises were settled by family conferences at the dinner table." *The Gumps* and *Gasoline Alley,* which first appeared in 1917 and 1919 respectively, were typical of an entire genre of family-centered comic strips which constituted one of the most popular forms of mass culture in the 1920s. The characters inhabiting these strips were distinguished primarily by their lack of distinction: decent, plain-looking, dependable, unexciting, independent but community-oriented people who were destined to live out their lives among neighbors just like themselves. Their very normality, the strips seemed to be saying, made them worth celebrating and emulating. Their virtues were those of the old America and when they strayed from these (for as normal people they had foibles) they were brought to account sharply.

A striking feature of the comic strips of the 1920's was their almost total lack of heroic figures. The central male in *Toots and Casper, Tillie the Toiler, Betty, Fritzi Ritz,* and ultimately, *Blondie,* were ineffectual, usually diminutive men whose entire lives revolved around the statuesque, beautiful women for whom the strips were named. It was from their wives or sweethearts (e.g., their present or potential families) that they derived meaning and purpose. The financial tycoon Daddy Warbucks of *Little Orphan Annie* was one of the decade's few prototypes of the incredibly powerful heroes who were to proliferate in the comic strips of the Great Depression. But in spite of the great wealth of her capitalist benefactor, Annie's triumphs in situation after situation were due, more often than not, to her own inner qualities and the innocence, goodness, and old-fashioned virtues of the average people who were always on hand to help her. The comic strips of the 1920s, with their quiet resignation, their emphasis upon steadiness, their celebration of the average, might appear to have been incongruous additions to newspapers whose front pages heralded the new, advertised the spectacular achievements of uncommon men, and called for endless change and progress. But they were a necessary addition, for they comprised the other half of the cultural equation that characterized the United States throughout the decade.

This web of ambivalence must be unraveled in order to reveal the meaning of any aspect of American culture in the Twenties. Serious artists and musicians attempted to come to terms with modern forms of painting and music at the same time they were returning to the themes and sources of an earlier America: the art of the Shakers, the Indians, and the colonial primitives, in painting; the tribal chants of the Indians, the spirituals of black slaves, the songs of cowboys and the Anglo-America folk, in music. Ernest Hemingway spoke for many members of his literary generation when he recalled that avant-garde Paris was a good place in which to think and write about his native Michigan. During the Twenties Americans found it far easier to come to terms with the new if it could be surrounded somehow by the aura of the old.

In their accounts of the "galloping materialism" of the 1920s, historians have made much of the secularization of American religion during the decade and the penchant Americans had for incorporating within the religious message the vulgarizations of American business rhetoric and ideology. The advertising executive Bruce Barton in his best-selling *The Man Nobody Knows* 1925, transformed Jesus into a twentieth century hustler, "the most popular dinner guest in Jerusalem" who "picked up twelve men from the bottom ranks of business and forged them into an organization that conquered the world." Comparisons like these were ubiquitous, but the reasons for them may not be quite as simple as we have assumed. It is entirely possible that modern businessmen were led to this rhetoric not out of supreme confidence in their standards and vocation but, on the contrary, because they were defensive and needed the ideals of Christ to justify and sell themselves to the American people. After announcing his aphorism, "The business of America is business," President Coolidge was quick to add this strained and obviously defensive analogy: "The man who builds a factory builds a temple, the man who works there worships there, and to each is due not scorn and blame but reverence and praise." "Would Isaiah be writing more Bibles if he were here today?" Henry Ford asked, and answered self-consciously, "He would probably be gaining experience; living down in the shops among workingmen; working over a set of blueprints. . . . There is no reason why a prophet should not be an engineer instead of a preacher."

Statements like these, when placed beside the rhetoric of businessmen who more often than not sounded like figures out of nineteenth century McGuffey Readers or Horatio Alger novels, indicate the need American business spokesmen still had for some noble purpose which stretched beyond mere material reward; they continually manifested an inability to accept the practices of modern business and technology purely in terms of practicality and efficiency. When Henry Ford declared, "I am more interested in people than I am in profits. . . . I don't give a hang for money as such, only as it helps me to help people with it," and when Herbert Hoover studded his speeches and writings with such words as "salvation," "devotion," "service," "dedication," "liberty," "vision," "courage," "faith," they were not derided by a cynical, materialistic generation but enshrined as two of the chief icons of America's business civilization. The production techniques of American business in the Twenties may have been new, but the images used to justify them were old and hallowed.

To stress the force of nostalgia and the presence of ambivalence is not to deny the realities of change. The desire to have things both ways—to accept the fruits of progress without relinquishing the fundamentals of the old order —explains many of the tensions in American life, but it has never led to complete paralysis. In spite of the persistent lag between actuality and perception, there has been a gradual acceptance of changes and a reordering of desires, expectations, and action throughout American history. Americans in the Twenties, as before and since, tended to turn to the past in their ideology and rhetoric more than in their actions. Still, the existence of this dualism between a past and future orientation is important for if it has not prevented action it has certainly impeded and shaped it. "The health of a people," Alfred North Whitehead has observed, "depends largely on their ability to question their inherited symbols in light of contemporary actualities, to keep them fluid, vibrant, and responsive." The 1920s had begun with the failure of President Wilson's prophecy concerning World War I. They were to end with the failure of President Hoover's prophecy that the United States was on the threshold of abolishing poverty and ensuring the promises of the American dream to all its citizens. The confused and ambivalent symbols and images with which the American people emerged from the 1920s made it all the more difficult and painful for them to cope with the material and psychic traumas that lay before them.

CHAPTER 15

THE GREAT DEPRESSION

As spectacular as the boom of the 1920s had been, the bust that ended the decade was even more incredible. As William E. Leuchtenburg points out in this selection, the economic and industrial gains of a decade of steady growth (with occasional sensational leaps) were wiped out in a matter of months. Although the origins of the great crash and the ensuing depression are debated by historians, economists, and even an occasional politician, the results are not. By every index available, the end result of the booming 1920s was an economic, industrial, and human disaster.

As Leuchtenburg indicates, the battle lines on the issue of what or who was responsible for this misfortune had formed by the time of the presidential campaign of 1932. The Democrats, led by Franklin D. Roosevelt, insisted that the origins were purely domestic. It was obviously to their advantage to heap all the blame on the head of the hapless Hoover. The fact that the Democrats, who controlled the House of Representatives, had been less than enthusiastic in cooperating with the President was quietly ignored. As might be expected, the Republicans attempted to locate the origins of the trouble as far from this country and their jurisdiction as possible. Europe was none too far; it was there that the Republicans claimed to find the origins of the disaster, and it was there, they maintained, that the problem had to be solved. Political figures who had prided themselves on being diplomatic isolationists suddenly realized and loudly proclaimed the large degree of economic interdependence that had risen between the two continents since the war. That neither the Democrats nor the Republicans had the faintest idea of how to ease the decline is clearly evident when one reads the platforms of the parties and the speeches of the candidates. Under such conditions, the advantage clearly lies with the party out of office. The year 1932 was no exception.

To one using the hindsight for which historians are justly famous, it is now fairly obvious that the arguments of both Republicans and Democrats contained elements of the truth. The domestic economy of the 1920s was altogether too speculative in nature and contained some rather large soft spots. Republican fiscal and monetary policy during the period was ill-founded and detrimental to national economic health. The economic collapse of Europe was both influenced by and itself greatly aggravated the problems in this country. The solutions to the problems of the period were complex and are debated to this day. Should Hoover have used the economic power of the federal government and, by so doing, would he have achieved the so-called multiplier effect (whereby government spending creates jobs and purchasing power, and so stimulates private investment)? The Senate Progressives, led by Robert La Follette, Jr., advocated this solution on humanitarian, not economic grounds. Many of the leading economists of the day thought that such proposals were not only foolish but also criminally wrong. Have we learned how to prevent the reoccurrence of such economic disasters? Most economists are confident that we have. It should be pointed out, however, that our fiscal and monetary safety devices have not been tested. It is also not at all evident that public and political opinion is prepared to use these devices when they are most effective —early in the crisis before its existence is clearly manifest.

There are a number of excellent works on the crash and the depression, but many of the better ones are so technical as to be of value primarily to the specialist. The most valuable on the crash itself for the general student are John K. Galbraith, *The Great Crash** (1955), and Robert Sobel, *The Great Bull Market** (1968). George Soule, *Prosperity Decade** (1947), and Broadus Mitchell, *Depression Decade* (1947),* survey the entire period. The election of 1932 and Roosevelt's response to the depression are well covered in the multivolume, biographical studies by Frank Freidel and Arthur M. Schlesinger, Jr. The latter's volume, *The Crisis of the Old Order** (1957), is an extremely literate and thorough survey informed by a strong pro-New Deal bias. Irving Bernstein, *The Lean Years** (1960), is an excellent study of labor's problems during the "boom," and Theodore Saloutos and J. D. Hicks, in *Twentieth Century Populism: Agricultural Discontent in the Middle West** (1951), show the underlying sickness of the farm belt in the full flush of the big bull market.

*Available in a paperback edition.

SMASHUP

WILLIAM E. LEUCHTENBURG

The prosperity of the 1920's produced the contagious feeling that everyone was meant to get rich. The decade witnessed a series of speculative orgies, from "get-rich-quick" schemes to the Florida real estate boom, climaxed in 1928 and 1929 by the Great Bull Market. Before the war, stock market investment had been almost wholly a preserve of the wealthy; in the 1920's clerks and bootblacks talked knowingly of American Can or Cities Service and bought five shares "on margin." In later years it was frequently said that by the end of the twenties "everyone was in the market," but there were actually fewer, probably far fewer, than a million people involved. What is closer to the truth is that millions of Americans followed the market with avid interest; it became, remarks Professor Galbraith, "central to the culture."

No one can explain what caused the speculative wave of 1928. It is true that credit was easy, but credit had been easy before without producing a speculative mania. Moreover, much of the speculation was carried on at rates of interest which by any reasonable standard were tight. More important were the sense of optimism which permeated the decade and the conviction that, especially in the economic world, anything was possible. . . . Since commodity prices were remarkably stable throughout the boom, economists were reassured that, despite the speculative fever, the economy was basically sound.

The volume of sales on the New York Stock Exchange leaped from 236 million shares in 1923 to 1,125 million in 1928. That was a year when everything one touched seemed to turn to gold: industrial stocks went up the astonishing total of 86.5 points. Customers crowded into brokers' offices in midmorning and stood staring at the blackboard or inspecting the tape until closing time. They borrowed money, bought more stock, watched the stock go up, and borrowed still more money to buy still more stock. By 1928 the stock market was carrying the whole economy. If it had not been for the wave of speculation, the prosperity of the twenties might have ended much earlier than it did. Coolidge's deflationary policies had withdrawn government funds from the economy, consumers had cut spending for durable goods in 1927, and the

SOURCE. William E. Leuchtenburg, *The Perils of Prosperity, 1914–1932*, pp. 241–268.
Copyright © 1958 by The University of Chicago Press. Reprinted by permission of The University of Chicago Press.

market for housing had been glutted as early as 1926. But with the economy sparked by fresh funds poured into speculation, a depression was avoided and the boom continued. . . .

In early September, 1929, the stock market broke, rallied, then broke again. By early October, Radio had tumbled 32 points, General Electric over 50 points, Steel almost 60 points. Still there was no panic. "Stock prices," announced Professor Irving Fisher of Yale, in what was to become a classic statement, "have reached what looks like a permanently high plateau." In the last week in October the situation turned suddenly worse. On October 23, rails and industrials fell 18 points. On Thursday, October 24, prices broke violently, and a stampede set in. The gains of many months were wiped out in a few hours. Radio opened at 68 3/4, closed at 44 1/2. For a few days a determined effort by bankers led by the House of Morgan held the market steady, but the next week the downward plunge resumed with reckless fury. On Monday U.S. Steel lost 17 1/2, Westinghouse 34 1/2, General Electric 47 1/2. The next day, Tuesday, October 29, was a day of sickening disaster. The ticker closed two and a half hours behind; when the last sales had been listed, industrial stocks had zoomed down 43 points. . . .

The prosperity of the 1920's had been founded on construction and the automobile industry. Residential construction, which had stood at five billion dollars in 1925, was down to three billion by 1929. The automobile industry continued to grow, but after 1925 it grew at a much slower rate, cutting back purchases of steel and other material; the cycle of events, whereby an increase in car production produced rapid increases in steel, rubber, glass, and other industries, now operated in a reverse manner to speed the country toward a major depression. By 1929 the automobile industry—and satellites like the rubber-tire business—were badly overbuilt. Since there was no new industry to take the place of automobiles and no policy of federal spending to provide new investment (Mellon, in fact, was working in the opposite direction), it was inevitable that as investment fell off and the rate of production slackened in the key industries, a serious recession would result.

There was no single cause of the crash and the ensuing depression, but much of the responsibility for both falls on the foolhardy assumption that the special interests of business and the national interest were identical. Management had siphoned off gains in productivity in high profits, while the farmer got far less, and the worker, though better off, received wage increases disproportionately small when compared to profits. As a result the purchasing power of workers and farmers was not great enough to sustain prosperity. For a time this was partly obscured by the fact that consumers bought goods on installment at a rate faster than their income was expanding, but it was inevitable that a time would come when they would have to reduce purchases, and the cutback in buying would sap the whole economy.

With no counteraction from labor unions, which were weak, or from government, which had no independent policy, business increased profits at twice the rate of the growth in productivity. So great were profits that many corporations no longer needed to borrow, and as a result Federal Reserve banks had only minimal control over speculation. With no other outlet, profits were plunged into the stock market, producing a runaway speculation.

The policies of the federal government in the 1920's were disastrous. Its tax policies made the maldistribution of income and oversaving by the rich still more serious. Its monopoly policies added to the rigidity of the market and left business corporations too insensitive to changes of price. Its farm policies sanctioned a dangerous imbalance in the economy. Its tariff policies made a difficult foreign-trade situation still worse. Its monetary policies were irresponsible; at critical junctures, the fiscal policy of the Coolidge administration moved in precisely the wrong direction. The administration took the narrow interests of business groups to be the national interest, and the result was catastrophe.

The market crash played a major role in precipitating the Great Depression. It shattered business confidence, ruined many investors, and wiped out holding company and investment trust structures. It destoyed an important source of long-term capital and sharply cut back consumer demand. Yet business would have been able to weather even the shock of the crash, if business had been fundamentally sound. The crash exposed the weaknesses that underlay the prosperous economy of the twenties—the overexpansion of major industries, the maldistribution of income, the weak banking structure, and the over-dependence of the economy on consumer durable goods. . . .

A year after the crash, six million men walked the streets looking for work. By 1932, there were 660,000 jobless in Chicago, a million in New York City. In heavily industrialized cities the toll of the depression read, as one observer noted, like British casualty lists at the Somme—so awesome as to become in the end meaningless, for the sheer statistics numbed the mind. In Cleveland 50 per cent were jobless, in Akron 60 per cent, in Toledo, 80 per cent. In Donora, Pennsylvania, only 277 of 13,900 workers held regular jobs. In the three years after the crash, 100,000 workers were fired on the average every week.

By 1932, the physical output of manufacturing had fallen to 54 per cent of what it had been in 1929; it was a shade less than production in 1913. All the gains of the golden twenties were wiped out in a few months. By the last year of the Hoover administration, the automobile industry was operating at only one-fifth of its 1929 capacity. As the great auto plants in Detroit lay idle, fires were banked in the steel furnaces on the Allegheny and the Mahoning. By the summer of 1932, steel plants operated at 12 per cent of capacity, and the output of pig iron was the lowest since 1896. Between 1929 and 1932, freight shipments were cut in half, and major railroad systems like the Missouri Pacific, the Chicago and North Western, and the Wabash passed into receivership.

The farmer, who had seen little of the prosperity of the 1920's, was devastated by the depression. The crash—and the ensuing financial debacle—destroyed much of what remained of his foreign markets. American foreign trade declined from $10 billion in 1929 to $3 billion in 1932. Foreign capital issues fell from $1500 million in 1928 to the abysmally low figure of $88 million in 1932. As foreign nations erected new barriers to American products and unemployment cut heavily into the domestic market, crop prices skidded to new lows. Wheat fell from $1.05 a bushel in 1929 to 39 cents in 1932, corn from 81 cents to 33 cents a bushel, cotton from 17 cents to 6 cents a pound, tobacco from 19 cents to 10 cents a pound. The result was catastrophic. Gross farm income fell from nearly $12 billion to the pitiful sum of $5 billion. . . .

The nation's first response to the depression was fatalistic. Business cycles were inevitable, the fatalists argued, and there was nothing to do but wait out this latest disaster. Any attempt to interrupt the process would only make matters worse. The *New York Times* contended that "the fundamental prescriptions for recovery [were] such homely things as savings, retrenchment, prudence and hopeful waiting for the turn." Businessmen, especially bankers, demanded a ruthless deflation. "To advise people to spend," declared one banker, "would be seditious." Above all, governments must reduce expenditures, and relief budgets must be cut to the bone. The depression revived an emphasis on Puritan virtues which the 1920's had rejected, and bankers linked their insistence on deflation to Calvinist morality. President John E. Edgerton told the National Association of Manufacturers in the autumn of 1930 that it was important to make people understand that the suffering of the unemployed was not the product of an economic breakdown but was the direct result of their moral infirmity.

The financial community purported to see the depression as a blessed occurrence which would improve the national character by chastening the spirit. The crash, announced the leading banking periodical, "should be highly beneficial." Nevertheless, as Gilbert Seides dryly remarked, "No one ever proposed to continue the depression in order to continue its benefits.". . .

President Hoover has been flayed by his critics as a tool of Wall Street and as a "do-nothing" President. He was neither. He strongly disapproved of the bankers' insistence on deflation, and he used governmental power to check the depression in an unprecedented manner. Hoover had little patience with men like Secretary Mellon, who urged him to "liquidate labor, liquidate stocks, liquidate the farmers, liquidate real estate." The President stepped up federal construction, urged state and local governments to accelerate spending, and gained promises of increased capital investment from the railroads and utilities. He summoned the leading businessmen of the country to a White House conference and obtained a pledge from them to maintain wage rates. Earlier in 1929, Congress had passed the Agricultural Marketing Act, which aimed to stabilize agriculture through federal encouragement of farm co-operatives. By 1930, a Grain Stabilization Corporation and a Cotton Stabilization Corporation were invading the open market to bolster crop prices.

Hoover's approach to unemployment relief was more orthodox. To provide relief for the jobless, Hoover relied on local government initiative and private charity. He created national committees of volunteers to solicit funds, but he set himself firmly against all proposals for federal relief. A federal dole would involve huge appropriations which would unbalance the budget and thus jeopardize the national credit, he thought. It would invite reckless spending on "pork-barrel" projects. Most important, federal relief projects, Hoover argued, would destroy the character of the recipients and create a class of public wards.

Within a few months, the assumptions on which Hoover based his relief policies were shot to bits. . . .

The worse the depression got, the less the cities did. New Orleans refused all new applicants, and St. Louis cut half the relief families from its rolls. Save for New York—and to a lesser extent Illinois, Pennsylvania, New Jersey, and Wisconsin—the state governments did almost nothing. As the situation in the automobile plants grew desperate, Michigan cut its relief funds from over $2 million in 1931 to $860,000 in 1932. More than 100 cities had no relief appropriations at all for 1932. . . .

In the cities, long queues of hungry men, their shoulders hunched against December winds, edged along sidewalks to get a bowl of broth from charity "soup kitchens." While most families were able to make out on shorter rations, the plight of the utterly destitute—and by 1932 they numbered millions—was appalling. In the St. Louis dumps, small groups of men, women, and children dug for rotten food. In Chicago, they stood outside the back doors of restaurants for leavings or scoured the market districts for spoiled fruit and vegetables. In the coal hills of Pennsylvania, families were fed on weeds and roots. While there were few deaths from starvation, 238 persons suffering from malnutrition or starvation were admitted to New York hospitals in 1931. Forty-five of them died.

In the three years after the crash, factory wages shrank from $12 billion to $7 billion. Although wages fell, the wage *rate,* which employers had promised Hoover they would maintain, held up remarkably well in the first two years of the depression. From the first, bankers declared a relentless war on the high-wage philosophy. *The Commercial and Financial Chronicle* conducted a persistent campaign for wage-slashing as "an intelligent step in the return of prosperity." "The man who relies upon the wage he receives for his daily toil,"

declared the *Chronicle,* "must realize that employers have suffered even as has
the employee, and much beyond the same." On September 22, 1931, U.S. Steel
announced a 10 per cent wage cut; General Motors, Bethlehem Steel, and other
corporations immediately followed. The wage front was broken. Within a year,
sweatshops had mushroomed all through the East. In one factory, 13-year-old
packing girls were paid 50 cents a day; in another plant, apron girls received
a daily wage of 20 cents.

To alleviate the misery of the depression and to use public funds to revive
investment, a group of Senate progressives demanded federal action. Senator
Robert Wagner of New York introduced bills for advance planning of public
works and to create a federal employment service and an agency to gather
unemployment statistics. Together with Wagner, Senators Robert M. La Follette, Jr., of Wisconsin, Edward P. Costigan of Colorado, and Bronson Cutting
of New Mexico advocated federal spending for public works and direct relief.
Hoover peremptorily opposed all these bills. While the relief situation was
rapidly nearing the point of total breakdown, Hoover issued sanguine statements minimizing the number of unemployed and the degree of suffering.

Hoover was quite right in issuing reassuring statements; it would have been
far worse if he had been panicky. It is also understandable that he would
attempt, at first, to rely on local initiative. Hoover's failure lay in his refusal
to admit the collapse of his program and in his rigid rejection of the need for
a new course. When the President's own relief experts reported that unemployment was mounting to incredible levels, he would not believe them. When they
urged him to launch a huge public works program, he disregarded them.
Because of "an aroused sense of public responsibility," Hoover claimed, "those
in destitution and their children are actually receiving more regular and more
adequate care than even in normal times."

In the spring of 1931, a slow upturn in production and employment led some
economists to believe that the United States was pulling out of the depression.
Then disaster struck from abroad. The withdrawal of American dollars from
Europe after the 1929 crash had created serious financial stringency in Europe.
In March, 1931, French bankers called in short-term German and Austrian
notes, a move made partly for political reasons. Unable to meet the demands,
the Kreditanstalt in Vienna buckled. The collapse of the greatest bank in
Austria in turn set off a chain reaction. Heavy withdrawals of gold from
Germany forced the Weimar Republic to default on its reparations payments.
Fearing Germany would go Communist, President von Hindenburg appealed
to Hoover for help.

In June, 1931, President Hoover proposed a one-year moratorium on reparations payments and intergovernmental debts. It was a superb move, but
Hoover received so little cooperation from the French that much of its value
was dissipated. In August, the British, who had gone to the aid of both Austria

and Germany, were caught short themselves. In September, Great Britain abandoned the gold standard. The British decision marked the virtual end of the system of international exchange of nineteenth-century capitalism. . . .

The European financial debacle created a fresh crisis in the United States. As Europeans demanded gold, American banks in turn had to call in their loans to American businesses, and a new wave of liquidations followed. When in October, 1931, Philadelphia's banks were threatened, President Hoover got the more substantial bankers of the country to set up a National Credit Corporation so that strong banks could bolster the weak ones. The strong banks, animated by a sense of *sauve qui peut,* refused to cooperate. . . .

Once the deflation threatened the financial structure, bankers were curiously unwilling to experience the spiritual benefits of chastening. Although they continued to advocate deflation for every other segment of the economy, the bankers demanded government protection from the consequences of deflation to themselves. Fearing that if the policy of deflation was not arrested, bankers would pull their own houses down, Hoover, in December, 1931, proposed the creation of a Reconstruction Finance Corporation. Based on the War Finance Corporation of World War I, the RFC was chartered by Congress in January, 1932, to lend funds to banks, railroads, building and loan associations, and similar institutions.

Hoover followed up the RFC with a series of other antideflationary measures. In January, 1932, new capital was provided for the Federal Land Banks. The Glass-Steagall Act released gold to meet foreign withdrawals and, by liberalizing Federal Reserve requirements, expanded credit. The Federal Home Loan Bank Act, aimed at saving the mortgage market, bolstered building and loan associations. In July, 1932, after Hoover vetoed the Garner-Wagner relief bill, which provided direct relief aid and vast public works, Congress passed a new law authorizing the RFC to lend money to states and municipalities for self-liquidating public works and to lend a smaller sum for relief to states whose resources were exhausted.

Although the RFC helped shore up railroads on the verge of bankruptcy and cut down, at least for a time, bank closings, it did nothing to get the economy rolling again. Bankers viewed the RFC not as a way to expand the volume of credit but as a means of preserving their own and other institutions from bankruptcy. The RFC virtually ignored its role as a public works agency; it moved with exasperating slowness in spending the public works and relief appropriations Congress granted it in 1932. The rest of Hoover's program met with even less success. The railroads and utilities, which had promised to expand construction, contracted their operations instead. New capital issues —investment in stocks and bonds—fell from $10 billion in 1929 to $1 billion in 1932. This was not enough new capital even to maintain the country's industrial plant. Although Hoover increased federal spending on public works, state and local governments cut back so sharply that total public construction declined. The grain and cotton corporations accumulated huge warehouses of surpluses they could not sell. Despite their efforts, the prices of grain and cotton plummeted, and the Federal Farm Board wound up with losses of $184 million. Disgusted with Hoover's insistence on voluntarism, the Board advocated federal compulsion to reduce farm production.

In the months after the crash, people continued to look to the business leaders they had revered in the 1920's to lift them out of the depression. As the months went by, and the outlook blackened, it became clear that the business titans were not miracle workers but as fallible as other mortals. Businessmen, who had claimed credit for the prosperity of the 1920's, were now blamed for producing the depression of the 1930's. . . .

In March, 1932, Ivar Kreuger, one of the most respected international financiers, committed suicide in his Paris apartment. When his affairs were disentangled, it was found that the Swedish Match King had fleeced American investors of a quarter of a billion dollars by duping Lee, Higginson and other presumably astute American investment firms. American financiers had permitted Kreuger to take $50 million in securities from the vaults of the International Match Company without anyone knowing it, and Lee, Higginson had sold Kreuger's issues to the American public without insisting on the elementary step of an independent audit. The same month, Samuel Insull's utility empire collapsed, with a total loss to investers of nearly $700 million. The stock of Insull Utility Investments fell from 107 1/2 in 1929 to 1 1/8 in March, 1932. Soon it was completely worthless. The scapegoat for other businessmen, Insull fled to Paris and crossed the Mediterranean in a dirty Greek steamer to avoid extradition to face a Cook County jury.

Nothing struck a harder blow at the prestige of American business than the phenomenon of want in the midst of plenty. While people went hungry, granaries bulged with wheat no one could sell. While people froze for lack of fuel in winter, snow drifted over the mouths of idle coal pits. With billions of dollars locked up in the banks, Iowa towns issued scrip and stores in the state of Washington issued and accepted wooden money. Knoxville, Atlanta, and Richmond printed their own currency. . . .

Technology was the god of the 1920's. When the depression struck, technology was denounced for bringing the curse of plenty. Men relentlessly sabotaged the production on which they had preened themselves in the Coolidge years. In 1932, Representative Hatton Sumners of Texas urged that the Patent Office cease giving patents on labor-saving devices. In the winter of 1930, Newark abandoned machines for hand excavation, and Minneapolis used picks and shovels. Boston stored away its snow-loading machines to give men work with snow shovels that winter. When Henry Ford, who had done as much as any man to mechanize agriculture, hired men to harvest crops on his farms, he equipped them only with old-fashioned hoes. Kansas, the most highly mechanized agricultural state in the country, restored hitching racks in front of courthouses.

Many Americans who had never had a "radical" thought before in their lives began to question the virtues of American capitalism. Scott Fitzgerald, who by the summer of 1932 was reading Karl Marx, wrote: "To bring on the revolution, it may be necessary to work inside the communist party." How, critics asked, could one justify a system that wilfully destroyed its crops and cast aside its machines? "When I think of what has been happening since unemployment began, and when I see the futility of the leaders," declared Father John A. Ryan, "I wish we might double the number of Communists in this country, to put the fear, if not of God, then the fear of something else, into the hearts of our leaders.". . .

As the bread lines lengthened, the mood of the country became uglier. In July, 1931, 300 unemployed men stormed the food shops of Henryetta, Oklahoma. An army of 15,000 pickets marched on Taylorville, Illinois, and stopped operations at the Christian County Mines in 1932. In Washington, D.C., 3,000 Communist "hunger marchers" paraded. None of these demonstrations matched in importance the rebellion of American farmers From Bucks County, Pennsylvania, to Antelope County, Nebraska, farmers banded together to prevent banks and insurance companies from foreclosing mortgages. When sheriffs attempted to carry out foreclosures, mobs of farmers, brandishing pitchforks and dangling hangman's nooses, persuaded the sheriffs to retreat. In Iowa—the center of stable Republican farm life—once prosperous farmers, leaving their neat white houses and rich lands behind, barricaded highways to prevent milk from getting to market in a vain effort to force up prices. In a national radio broadcast, John A. Simpson, president of the National Farmers' Union, denounced the wealthy as "cannibals that eat each other and who live on the labor of the workers.". . .

Demanding immediate and full payment of bonuses for their service in World War I, an army of 15,000 to 20,000 unemployed veterans moved on Washington in the spring of 1932. The House passed the bonus bill, but when the Senate voted the bill down by an overwhelming margin, half the men left the city. The rest stayed on; they had no jobs, no homes, no place else to go. Most of them lived in mean shanties on the muddy Anacostia flats, some camped in unused government buildings. General Glassford, the head of the District, treated the men with decency and with discretion, but, as the men stayed on day after day, Hoover and his officials panicked. On July 28, 1932, the Government decided precipitately to evict a group of bonus marchers from vacant government buildings on Pennsylvania Avenue. Two veterans were killed and several District police were injured in a scuffle that followed. President Hoover summoned the U.S. Army to take over.

With machine guns, tanks, and tear gas, brandishing sabers and drawn bayonets, the Army, in full battle regalia, advanced on the ragged group of bonus marchers. Led by the Army Chief of Staff, Douglas MacArthur (Dwight Eisenhower and George Patton were two of his junior officers) the Army dispersed the marchers and burned their billets. Hoover, whose attack on the veterans had aligned much of the country against him, made matters worse by releasing a report of the Attorney-General accusing the bonus army of being composed of Communists and criminals. General MacArthur, who called the veterans "a mob . . . animated by the essence of revolution" added to the sense that the government had lost its sense of proportion. If Hoover had "let it go on another week," MacArthur declared, "I believe that the institutions of our Government would have been very severely threatened."

By the summer of 1932, Hoover was subject to open contempt. None of his efforts seemed to do much good, and a great deal that he had said was less than honest. The country was convinced that Hoover, who more than any American of his generation had won the reputation of Great Humanitarian, was a cold-hearted man, indifferent to suffering. Scurrilous biographies were circulated accusing Hoover of having indulged in slave-trading, profited from Belgian relief, and even having caused the execution of Nurse Edith Cavell. His name became a trademark for every artifact of the depression. Men who slept on park benches dubbed the newspapers with which they covered themselves "Hoover blankets." A pocket turned inside out was a "Hoover flag." In the Southwest, harvest hands sang "Hoover made a souphound outa me."

Hoover was victimized by the excessive expectations which public relations men had built up in 1928. A man of great administrative ability, he possessed almost no political gifts. He had an aversion to the tortuous practices of democracy. Lacking skill at political maneuver, he met every situation with the directness of a rhinoceros. No one could question his devotion to his office. Hoover, observes Allan Nevins, worked "as hard as any resident of the White House since James K. Polk worked himself to death there." But, apart from his political failings and his questionable economic policies, he did not have the personality to inspire the people. . . . When asked to stir the people, President Hoover would tell his friends glumly: "I have no Wilsonian qualities."

Since it seemed almost certain that the Democrats would win in November, a keen contest developed for the Democratic presidential nomination. When New York's Governor Franklin D. Roosevelt won re-election by a landslide in 1930, he immediately established himself as the leading contender. A distant cousin of Theodore Roosevelt, he had much of Teddy's gusto. Although he took some time to grasp the seriousness of the depression—he dismissed it at first as a "little Flurry down town"—he soon was meeting it with Rooseveltian vigor. His economics was Victorian; at the Governor's Conference in Salt Lake

City in June, 1930, Roosevelt attacked Hoover for attempting to violate the natural laws of economics and the principle of laissez faire. Yet Roosevelt established the first state relief agency in the country and by 1932 had won almost every progressive in the party to his cause. In his humanitarian approach to politics, in his love of experimentation, and in his impatience with economic fatalism, Roosevelt suggested that beneath his cautious platitudes lay the promise of an audacious program.

The fight for the Democratic nomination quickly settled down to a stop-Roosevelt campaign. Al Smith, piqued by Roosevelt's rise to eminence while Smith's fortunes were declining and riled at Roosevelt's refusal to retain Smith's advisers in Albany, led the opposition. Although the conflict was essentially a clash of personalities, Smith injected an ideological note in the campaign as well, for he was aligned with the most conservative elements in the Democratic party. When Roosevelt in April, 1932, pleaded for "the forgotten man at the bottom of the economic pyramid," Smith, his face red with anger, retorted, "This is no time for demagogues." Although it seemed unlikely that Smith could win the Democratic nomination himself, it was quite conceivable that Smith could muster enough votes to block Roosevelt's nomination and throw the honor to someone else. Of the myriad of other candidates, John Garner, the Democratic Speaker in the House, had the strongest support, but astute observers believed that, if the convention deadlocked, the nomination might well go to Wilson's Secretary of War, Newton Baker, an internationalist who was conservative on economic issues.

At the Democratic convention in Chicago in June, Roosevelt took a sizable lead over his nearest rivals, Smith and Garner, but when, after three ballots, Roosevelt was unable to obtain the two-thirds vote necessary for victory, it appeared that he might be denied the nomination. At this critical juncture, California decided to throw its Garner votes to Roosevelt. The reasons for the California decision are not certain, but there is a persistent belief that it was based on the determination of William Randolph Hearst to prevent the convention from turning to the internationalist Baker. Even more important was Garner's refusal to permit the Democratic party to deadlock and destroy itself as it had in 1924. On the fourth ballot, Senator William McAdoo, whose presidential hopes had been frustrated by Smith in 1924, announced California's switch. As he stalked to the platform, he allegedly whispered: "Here's where I even up scores." The California vote turned the tide for Roosevelt; Garner, possibly as the result of an informal deal, gained the vice-presidential nomination.

Neither convention seemed as concerned about the depression as it did about the prohibition issue. "Here we are in the midst of the greatest crisis since the Civil War," wrote John Dewey, "and the only thing the two national parties seem to want to debate is booze." Save for prohibition—the Democrats were wringing wet, while the Republicans hedged—there were few important differences between the parties. The one major distinction established during the campaign was that Roosevelt, who, for an old Wilsonian, had become strongly nationalist, traced the depression to domestic causes, while Hoover emphasized its European origins.

At times, Roosevelt's campaign speeches anticipated the New Deal; he talked of the need for experimentation, indorsed social welfare legislation, outlined the idea of the Civilian Conservation Corps, and urged public power development and government regulation of utilities. But a great deal of what he said was double talk. While he promised expensive national reforms, he pledged at the same time a 25 per cent cut in the budget and censured Hoover's administration as "the greatest spending administration in peace times in all our history"—one which had "piled bureau on bureau, commission on commission.". . . His tariff policy was contradictory; his farm speech at Topeka was designed to mean all things to all men. Running safely ahead, Roosevelt saw no point in unnecessary militancy. On Election Day, the country gave Roosevelt 22,800,000 votes to Hoover's 15,750,000. Roosevelt captured all but six states; he swung every state south and west of Pennsylvania.

The vote was less triumph for Roosevelt than a rejection of Hoover. . . .

CHAPTER 16

THE PRESIDENCY OF HERBERT HOOVER

One of the great ironies of United States history is that the full blame of the Great Depression should fall on the man who had so little responsibility for the policies that led to it and who labored so hard to end it—Herbert Hoover. It is also ironic, as Carl Degler points out in the following essay, that Hoover, a symbol of progressivism in the 1920s, should be forever incarnated as the archetype of reaction. Hoover began his public career as a humanitarian. He went out of office roundly despised and ridiculed as callous and heartless. This alone justifies the description of his term as President as an "ordeal."

It has been an article of faith in liberal circles since the 1930s that Hoover, as President, was inept, regressive, and unfeeling. Until the 1960s this opinion had been reinforced by the historical accounts of the man and his term in office. His predecessors received credit for the boom and his successor was credited with bringing the nation through the post crash crisis. The Hoover years were viewed as a dismal interlude between the colorful excesses of the Jazz Age and the exhilarating dynamism of the New Deal. Studies of the last two decades, like the following selection, have done much to reverse this view.

Although the reinterpretations do much to improve Hoover's historical image, they do not answer all the questions about his presidency, nor do they leave him without political flaws. Why, for example, was Hoover so adamantly opposed to direct welfare grants? He had approved such aid to the Belgians in the World War I years. Were not the victims of the depression as innocent and helpless as the victims of the war? Why did the concept of the balanced budget hold such a fatal attraction, not only to Hoover but also to the other leading politicians of the time? What was there about Hoover's personality that made him unbending and unwilling to change, to admit error, or to try something new? How valid is Degler's suggestion that Hoover's climb from poverty to success greatly influenced his reaction to possible solutions to the Great Depression?

The student interested in going more deeply into these matters should read the works suggested for the preceding topic. For a more detailed analysis of the Hoover period, see Joan Hoff Wilson, *Herbert Hoover, Forgotten Progressive* (1975); Harris Warren, *Herbert Hoover and the Great Depression** (1959); and Albert U. Romasco, *The Politics of Abundance: Hoover, the Nation and the Depression** (1965).

*Available in a paperback edition.

THE ORDEAL OF HERBERT HOOVER

CARL N. DEGLER

In 1958 Herbert Hoover published a book about his old chief entitled *The Ordeal of Woodrow Wilson*. Wilson's struggle for the League was short and his part in it has gained lustre with passing years. Not so with the ordeal of Herbert Hoover. The Great Depression was considerably longer and his reputation has never been free from the memory of that ordeal. Today, in fact, there are two Hoovers. The first is the living man, the former President who has unstintingly and very capably served Democratic and Republican Administrations alike. He is the Hoover of nation-wide birthday celebrations, of rhapsodic editorials, of admiring Republican national conventions. That conception bears almost no relation to the second, the historical Hoover. In the history books his Administration is usually depicted as cold-hearted, when not pictured as totally devoid of heart, inept, or actionless in the face of the Great Depression. Simply because of the wide gulf between the two Hoovers it is time to try to answer the question William Allen White posed over thirty years ago. Writing an evaluation of Hoover's Administration in the *Saturday Evening Post* of March 4, 1933, White closed his piece with the following words: "So history stands hesitant waiting for time to tell whether Herbert Hoover . . . by pointing the way to social recovery . . . is the first of the new Presidents . . . or whether . . . he is the last of the old."

The notion of two Hoovers should never have grown up; his life and views were too consistent for that. During Hoover's tenure of office, Theodore Joslin, his press secretary, undertook to examine closely all the President's utterances and writings of the preceding ten or eleven years. "In all of those million-odd words, dealing with every important subject," Joslin reported in 1934, "the number of times he reversed himself or modified an important position could be counted on the fingers of one hand." And so it has remained even after March 4, 1933.

Nor were those principles, to which Hoover held so consistently, simply conservative ones, as has so often been assumed. In 1920, for example, when Hoover's political career began, he was the darling of the progressives who still

SOURCE. Carl N. Degler, "The Ordeal of Herbert Hoover," *The Yale Review*, LII (Summer 1963), pp. 563–583. Copyright © 1963 by *The Yale Review*. Reprinted by permission of *The Yale Review*.

clustered about the figure of the fallen Wilson. College and university faculties were calling upon Hoover to run for president that year—on either ticket. Indeed, his silence as to which party he belonged to for a time caused his name to figure as prominently in Democratic primaries as in Republican. For example, he received the most votes by far in the Michigan Democratic primary that year. That year, too, Franklin Roosevelt, who was also a member of Woodrow Wilson's Administration, wrote Josephus Daniels that Herbert Hoover "is certainly a wonder, and I wish we could make him President of the United States. There could not be a better one." (Nor did Roosevelt's enthusiasm cool until much later. In 1928 he refused to write an article against Hoover's candidacy because Hoover was "an old personal friend.")

Hoover's principles were distinctly and publicly progressive. In 1920, for example, he defended the principle of collective bargaining and the right to strike—two very unpopular principles at that date—before a frosty Chamber of Commerce in Boston. As Secretary of Commerce in the Harding Administration he opposed the sweeping federal injunction against the railroad strikers and worked with Harding to have the steel industry abandon the twelve-hour day. In his book of guiding principles, *American Individualism,* which was published in 1922, he was careful to distinguish his views from laissez-faire capitalism. The American way, he insisted, "is not capitalism, or socialism, or syndicalism, nor a cross breed of them." It did include, though, government regulation in order to preserve equality of opportunity and individual rights. . . . While Secretary of Commerce in the 1920's he instituted much needed regulations for the burgeoning radio and airplane industries. It was Herbert Hoover who said in 1922 at the first conference on radio that "the ether is a public medium and its use must be for the public benefit. The use of radio channels is justified only if there is public benefit. The dominant element of consideration in the radio field is, and always will be, the great body of the listening public, millions in number, country-wide in distribution." . . . In 1928 he was recommending that a three billion dollar reserve of public works be built up to serve as an economic stabilizer in times of recession.

In short, though he served both Harding and Coolidge, Herbert Hoover was not of their stripe. . . . Moreover, unlike Coolidge, Hoover did not publicly ignore the scandals that rocked the Harding Administration. In June, 1931, while dedicating the Harding Memorial at Marion, Ohio, Hoover went out of his way to speak of the tragedy of Warren Harding and the enormity of the betrayal of a public trust by Harding's friends.

Hoover's record as president contains a number of truly progressive achievements. Although he cannot take credit for initiating the Norris-LaGuardia Act of 1932, the fact remains that one of the most important prolabor acts in the whole history of American labor was signed by Herbert Hoover. Like other progressives, he sponsored legislation for conservation like the giant Boulder Dam project and the St. Lawrence Seaway.

But perhaps the most striking example of Hoover's willingness to recognize the new role of government in dealing with the complexities of an industrial economy was his breaking precedent to grapple directly with the Depression. . . .

Within a matter of weeks after the great crash of the stock market at the end of October, Hoover called a meeting of prominent business, labor, and farm leaders to work out plans for preventing the market crash from adversely affecting the rest of the economy. A week later he met for the same purpose with railway presidents. The economic leaders agreed to his plan of holding the line on wages and encouraging industrial expansion. In his annual message to Congress in December 1929, Hoover proudly told of these and other efforts his Administration had made to stem the economic decline. These efforts, he said, "must be vigorously pursued until normal conditions are restored." In January he continued to expand public works on Boulder Dam and on highway construction. By the end of July 1930, the Administration had got underway $800 million in public works, and the President called upon the states and local units of government to follow the national government's example in order to provide as much employment as possible.

The President was well aware of the unprecedented character of his swift anti-depression action. He said as much in his message to Congress in December 1929; he made the same point more explicitly at the Gridiron dinner in April 1930. The country, he said, had avoided the dole and other unsatisfactory devices to meet unemployment by "voluntary cooperation of industry with the Government in maintaining wages against reductions, and the intensification of construction work. Thereby we have inaugurated one of the greatest economic experiments in history on a basis of nation-wide cooperation not charity."

At first Hoover was optimistic about the effects of his program. Several times during the first year he compared the economic decline with that of 1921-22, usually with the observation that the earlier one was the more difficult. As he told the Chamber of Commerce in May 1930, the amount of public works contracted for was already three times the amount in the corresponding period of the previous "great depression."

Yet his optimism did not keep him from action. One thing he emphasized was the necessity of learning from this Depression about the prevention of future ones. He advocated better statistical measures and reform of the banking structure to prevent the drain of credit from productive to speculative enterprise, such as had led to the stock market boom and crash. Moreover, although he emphasized from the beginning that the Depression was "worldwide" and that its "causes and its effects lie only partly in the United States," he did not use this as an excuse for inactivity. . . . In October 1930 he told the American Bankers Association that depressions were not simply to be borne uncomplainingly. . . .

Hoover also told the bankers that he could not condone the argument which had been reported from some of them that the people would have to accept a lower standard of living in order to get through the Depression. Such a suggestion, he said, could not be countenanced either on idealistic or on practical grounds. . . . Several times during the Depression Hoover made it clear that the government had a responsibility to employ as many as possible as its contribution to the mitigation of the unemployment which was growing alarmingly.

The failure of the economy to respond to treatment and the loss of many Republican seats in the elections of 1930 caused Hoover for a while to place new emphasis upon the foreign sources of the Depression. At the end of 1930 he told the Congress that the "major forces of the depression now lie outside of the United States." In fact, though, the real collapse of the European economy was still almost six months away. Hoover was most fearful that the growing Congressional demands for new expenditures would throw the budget out of balance. . . . "We cannot legislate ourselves out of a world economic depression; we can and will work ourselves out."

The last sentence, because it was obviously too sweeping to be accurate, was to plague him for years. More important, he quite clearly did not believe it himself, since he later advocated legislation for just the purposes he said it could not serve. In the very next month, for example, he explained at some length to a group of Republican editors just how much the Administration had been doing to extricate the country from the Depression. . . . Unlike previous administrations, he continued, his had expanded, instead of curtailing, public works during a depression. Public works expenditures, both by the federal and state governments, he said, continued to increase. Some two billion dollars were being spent, and a million men were employed on these projects. Aid was also being given to farmers in the drought areas of the South and the Middle West.

That Hoover truly favored action over patient waiting for the storm to lift was further shown in his elaborate twelve-point program for recovery presented in his annual message in December 1931. Among his recommendations was the Reconstruction Finance Corporation, which would become one of the major agencies of his Administration and of the New Deal for stabilizing banks and aiding recovery. At a press conference the same month he emphasized anew the desirability of domestic action. . . . By early February 1932 the Reconstruction Finance Corporation was in operation. That same month he persuaded the Congress to enact the Glass-Steagall banking bill, which increased the bases for Federal Reserve bank reserves and thus expanded and conserved gold. The purpose of the RFC was to shore up failing banks and other financial institutions caught in runs upon their deposits. With the permission of the Interstate Commerce Commission, the RFC could also extend financial aid to railroads.

Beyond these operations, though, the President would not let the lending agency go. Especially did he resist federal aid to the unemployed, although the demands for it were growing monthly. He even opposed Congressional appropriations to the Red Cross on the ground that they would dry up private sources of relief funds. . . . He did urge the citizenry generously to support, as he did himself, private charities, like the Red Cross, which were carrying so much of the burden of unemployment relief. At no time, of course, did Hoover object to helping the unemployed; he was no Social Darwinist arguing for the survival of only the fittest. Again and again, using the most idealistic language, he called upon Americans to extend a hand to those fellow citizens in need. But as much as he publicly and privately deplored the suffering which the economic crisis brought, he feared and deplored even more the effects which would be sure to follow if the federal government provided relief to the unemployed. Nowhere was the rigidity of Hoover's highly trained, agile, and well-stocked intellect more apparent than in this matter. Throughout his years as president, despite the cruelest of sarcastic barbs in the press and from the public platform, he held to his position.

Yet surprising as it may seem today, for a long time the country was with him. This was true even during 1931 and early 1932 when it was becoming increasingly evident that private charities, municipal relief funds, and even the resources of the states were inadequate to meet the costs of providing for ten or eleven million unemployed. Already in August 1931 Governor Franklin Roosevelt had told the New York legislature that unemployment relief "must be extended by government—not as a matter of charity but as a matter of social duty." Yet, as late as February 1932 the country was still following Hoover's view of relief and not Roosevelt's. This was shown by the fate of a bill sponsored by liberal Senators Robert M. La Follette, Jr. of Wisconsin and Edward F. Costigan of Colorado to provide federal money to the states for relief. The bill was defeated by a vote of 48 to 35. Democratic Senators made up some forty percent of the votes which killed the measure.

By May 1932, though, the pressure for some federal assistance in relief matters was building up fast. The National Conference of Social Workers, which in the previous year had refused to endorse the principle of federal relief, now switched to supporting it. More important from Hoover's standpoint was the announcement by Senator Joseph Robinson, the conservative Democratic leader in the Senate, that he was joining the liberals in favoring federal relief. Within two days the President announced, after consultation with Robinson, that the RFC would hereafter lend money to the states if their resources for relief were exhausted. The next day the President defended the extraordinary powers of the RFC as necessitated by the economic emergency. . . .

Soon thereafter, though, the President demonstrated that he would not take another step toward putting the federal government into the relief field. Two bills by Democrats which went beyond his limits were successfully vetoed. After Congress had adjourned in July 1932, he issued a nine-point program for economic recovery, but most of the items on it were old and the rest were only recommendations for exploratory conferences. By the summer of 1932, then, the Hoover program for recovery had been completed; his principles would permit him to go no further.

As one reviews the actions which Hoover took it is impossible to describe him as a do-nothing president. He was unquestionably one of the truly activist presidents of our history. But he was an activist within a very rigid framework of ideology. Of all American presidents, Herbert Hoover was probably the most singlemindedly committed to a system of beliefs. His pragmatism was well hidden and what there was of it emerged only after great prodding from events. To a remarkable degree, one can observe in his acts as president those principles of individualism which he set forth so simply in his book ten years before. The very same principle, for example, which prevented his sanctioning federal relief to the unemployed, dictated the tone and content of his veto of the bill to create a government corporation to operate Muscle Shoals. The government, he said, should not compete with private enterprise. . . . It was the same belief in individual freedom and cooperation which kept him from accepting a governmental system of old age and unemployment insurance. He advocated such measures only when undertaken voluntarily and through private insurance companies.

Even the Reconstruction Finance Corporation, perhaps his most enduring anti-depression agency, was created to assist private business, not to supplant it. True, it was a credit agency in competition with private enterprise, but it was designed to perform tasks which no private institution dared risk; the competition was therefore minimal if not nonexistent. Moreover, although it has been frequently alleged that the RFC lent money to corporations while the Administration denied relief to the unemployed, in Hoover's mind the distinction was crucial and real. The RFC was making loans which would be repaid —and most were—when the banks got back on their feet; it was not making grants. Even when Hoover did permit the RFC to lend money to the states for relief purposes he still insisted that no grants of federal funds be made.

But there was an even more important social justification for agencies like the RFC and the Federal Home Loan Board, which Congress created in July 1932 at the President's request. Hoover recognized as no president had before that the welfare of society was dependent upon business and that government, therefore, must step in. He did this, not because, as some critics said, he favored business over the common people, but because he recognized that if the banks failed the economy would collapse, savings would be lost, and jobs destroyed. The RFC and the Federal Home Loan Board, in effect, socialized the losses of financial institutions by using government to spread their obligations through society. Hoover was not prepared, though, to socialize the losses of the unemployed. That step in ameliorating the impact of the Depression was undertaken by the New Deal through the WPA and other relief agencies. In this respect Hoover was a transitional figure in the development of the government as an active force in the economy in times of depression. He was the first to smash the old shibboleth of government unconcern and impotence.

Perhaps his long-term role was even greater. In the face of great opposition and much outright hostility, he made a determined and even courageous effort to give the business community and voluntary private agencies a chance to show whether they could bring the nation out of a depression. Their failure to do so gave a moral as well as a political impetus to the New Deal. Just as after Munich no one could say the West had not done its utmost to meet Hitler halfway, so after Hoover's Administration no one could say that government had rushed in before other social or economic agencies had been given a try. That this was so goes a long way toward explaining the remarkable consensus among Americans ever since the 1930's that government has the prime responsibility for averting or cushioning the effect of a depression.

A second principle which stopped Hoover from permitting the federal government to provide relief was his conviction that the budget must not be unbalanced. As early as February 1930 he warned the Congress against extravagance and told of his own efforts to economize. Economy was essential, he emphasized, in order to avoid increasing taxes. But as decreasing revenues began to fall behind expenditures, Hoover's concern to keep the budget in balance overcame his reluctance to increase taxes. On July 1, 1931 the deficit was almost $500 million—an astronomical figure in those days when the total federal budget was less than $4 billion. In December of that same year Hoover recommended an increase in taxes. When Congress proved dilatory he told a press conference in March 1932 that a balanced budget "is the very keystone to recovery. It must be done." Anything less would undo all the recovery measures. . . .

Hoover recommended a manufacturers' sales tax as the chief new revenue device, in which suggestion he was joined by the new Democratic Speaker of the House, John Nance Garner of Texas. Garner enjoyed a reputation for being hostile to business and something of a radical in the old Populist tradition, but in the matter of bringing the budget into balance he stood four-square with the President. Congress did not pass the sales tax, but it did pass one of the largest peacetime tax increases in American history.

Today it seems incredible that in a time of economic slump when consumer purchasing power was the principal requirement for recovery, the nation should elect to take money out of the hands of consumers. Yet this was precisely what the bill, recommended and signed by the Republican President and passed by the Democratic House, entailed. In fact, when in the course of the debate the House seemed hesitant about increasing taxes, the Democratic Speaker, John Garner, could not contain his anxiety. Conspicuously forsaking the Speaker's chair, Garner advanced to the well of the House to make an earnest plea for more taxes. At the conclusion of his speech, he asked "every man and every woman in this House who . . . is willing to try to balance the budget to rise in their seats." Almost the whole House, with its majority of Democrats, rose to its feet, to a growing round of applause. When he asked those who did not want to balance the budget to rise, no one did. The overwhelming majority of the newspapers of the country strongly commended the Congress in June 1932 for its efforts to balance the budget through increased taxes.

During the campaign of 1932 the Democrats continued to equal or even outdo Hoover in their slavish adherence to the ideal of a balanced budget. Franklin Roosevelt, for example, unmercifully attacked the Administration for its extravagance and its unbalanced budget, calling the fifty percent increase in expenditures since 1927 "the most reckless and extravagant past that I have been able to discover in the statistical record of any peacetime government anywhere, any time." He promised a cut of 25 percent in the budget if he were elected. Nor was this simply campaign oratory. As Frank Freidel has observed in his biography, Roosevelt was perfectly sincere in his dismay at the Hoover deficit and he would continue to be regretful about deficits until well after 1933.

From the record, then, it is evident that Democrats were in no better theoretical position to deal with the Depression than Hoover. Leaders of both parties thought of the government as a large household whose accounts must be balanced if national bankruptcy were to be avoided. Neither party could conceive of the central role which government must play in the economy in an industrial society in time of depression. It would take the whole decade of the New Deal and the continuance of the Depression before that fact would be learned by leaders and people alike.

Despite his fixation on the question of the budget, Hoover's conception of the Depression was sophisticated, rational, and coherent; the remedies he suggested were equally so, given his assumptions. In trying to find a way out, Hoover placed most reliance on what modern economists would call the "expectations" of businessmen. If businessmen feel that times are good or at least that they are getting better, they will invest in new plants and equipment, which in turn will employ men and create purchasing power. In substance, the remedies Hoover offered were designed to raise the expectations of businessmen and to maintain purchasing power until the economy picked up again. His first step was securing agreement among businessmen to hold the line on wages in order to keep purchasing power from falling. (And, by and large, as a result of his efforts, wage rates did not fall until the middle of 1931, but employment did, with, unfortunately, the same effect.) A second step in his program was to use government to help out with public work projects and, when private agencies proved inadequate, to provide credit through agencies like the RFC and the Home Loan Board. Finally, as a third arrow in his anti-depression quiver, Hoover sought, through the prestige of his office, to create that sense of confidence and approaching good times which would encourage businessmen to invest. As it turned out, though, he gambled and lost. . . .

The Hoover recovery program failed, but probably no government program then thought permissible could have been any more successful. Certainly the New Deal with its more massive injection of government money into the economy succeeded little better. It ended the decade with 9.5 million still unemployed, and industrial production remained below the 1929 level throughout the 1930's except for a brief period in late 1936 and early 1937. On the other hand, most of the countries of Western and Central Europe regained the 1929 level of production by early 1935.

Part of Hoover's ordeal during the Great Depression undoubtedly derived from his personality, which, for a president, was unusual. Indeed, until he became President he had rarely been connected with government other than in an office which was nonpartisan or which he soon made so. Outwardly, at least, he was far removed from the stereotype of the politician; he would not slap a back or utter a guffaw. He appeared shy in public, though stolid was a more accurate description. A bulky man of over 200 pounds, standing almost six feet when he entered the White House, he gave a paradoxical impression of conservative solidity and beaming youth at the same time. His public speech, like his writing, was formal, often stiff, and sometimes bordered on the pedantic. Early in Hoover's Administration, soon after the stock market crash, William Allen White, a Hoover supporter, spotted the new President's weakness. "The President has great capacity to convince intellectuals," he wrote. "He has small capacity to stir people emotionally and through the emotions one gets to the will, not through the intellect." Even Hoover's press secretary recognized that he "experienced the greatest difficulty in interpreting himself and his acts to the public.". . .

In view of his poor public image, it is not surprising that for most of his presidency, Hoover's relations with the press were strained when not downright painful. Although he continued the press conferences which Wilson had begun, they were formal affairs with written questions; many reporters were convinced that the President concealed more than he revealed in the meetings. But it was probably Hoover's sensitivity to criticism that worked the real damage. His annual addresses to newspapermen at the Gridiron Club, which, as was customary, mercilessly lampooned his administration, often carried an edge, betraying his sensitivity to the press corps' jibes. . . .

Yet despite his difficulties as a public figure, in private Hoover was neither phlegmatic nor shy. In fact he was extremely convivial, seeking constant company, whether at the White House or at his retreat on the Rapidan in the Blue Ridge Mountains. His wife told Joslin that the President could not be happy without numbers of people around him. His friends cherished his constant flow of stories and he delighted in his cigars and pipe. He was an outdoor type of man, reveling in fishing and hiking. Although he liked a joke, he rarely laughed out loud, though his friends knew well his soft chuckle. . . .

Part of the reason Hoover resented the barbed comments of the press was that he worked so hard. It was as characteristic of Herbert Hoover that he was the first president to have a telephone on his desk as it was characteristic of Calvin Coolidge that he refused to have one. Hoover rose at 6 a.m. each morning, joined a group of his friends for a brisk half-hour session with a five pound medicine ball on an improvised court on the White House grounds, then went in to breakfast. He was at his desk by 8:30. He worked steadily all day, smoking incessantly, and usually well into the night. Often he would wake up in the middle of the night and pore over papers or write for an hour or two before going back to sleep. Nevertheless, he rose at the same early hour. Subordinates were not always able to keep up with his pace; some had to be dispatched to rest, but Hoover, miraculously, never succumbed to his self-imposed regiment. His secretary reports that he was not sick a single day of the four years he spent in the White House. A few days at the camp on the Rapidan or a short trip usually sufficed to restore his energies and his will to work. . . .

Aside from the circumstances in which he found himself as President, one of the reasons the office was "hell" was that Hoover was a poor politician. Often it is said that he did not like politics, or even that he was above politics. Both statements describe the image he held of himself, but many of Hoover's actions while in office are clearly partisan and political. . . . In December 1931, when some voices were calling for a coalition government to deal with the worsening depression, Hoover made it clear that he would have nothing to do with Democrats. . . . On the other hand, he would appoint Democrats to office, as he did former Senator Atlee Pomerene to head the RFC when he wanted that office to win support from Democrats. Nor was he devoid of political dramatics. In September 1931 he made a quick descent upon the American Legion Convention in Detroit in a successful effort to stop the Legion from going on record in favor of a bonus for veterans. By going all the way to Detroit, speaking for eleven minutes, and then immediately leaving for Washington again, he demonstrated the importance of his message and the weight of the schedule of work he pursued in Washington. Moreover, as the account written by his Press Secretary Joslin makes clear, he was no more above benefiting from parliamentary trickery in Congress than the next politically-minded president. . . . Hoover suffered deeply when attacked, and he did not turn the other cheek. As William Allen White, who supported and admired the President, wrote in 1933, "he was no plaster saint politically. He had, during his three years, rather consistently and with a nice instinct chosen to honor in public office men of a conservative type of mind." Moreover, the behind-the-scenes circumstances of his nomination in 1928 and his renomination in 1932, both of which were steam-roller operations, should remove any doubts about his willingness and ability to use devices and tactics quite customary in politics.

No, it was not that he was above politics or that he really despised the operations of politicians. His difficulty was that he was temperamentally incapable of doing what a politician has to do—namely, to admit he could be wrong and to compromise. In the whole volume of his memoirs devoted to the Depression there is not a single mention of a major error on his part, though his opponents are taxed with errors in every chapter. Over a hundred pages of the volume are devoted to the answering of every charge of Franklin Roosevelt in 1932. Nowhere, though, does he notice that in 1932, he himself in his speech at Detroit incorrectly quoted Roosevelt and then proceeded to criticize at length his opponent for something he never said. This inability to admit error, to compromise, William Allen White recognized in 1931 as Hoover's undoing. . . . Hoover's inability to admit error and the seriousness with which he viewed himself are both illustrated in another incident during the campaign of 1932. One of the Democrats' favorite sports that year was recalling, with appropriate sounds of derision, Hoover's remarks in 1928 to the effect that the United States was well on the way to abolishing poverty. Hoover, instead of admitting he had been somewhat optimistic, once again donned his hair shirt and stolidly endorsed the earlier statement because, as he said, it expressed the ideals for which Americans stood. Yet this was in the middle of the Depression and he was running for reelection.

In good times, Herbert Hoover's humble birth might have been an asset, but in the Great Depression it was not. Left an almost penniless orphan at nine, Hoover became a world figure and a millionaire before he was forty-five. With such spectacular success behind him it was understandable that he should think, albeit mistakenly, that anyone could achieve at least half as much as he. Undoubtedly his own experience fostered his insistence, throughout his life, that individual initiative was the prime motive force in a good society. What to other men appear as obstacles or handicaps, to the self-made man appear, at least in retrospect, as goads or incentives. Like most such men, Hoover attributed his success to will. . . . To such a man individual effort seems capable of moving mountains unaided; he is loath to see it shunted aside by collective action even in times of economic dislocation. The self-made man can indeed be the wrong man at such times.

Nor was it an accident that the other prominent self-made politician of the time, Alfred E. Smith, was also doubtful about the virtues of government aid to the unemployed, that he should attack Franklin Roosevelt for accusing the Hoover Administration of aiding the corporations and ignoring the poor. . . . In a short time, Smith's views, like Hoover's, would bring him to outright opposition to the New Deal. It is not without significance in this respect that Roosevelt, who came to represent government benevolence toward the unemployed, was no self-made man, but lived securely and unadventurously on inherited wealth.

The differences in social origins of Roosevelt and Hoover, of course, are only one facet of the divergence between the Hoover Administration and the New Deal. Indeed, since the 1930's it has become commonplace to see Hoover and Roosevelt as opposites. Certainly there are differences—and important ones— between the administrations of the two Presidents, but we are now far enough removed from both to recognize also the real continuity between them that William Allen White was prescient enough to foresee dimly. When the two administrations are seen against the backdrop of previous administrations and earlier social attitudes, the gulf between them shrinks appreciably. Both men, it is worth recalling, were protégés of Woodrow Wilson; both of them, therefore, accepted a role for government in the economy which added up to a sharp departure from laissez-faire. Both, in the course of their respective administrations, drew upon their experiences in the First World War, where they had seen government intervening in the economy. Hoover's RFC, for example, was frankly modeled, as he said, after the War Finance Corporation. Both saw big business standing in need of controls, and, for a while, both believed that cooperation between business and government was the best way to achieve that control. Hoover, for instance, cited the Federal Reserve System as the ideal kind of business and government cooperation for purposes of regulating the economy; Roosevelt in the NRA also placed his trust in controls worked out through business and government cooperation. Moreover, both Roosevelt and Hoover took the view that it was government's responsibility to do something about a depression; neither man was willing to subscribe to the view which prevailed before 1929—namely, that economic declines were simply natural phenomena through which the nation struggled as best it could and that government could not be expected to do much about them.

Finally, it is also worth noticing that the temperament of the two men, their conceptions of America and of its future are much closer than the conventional picture paints them. . . . All through the Depression, Hoover's unvarying theme was that all this would pass and the essential vigor of the American economy would reassert itself. Undoubtedly he counted too heavily on the influence of his words to overcome the lack of business confidence, but there is no question of his optimistic outlook. One measure of it was the shock he received when he read Roosevelt's address to the Commonwealth Club in San Francisco. That was the speech in which Roosevelt talked about the frontier being ended and opportunities for economic growth being limited. . . . Although historians have frequently referred to the Commonwealth Club address as the one clear indication during the campaign of 1932 of the philosophy behind the New Deal, we now know that the speech was neither written by Roosevelt, nor read by him before he appeared before his audience. As Rexford Tugwell has pointed out, the Commonwealth Club address, which Berle and he wrote, did not reflect Roosevelt's true attitude toward the American economic future. Indeed, its very singularity among Roosevelt's campaign speeches demonstrates how foreign it was to Roosevelt's feelings and convictions. The speech belied his abundant enthusiasm for the future, and his deep faith in the country and its capacities. Moreover, he soon contradicted its import in his Inaugural Address, when he electrified the country with the cry, "All we have to fear is fear itself."

How ironical that those words of Roosevelt should be so well known, when it was Herbert Hoover who all along had been saying the same thing—in less graphic and less credible language, to be sure—but saying it nonetheless. That fact, too, contributed to the ordeal of Herbert Hoover.

CHAPTER 17

THE NEW DEAL: THE BEGINNING

Few historians would deny that the first three months of the presidency of Franklin D. Roosevelt, the famous Hundred Days, was one of the most dramatic periods in American political history. In early 1933 the country was in the full grip of the depression. Industrial production was spiraling downward, the banking system was in a state of near-total collapse, and no one in authority seemed to know what to do. Then came the inauguration of the new President and, with his buoyant address, an injection of hope into the popular bloodstream.

The new President, as the following selection shows, did not let this feeling of euphoria die. He called the Congress into special session and, working closely with his advisers, he began to shower the legislators with proposals aimed at recovery. Few segments of the economy were untouched, but the thrust of the first New Deal legislation was toward restoring economic vitality rather than reforming the country's economic institutions. Later, some of the President's liberal supporters were to complain that fundamental changes had not been made when these institutions lay powerless to resist radical alteration.

Could the President, had he so desired, have secured the passage of legislation that would have seriously modified the country's principal economic institutions, for example, banking? Was his victory at the polls a mandate for radical reform? If so, how radical? If not, what was his mandate from the people? In reality, does an American election victory actually confer any mandate? How successful were Roosevelt's measures for recovery? Finally that perennial question—was this phase of the New Deal evolutionary or revolutionary?

In addition to the works cited for the preceding selections, Daniel Fusfeld, *The Economic Thought of Franklin D. Roosevelt and the Origins of the New Deal* (1956), is valuable. Raymond Moley, *After Seven Years* (1939), gives an insider's view of the period. Daniel McCoy in his exciting volume, *Angry Voices*

(1958), covers the left-wing opposition to the New Deal. William E. Leuchten-burg, *Franklin D. Roosevelt and the New Deal** (1963), is a prizewinning volume, and Paul K. Conklin presents a brilliant critical analysis in *The New Deal** (rev. ed., 1975).

*Available in a paperback edition.

PROLOGUE: THE HUNDRED DAYS

ARTHUR M. SCHLESINGER, JR.

Saturday, March 4, 1933. "This nation asks for action, and action now. . . . We must act, and act quickly." The great mass before the Capitol, huddling in the mist and wind under the sullen March sky, responded with a burst of applause. The new President moved on to his conclusion.

In this dedication of a Nation we humbly ask the blessing of God. May He protect each and every one of us. May He guide me in the days to come.

Then the flourish of cavalry bugles, and the call to the inaugural parade, and Franklin Delano Roosevelt, his face still set and grim, entered his car to review the marchers from the stand in front of the White House.

Through the country people listened to their radios with a quickening hope. Nearly half a million of them wrote letters to the White House in the next few days. People said: "It was the finest thing this side of heaven"; and "Your human feeling for all of us in your address is just wonderful"; and "It seemed to give the people, as well as myself, a new hold upon life." "Yours is the first opportunity to carve a name in the halls of immortals beside Jesus," wrote one. "People are looking to you almost as they look to God," wrote another.

But others could not suppress anxiety. Eleanor Roosevelt called the inauguration "very, very solemn and a little terrifying"—terrifying "because when Franklin got to that part of his speech when he said it might become necessary for him to assume power ordinarily granted to a President in war time, he received his biggest demonstration." What could this mean for the baffled and despairing nation? "One has a feeling of going it blindly," she said, "because we're in a tremendous stream, and none of us knows where we're going to land."

II

. . . So the first day ended in suspense. And on the next, the new President (as he later recalled it), wakening with a pressing sense of work to be done, ate an early breakfast and had himself wheeled over to his new office. There,

SOURCE. Arthur M. Schlesinger, Jr., *The Coming of The New Deal*, pp. 1-23. Copyright © 1958 by Arthur M. Schlesinger, Jr. Reprinted by permission of Houghton Mifflin Company.

seated for the first time in the presidential chair, he found himself suddenly alone in an empty room. The desk was empty, the drawers were empty, the President could not even find pencil and pad to make a note. He looked for buzzers on the desk, but found no button to push, no way to signal the outside world. He sat for a moment, the great chamber echoing and silent, the center of action cut off from the nation at the moment of crisis. At last he bestirred himself and gave a mighty shout, which brought Missy LeHand and Marvin McIntyre running from adjacent rooms. For others, the story, as he used to tell it, seemed a skit on his physical helplessness. For himself—or so at least Rexford G. Tugwell surmised—the predicament was a parable of the national helplessness, extending for a dreadful moment even to what Wilson had called "the vital place of action in the system."

It was hard to understate the need for action. The national income was less than half of what it had been four short years before. Nearly thirteen million Americans—about one quarter of the labor force—were desperately seeking jobs. The machinery for sheltering and feeding the unemployed was breaking down everywhere under the growing burden. And a few hours before, in the early morning before the inauguration, every bank in America had locked its doors. It was now not just a matter of staving off hunger. It was a matter of seeing whether a representative democracy could conquer economic collapse. It was a matter of staving off violence, even (at least some so thought) revolution.

Whether revolution was a real possibility or not, faith in a free system was plainly waning. Capitalism, it seemed to many, had spent its force; democracy could not rise to economic crisis. The only hope lay in governmental leadership of a power and will which representative institutions seemed impotent to produce. Some looked enviously on Moscow, others on Berlin and Rome; abroad there seemed fervor, dedication, a steel determination. Could America match this spirit of sacrifice and unity? "What does a democracy do in a war?" said Al Smith, the former governor of New York, who had been the Democratic party's candidate for President in 1928. "It becomes a tyrant, a despot, a real monarch. In the World War we took our Constitution, wrapped it up and laid it on the shelf and left it there until it was over." "Even the iron hand of a national dictator," said Alfred M. Landon of Kansas, "is in preference to a paralytic stroke. . . . If there is any way in which a member of that species, thought by many to be extinct, a Republican governor of a mid-western state, can aid [the President] in the fight, I now enlist for the duration of the war."

III

The first priority was the banking system. Before anything else could be done, it seemed imperative to clear the financial arteries of the economy. The outgoing President had asked the President-elect in February to join with him in meeting the banking crisis. But Herbert Hoover had stipulated that cooperation was to be on his own terms; this meant, as he privately confided to a friend, the ratification by Roosevelt of "the whole major program of the Republican Administration" and "the abandonment of 90% of the so-called new deal." Roosevelt, angered at the proposal that he renounce the policies on which he had won the election, broke off negotiations. . . .

He had already settled on the main lines of his attack. Before arriving in Washington, he had rough drafts of two presidential proclamations: one calling a special session of Congress; the other declaring a bank holiday and controlling the export of gold by invoking forgotten provisions of the war-time Trading with the Enemy Act. On Saturday night, a few hours after the inauguration, Secretary of the Treasury [William] Woodin agreed to have emergency banking legislation ready for Congress when it convened on Thursday, March 9. After lunch on Sunday, Roosevelt called the cabinet together to complete the program of action. Woodin, after a morning of conferences, reported that the bankers, hastily summoned from across the country, had no plan of their own. Attorney-General Cummings then gave his official assent to the use of the Trading with the Enemy Act. This prepared the way for the two proclamations, and they were issued in the next four hours.

With the declaration of the bank holiday, the administration bought time —eighty hours until Congress reconvened—to work out a plan for reviving the banks. Old officials and new labored together day and night in the Treasury. Ogden Mills, Hoover's Secretary of the Treasury, exhorted the group to produce a program; if they couldn't, let "the President and Mr. Woodin tell us to get the devil out of here and get some men who can." We had "forgotten to be Republicans or Democrats," wrote Raymond Moley, the chief of Roosevelt's campaign brain trust, now an Assistant Secretary of State. "We were just a bunch of men trying to save the banking system."

The decision to save the system rather than to change it had come about almost by inadvertence. The first problem, as the President saw it, was to banish fear. If he was to restore confidence in the system, he had to offer policies which bankers themselves would support. And he had no real alternative to the restoration of the existing structure. It is true that Rexford G. Tugwell, another member of the campaign brain trust, now Assistant Secretary of Agriculture, had a scheme by which the postal savings system would take over the deposit and checking transactions of banks, while separate corporations would assume the job of commercial credit; but Tugwell's advice was not sought in the banking crisis. Indeed, as Tugwell later acknowledged, Wall Street and the orthodox economists had a monopoly of *expertise* in this area. America had no one outside the charmed circle, like John Maynard Keynes in Britain, who might have conceived a genuine reform.

There was restiveness in Congress about the President's approach. "I think back to the events of March 4, 1933," Senator Bronson Cutting of New Mexico later wrote, "with a sick heart. For then . . . the nationalization of banks by President Roosevelt could have been accomplished without a word of protest. It was President Roosevelt's great mistake." On the night before Congress convened, Senators Robert M. La Follette, Jr., of Wisconsin and Edward P. Costigan of Colorado, two leading progressives, called at the White House to urge Roosevelt to establish a truly national banking system. But they found Roosevelt's mind made up. . . .

IV

For the country, the proclamation of the holiday ushered in almost a springtime mood. The closing of the banks seemed to give the long economic descent the punctuation of a full stop, as if this were the bottom and hereafter things could only turn upward. Anything was better than nagging uncertainty. Now everyone knew where he stood. People enjoyed the sense of common plight. They made jokes and wrote out checks and accepted scrip and adjusted themselves with good cheer to the bankless economy.

But Washington, where the banking system was to be saved, could not be so philosophical. The ever approaching deadline stretched already taut nerves to the breaking point. Phones rang incessantly with excited calls from distant cities. The corridors of the Treasury echoed with rumor, fear, and fantasy. Bankers went to pieces under the pressure, and brain trusters showed the strain. Yet the old Treasury team, led by Mills and his Undersecretary, Arthur A. Ballantine, remained cool; and the new Treasury chief was displaying unexpected qualities of poise and endurance. . . .

By Monday a variety of proposals were under discussion at the Treasury. Many bankers demanded that the government issue scrip as it had during the panic of 1907. This idea assumed that the banks had too little currency on hand to meet national needs on reopening. The Hoover administration, in one of its last acts, had actually prepared a joint resolution to provide for the issuance of currency by clearinghouses. But, on reflection, the Treasury group, now reinforced by George L. Harrison of the New York Federal Reserve Bank and George W. Davison of the Central Hanover Bank, turned against this proposal. They favored instead a plan devised by Dr. E. A. Goldenweiser of the Federal Reserve Board whereby currency could be issued under the Federal Reserve Act against bank assets. If the first essential was to restore confidence, then Federal Reserve notes would be far less disturbing than clearinghouse script. Woodin, after spending Monday evening, so it was said, dozing and strumming his guitar, adopted the Goldenweiser ideal.

For the rest, the banking bill, as it took shape in the next frenzied days, gave the Secretary of the Treasury power to prevent gold hoarding and to take over gold bullion and currency in exchange for paper; and it provided for the review and reopening of the closed banks under a system of licenses and "conservators." In the Treasury, men worked around the clock to translate the broad plan into legislative language, pausing only for coffee, a shower, or a snatch of sleep. On Wednesday afternoon a draft went to the White House. That evening Roosevelt presented the legislation to a conference of congressional leaders from both parties. A newspaperman asked Woodin whether the bill was finished. "Yes, it's finished," said Woodin wryly. "My name is Bill and I'm finished too."

On Thursday, March 9, at noon, a breathless five days after the inauguration, Congress convened. Almost at once it received a message from the President: "I cannot too strongly urge upon the Congress the clear necessity for immediate action." Chairman Henry B. Steagall of the Banking and Currency Committee read aloud the only available copy of the proposed banking legislation. Debate was limited to forty minutes, and even before this time expired members began calling "Vote! Vote!" Shortly after four o'clock, the House passed unanimously and without a roll call the bill few of its members had ever seen. In the meantime, the Senate, which had been awaiting printed copies, decided to substitute the House version and open its own debate. Huey Long of Louisiana, trying to amend the bill, succeeded only in provoking Carter Glass of Virginia, once Secretary of the Treasury under Woodrow Wilson, into white-faced rage; Long's amendment was shouted down. Just before seven-thirty, the Senate passed the bill 73 to 7. An hour later, it was at the House. The whole affair, from the first introduction to the final signature, had taken less than eight hours.

Not for years had Congress acted with such speed and decision. And already, before the passage of the bill, the Secretary of the Treasury had issued regulations permitting urgent transactions to go ahead. Though technical hitches prevented banks from reopening on Friday, March 10, as Roosevelt wished, the basic procedures were nonetheless now established. Gold and deposits were flowing back into the system. After the weekend, the people could look forward with assurance to orderly reopening.

V

Roosevelt had first thought of putting through the emergency banking legislation and sending Congress home. But the momentum generated by the banking bill now seemed too valuable to waste. On Wednesday night Henry Wallace and Rex Tugwell raised the possibility of keeping Congress in session long enough to enact a farm program. And, even more insistently, Roosevelt's budget director, Lewis W. Douglas, argued that the President should seize the opportunity to do something about government economy. . . .

Douglas's passion for economy was part of his larger belief that economic order—indeed, civilization itself—rested on fiscal credit. "The country's future depends upon it," he exclaimed, "—upon a balanced budget and an end to wild extravagance." Under the spendthrift Hoover administration, Douglas declared, America had been going "the identical way that Germany went in the years just after the war." The only hope was a drastic reversal in government fiscal policy. "If we fail to practice economy, if we do not balance the budget, then we shall have created a malevolent wheel which is revolving constantly in an adverse direction and which inevitably means the complete economic collapse of the United States. . . . It would mean plunging the whole world into darkness."

Nor did Douglas want to balance the budget by increasing taxes. A larger tax burden, he felt, would have economic effects almost as deplorable as deficit spending itself. The solution was to cut government spending—taper off subsidies to farmers, to business, to public works, to veterans, even to national defense. "To those who say, 'You must not cut the army, for instance,'" Douglas declared, "I say, which is more important? A national defense which is perfectly futile, if the credit of the government collapses, or an unimpaired credit of your government? For myself, I say 'An unimpaired credit of the government.' For it is upon that, that all human values of our people ultimately rest."

For Douglas, the essence of the Roosevelt program was the pledge, rashly made in a speech at Pittsburgh during the 1932 campaign, to reduce the cost of government 25 per cent—to move toward what Roosevelt had then called "the one sound foundation of permanent economic recovery—a complete and honest balancing of the Federal budget." Once the budget was balanced, Douglas believed, confidence would return, frozen loans would thaw out, credit would expand, and recovery would be assured. But his experience in the House had convinced him that Congress could never bring itself to cut government spending. The only way to effect genuine retrenchment, he had come to think, was through the delegation of power to the Executive. During the interregnum, Roosevelt and Douglas had discussed the wartime grants of authority which Congress had made to Woodrow Wilson. Now in the first week of power, with Congress in a mood of unwonted acquiescence, it seemed the right time to request such delegations again.

On Thursday night, March 9, only an hour after he had signed the Emergency Banking Act, Roosevelt outlined an economy program to congressional leaders. With bland amiability, Roosevelt presented his proposals: reorganization of the veterans' pension system and reduction of pensions, to be accomplished through delegation of authority to the President; a reduction of congressional salaries; a reduction of Federal salaries—all designed to save the budget half a billion dollars. The politicians listened with incredulity. . . .

VI

Roosevelt spoke with deep sincerity. His fiscal notions were wholly orthodox. He saw little difference so far as budgets were concerned between a household or a state government on the one hand and the federal government on the other. In either case, Micawber was right: more income than expenditure—happiness; more expenditure than income—misery. . . .

For a moment, however, the economy bill seemed to break the presidential spell. In the House, the Democratic caucus declined to support the President. Some Democrats were doubtless motivated by old obligations to the veterans' lobby or by old fears of its retaliatory power. Yet others honestly—and plausibly—believed that it made no sense to cut government spending when the overriding economic need was for more spending everywhere in the economy. A number of liberal Democrats—Gordon Browning of Tennessee, Wright Patman of Texas, John Rankin of Mississippi, Fred Vinson of Kentucky, James Mead of New York, John McCormack of Massachusetts—abandoned the President. However, the conservative Democrats, led by John McDuffie of Alabama, maintained parliamentary control; and, with the expert assistance of an economy-minded Republican, John Taber of New York, McDuffie was able to get the bill through the House on Saturday by a vote of 266-138, two days after the banking bill, one week after the inauguration.

The second Sunday of the Roosevelt administration was no day of rest for the President. Over supper at the White House Roosevelt remarked, "I think this would be a good time for beer." Louis Howe produced a copy of the Democratic platform; and, late in the evening, Roosevelt wrote a brief message based on the platform calling for the modification of the Volstead Act in order to legalize beer and light wines. On Monday the 13th, Congress received the new message; on the same day, the economy bill passed its first test in the Senate. On Tuesday the House, ignoring the Anti-Saloon League and the Women's Christian Temperance Union, voted for 3.2 beer. On Wednesday the Senate voted 62 to 13 for economy and on Thursday 43 to 30 for beer: the two most powerful lobbies in Washington—the veterans and the prohibitionists— were now in rout. A Treasury bond issue on March 13 was oversubscribed in a single day. On the 15th, the securities markets, closed during the bank holiday, reopened in a bullish mood. In the meantime, banks were reopening, and deposits were exceeding withdrawals. The acute panic was evidently at an end.

VII

And the President during these days spoke not only to Congress. He also addressed himself directly to the people. The day before Congress convened, he held his first presidential press conference. Over a hundred skeptical reporters crowded into the executive office. They found, not the dour irritability to which White House correspondents were accustomed, but a gay and apparently open friendliness. The President hoped, he told the press, that these meetings could be enlarged additions of the "very delightful family conferences I have been holding in Albany." "No more written questions," he said; no more "presidential spokesmen." Instead he proposed a free exchange between the Executive and the newsmen, to be made the more effective by defining some information as "background," not for attribution to the White House, and by putting other remarks "off the record" entirely. "I am told that what I am about to do will become impossible," Roosevelt said, "but I am going to try it." As he launched into a frank discussion of the banking crisis, his enjoyment of the give-and-take with the press was obvious. When the conference ended, the newspapermen broke into spontaneous applause.

On Sunday evening, March 12, at the conclusion of the first week, Roosevelt made even more direct contact with the nation in the first of what came to be called his "fireside chats." His purpose was to reassure people that their savings in closed banks were secure. . . . In plain language Roosevelt analyzed the banking crisis and forecast the steps which lay ahead. "Let us unite in banishing fear," he concluded. ". . . It is your problem no less than it is mine. Together we cannot fail." The President took a complicated subject like banking, said Will Rogers, and made everybody understand it, even the bankers. . . .

Even conservatives joined in the applause. After all, Roosevelt had saved the old banking system, cut government spending, struck at prohibition, and displayed no evidence of radicalism. Henry L. Stimson, Hoover's Secretary of State, who had heard the inaugural address with much suspicion, now wrote the President, "I am delighted with the progress of your first week and send you my heartiest congratulations." William Randolph Hearst said, "I guess at your next election we will make it unanimous." Hamilton Fish proudly pronounced the new regime "an American dictatorship based on the consent of the governed without any violation of individual liberty or human rights." Newton D. Baker described Roosevelt as "a providential person at a providential moment." Cardinal O'Connell called him "a God-sent man." . . .

VIII

Above all, the presidential mansion itself embodied the new spirit. Colonel Starling, head of the President's Secret Service detail, took the Hoovers to the railroad station on Inauguration Day. When he returned a few hours later, he found the White House, he said "transformed during my absence into a gay place, full of people who oozed confidence." Rudolph Forster, the dignified and self-contained Executive Clerk who had served every President since McKinley, later said, "I would not have believed that twenty-four hours could make the difference that those did when the last people moved out of here and these new ones moved in." Where once glumness and formality had ruled, there was now a mixture of levity and high seriousness, of solemnity and exhilaration; the public business went on, but one seemed to hear in the distance barking dogs and voices of children. . . .

The day before inauguration, Roosevelt, making a ceremonial visit at the White House, had suggested that the outgoing President need not return his call. Hoover had coldly replied, "Mr. Roosevelt, when you are in Washington as long as I have been, you will learn that the President of the United States calls on nobody." But Hoover's Washington vanished in the new informality. Only five days after Hoover made this remark, Felix Frankfurter reminded Roosevelt that it was Oliver Wendell Holmes's ninety-second birthday. Before March 8 was over, the President had taken enough time from the banking crisis to negotiate the steep stairs at I Street and pay his personal respects. "We face grave times," Roosevelt said to the old Justice. "What is your advice?" The Civil War veteran replied without hesitation: "Form your ranks and fight!" ("A second-class intellect," Holmes said of Roosevelt later, "—but a first-class temperament!")

An even more striking contrast with his predecessor came in May when a second installment of the Bonus Expeditionary Force descended on Washington. The Roosevelt tactic, instant and instinctive, was to kill by kindness. Instead of the shacks at Anacostia and the hostility of police and Army, Roosevelt offered the veterans an Army camp, three meals a day, endless supplies of coffee, and a large convention tent, where the leaders could orate to their hearts' content. The Navy Band played for the veterans; Army doctors ministered to their ills; dentists pulled their teeth; the President conferred with their leaders; and, as a climax, Mrs. Roosevelt and Louis Howe drove out one rainy spring day in a blue convertible. While Howe dozed in the car, Mrs. Roosevelt walked through ankle-deep mud and led the vets in singing "There's a long, long trail a-winding." "Hoover sent the Army," said one veteran; "Roosevelt sent his wife." In two weeks, most of the veterans went affably into the Civilian Conservation Corps, and the Second B.E.F. had met a painless Waterloo. . . .

Somehow Roosevelt kept all the reins in his hand. He seemed to thrive on crisis. Reporters took from his press conferences images of urbane mastery, with the President sitting easily behind his desk, his great head thrown back, his smile flashing or his laugh booming out of the pleasure of thrust and riposte. He saw agitated congressmen, panicky businessmen, jealous bureau-crats; he kidded the solemn, soothed the egotistical, and inspired the down-hearted. There remained too a sense of ambiguity and craftiness. He could be hard and frightening when he wanted to be, and he played the political game with cold skill. Charm, humor, power, persuasion, menace, idealism—all were weapons in his armory.

IX

The first explosive week, which saw the Emergency Banking Act, the economy drive, the attack on prohibition, and the dramatic display of presi-dential leadership, was only the beginning. As yet, Roosevelt had done nothing to carry out the New Deal he had proclaimed during the campaign. On Thursday, March 16, the admininistration took a new turn. On that day Roosevelt sent Congress a message calling for the national planning of agricul-ture. This was the first of a series of proposals designed to reorganize one after another the basic aspects of American economic life. In the next weeks the New Deal proper began to unfold.

And with the New Deal came the New Dealers. Depression, by cutting off normal outlets in law practice or in the universities, had made men of intellec-tual ability available as never before; and government had never been so eager to hire them. Like circles beyond circles, both the legal network and the academic network were limitless. With each prominent New Dealer acting as his own employment agency, Washington was deluged with an endless stream of bright young men. "If ability could be measured in a tin bucket," Willard Kiplinger wrote in the journal of the United States Chamber of Commerce in 1934, "I should say that the Roosevelt administration contained more gallons of ability than any of its recent predecessors." They brought with them an alertness, an excitement, an appetite for power, an instinct for crisis and a dedication to public service which became during the thirties the essence of Washington. "No group in government," said Arthur Krock, "has ever been more interesting, dull, brilliant, stupid, headstrong, pliable, competent, ineffi-cient; more honorable in money matters, more ruthless in material methods." Their *elan,* their bravado, their sense of adventure, their cocky assurance, their inexhaustible activism were infectious. They often were irritating, but they always were alive. . . .

Who were the New Dealers? They represented all classes—from the well-born, like Franklin Roosevelt, Averell Harriman, Francis Biddle, to the sons of poverty, like Harry Hopkins—but they were predominantly middle class. They represented a variety of occupations; but they were mostly lawyers, college professors, economists, or social workers. They came from all parts of the land and from both city and country, though most of them had been educated in state universities or in Ivy League colleges, and many had their first political experience in the fight for decent city government. They were all ages, though most of them were born between 1895 and 1905. But the common bond which held them together, as Herman Kahn has acutely noted, was that they were all at home in the world of ideas. They were accustomed to analysis and dialectic; and they were prepared to use intelligence as an instrument of government. They were more than specialists. As Kahn has further pointed out, they were—or considered themselves—generalists, capable of bringing logic to bear on any social problem. They delighted in the play of the free mind.

They were by no means of a single school. Indeed, they represented divergent and often clashing philosophies. The laissez-faire liberalism of the Democratic party, dedicated, in the tradition of Grover Cleveland, to sound money, fiscal orthodoxy, and tariff reduction, found its voices in Lewis Douglas and Cordell Hull and its first victory in the Economy Act. The agrarian tradition, stronger in the Congress than in the administration, harking back to William Jennings Bryan and demanding monetary inflation as a means of turning the terms of trade more favorably to the farmer, soon expressed itself in the Thomas amendment to the Agricultural Adjustment Act and in the devaluation policy. The trust-busting liberalism of the Brandeis-Wilson school, seeking to liberate the economy from business bigness, spoke especially through Professor Felix Frankfurter of Harvard and shortly achieved the Securities and Glass-Steagall Acts. And to these traditional Democratic strains there was now added an infusion of the Theodore Roosevelt-Herbert Croly Progressivism of 1912, finding advocates from Raymond Moley on the right to Rexford Tugwell on the left, and seeking to counter the anarchy of competition by government-business collaboration.

They often suffered frustration and disillusion. They worked to the edge of collapse. They had moments when they hated Washington and government and Roosevelt. Yet for most of them this was the happiest time and the deepest fulfillment they would ever know. "It was one of the most joyous periods of my life," wrote Thomas L. Stokes as a newspaperman covering Roosevelt's arrival in Washington. "We came alive, we were eager." It was, said Tugwell in retrospect, a "renaissance spring" when men were filled with courage beyond natural instincts, with hopes beyond reasonable expectation, with a belief in human possibility which it would take a good deal of betrayal to break down—"a time of rebirth after a dark age." The memories would not soon fade —the interminable meetings, the litter of cigarette stubs, the hasty sandwich at the desk or (if there was time) the lazy lunch along the sun-drenched wharves by the Potomac, the ominous rumor passed on with relish, the call from the White House, the postponed dinner, the neglected wife, the office lights burning into the night, the lilacs hanging in fragrance above Georgetown gardens while men rebuilt the nation over long drinks, the selflessness, the worry, the mistakes, the achievement. At his worst, the New Dealer became an arrant sentimentalist or a cynical operator. At his best, he was the ablest, most intelligent, and most distinguished public servant the United States ever had.

X

In the three months after Roosevelt's inauguration, Congress and the country were subjected to a presidential barrage of ideas and programs unlike anything known to American history. On adjournment on June 15, 1933, the President and the exhausted 73rd Congress left the following record:

March 9   —   The Emergency Banking Act

March 20   —   The Economy Act

March 31   —   Establishment of the Civilian Conservation Corps

April 19   —   Abandonment of the gold standard

May 12   —   The Federal Emergency Relief Act, setting up a national relief system

May 12   —   The Agricultural Adjustment Act, establishing a national agricultural policy, with the Thomas amendment conferring on the President powers of monetary expansion

May 12   —   The Emergency Farm Mortgage Act, providing for the refinancing of farm mortgages

May 18   —   The Tennessee Valley Authority Act, providing for the unified development of the Tennessee Valley

May 27   —   The Truth-in-Securities Act, requiring full disclosure in the issue of new securities

June 5   —   The abrogation of the gold clause in public and private contracts

June 13   —   The Home Owners' Loan Act, providing for the refinancing of home mortgages

June 16   —   The National Industrial Recovery Act, providing both for a system of industrial self-government under federal supervision and for a $3.3 billion public works program

June 16 — The Glass-Steagall Banking Act, divorcing commercial and investment banking and guaranteeing bank deposits

June 16 — The Farm Credit Act, providing for the reorganization of agricultural credit activities

June 16 — The Railroad Coordination Act, setting up a federal Coordinator of Transportation.

This was the Hundred Days; and in this period Franklin Roosevelt sent fifteen messages to Congress, guided fifteen major laws to enactment, delivered ten speeches, held press conferences and cabinet meetings twice a week, conducted talks with foreign heads of state, sponsored an international conference, made all the major decisions in domestic and foreign policy, and never displayed fright or panic and rarely even bad temper. His mastery astonished many who thought they had long since taken his measure. . . .

The combination of power and delight was irresistible to people used to neither in the White House; it gave Americans new confidence in themselves. Roosevelt pressed home the recovery of morale. "When Andrew Jackson, 'Old Hickory,' died," he said in July, "someone asked, 'will he go to Heaven?' and the answer was, 'He will if he wants to.' If I am asked whether the American people will pull themselves out of this depression, I answer, 'They will if they want to.' "

Before March 4, America was in a state of extreme shock. No one would ever know, General Hugh S. Johnson later said, "how close were we to collapse and revolution. We could have got a dictator a lot easier than Germany got Hitler." "I do not think it is too much to say," wrote Tugwell, "that on March 4 we were confronted with a choice between an orderly revolution—a peaceful and rapid departure from past concepts—and a violent and disorderly overthrow of the whole capitalist structure." "At the end of February," wrote Walter Lippmann, "we were a congeries of disorderly panic-stricken mobs and factions. In the hundred days from March to June we became again an organized nation confident of our power to provide for our own security and to control our own destiny."

By bringing to Washington a government determined to *govern*, Roosevelt unlocked new energies in a people who had lost faith, not just in government's ability to meet the economic crisis, but almost in the ability of anyone to do anything. The feeling of movement was irresistible. Washington, Arthur Krock reported, was experiencing the sensation of a man traveling on a life-and-death errand thousands of miles away who suddenly found himself switched from an ox cart to an airplane. "Never was there such a change in the transfer of government." Justice Harlan Stone of the Supreme Court wrote his old friend Herbert Hoover two months after the shift in administration, "To judge by the rapidity of changing events, as many decades might have passed." And there could be no question, Krock added, who was responsible: "The President is the boss, the dynamo, the works."

For a deceptive moment in 1933, clouds of inertia and selfishness seemed to lift. A despairing land had a vision of America as it might some day be. "For the first time since we can remember," said Frances Perkins, "we are trying to be a unified people." Anne O'Hare McCormick described the response as "the rising of a nation." "It's more than a New Deal," said Harold Ickes. "It's a new world. People feel free again. They can breathe naturally. It's like quitting a morgue for the open woods." "We have had our revolution," said *Collier's*, "and we like it." . . .

CHAPTER 18

WORLD WAR II: THE HOME FRONT

In terms of staunch commitment to fundamental national principles, World War II has traditionally been seen as a bright spot in American history. Particularly in the complex, divisive, uncertain years of the 1960s, 1970s, and 1980s, Americans could look back with satisfaction to a time when the nation was wholeheartedly engaged in an ennobling struggle against gigantic evil. There was never any question about the rightness of the nation's course. From 1941 to 1945 Americans labored and fought, struggled and sacrificed, and suffered and died in a crusade against corruption and racism on an international scale. Well might Americans take pride in their country's stance in that time of global crisis and confrontation.

It is in this light that the following selection, from Roger Daniels' study of *Concentration Camps USA,* is particularly sombering. For at the same time that Americans were enthusiastically united in militant opposition to Axis aggression, in the name of human rights and antiracism, they themselves were indulging racist prejudices and fears in their treatment of both Japanese aliens and Japanese-American citizens, particularly on the West Coast. In this selection, Professor Daniels shows that American distrust and fear of Japanese residents did not develop suddenly in the years just before Pearl Harbor in response to Japanese aggression in the Pacific. Instead, anti-Japanese racism was deeply rooted, and as early as the 1890s some Americans, among them publicists and governmental officials, had begun to develop a phobia about an imminent Japanese attack on the American West Coast. It was the pervasiveness of anti-Japanese racism and the acuteness of the fear of Japanese invasion that led, in the aftermath of Pearl Harbor, to the mass removal and internment in concentration camps of over 100,000 Japanese residents.

The story of what happened to Japanese-Americans in the war years is straightforward and evident. What is not so clear is why it happened. In reading this selection, students should concentrate on the following questions.

What were the causes of the anti-Japanese racist attitudes that developed on the West Coast? Was the fear and distrust of Japanese-Americans logical and rational; did Japanese-Americans present any real dangers to the United States? Finally, to what extent have Americans outgrown propensities toward ethnocentrism and racism? Have we as a nation matured to the point that similar shameful treatment of people can never happen again?

Excellent treatment of this subject is found in two studies by Roger Daniels, *The Politics of Prejudice* * (1962), and *Concentration Camps USA: Japanese Americans and World War II* * (1971). For broader consideration of the home front, see John M. Blum, *V Was for Victory: Politics and American Culture During World War II* (1976), and Richard Polenberg, *War and Society: The United States, 1941–1945* (1972).

*Available in a paperback edition.

PEARL HARBOR AND THE YELLOW PERIL

ROGER DANIELS

If the attack on Pearl Harbor came as a devastating shock to most Americans, for those of Japanese ancestry it was like a nightmare come true. Throughout the 1930s the Nisei generation dreaded the possibility of a war between the United States and Japan; although some in both the Japanese and American communities fostered the illusion that the emerging Nisei generation could help bridge the gap between the rival Pacific powers, most Nisei, at least, understood that this was a chimera. As early as 1937 Nisei gloom about the future predominated. One Nisei spoke prophetically about what might happen to Japanese Americans in a Pacific war. Rhetorically he asked his fellow Nisei students at the University of California:

. . . what are we going to do if war does break out between United States and Japan? . . . In common language we can say "we're sunk." Even if the Nisei wanted to fight for America, what chances? Not a chance! . . . our properties would be confiscated and most likely [we would be] herded into prison camps—perhaps we would be slaughtered on the spot.

As tensions increased, so did Nisei anxieties; and in their anxiety some Nisei tried to accentuate their loyalty and Americanism by disparaging the generation of their fathers. Newspaper editor Togo Tanaka, for example, speaking to a college group in early 1941, insisted that the Nisei must face what he called "the question of loyalty" and assumed that since the Issei were "more or less tumbleweeds with one foot in America and one foot in Japan," real loyalty to America could be found only in his own generation. A Los Angeles Nisei jeweler expressed similar doubts later the same year. After explaining to a Los Angeles *Times* columnist that many if not most of the older generation were pro-Japanese rather than pro-American, he expressed his own generation's fears. "We talk of almost nothing but this great crisis. We don't know what's going to happen. Sometimes we only look for a concentration camp."

While the attention of Japanese Americans was focused on the Pacific, most other Americans gave primary consideration to Europe, where in September

SOURCE. Roger Daniels, *Concentration Camps USA: Japanese Americans and World War II*, pp. 26–29, 31–41. Copyright © Roger Daniels Reprinted by permission.

1939 World War II had broken out. Hitler's amazing blitzkrieg against the west in the spring of 1940—which overran, in quick succession, Denmark and Norway and then Holland, Belgium, Luxembourg, and France—caused the United States to accelerate its defense program and institute the first peacetime draft in its history. Stories, now known to be wildly exaggerated, told of so-called fifth column and espionage activities, created much concern about the loyalty of aliens, particularly German-born aliens, some 40,000 of whom were organized into the overtly pro-Nazi German-American Bund. As a component part of the defense program, Congress passed, in 1940, an Alien Registration Act, which required the registration and fingerprinting of all aliens over fourteen years of age. In addition, as we now know, the Department of Justice, working through the Federal Bureau of Investigation, was compiling a relatively modest list of dangerous or subversive aliens—Germans, Italians, and Japanese—who were to be arrested or interned at the outbreak of war with their country. The commendable restraint of the Department of Justice's plans was due, first of all, to the liberal nature of the New Deal. The Attorney General, Francis Biddle, was clearly a civil libertarian, as befitted a former law clerk of Oliver Wendell Holmes, Jr.

Elsewhere in the government however, misgivings about possible fifth column and sabotage activity, particularly by Japanese, were strongly felt. For example, one congressman, John D. Dingell (D-Mich.), wrote the President to suggest that Japanese in the United States and Hawaii be used as hostages to ensure good behavior by Japan. In August 1941, shortly after Japanese assets in the United States were frozen and the Japanese made it difficult for some one hundred Americans to leave Japan, Dingell suggested that as a reprisal the United States should "cause the forceful detention or imprisonment in a concentration camp of ten thousand alien Japanese in Hawaii. . . . It would be well to remind Japan," he continued, "that there are perhaps one hundred fifty thousand additional alien Japanese in the United States who [can] be held in a reprisal reserve."

And, in the White House itself, concern was evidenced. Franklin Roosevelt, highly distrustful of official reports and always anxious to have independent checks on the bureaucracy, set up an independent "intelligence" operation, run by John Franklin Carter. Carter, who as the "Unofficial Observer" and "Jay Franklin" had written some of the most brilliant New Deal journalism and would later serve as an adviser to President Harry S Truman and Governor Thomas E. Dewey, used newspapermen and personal friends to make special reports. In early November he received a report on the West Coast Japanese from Curtis B. Munson. His report stressed the loyalty of the overwhelming majority, and he understood that even most of the disloyal Japanese Americans hoped that "by remaining quiet they [could] avoid concentration camps or irresponsible mobs." Munson was, however, "horrified" to observe that dams, bridges, harbors, power stations, etc., are wholly unguarded. The harbor of San Pedro [Los Angeles' port] could be razed by fire completely by four men with hand grenades and a little study in one night. Dams could be blown and half of lower California could actually die of thirst. . . . One railway bridge at the exit from the mountains in some cases could tie up three or four main railroads.

Munson felt that despite the loyalty or quiescence of the majority, this situation represented a real threat because "there are still Japanese in the United States who will tie dynamite around their waist and make a human bomb out of themselves." This imaginary threat apparently worried the President too, for he immediately sent the memo on to Secretary of War Henry L. Stimson, specifically calling his attention to Munson's warnings about sabotage. In early December, Army Intelligence drafted a reply (which in the confusion following Pearl Harbor was never sent) arguing, quite correctly as it turned out, that "widespread sabotage by Japanese is not expected . . . identification of dangerous Japanese on the West Coast is reasonably complete." Although neither of these nor other similar proposals and warnings was acted upon before the attack on Pearl Harbor, the mere fact that they were suggested and received consideration in the very highest governmental circles indicates the degree to which Americans were willing to believe almost anything about the Japanese. This belief, in turn, can be understood only if one takes into account the half century of agitation and prophecy about the coming American-Japanese war and the dangers of the United States being overwhelmed by waves of yellow soldiers aided by alien enemies within the gates.

This irrational fear of Oriental conquest, with its racist and sex-fantasy overtones, can be most conveniently described as the "yellow peril," a term probably first used by German Kaiser Wilhelm II about 1895. . . . [By] the end of the century, a potential predator had appeared; in 1894 formerly isolated and backward Japan won its first modern naval battle, defeating the Chinese off the Yalu River. The very next year, the prince of Jingoes, Henry Cabot Lodge, then a Republican congressman from Massachusetts, warned Congress that the Japanese "understand the future . . . they have just whipped somebody, and they are in a state of mind when they think they can whip anybody." In 1898, during the discussion of the American annexation of Hawaii, Senator Cushman K. Davis (R-Minn.), chairman of the Senate Foreign Relations Committee, warned his colleagues that the mild controversy with Japan over Hawaii was merely "the preliminary skirmish in the great coming struggle between" East and West.

These still nascent fears about Japan were greatly stimulated when the Japanese badly defeated Russia in the war of 1904–1905, the first triumph of Asians over Europeans in modern times. The shots fired at Mukden and in the Straits of Tushima were truly shots heard round the world. Throughout Asia the Japanese victory undoubtedly stimulated nationalism and resistance to colonialism; in Europe, and particularly in the United States, it greatly stimulated fears of conquest by Asia. Shortly after the end of that war the "yellow peril" was adopted by its most significant American disseminator, newspaper mogul William Randolph Hearst. Although the theme of possible Japanese attack had been initiated by a rival paper, the San Francisco *Chronicle,* it was Hearst's San Francisco *Examiner,* as well as the rest of his chain, which made the theme of danger from Asia uniquely its own. . . .

Even during World War I, when Japan fought Germany, anti-Japanese military propaganda did not cease; the publication of the infamous Zimmermann telegram of early 1917 which proposed a German-Mexican-Japanese alliance against the United States further inflamed American, and particularly Pacific Coast, feeling, even though Japan, interested in annexations in the Pacific and on the East Asian Mainland, clearly wanted to have nothing to do with it. During and after the war a number of anti-Japanese movies, which showed the Japanese actually invading or planning to invade the United States, were produced and shown in theaters throughout the country; some of the most noxious were made by the motion picture arm of the Hearst communications empire. Sunday supplements and cheap pulp magazines featured the "yellow peril" theme throughout the 1920s and 1930s and a mere inventory of "yellow peril" titles would cover many pages. It is impossible, of course, to judge with any accuracy the impact or influence of this propaganda, but it seems clear that well before the actual coming of war a considerable proportion of the American public had been conditioned not only to the probability of a Pacific war with Japan—that was, after all, a geopolitical fact of twentieth-century civilization—but also to the proposition that this war would involve an invasion of the continental United States in which Japanese residents and secret agents would provide the spearhead of the attack. After war came at Pearl Harbor and for years thereafter many Japanophobes insisted that, to use Wells's phrase, "the Yellow Peril was a peril after all," but this is to misunderstand completely Japan's intentions and capabilities during the Great Pacific War. The Japanese military planners never contemplated an invasion of the continental United States, and, even had they done so, the logistical problems were obviously beyond Japan's capacity as a nation. But, often in history, what men believe to be true is more important than the truth itself because the mistaken belief becomes a basis for action. These two factors—the long racist and anti-Oriental tradition plus the widely believed "yellow peril" fantasy—when triggered by the traumatic mechanism provided by the attack on Pearl Harbor, were the necessary preconditions for America's concentration camps. But beliefs, even widely held beliefs, are not always translated into action. We must now discover how this particular set of beliefs—the inherent and genetic disloyalty of individual Japanese plus the threat of an imminent Japanese invasion—produced public policy and action, the mass removal and incarceration of the West Coast Japanese Americans.

* * * * *

As is well known, despite decades of propaganda and apprehension about a Pacific war, the reality, the dawn attack at Pearl Harbor on Sunday, December 7, 1941, came as a stunning surprise to most Americans. Throughout the nation the typical reaction was disbelief, followed by a determination to close ranks and avenge a disastrous defeat. Faced with the fact of attack, the American people entered the war with perhaps more unity than has existed before or since. But if a calm determination to get on with the job typified the national mood, the mood of the Pacific Coast was nervous and trigger-happy, if not hysterical. A thousand movies and stories and reminiscences have recorded the solemnity with which the nation reacted to that "day of infamy" in 1941. Yet, at Gilmore Field, in Los Angeles, 18,000 spectators at a minor league professional football game between the Hollywood Bears and the Columbus Bulldogs "jumped to their feet and cheered wildly when the public address system announced that a state of war existed between Japan and the United States."

The state's leading paper, the Los Angeles *Times* (Dec. 8, 1941), quickly announced that California was "a zone of danger" and invoked the ancient vigilante tradition of the West by calling for

alert, keen-eyed civilians [who could be] of yeoman service in cooperating with the military authorities against spies, saboteurs and fifth columnists. We have thousands of Japanese here. . . . Some, perhaps many, are . . . good Americans. What the rest may be we do not know, nor can we take a chance in the light of yesterday's demonstration that treachery and double-dealing are major Japanese weapons.

Day after day, throughout December, January, February, and March, almost the entire Pacific Coast press (of which the *Times* was a relatively restrained example) spewed forth racial venom against all Japanese. The term Jap, of course, was standard usage. Japanese, alien and native-born were also "Nips," "yellow men," "Mad dogs," and "yellow vermin," to name only a few of the choicer epithets. *Times* columnist Ed Ainsworth cautioned his readers "to be careful to differentiate between races. The Chinese and Koreans both hate the Japs more than we do. . . . Be sure of nationality before you are rude to anybody." (*Life* Magazine soon rang some changes on this theme for a national audience with an article—illustrated by comic strip artist Milton Caniff, creator of *Terry and the Pirates*, and, later, *Steve Canyon*—which purported to explain how to tell "Japs" from other Asian nationalities.) The sports pages, too, furnished their share of abuse. Just after a series of murderous and sometimes fatal attacks on Japanese residents by Filipinos, one sports page feature was headlined FILIPINO BOXERS NOTED FOR COURAGE, VALOR.

Newspaper columnists, as always, were quick to suggest what public policy should be. Lee Shippey, a Los Angeles writer who often stressed that *some* Japanese were all right, prophetically suggested a solution to California's Japanese problem. He proposed the establishment of "a number of big, closely guarded, closely watched truck farms on which Japanese-Americans could earn a living and assure us a steady supply of vegetables." If a Nazi had suggested doing this with Poles, Shippey, a liberal, undoubtedly would have called it a slave labor camp. But the palm for *shrecklichkeit* must go to Westbrook Pegler, a major outlet of what Oswald Garrison Villard once called "the sewer system of American journalism." Taking time off from his vendettas with Eleanor Roosevelt and the American labor movement, Pegler proposed, on December 9, that every time the Axis murdered hostages, the United States should retaliate by raising them "100 victims selected out of [our] concentration camps," which Pegler assumed would be set up for subversive Germans and Italians and "alien Japanese."

Examples of newspaper incitement to racial violence appeared daily (some radio commentators were even worse). In addition, during the period that the Japanese Americans were still at large, the press literally abounded with stories and, above all, headlines, which made the already nervous general public believe that military or paramilitary Japanese activists were all around them. None of these stories had any basis in fact; amazingly, there was not one demonstrable incident of sabotage committed by a Japanese American, alien or native-born, during the entire war. Here are a few representative headlines.

JAP BOAT FLASHES MESSAGE ASHORE

ENEMY PLANES SIGHTED OVER CALIFORNIA COAST

TWO JAPANESE WITH MAPS AND ALIEN LITERATURE SEIZED

JAP AND CAMERA HELD IN BAY CITY

VEGETABLES FOUND FREE OF POISON

CAPS ON JAPANESE TOMATO PLANTS POINT TO AIR BASE

JAPANESE HERE SENT VITAL DATA TO TOKYO

CHINESE ABLE TO SPOT JAP

MAP REVEALS JAP MENACE

NETWORK OF ALIEN FARMS COVERS STRATEGIC DEFENSE AREAS OVER
SOUTHLAND

JAPS PLAN COAST ATTACK IN APRIL WARNS CHIEF OF KOREAN SPY BAND

In short, any reading of the wartime Pacific Coast press—or for that matter
viewing the wartime movies that still pollute our television channels—shows
clearly that, although a distinction was continually being made between
"good" and "bad" Germans (a welcome change from World War I), few
distinctions were ever made between Japanese. The evil deeds of Hitler's
Germany were the deeds of bad men; the evil deeds of Tojo and Hirohito's
Japan were the deeds of a bad race. While the press was throwing fuel on the
fires of racial animosity, other faggots were contributed by politicians, federal
officials, and, above all, the military. The governor of California, Culbert L.
Olson, a liberal Democrat, had insisted, before Pearl Harbor, that Japanese
Americans should enjoy all their rights and privileges even if war with Japan
came, and correctly pointed out that equal protection under the law was a
"basic tenet" of American government. But Olson's constitutional scruples
were a casualty of Pearl Harbor: on December 8, the governor told the press
that he was thinking of ordering all Japanese, alien and citizen, to observe
house arrest "to avoid riot and disturbance."

The Department of Justice, working through the FBI and calling on local
law enforcement officials for assistance and detention, began roundups of what
it considered "dangerous" enemy aliens. Throughout the nation this initial
roundup involved about 3000 persons, half of whom were Japanese. (All but
a handful of these lived on the Pacific Coast.) In other words the federal
officials responsible for counterespionage thought that some 1500 persons of
Japanese ancestry, slightly more than 1 percent of the nation's Japanese population, constituted some kind of threat to the nation. Those arrested, often in
the dead of night, were almost universally of the immigrant, or Issei, generation, and thus, no matter how long they had lived here, "enemy aliens" in law.
(It must be kept in mind that American law prohibited the naturalization of
Asians.) Those arrested were community leaders, since the government, acting
as it so often does on the theory of guilt by association, automatically hauled
in the officers and leading lights of a number of Japanese organizations and
religious groups. Many of these people were surely "rooting" for the Emperor
rather than the President and thus technically subversive, but most of them
were rather elderly and inoffensive gentlemen and not a threat to anything.
This limited internment, however, was a not too discreditable performance for
a government security agency, but it must be noted that even at this restrained
level the government acted much more harshly, in terms of numbers interned,
toward Japanese nationals than toward German nationals (most known mem-

bers of the German-American Bund were left at liberty), and more harshly toward Germans than to Italians. It should also be noted, however, that more than a few young Nisei leaders applauded this early roundup and contrasted their own loyalty to the presumed disloyalty of many of the leaders of the older generation.

In addition to the selective roundup of enemy aliens, the Justice Department almost immediately announced the sealing off of the Mexican and Canadian borders to "all persons of Japanese ancestry, whether citizen or alien." Thus, by December 8, that branch of the federal government particularly charged with protecting the rights of citizens was willing to single out one ethnic group for invidious treatment. Other national civilian officials discriminated in other ways. Fiorello La Guardia, an outstanding liberal who was for a time director of the Office of Civilian Defense as well as mayor of New York, pointedly omitted mention of the Japanese in two public statements calling for decent treatment for enemy aliens and suggesting that alien Germans and Italians be presumed loyal until proved otherwise. By implication, at least, Japanese were to be presumed disloyal. Seventeen years earlier La Guardia had been one of three congressmen who dared to speak in favor of continuing Japanese immigration, but in December 1941 he could find nothing good to say about any Japanese.

Even more damaging were the mendacious statements of Frank Knox, Roosevelt's Republican Secretary of the Navy. On December 15 Secretary Knox held a press conference in Los Angeles on his return from a quick inspection of the damage at Pearl Harbor. As this was the first detailed report of the damage there, his remarks were front-page news all across the nation. Knox spoke of "treachery" in Hawaii and insisted that much of the disaster was caused by "the most effective fifth column work that's come out of this war, except in Norway." The disaster at Pearl Harbor, as is now generally acknowledged, was caused largely by the unpreparedness and incompetence of the local military commanders, as Knox already knew. (The orders for the relief of Admiral Kimmel were already being drawn up.) But the secretary, who, as we shall see, harbored deep-felt anti-Japanese prejudices, probably did not want the people to lose faith in their Navy, so the Japanese population of Hawaii—and indirectly all Japanese Americans—was made the scapegoat on which to hang the big lie. (Knox, it should be remarked, as a Chicago newspaper publisher in civilian life, had a professional understanding of these matters.)

But the truly crucial role was played by the other service, the United States Army. The key individual, initially, at least, was John L. De Witt, in 1941 a lieutenant general and commander of the Western Defense Command and the 4th Army, both headquartered at San Francisco's Presidio. Despite these warlike titles, De Witt, who was sixty-one years old and would be retired before the war's end, was essentially an administrator in uniform, a staff officer who had specialized in supply and had practically nothing to do with combat during his whole Army career. Even before Pearl Harbor, De Witt had shown himself to be prejudiced against Japanese Americans. In March 1941, for example, he found it necessary to complain to Major General William G. Bryden, the Army's Deputy Chief of Staff, that "a couple of Japs" who had been drafted into the Army, were "going around taking pictures." He and Bryden agreed to "just have it happen naturally that Japs are sent to Infantry units," rather than to sensitive headquarters or coast defense installations. De Witt's prejudices, in fact, extended all along the color line. When he discovered that some of the troops being sent to him as reinforcements after Pearl Harbor were Negro, he protested to the Army's chief of classification and assignment that

you're filling too many colored troops up on the West Coast. . . . there will be a great deal of public reaction out here due to the Jap situation. They feel they've got enough black skinned people around them as it is. Filipinos and Japanese. . . . I'd rather have a white regiment. . . .

Serving under De Witt, in December 1941, as the corps commander in charge of the defense of Southern California, was a real fighting man, the then Major General Joseph W. Stilwell, the famed "Vinegar Joe" of the heartbreaking Burma campaigns. His diary of those days, kept in pencil in a shirt-pocket notebook, gives an accurate and pungent picture of the hysteria and indecisiveness that prevailed at De Witt's headquarters and on the Coast generally.

Dec. 8
Sunday night "air raid" at San Francisco . . . Fourth Army kind of jittery.
Dec. 9
. . . Fleet of thirty-four [Japanese] ships between San Francisco and Los Angeles. Later —not authentic.
Dec. 11
[Phone call from 4th Army] "The main Japanese fleet is 164 miles off San Francisco." I believed it, like a damn fool. . . .
    Of course [4th Army] passed the buck on this report. They had it from a "usually reliable source," but they should never have put it out without check.
Dec. 13
Not content with the above blah, [4th] Army pulled another at ten-thirty today. "Reliable information that attack on Los Angeles is imminent. A general alarm being considered. . . ." What jackass would send a general alarm [which would have meant warning all civilians to leave the area including the workers in the vital Southern California aircraft industry] under the circumstances. The [4th] Army G-2 [Intelligence] is just another amateur, like all the rest of the staff. Rule: the higher the headquarters, the more important is *calm*.

Stilwell's low opinion of General De Witt was apparently shared by others within the Army; shortly after Vinegar Joe's transfer to Washington just before Christmas, he noted that Lieutenant General Lesley J. McNair, Deputy Commander, Army Ground Forces, had told him that "De Witt has gone crazy and requires ten refusals before he realizes it is 'No'." De Witt, it must be understood, was a cautious, conservative officer in the twilight of his career. He saw, throughout the Army, younger men being promoted into key posts; his contemporary, Lieutenant General Walter C. Short, the Army commander in Hawaii, was in disgrace. With misplaced concreteness De Witt apparently decided that there would be no Pearl Harbors on the West Coast. It is interesting to note that the cautious De Witt, in safe San Francisco, was more alarmed by the famous "war warning" telegram of November 27 than was Short in exposed Honolulu, and had the former been the Hawaiian commander, the Army at least, might have been in a more advanced state of readiness. But after Pearl Harbor, caution turned into funk; no one who reads the transcripts of De Witt's telephone conversations with Washington or examines his staff correspondence can avoid the conclusion that his was a headquarters at which confusion rather than calm reigned, and that the confusion was greatest at the very top.

It was in this panic-ridden, amateurish Western Defense Command atmosphere that some of the most crucial decisions about the evacuation of the Japanese Americans were made. Before examining them, however, it should be made clear that the nearest Japanese aircraft during most of December were attacking Wake Island, more than 5000 miles west of San Francisco, and any major Japanese surface vessels or troops were even farther away. In fact, elements of the Luftwaffe over the North Atlantic were actually closer to California than any Japanese planes. California and the West Coast of the continental United States were in no way seriously threatened by the Japanese military. This finding does not represent just the hindsight of the military historian; the high command of the American army realized it at the time. Official estimates of Japanese capabilities made late in December concluded correctly that a large-scale invasion was beyond the capacity of the Japanese military but that a hit-and-run raid somewhere along the West Coast was possible.

In the days just after Pearl Harbor there was no concerted plan for mass incarceration. As evidence of this, on December 9 General Brehon Somervell, the Army's G–4 (Supply), ordered the construction of "facilities for the internment of alien enemies and other prisoners of war"; the three facilities authorized within De Witt's Western Defense Command had a total capacity of less than 2000, a figure consistent with the number of enemy aliens the FBI was in the process of rounding up. But De Witt and his nervous headquarters staff, ready to believe anything, soon began to pressure Washington for more drastic action against the presumably dangerous enemies in their midst.

The first proposal by the Army for any kind of mass evacuation of Japanese Americans was brought forward at a De Witt staff conference in San Francisco on the evening of December 10. In the language of a staff memo, the meeting considered "certain questions relative to the problem of apprehension, segregation and detention of Japanese in the San Francisco Bay Area." The initial cause of the meeting seems to have been a report from an unidentified Treasury Department official asserting that 20,000 Japanese in the Bay Area were ready for organized action. Apparently plans for a mass roundup were drawn up locally, and approved by General Benedict, the commander of the area, but the whole thing was squelched by Nat Pieper, head of the San Francisco office of the FBI, who laughed it off as "the wild imaginings" of a former FBI man whom he had fired. The imaginings were pretty wild; the figure of 20,000 slightly exceeded the total number of Japanese men, women, and children in the Bay Area. But wild or not, De Witt's subordinate reported the matter to Washington with the recommendation that "plans be made for large-scale internment." Then on December 19 General De Witt officially recommended "that action be initiated at the earliest practicable date to collect all alien subjects fourteen years of age and over, of enemy nations and remove them" to the interior of the United States and hold them "under restraint after removal" to prevent their surreptitious return. (The age limit was apparently derived from the federal statutes on wartime internment, but those statutes, it should be noted, specified males only.)

De Witt was soon in touch with the Army's Provost Marshal General, Allen W. Gullion, who would prove to be a key figure in the decision to relocate the Japanese Americans. Gullion, the Army's top cop, had previously served as Judge Advocate General, the highest legal office within the Army. He was a service intellectual who had once read a paper to an International Congress of Judicial Experts on the "present state of international law regarding the protection of civilians from the new war technics." But, since at least mid-1940, he had been concerned with the problem of legally exercising military control over civilians in wartime. Shortly after the fall of France, Army Intelligence took the position that fifth column activities had been so successful in the European war in creating an internal as well as an external military front that the military "will actually have to control, through their Provost Marshal Generals, local forces, largely police" and that "the Military would certainly have to provide for the arrest and temporary holding of a large number of suspects," alien and citizen.

Gullion, as Judge Advocate General, gave his official opinion that within the United States, outside any zone of actual combat and where the civil courts were functioning, the "Military . . . does not have jurisdiction to participate in the arrest and temporary holding of civilians who are citizens of the United States." He did indicate, however, that if federal troops were in actual control (he had martial law in mind), jurisdiction over citizen civilians might be exercised. Although martial law was never declared on the Pacific Coast, Chief of Staff George C. Marshall did declare the region a "Theater of Operations" on December 11. This declaration, which was not made with the Japanese Americans in mind, created the legal fiction that the Coast was a war zone and would provide first the Army and then the courts with an excuse for placing entirely blameless civilian citizens under military control.

By December 22 Provost Marshal General Gullion, like any good bureaucrat, began to campaign to enlarge the scope of his own activities, an activity usually known as empire building. He formally requested the Secretary of War to press for the transfer of responsibility for conduct of the enemy alien program from the Department of Justice to the War Department. This recommendation found no positive response in Stimson's office, and four days later Gullion was on the telephone trying to get General De Witt to recommend a mass roundup of all Japanese, alien and citizen. Gullion told the Western Defense commander that he had just been visited by a representative of the Los Angeles Chamber of Commerce urging that all Japanese in the Los Angeles area be incarcerated. De Witt, who would blow hot and cold, was, on December 26, opposed. He told Gullion that

I'm very doubtful that it would be common sense procedure to try and intern 117,000 Japanese in this theater. . . . An American citizen, after all, is an American citizen. And while they all may not be loyal, I think we can weed the disloyal out of the loyal and lock them up if necessary.

De Witt was also opposed, on December 26, to military, as opposed to civilian, control over enemy aliens. "It would be better," he told Gullion, if "this thing worked through the civil channels."

While these discussions and speculations were going on all about them, the West Coast Japanese in general and the citizen Nisei in particular were desperately trying to establish their loyalty. Many Japanese communities on the Coast were so demoralized by the coming of war that little collective action was taken, especially in the first weeks after Pearl Harbor. But in Los Angeles, the major mainland center of Japanese population, frantic and often pitiful activity took place. Most of this activity revolved around the Japanese American Citizens League, an organization, by definition, closed to Issei, except for the handful who achieved citizenship because of their service in the United States armed forces during World War I. Immediately following Pearl Harbor the Japanese American Citizens League (JACL) wired the President, affirming their loyalty; the White House had the State Department, the arm of government usually used to communicate with foreigners, coolly respond by letter that "your desire to cooperate has been carefully noted." On December 9 the JACL Anti-Axis Committee decided to take no contributions, in either time or money, from noncitizens, and later, when special travel regulations inhibited the movement of aliens, it decided not to help Issei "in securing travel permits or [giving] information in that regard." In addition, Nisei leaders repeatedly called on one generation to inform on the other.

On the very evening of Pearl Harbor, editor Togo Tanaka went on station KHTR, Los Angeles, and told his fellow Nisei:

As Americans we now function as counterespionage. Any act or word prejudicial to the United States committed by any Japanese must be warned and reported to the F.B.I., Naval Intelligence, Sheriff's Office, and local police. . . .

Before the end of the week the Los Angeles Nisei had set up a formal Committee on Intelligence and had regular liaison established with the FBI. These patriotic activities never uncovered any real sabotage or espionage, because there was none to uncover. Nor did it provide the protective coloration that the Nisei hoped it would; race, not loyalty or citizenship, was the criterion for evacuation. It did, however, widen the gap between the generations, and would be a major cause of bitterness and violence after the evacuation took place.

CHAPTER 19

AMERICAN DIPLOMACY IN WORLD WAR II

Two things stand out above all others when one reviews the workings of Allied diplomacy during World War II: (1) The Allies were both individually and collectively looking beyond the war's end to a future reshaping of the world, and (2) their postwar goals were ofttimes hazy and almost never the same. Nevertheless, the early realization that the defeat of the Axis must precede any global settlement dictated Allied cooperation at the strategic and, on occasion, even the tactical level. The history of American diplomatic endeavors is thus a story of attempts to cooperate with diverse leaders, such as Josef Stalin, Winston Churchill, Charles de Gaulle, and Chiang Kai-shek, each of whom represented divergent interests. The strong personality of Franklin D. Roosevelt was in itself an additional complication. It is hardly surprising that these efforts at cooperation occasionally failed. That they worked at all is an indication of how strongly the common enemy was feared and detested.

A cursory reading of the following selection would lead one to believe that President Roosevelt was at times ill-informed, ill-advised, and naive. On closer study, however, it appears that his basic fault lay in his attempt to force events to conform to his vision of a peaceful, free, postwar world—an ideal beyond his, and perhaps anyone's, diplomatic reach. Given Churchill's desire to cling to the vestiges of empire, Stalin's paranoid suspicion, de Gaulle's dreams of French hegemony in Western Europe, the internal rot of Chiang's government, and the rising expectations of the colonial areas of the world, it appears obvious that no one figure or, for that matter, no one nation could have averted the conflicts that inevitably arose. In this selection, Gaddis Smith has done a masterful job of synthesizing a large, complex body of material without dangerously oversimplifying either the problems or the attempted solutions.

But, as in all good historical writing, new questions emerge from Professor Smith's explanations and conclusions. Was Roosevelt justified in believing that he could charm Stalin into trusting the West? Was Stalin justified in his demands that the Allies open a second front in Europe to relieve some of the pressure on the Russian forces? Given the improvements in armored and aerial warfare, was there any justification for the British fear of a World War I type stalemate if the West should invade the European continent early in the war? Why did Roosevelt and his advisers place such confidence in the Chinese? Last, and perhaps most important, was there ever any real hope that the "Big Four" could reach a common agreement on the nature of the postwar world and then work in conjunction to attain that goal?

One of the most provocative volumes ever written on American diplomatic history is George F. Kennan, *American Diplomacy, 1900–1950** (1951). Its section on this period is most pertinent. The standard account of Big Three diplomacy is Herbert Feis, *Churchill, Roosevelt, and Stalin: The War They Waged and the Peace They Sought** (1957). This volume cannot be ignored by serious students. Robert E. Sherwood, *Roosevelt and Hopkins** (1948), is a dated account that virtually canonizes Roosevelt, but it contains valuable material. D. F. Fleming, *The Cold War and Its Origins, 1917–1960*, 2 vols. (1961), relates wartime diplomacy to the events that followed it. Herbert Feis, *The China Tangle** (1953), is more explicit on Asian policy than the foregoing volumes, and George F. Kennan, *Russia and the West Under Lenin and Stalin** (1961), furnishes the same in-depth insight into Soviet affairs during World War II.

*Available in a paperback edition.

THE NATURE OF WARTIME DIPLOMACY

GADDIS SMITH

American public opinion changed before the spectacle of unchecked Nazi aggression. President Franklin D. Roosevelt won support for military and naval preparedness and material aid to Great Britain. The United States became the "arsenal of democracy." Congress put aside the neutrality laws and passed the lend-lease program in March 1941. Three months later Hitler attacked Russia. Americans forgot their dislike for the Soviet state and extended aid. Roosevelt claimed that his aim was to keep the United States out of war, but by late 1941 the American people realized that the higher aim of checking Axis aggression might soon make entry into war inevitable. On the Atlantic the American navy was skirmishing with German U-boats. In the Pacific Japan might strike at any moment against the tightening web of American economic warfare. The blow came at Pearl Harbor, December 7, 1941. The United States was at war with Japan. Germany and Italy immediately declared war on the United States. The period of equivocal undeclared war was over.

Repeatedly and without success the United States had tried various unconditional approaches to peace and security: neutrality in 1914, idealism in 1918, isolation in the 1930's. Now the nation sought security by the unconditional defeat of the enemy. Since the enemy's existence was deemed the only significant cause of insecurity, men now assumed that a world consistent with American ideals and interests would emerge once the Axis powers were destroyed. Freed from enslavement and the fear of Axis aggression, all nations would embrace American ideals of democracy and peaceful conduct. If a misguided ally—Great Britain, for example—showed a tendency to stray from these ideals, a little friendly diplomatic persuasion would be sufficient to return her to the paths of righteousness. Absolute victory was achieved after four years and some effort had been made to change the behavior of allies, but Americans discovered in sorrow that peace was still unsecured. At the moment of victory in 1945 American leaders were on the verge of the realization that there were no unconditional solutions and that final, complete security in the twentieth century was unattainable.

SOURCE. Gaddis Smith, *American Diplomacy During The Second World War, 1941–1947,* pp. 2–19. Copyright © 1965 by John Wiley & Sons, Inc. Reprinted by permission of John Wiley & Sons, Inc.

The first diplomatic objective on the road to unconditional victory was coordination of the American, British, and Russian efforts. This was the task of the three heads of government: President Roosevelt, Prime Minister Winston S. Churchill, and Premier Josef V. Stalin. While the Big Three at the summit decided grand strategy and ambiguously discussed fundamental objectives of the war, their subordinates bargained to allocate materials, provide shipping, build bases, assign troops, and develop new weapons. The great decisions were tied to the outcome of the lesser and all required international negotiation. Diplomacy, instead of retiring to the sidelines until the fighting was over, became indispensable to every aspect of the war and thus to the life of the United States.

In December 1941 the potential power of the United States was great, but the immediate outlook was disastrous, far more disastrous than the American public realized. The navy was crippled; the army was an expanding swarm of civilians without sufficient equipment, training, or experienced officers; and industry was only partially converted from peacetime production. Germany controlled western Europe and her armies were wintering deep in Russia. Who dared predict that Russia could withstand the onslaught through another summer? Elsewhere German armies seemed on the verge of driving the British from Egypt and taking the vital Suez Canal. At any moment Franco in Spain might snatch Gibraltar. Hitler could then close the Mediterranean, dominate North Africa and the Middle East while choking the United Kingdom with a cordon of submarines in the Atlantic. The western hemisphere would be directly threatened. In Asia and the Pacific the only limit to Japan's wave of conquest was her own decision not to move beyond certain lines. Half of China, the Philippines, Indochina, Burma, Malaya, the Netherlands East Indies, and scores of smaller island groups were in her grasp. Would she seize India, Australia, Siberia, Hawaii? What could stop her? Anything was conceivable.

Fortunately, American diplomacy responded less to the immediate military peril, which might have been paralyzing, than to an optimistic view of the nation's historical experience and to the buoyantly confident personality of the commander-in-chief, Franklin D. Roosevelt. Americans later were to be led astray by too much optimism, but, on the dark morrow of Pearl Harbor, optimism enabled men to begin planning for victory. Notwithstanding the pain and humiliation of retreat in the Pacific, attention was turned first to coordinating strategy for the defeat of Germany. This priority was maintained on the sound assumption that Germany without Japan would be as strong as ever, whereas Japan without Germany could not long stand alone.

The remembered experience of the First World War exercised a profound effect on the diplomacy of European strategy. Americans had misleading and rather happy memories. In the summer of 1918 large numbers of American troops faced the enemy for the first time. By November the war was over. Admittedly, circumstances were now radically different, but the experience of 1918 combined with a natural optimism led Americans to favor a strategy of direct attack as soon as possible (preferably 1942 but certainly 1943) across the Channel on the center of German power.

The favored strategy of Great Britain, also based in large measure on experience of the First War, was totally different. From the autumn of 1914 until the summer of 1918, while the United States remained neutral or in a state of preparation, Great Britain and France had seen an entire generation of young manhood die in the stinking trenches of the western front. For four years gains and losses were measured in yards, casualties in millions. Now, twenty-five years later, France was conquered and Britain, having narrowly rescued her small army at Dunkirk, stood alone in Europe. What Englishman could advocate a deliberate return to the horrors of the continent before all other methods of attacking the enemy had been exhausted and victory assured? Certainly not Churchill, who had in the First War been a leading, if unsuccessful, critic of the stationary slaughter of the trenches. In the Second War Churchill, expressing his own and his nation's convictions, argued tirelessly against a premature frontal attack. By no means all of his alternative proposals were adopted, but he did succeed in postponing the main attack until Anglo-American strength was overwhelming. Until that attack came, in June 1944, the competition between the two strategies—the massive direct assault versus shifting operations on the periphery—was a central theme in Anglo-American diplomacy to which all other issues were in some way related.

Russia, the third great ally, had only one possible strategy: maximum defensive pressure against Germany while urging the United States and Great Britain to open the second front in Europe without delay and simultaneously hoping that Japan, a neutral in the Russo-German war, would not attack in Siberia. The keynote of Russian diplomacy was surly suspicion compounded from Marxist-Leninist-Stalinist theories, Russia's warped memory and interpretation of events since 1917, and anticapitalist propaganda which Soviet leaders no doubt had come themselves to believe. According to the Russian view, the capitalist nations had sought to strangle the Soviet Union at birth from 1917 to 1920, but having failed had sought in the 1930's to save their own necks by turning Hitler against Russia. Current Anglo-American friendliness was, in Soviet eyes, the product of fear and the mask to a continuing hope that Russia would bleed to death. Postponement of the second front in Europe was simply an expression of this hope.

British and American leaders were angered and hurt by the Soviet calumny, but they differed in their opinions of how to deal with it. The British were relatively unruffled and stoical. Russian suspicions were a fact of life to the British. Russian demands for an immediate second front were understandable, but must be firmly refused until the time was ripe. The idea that Russia might make a separate peace with Germany, as at Brest-Litovsk in 1918, if she did not receive full satisfaction from the West was dismissed by the British as nonsense. Similarly, the British argued that Russian cooperation or the lack of it in the postwar world would depend on the power structure at the time and not on fanciful Russian gratitude for favors which the West could not afford to grant.

The American attitude toward Russia was not monolithic, but the dominant view, to which President Roosevelt subscribed, was conciliatory, indulgent, and tinged with the vague fear that an unappeased Russia might make a separate peace. Roosevelt and his closest advisers were far readier than the British to meet Russian demands, to see an element of truth in Russian distortion of the past, and to insist that the way to win Russian trust was to begin by trusting, and making every possible allowance for Russian unpleasantness. Furthermore, Americans proclaimed time and again that the future peace of the world depended not on the balance of power but on the closest possible cooperation with Russia. That cooperation could and must be assured while the war was still in progress. In short, Americans were pessimistic concerning what Russia might do if her wishes were not met, but they were essentially optimistic in their belief that Western attitudes could shape Russian behavior both during and after the war. The ramifications of this Anglo-American-Soviet interplay appear everywhere in the diplomacy of the war. They affected the debate over grand strategy and they touched such questions as shipping and allocation of supplies. They lay behind the formulation of war aims for Europe, for Asia, and for the nature of the United Nations. In that interplay can be found some of the origins of the Cold War.

American optimism extended to the war against Japan. This segment of the conflict remained second priority until the day of victory in Europe, but it absorbed an increasing amount of diplomatic energy and military resources. The ocean war on the Pacific was an American show and required few diplomatic arrangements, but on the mainland of Asia diplomacy encountered its most complicated, difficult, and frustrating task: the support of China. Of all the allies of the United States, China excited the highest hopes and ultimately provided the most crushing disappointment. The reasons are embedded in both Chinese and American history as well as in the hard realities of geography and military power during the war. Had the China of Chiang Kai-shek conformed to the romantic image cherished widely in the United States all would have been well. According to this image, which had flourished since the early nineteenth century, China was yearning and able to follow in the ways of its one benefactor and friend, the United States. If China could only be freed from the bondage of foreign oppression, an efficient, modern democracy would emerge. The Japanese occupation was a serious obstacle on this road to freedom, but, according to American illusion, the full moral support of the United States plus whatever equipment could be spared would bring ultimate triumph and a united, independent China, one of the four great powers (along with the United States, Russia, and Britain) upon whose permanent friendship the peace of the world would depend.

Such was the dream. Before long it became a nightmare. First, as in other areas of war, came the conflict of basic strategies. Naturally, Chiang Kai-shek considered that the center of the war was in China and that he should receive as much American support as he needed in order to preserve his position against the Communists and other domestic foes and then defeat the Japanese. For the United States, however, world strategy placed China fourth in line as a recipient of supplies: behind Anglo-American operations in Europe, behind Russia, and behind the naval war in the Pacific; and at no time was the United States willing to see its limited aid to China used for any purpose except the waging of war against Japan. Next came the problem of geography and logistics. Because Japan soon controlled all the land and water routes into China, every ton of supplies had to be transported first to northeastern India and then flown "over the Hump" at astronomical expense. For equal expenditure the United States could deliver hundreds of tons of supplies to England for every ton delivered in China. Last and most important was the relationship of the irreconcilable conflict between Chiang's government and the Communists. Few Americans could comprehend the murderous bitterness of this antagonism or why the Chinese could not forget their differences, like good Democrats and Republicans in the United States, in the patriotic struggle against Japan. Throughout the war and for more than a year afterward, it was American policy to seek to unify the Chinese factions. Seldom has an effort been so futile.

But in the days after Pearl Harbor none of these dismal facts about China was understood. Roosevelt, his advisers, and the American people looked forward to a triumphant partnership. Thus, in every quarter of the globe American diplomacy, sustained by an optimistic reading of the past and an unreal attitude toward the present, began its wartime tasks.

A factor that influenced the style and results of American wartime diplomacy as much as the nation's optimistic interpretation of the past was the personality of President Roosevelt. He took crucial diplomatic negotiations more completely into his own hands than any president before or since. One way to examine Roosevelt's qualities as a diplomat is to compare him with Woodrow Wilson. There was nothing cheerful about Wilson's solemn crusade of Christian good against the forces of evil. Roosevelt, in contrast, always gave the appearance of a happy man, sometimes to the point of an unbecoming and inappropriate frivolity. Wilson found it hard to like the individuals with whom he was forced to deal; Roosevelt's first instinct was to like everybody. Wilson was solitary; Roosevelt loved the crowd, huge parties, the feeling of presiding over a numerous family.

Associates found both Wilson and Roosevelt difficult to work with, but for different reasons. Wilson enjoyed admitting that he had a "one track mind." For long periods he would concentrate on a single issue and ignore others of equal importance. Roosevelt's mind, in contrast, was trackless. He would dabble in a dozen questions simultaneously and acquire a superficial acquaintance with thousands of details in which Wilson would have had no interest. Subordinates found it difficult to keep Roosevelt's mind focused for long on any one problem. He loved to ramble and he seldom studied deeply.

Wilson was stubborn and opinionated; his dislike for advice that did not conform with his own conclusions often became dislike for the adviser. Roosevelt, on the other hand, had a compulsion to be liked. In dealing with others he would feign agreement with an opinion rather than produce disappointment. In domestic politics this habit of trying to please everyone caused confusion but no lasting harm. When Roosevelt's final views on an issue emerged, the man who had been misled could resign. Many did.

But this Rooseveltian technique had doleful results when applied to international affairs, where all the favorable conditions that Roosevelt enjoyed at home were missing. Disagreements in domestic affairs were over means, not basic objectives. All Americans desired a healthy economy, an end to unemployment, and a broadening of security among the whole population. There were no disagreements that could not be faced and thrashed out by reasonable men of good will. But how different the conduct of international affairs, especially in the emergency conditions of a world war. The nations in uneasy coalition against the Axis disagreed not only on the means of winning the war, but also on fundamental objectives for the future. Differences were too profound to be dissolved by geniality, and disgruntled allies, unlike subordinates, could not be ignored. Roosevelt either forgot these truths, or else believed that his power to make friends was so irresistible that all opposition could be charmed out of existence. He was wrong.

There was another unfortunate connection between domestic politics and Roosevelt's diplomacy. As the most successful American politician of the century, Roosevelt had a superb sense of how much support he could command for his domestic programs. But in his understanding of what the people would accept in foreign affairs he was timid and unsure. Often he shied away from problems that needed to be confronted—Russian treatment of Poland, for example—because he feared that publicity might lose votes. He overestimated the strength of isolationism and underestimated the ability of the American people to absorb bad news and undertake new responsibility. As a result Roosevelt sometimes gave the public a falsely optimistic picture of our diplomacy, especially in regard to Russia and China. He also gave the Russians the impression that the United States would probably withdraw into partial isolation after victory and that Russia, therefore, need not worry about American opposition to her postwar ambitions in Europe.

Two further traits of Roosevelt's character should be noted. The President had a small boy's delight in military and naval problems. Under the Constitution he was commander-in-chief of the armed forces and he set out to give practical as well as theoretical meaning to the title. Much of his time was spent in close consultation with military and naval authorities. Usually, he took the advice of the chiefs of staff, but on occasion he made important military decisions independently. Roosevelt's fascination with strategy and tactics intensified the American emphasis on military objectives to the neglect of those long-range political conditions to which military operations should always be subordinate. For example, in 1944 and 1945 Roosevelt concentrated so hard on the military objective of bringing Russia into the war against Japan that he seriously weakened American bargaining power in the settlement of permanent political objectives in Europe and Asia.

Finally, Roosevelt, unlike Wilson, was a pragmatist who lived in a world in which good and bad were somewhat mixed. He had no qualms about further blending the two, and for settling by way of compromise for the best that seemed available. Roosevelt was no metaphysician losing sleep by wondering if evil means could contaminate a worthy end. He was more inclined to act and let the historians worry about the philosophical problems involved in his behavior. The historian must conclude, however, that much of Roosevelt's diplomacy fails of justification even on its own terms. Too often the means were questionable and the results worse.

Roosevelt's character produced the worst results in his diplomacy with Stalin; with Churchill the best. Churchill and Roosevelt enjoyed the closest personal and official relationship that has ever existed between an American president and the head of another government. It was not, however, a relationship of equality. Roosevelt had the power and Churchill the ideas. Churchill, acutely aware of the British Empire's dependence on the United States, kept Roosevelt informed and entertained with an almost daily stream of incomparably lucid and persuasive letters and telegrams. Frequently, he traveled to meet Roosevelt in Washington, at Hyde Park, or in Canada. Roosevelt never went to Churchill in Great Britain, although both Roosevelt and Churchill did meet Stalin on or near his home ground. Churchill's sincere liking for Roosevelt, his understanding of the President's character, and above all the range and penetration of his intellect served the British Empire and the Anglo-American cause well. No other man could have won Roosevelt's approval to such a large measure of British policy. But sometimes Roosevelt and his advisers did refuse Churchill's requests. On those occasions Churchill gave way with a grace that was as uncharacteristic of his past political behavior as it was serviceable for the preservation of the even tenor of Anglo-American relations.

Roosevelt's personal relations with Stalin were the least effective aspect of his diplomacy. The President met Stalin's displays of temper, suspicion, and churlish obstructionism with redoubled efforts at conciliation. Early in the war he tried to please Stalin by an implied promise of an immediate second front, and later he remained silent in the face of barbarous Soviet conduct in Poland. Sometimes he tried to win Stalin's confidence by ridiculing Churchill and hinting at a Soviet-American alignment against British colonialism. In personal relations and in diplomacy it is unwise and dangerous to pretend to denounce a proven friend in order to ingratiate oneself with a third party. Churchill bore the humiliation manfully; Stalin was not fooled. He listened to Roosevelt's chatter, said little himself, and coolly pushed the Soviet advantage in Europe and Asia without regard to the idealistic principles of political liberty to which Russia, as one of the United Nations, had subscribed. Stalin acted on the assumption, which Roosevelt's words and behavior amply confirmed, that the United States would raise no effective opposition to hostile Russian expansion. By the time Roosevelt's policy was reversed after the war, the Russian position had been consolidated, and the lines of the Cold War drawn.

The results of Roosevelt's personal diplomatic contact with the proud and haughty leaders who ranked just below the triumvirate, Chiang Kai-shek of China and Charles de Gaulle of France, were poor. Chiang and de Gaulle were similar in many ways. Each claimed to represent a great power suffering from temporary adversity; each was quick to resent the slightest reflection on his personal prestige or the sovereign prerogatives of his nation. Roosevelt, however, treated the two leaders in opposite fashion, acting more in terms of his preconceived notions about France and China than the actual situation. The President was an infatuated captive of the myth that China under Chiang Kai-shek was one of the world's great powers and deserved to be treated as such. He even toyed with the idea of giving Chiang a voice in the settlement of European affairs. No amount of evidence concerning Chiang's maladministration, the disunity of the country, the strength of the opposition, or the inefficiency of the Kuomintang armies appeared capable of shaking Roosevelt's illusion, at least until the closing months of the war.

For modern France, in contrast, Roosevelt had acquired an attitude of contempt as extreme as his admiration for China. He considered France a source of decay in the world, a politcally and socially sick nation which by laying down before Hitler and giving way to the Japanese in Indochina had forfeited the right to be respected. Roosevelt saw de Gaulle as a pompous adventurer who represented only a clique of followers and who secretly intended to assume the dictatorship of his country after the liberation. Ultimately, Roosevelt's attitudes led to severe friction with France and to bitter misunderstandings on the part of the American people when Chiang Kai-shek collapsed so ignominiously in his civil war with the Communists.

Although wartime diplomacy, pervasively influenced by the personality of President Roosevelt, dealt principally with military operations, one overriding question was always present: what kind of world did each of the three major allies desire after the war? Each power sought, first of all, a victory that would prevent recurrence of a war as catastrophic as the one in which the world was then involved. American leaders gradually developed among themselves some broad ideas on how this might be done, but they believed that their objectives could best be achieved if specific discussions concerning the future were postponed until the fighting was over. Assuming that no postwar problem could be as important or difficult as the defeat of the Axis and that there would be time enough after victory to make detailed arrangements, they were insensitive to the way in which the conduct of war can prejudice the results.

From the American point of view, there were several ways that the goal of postwar security might be sought. Isolation had failed and was now discredited, more thoroughly than Roosevelt realized. A unilateral armed *Pax Americana* in which every threat to security was instantaneously smashed by the exercise of the superior force of the United States was technically worth considering, but was not politically or morally tolerable. A *Pax Anglo-Americana* in which the United States and Great Britain together ran the world had appeal for some Americans, and briefly for President Roosevelt, but it, too, was not feasible. Roosevelt until 1944 favored a peace secured by the armed cooperation of "the Four Policemen": the United States, Russia, China, and Great Britain—in that order of importance. Little countries would be required to keep quiet and take orders. This concept had numerous flaws. A power vacuum would be left in western Europe where, according to Roosevelt, neither Germany nor France would again be factors in world politics. This would be especially dangerous if Roosevelt's assumption of an identity of interest between Russia and the West proved unfounded. In Asia there was considerable doubt whether the Chiang Kai-shek regime in China could survive, much less serve as a policeman for others. In addition, the outcry of small nations at being herded about by the great powers would be too loud to ignore in the United States and Great Britain, countries which prided themselves on respecting the rights of others.

Churchill felt that Roosevelt intended to relegate Great Britain to a position of undeserved and unrealistic inferiority while encouraging the disintegration of the British Empire, a development which Churchill resisted with skill and energy. The Prime Minister's own program for securing the peace was equally objectionable to most Americans. Churchill, a strong believer in the traditional

British reliance on the balance of power, assumed that the fate of Europe still determined the fate of the world; that there was a basic conflict of interest between Russia and the West; that these differences should be faced openly and realistically; that western Europe had to be rehabilitated as quickly as possible with France and eventually Germany rejoining the continent's power structure; that the United States ought to cooperate with Britain in rebuilding Europe and be prepared, if necessary, to oppose Russian ambitions. Churchill believed that colonial peoples should receive increased self-government, but that the imperial powers should continue to exercise responsibility for their colonies in the interests of world stability.

Roosevelt abandoned the concept of "the Four Policemen" in favor not of Churchill's balance of power program but in response to the rising enthusiasm in the United States for the formation of a universal collective security organization, the United Nations. Secretary of State Cordell Hull, for example, argued that postwar antagonism between Russia and the West was unthinkable and that a third world war was the only conceivable alternative to full cooperation. Great power cooperation must be embedded in a world organization, a resurrection of the Wilsonian League of Nations. From 1944 onward Roosevelt and his advisers were fully committed to the early establishment of the United Nations as the only way to lasting peace. They became increasingly suspicious of Churchill's ideas. Ironically, many Americans came to believe that British imperialism and continued adherence to the idea of the balance of power were greater threats to security than anything Soviet Russia might do.

This does not mean that American leaders were hostile to Great Britain; rather they looked upon Britain as a misguided friend unfortunately wedded to dangerous and outmoded patterns of behavior. It was the duty of the United States to set this friend right for her own good and the good of the world. Russia, in contrast, was seen as the unfairly maligned giant, a bear too long harassed by an unsympathetic world. Russia had been so badly treated in the past that it was now necessary for the United States and Great Britain to make an extra effort to be warm and understanding. Roosevelt and many of his advisers believed that inwardly the Soviets yearned to be friends with the West, but were too scarred with unhappy memories to take the initiative. Russia's enormous loss of life in the war, approximately ten times Anglo-American losses, strongly reinforced the sympathetic American attitude. How callous it seemed to think ill of a nation that was suffering so horribly in what Americans thought of as the common cause of humanity against the barbaric Axis. In the face of this suffering, to treat Russia as a potential adversary, as the British were inclined to do, would perpetuate the atmosphere of suspicion.

While Roosevelt, Churchill, and their advisers privately wrestled with different theories for the maintenance of peace, the official public declaration of

Anglo-American war aims remained the Atlantic Charter, a generalized statement drafted by the two leaders in August 1941, and subsequently accepted by all countries joining the war against the Axis. The Atlantic Charter denied that its adherents sought self-aggrandizement; it condemned territorial changes against the will of the peoples concerned, and favored self-government, liberal international trading arrangements, freedom from fear and want, and permanent security against aggression. Soviet Russia adhered to the Charter with the capacious qualification that "the practical application of these principles will necessarily adapt itself to the circumstances, needs, and historic peculiarities of particular countries." In other words, Russia would not be deflected in the slightest by the Charter from the pursuit of her own aims in her own way.

Roosevelt thought that Russia wanted nothing but security from attack and that this could easily be granted. Personally uninterested in theory and President of a country where ideological passion was out of style, Roosevelt tended to assume that national security meant approximately the same thing in Moscow as it did in Washington. Unfortunately, even the Russians could not say where the line lay between the normal requirements of national security and the imperatives of Communist ideology. Russia's minimum territorial objectives in Europe were clearly stated. They included restoration of the June 1941 boundary, which meant that Russia would enjoy the full fruits of the 1939 Nazi-Soviet pact, specifically the annexation of the three Baltic states, nearly half of prewar Poland, and pieces of Finland and Rumania. Germany was to be dismembered into a cluster of weak separate states and hunks of territory were to be given to Poland and Russia. Politically, Russia insisted on "friendly" governments along her central European borders. In practice this came to mean Communist regimes imposed by totalitarian means. In Asia the Soviets sought the expulsion of Japan from the mainland and the restoration of Russia's position as it existed at the height of Tsarist imperial power in 1904. This would entail serious limitations on Chinese sovereignty in Manchuria.

The United States shared these aims as far as they applied directly to Germany and Japan, but everything beyond that was in actual or potential conflict with the Atlantic Charter. By postponing decisions on these conflicts, Roosevelt convinced himself that he was preventing discord with Russia without making concessions that violated the Charter. But inwardly the President was quite prepared to concede these Russian aims on the assumption that once they were attained Russia would feel secure and would cooperate without reservations in the new world organization.

In retrospect it seems clear that Roosevelt's basic assumption was false. The evidence indicates that Soviet leaders believed that their state and ideology could never be secure as long as the world contained any large concentration of non-Communist power. Defensively they could assign no limits to the requirements of security; offensively they were under a compulsion rooted in Russian history as well as Communist ideology to expand the area of their domination wherever practical. Russian security and expansion were two sides of the same coin. A collective security organization was for the Russians an instrument to be joined or abandoned solely in terms of its usefulness in advancing Russian power in a world of irreconcilable conflict between capitalism and Communism; it was not the beneficent organization of universal cooperation envisioned by the more idealistic Americans.

Historically, most wars have been accompanied by considerable diplomatic contact between enemies; the two sides test each other's determination and bargain quietly over terms while the guns are still firing. In the Second World War, the war of unconditional surrender, the United States engaged in little diplomacy of this type. Germany and Japan, however, carried on negotiations within their spheres which significantly influenced the outcome of the war. To generalize, the Axis lost through blundering many of the advantages gained by force of arms. Had Germany and Japan been so skilled at dealing with each other, with neutrals, and with conquered peoples as they were in launching military offensives, the plight of the Allies would have been far more drastic than it was. Instead, Axis diplomacy was one of the greatest assets enjoyed by the Allies.

Hitler and the militarists of Japan came to power because the German and Japanese people were dissatisfied with the conditions that prevailed after the First World War and found a totalitarian new order appealing. In like manner, Germany and Japan scored great initial military success because many of their adversaries lacked the will to take risks in defense of an international status quo which had not brought security, prosperity, or happiness. In order to exploit this advantage it was necessary for Germany and Japan to coordinate their activities and to convince the neutrals and the conquered that, as their propaganda claimed, the new orders for Europe and Asia offered genuine benefits for those willing to cooperate. They failed utterly on both counts.

In every war between coalitions one group seeks to drive wedges into the other. It was not necessary for the Allies to seek to separate Germany and Japan because they were never together, notwithstanding the alliance signed in September 1940. The two countries were profoundly suspicious of each other and withheld information with a fervor of secrecy more appropriate among enemies. The major, fateful decisions of each—Germany's invasion of Russia and Japan's attack on the United States—were made without informing the other in advance. Ultimately, these decisions meant defeat; perhaps it could not have been otherwise given the inferiority of the Axis in population and economic resources. But true coordination diplomatically arranged might have placed the outcome in doubt.

Geographical separation was, of course, a huge obstacle to coordination, but military action might have brought the two countries into contact. Far more divisive was ideological antipathy. Japanese propaganda stressed opposition to European imperialism and appealed to the idea of Asia for the Asians. It was thus most difficult to sympathize with the boundless growth of German power. Would Germany insist on acquiring new imperial status in the Far East? The Japanese could not be sure. Hitler's ideological dislike for the Japanese was even stronger. He was a believer in "the Yellow Peril" and found the spectacle of Japanese victories over white people most disturbing even when the whites were his enemies. In short, there was "a fundamental inconsistency in the alliance between Nazi Germany, the champion of the concept of Nordic racial superiority, and Japan, the self-appointed defender of Asia against Western imperialism." In March 1942, to illustrate this point, Hitler is reported to have indulged in the thought that it would be satisfying to send England twenty divisions to help throw back the yellow horde.

Few countries have ever been so brutally and selfishly nationalistic as Germany and Japan during the Second World War. They went to war to satisfy that nationalism and lost partly because their nationalism prevented their cooperation. Still less could they cooperate with smaller countries and colonial peoples who had no love for the Allies and who might have been made into effective collaborators if the Axis had tried seduction instead of rape. In Europe Hitler had an opportunity of winning support from anti-Communists in the Balkans, Poland, and the Ukraine. But he imposed slavery where he might have made friends. He could have had far greater support from Vichy France and Franco's Spain if he had decided to offer them advantages in the new Europe. Different diplomacy and military strategy could have brought Hitler control of the Mediterranean and all of North Africa. He then might have exploited anti-British sentiment in the Middle East and brought that sparsely defended and crucial area into his orbit. India was also susceptible to anti-British appeals and if India fell, Germany and Japan would be united in control of the southern rim of Eurasia. This would have brought incalculable adversity to the Allies.

Similarly, in Asia Japan had great opportunities as she conquered colonies whose populations longed to be rid of European rule. By acting genuinely in tune with their propaganda and granting some scope to the national aspirations of these peoples, the Japanese might have forged a chain of allies across Southeast Asia. In many places they did receive a tentative welcome at first, but soon the arrogance and brutality of conquerors produced bitter hatred. The colonial peoples knew that European imperialism was bad, but Japanese imperialism was worse.

CHAPTER 20

PRESIDENT HARRY TRUMAN: DOMESTIC AFFAIRS

When Harry S. Truman was thrust into the presidency, little was publicly known about his views on domestic policies, other than that he had regularly supported President Roosevelt as a senator. It soon became obvious that he was not as decisive on the domestic scene as he was in dealing with matters of foreign policy. As André Maurois points out, he would vacillate at times between opposing sets of advisers, thereby creating confusion and adding to the impression that he was, indeed, not big enough for the job.

The problems he faced were certainly great. He had to preside over a much larger demobilization than that of 1918 in such a way as to avoid the economic dislocations of the earlier period. After 1946 he was handicapped by a Republican Congress, loyal to the domestic policies of the conservative Robert A. Taft. However, he was immensely aided by the earlier enactment, in June 1944, of one of this country's most farsighted pieces of legislation, the so-called GI Bill. Not only did this legislation pave the way for the returning soldier to establish a business or to buy a house, but it contained provisions making it possible for him to remain out of the labor market entirely. The educational provisions of the act were intended primarily to enable the veteran to go to college or to trade school, thereby increasing his skill, income, and taxability. Hence, the act would clearly work to further the nation's economic strength in the long run. But the legislation provided an extra short-term benefit in keeping many ex-soldiers enrolled in school and out of the labor force, thus stretching out the period of economic adjustment for several years. The threat of heavy unemployment was markedly reduced. The gain to the individuals, many of whom otherwise would never have pursued further education, is incalculable. A virtual social revolution was assured.

As yet, no historian has given a satisfactory explanation for Truman's wavering in his handling of domestic policy prior to 1948. Was it merely his executive inexperience? If so, why was he more resolute in dealing with foreign affairs? Could it be that his greater familiarity with domestic questions and their backgrounds made him more hesitant to deal with those problems? In interpreting this period, the student is immediately struck by the fact that Truman's domestic program was not enacted. Of what importance is legislative success in measuring the strength and impact of a presidential administration? What other criteria could be used to guage the historic contribution of an administration?

An increasing body of scholarly work deals with this topic. It is covered in a popular vein by Eric Goldman in *The Crucial Decade—And After: America, 1945–1960** (1960). For accounts that focus direcly on the Truman administration, see Cabell Phillips, *The Truman Presidency** (1966); A. L. Hamby, *Beyond the New Deal: Harry S Truman and American Liberalism** (1973); B. J. Bernstein, ed., *Politics and Policies of the Truman Administration* (1970); and Robert J. Donovan, *Conflict and Crisis: The Presidency of Harry S Truman* (1977).

*Available in a paperback edition.

THE TRUMAN ERA

ANDRÉ MAUROIS

The Truman era—a commonly used expression; and it is a fitting and a discreet tribute to that Harry Truman who, having commanded a battery of artillery in 1918 and having run a not very prosperous haberdasher's shop, suddenly found himself burdened with the world's most important affairs. It means that, unpretentiously, but not without strength, Truman left his own personal mark upon some years of history. He was no Roosevelt who, like Moses, led his people through the desert of the depression and the trials of the war toward an awareness of their social and international responsibilities. Truman's ambition was rather to be a Joshua, the faithful lieutenant who, after the prophet's meeting with his God and the proclamation of the Tables of the Law, undertook the application of them. The war was won, the social legislation passed, the Promised Land in sight. He had the right to hope for a presidency during which a lasting peace would reward the American people for the sacrifices they had made.

It is said that the morning after VJ Day, the President changed the little gun that stood on his desk for a miniature plow. He liked artless symbols of this kind. In Independence, it was the simple virtues that counted—honesty, straighforwardness, family affection. He loved accompanying his daughter Margaret, the singer, on the piano, and writing to his ninety-two-year-old mother. The comradeship of the Senate pleased him; so did the feeling that there he had the right to look the most powerful man in the eye, since no one could reproach him with the wrongful gaining of a single dollar. In his heart of hearts, he would have liked to see all the nations of the earth adopt the moral standards of Independence, Missouri. But the nations of the earth possessed neither his common sense nor his humility, and for eight years, he was to learn the ways of a very rough calling. As he says himself, in his *Memoirs,* the vice-presidency had hardly prepared him for it at all. During the year that preceded Roosevelt's death, he had scarcely seen him eight times. But he did hold one trump card—his knowledge of history. He knew how Lincoln before him had dealt with difficult demagogue generals. He knew that all nations

SOURCE. André Maurois, *The New Freedom to the New Frontier: A History of the United States from 1912 to the Present,* pp. 247–249, 254–262, and 265–268. Copyright © 1963 by David McKay Company, Inc. Reprinted by permission of David McKay Company, Inc.

sometimes have their fits of hysteria. He had read of the Salem witches and the Ku Klux Klan. He was well acquainted with the life of Andrew Johnson who, like himself, woke up to find that he was the successor of a great president. "History taught me that the leader of any country, in order to assume his responsibilities as a leader, must know the history, not only of his own country, but of all the great countries."

His countrymen, astonished at seeing Truman in Roosevelt's seat, thought of him at first as an average American and nothing more. This was a serious mistake. An "average man" would not have possessed his personality, or his wide reading, or his courage. He began by keeping Roosevelt's favorite advisers, but later he did not hesitate to discard those who, like Byrnes, Wallace, and MacArthur, tried to oblige him to follow policy of which he disapproved: on the other hand, when he thought men (Marshall, Clifford, Acheson, and Kennan, for example) good judges of the situation, he accepted their advice. They supplied plans of action: the merit of applying them, in the face of violent opposition, belonged to him alone. The Truman era: yes, the phrase is just, for it was he who guided world events that, without him, would have taken a very different and even more dangerous turning. . . .

II

It was widely held that the transition from a war economy to one of peace could not be made without a serious depression. This had happened after the First World War; and the United States had been even more deeply disturbed and for a longer time by the second. Would a capitalist economy be able to withstand the trial? Stalin expected a crisis in America similar to that of 1929. "It was clear," says Truman in his memoirs, "that his foreign policy was based upon this expectation." Stalin supposed that by delaying settlement he would have a weakened America before him, incapable of helping her allies and ready to make all manner of concessions. This was not bad reasoning. If a major depression had followed the war, it is possible that the Americans might, out of discouragement and bitterness, have turned back to isolationism. But instead of a crisis, the United States was to experience an unprecedented prosperity.

In 1933, the national income was 39.6 billion dollars: by 1940, it had risen to 81.3 billion dollars. It reached 182.8 billion in 1945. There was no unemployment, and savings were abundant. It might have been supposed that the sudden cancellation of war contracts would be a terrible blow to production. But no, everything passed off very well. The needs of the private citizen had been very meagerly served for the last five years, and now that the war was over they were quite capable of absorbing more than the country could produce. Instead of crisis, the threat was rather that of inflation. The people were well off, and they competed for nonexistent goods. There was a shortage of housing and cars, and soon even meat was scarce. Prices rocketed. But the prosperity went on. From 1946 to 1953, during the Truman era, the population increased by 21 percent, the national income by 37 percent, and personal incomes, after payment of taxes, by 20 percent. It had been said with great anxiety, "Sixty million jobs will be needed after the war." Sixty-two million were available. In spite of the inflation, the people's buying power increased.

It has already been said that the demobilization was too rapid. But how was it possible to resist the pressure of the soldiers and their families, and of the workers whom the war factories had taken far from their homes? The soldiers were tired of military life and the workers of canteens and dormitories, and both rushed back to their houses, their farms, their spouses, and their children. There were positive riots in the army in 1946, when attempts were made to slow down the rate of release. As early as the summer of that year, the huge wartime "armadas" had been reduced to peacetime strength. This hastiness created great dangers in foreign policy. It might also have been supposed that it would do the same for the country's economy, by suddenly throwing ten million men into the labor market. But earlier on, a most prudent law had been passed, a law the public called the GI Bill of Rights. It provided for a great deal of help in many forms for the ex-servicemen: scholarships to prepare for a profession or a trade; four years at a university, with books free; grants of money for those who could not find work; employment agencies; loans for the purchase of houses, businesses, or farms. In short, huge funds to tide over the transition.

The tens of billions of dollars thus spent were the best possible investment for the nation. Good minds that in ordinary times might have been wasted received the education they deserved. There was feeling that justice had been done, and this appealed to thousands of men who up until then had supposed that the university was a luxury for the rich. The present writer was at that time teaching in an American university. The veterans easily held the lead in all the classes. One of them wrote to him,

It was the army that gave me the only worthwhile education—learning to rely on nobody but myself. Before that I lived in a fictitious world. I loved sentimentality. Now I have moved from the world of words to the world of deeds. It was battle, and not the blackboard, that taught me that the solution of a geometrical problem decided whether I was to come under murderous shellfire or not. . . . It was contact with reality that taught me the difference between a fine book, such as *War and Peace,* and the stupidity of some nondescript piece of propaganda.

Another wrote,

The war gave me the opportunity of seeing many different nations in every climate under the sun. I shall never be an isolationist again. I am too well aware how everything in the world links up with everything else.

These men and women came back from the war more devoted to equality than they had been before. Some had suffered from what they called the caste system when they were in the army. One sergeant told how the officers had built a club, in one of the Pacific islands, and had surrounded it with notices "Restricted Area. Officers only"; the enlisted men built a bigger, better club, and wrote on the lane leading to it, "Restricted. Enlisted men only." No one would go back to "underprivileged" jobs. Neither industry nor farming found it easy to recruit laborers. The Truman era was a time of great hopes and of happy dreams. It was thought that the recently discovered antibiotics were going to overcome even the worst diseases. It was foretold that presently new sources of energy would allow men to work shorter hours but nevertheless receive higher pay. This was the time at which Fred Vinson, the director of reconversion, said, "The Americans are in the difficult—and agreeable—position of having to learn how to live half as well again as they have ever lived before." People had not begotten many babies during the great depression: prosperity and the return of the soldiers suddenly set up a new record in this field.

The reconversion of industry, however, raised many difficult problems. As early as VJ Day, Truman had set up a program: the cancellation of war contracts as soon as possible; the freezing of prices and rents until competition should operate again, in order to prevent inflation; the maintenance of wages at their current level, for the same reasons; the retention of wartime controls on production only to the extent necessary to prevent bottlenecks and the cornering of raw materials; and the provision of full employment. It was a reasonable program; but reason is not the prime mover among mankind, and each blamed that part of the program that inconvenienced him. The unions would have liked prices to be frozen while wages were left free. "During the war," they said, "the workers did in fact work overtime. If we are returned to the forty-hour week, with the same pay, our purchasing power will drop." The employers, for their part, maintained that business conditions did not allow them to increase wages and proved this was so by impressive statistics, to which the unions replied with more statistics, equally impressive.

Truman, torn between the New Dealers in his Cabinet on the one hand and by some of the conservatives in his party on the other, wavered first this way and then the other. One day, he told livestock dealers that he would maintain price controls on meat; three weeks later, he took them off. The fact of the matter was that $48,000,000,000 of savings and a reduction of $6,000,000,000 in taxes was giving all classes of the population an enormous purchasing power just at a time when there was not much to buy. As for the President, his opponents claimed that he was behaving neither like a real believer in the New Deal nor as an adversary of it, but rather like a man who yields to the strongest pressure at each successive moment. Hence a flood of criticism. "To err is Truman," they said: or, as one might put it, *"Errare Trumanum est."*

In 1946, there began a time of strikes. Some were of no importance, but the long-drawn-out strike of miners made the government uneasy. It appeared to be dangerous, not only for the country, whose factories it might bring to a halt, but for Europe, to whom America had promised coal. The question of pay was complicated by questions of prestige. It was rumored that the former friends, John L. Lewis, of the miners, and Philip Murray, of the CIO, had quarreled, and that if one of them gained a concession the other at once had to get something better. The soft-spoken Murray, a gentle Scot, owed his authority to reason: John L. Lewis, who had the face of a Danton, fascinated the mineowners by his romantic eloquence. "Lewis," said one of these big employers, "speaks an English worthy of Winston Churchill." During the pauses between sessions, he would go to the window, gaze at the trees and the flowers, and improvise a couplet upon spring, scattered with quotations from Shakespeare. Both sides were in agreement upon the most important point, the setting up of a fund to look after the miners' health and security. But Lewis wanted to be the sole administrator of the fund; whereas the employers thought that they too should have a say in its management.

With the midterm election of 1946 in view, Truman maneuvered carefully. He needed the unions. His friends in Independence, Missouri, pitied him: "Poor Harry. He is having a very difficult presidency." Yet in the middle of the strike, he arrived on his airplane "The Sacred Cow" to greet his old mother on Mother's Day. He could understand and direct the most important affairs of the nation, but for all that he remained a small-town man at heart. "Being president is only a beginning for him," said one of his friends. "His real ambition is to be governor of Missouri." An opponent replied, "Under him, Pennsylvania Avenue has turned into Main Street."

But Main Street's intelligence is not to be despised. When in their turn the railways threatened to go on strike, Truman reacted strongly. He requisitioned both mines and railways, and he was in the act of delivering an almost violent message to Congress when he was handed a paper. The strike was over: he had won. It was a bitter victory, and it left rancor behind it. The Americans had accepted compulsory military service but only with great reluctance, and the use of its harsh discipline to prevent a strike seemed to them unconstitutional. On the other hand, the distraction in the railroad stations at the mere announcement of the possibility of a strike proved how right the President had been in dreading an interruption of a public service in this vast country.

Public opinion was turning against him. It objected to Truman's optimism, to what it unfairly termed his platitudes, and even to his filial affection. People said with a sneer, "Every day is Mother's Day at the White House." The Republicans invented a most successful slogan for the 1946 campaign, the campaign for the election of the Eightieth Congress: "Had enough? Have you had enough of strikes, of Cabinet officers who contradict one another, of ambivalent policy, of inflation, of expensive living, of atomic bombs?" The public opinion institutes, which are no more infallible than weather bureaus but which are reasonably exact in showing a general tendency, had shown 87 percent of Americans as favorable to Truman at the time of his honeymoon with the nation—a record figure. A little before the 1946 Congressional election, the percentage had dropped to 35 percent. To the question "Had enough?" the electors replied, "Yes, we have had enough," and they sent a Republican Congress to Washington. Senator Taft was going to have his hour, unless. . . .

III

Unless everything changed. In politics it is almost always forgotten that situations evolve by themselves. Very soon meat became plentiful once more; the housewives calmed down; the strikes stopped because the union leaders felt them to be unpopular. The great body of the citizens were living better than they had before the war, and they knew it. "The American Meat Institute issued the most revealing figures. Before the war, housewives had turned to macaroni, egg and cheese mixtures, or some other inexpensive dish for half the family meals; in 1947, the average American ate meat five out of seven nights a week." And it was not only the standard of living that was getting better. The average American's dignity and feeling of equality were also increasing. The workers had won solid gains. Truman had caused a very important law to be passed in 1946, the Full Employment Act, under the provisions of which the country was to be divided into economic regions. If, in any of these regions, there was a threat of unemployment, the government would deal with the situation by grants or by undertaking public works. In other words, the government would set about a true planning of the economy. It would not dictate production plans to industry; but, knowing the estimates of private enterprise, it would supplement them with a program designed to maintain full employment. It would be the duty of a Council of Economic Advisers, which the act set up in the executive branch, to tell the President of any signs of weakness in the economy and to suggest means of dealing with them. The Act created also, within the Congress, a Joint Committee on the Economic Report that was to analyze the data contained in the annual report of the council and to initiate legislation on the basis of recommendations by the President.

Equally important was the contract between General Motors, the great car manufacturers, and the United Auto Workers Union. For the first time, a sliding scale of prices and wages was established, with automatic revision every three months, so as to maintain purchasing power. Furthermore, an annual increase in real wages was to take into account increased production: there were also clauses dealing with social security—pensions, medical insurance, and life insurance arranged by the automobile industry. The workers' status was getting better. Strikes were less frequent.

But the Eightieth Congress, with its Republican majority, had come to Washington with the conservatives, so long defeated by the New Deal, thirsty for revenge. These fifteen years past, they had felt a homesick longing for laissez-faire and free enterprise. The war had rendered them powerless. Sadly they had seen a new America, the America of Roosevelt's friends, the intellectuals and the unions, taking on an ever greater importance. Their favorite spokesman was Senator Taft.

The Taft family, which had not long before given the United States a likable and upright president, later chief justice, had for a great while symbolized respectability mingled with culture and a love for tradition in the city of Cincinnati, as the Lodge family had in Boston. Senator Taft, although he had been a brilliant student at Yale and Harvard, refused the label "intellectual" in the disagreeable sense that he attributed to the word. "Basically, Taft amounted to a call for counterrevolution against the half century of revolution." A revolution that had been begun, it may be observed, by the Republican Teddy Roosevelt. Filled with sincerity and an undeniable civic courage, Taft stood up for the old American liberties against all these dubious novelties, these plans, subsidies, and international engagements. In a word, he would have liked to live in 1900, and it was his misfortune to be living in 1946. He was certainly the only man capable of telling the farmers, his electors, that farm prices were too high. At the height of the furor over meat prices, reporters asked the Senator for his solution, and he replied, "Eat less." It was the purest Taftiana—in its magnificent tactlessness and its bedrock assumption that a real American solved his own problems.

The great aim of Taftism (and of the Eightieth Congress, which was hostile to Truman) was to reestablish the balance between management and workers in the industrial world by restraining "the unions' excesses." In 1946, Truman himself had approved a law that forbade "featherbedding," that is to say, bringing pressure to bear on an employer to oblige him to engage more hands than he needed and paying for work not actually performed. In 1947, Congress passed the Taft-Hartley Act that did not undo all the unions' victories, but that did forbid them to insist upon a "closed shop," in which all workers necessarily belonged to a union. It also forbade them to refuse genuine negotiations, and, more widely, it outlawed all "unfair practices." The law allowed employers to sue unions for breach of contract. It provided for "cooling-off periods," or pauses for thought before a strike, and it authorized the President to use the right of injunction if the strike threatened the health of the nation or the security of the state. It forbade the unions to make grants to political parties and compelled them to submit their yearly accounts to the Department of Labor. The great workers' unions at once protested violently against what they called "a slave labor law." Truman vetoed it. Congress passed the law over his veto. The repeal of the Taft-Hartley Act was to be a major political issue for years. Meanwhile, it did not prevent the unions, which still had the right of negotiating collective contracts, from successfully struggling to improve their members' economic position.

The chief reasons for the relative stability of the American economy after the Second World War was in fact the progress that had been made in the redistribution of income and the huge amount of goods and equipment the Cold War military buildup and economic aid to the war-ravaged countries required. The current that had for so long carried purchasing power toward the same class and that had brought about a dangerous concentration of wealth had been reversed. The current in the opposition direction was not yet a very brisk one, but there was no doubt about which way it was flowing. In 1941, 29 percent of American families had an income of less than $500; in 1947, 8.4 percent. In 1941, only 4 percent of families earned between $4,000 and $5,000 a year; in 1947, 12.8 percent. Poverty, alas, had not been wiped out. The pyramid was not breaking down quickly: far from it. But a vast, slow leveling was really taking place. The welfare of all had become the aim, at least the long-term aim, of most. Crises were still possible, but it seemed that there were compensatory mechanisms that allowed them to be dealt with. Even the farmers, well supported by the government, had recovered, if not prosperity, then at least a position of decent steadiness. It may not have been Paradise, but it was certainly no longer Hell.

After the 1946 election, Truman's opponents had said, "This is not an election; it is a rout." They were wrong: it was only a hard knock, and in the course of his jolting career the President had received plenty of them. The artilleryman decided to correct the range. He adroitly gloried in the opposition of Congress. It insisted upon economies and cut taxes: Truman replied that the savings would be made at the expense of social reforms and the national defense. He proposed a program of greater aid for farmers and equality of rights for racial minorities, thus making sure of important blocks of votes for the presidential election of 1948. "He is not a statesman, he is a politician," said one of his opponents. Truman replied, "You had to have a politician to make a statesman." Foreign policy was to give him the opportunity of showing that he was a statesman as well. . . .

V

Harry Truman had gone to the White House in 1945 not because he had been elected president by the American people but because Roosevelt was dead. To stay there after 1948, he had to win an electoral victory and win it alone. Very much alone, indeed. For his party, with the exception of a few particular friends, did not want him as candidate. "You can't win, Harry," they told him. He had against him the right wing of the Democratic party, the Southerners, because he had shown himself favorable to the Negroes, and, more widely, because they thought him too "advanced." At the same time, certain intellectuals, fellow travelers belonging to the left wing of the party, thought that if Henry Wallace founded a "progressive" party, he would win ten million votes. The Democratic politicians, the bosses, asserted that with Truman as their candidate the party was heading for such a defeat that it would never recover. Why this withdrawal from Truman? Because a policy of compromise had disappointed the ultras of either extremity; because many thought he had not the caliber to be a president; and lastly because he had "shot at Santa Claus" by vetoing tax reduction.

The Republican convention made his task harder still by choosing as their candidate not Taft, who had many enemies but (as in 1944) Governor Dewey, who was more neutral and, like Vandenberg, in favor of a generous international policy; furthermore, Dewey himself was quite near to Truman's social ideas. It was Taft's natural and just ambition to be president, and this nomination, as were the 1944 and 1952 ones, was a tragedy for him. He had sacrificed his career to his principles.

The Democratic convention, which came after, searched desperately for a new candidate. There had been talk among Democrats, including Truman himself in the early days of his presidency, of offering the nomination to Eisenhower. But Eisenhower was politically inclined toward the Republicans. Truman's desire for renomination steadily increased; so nothing came of the Eisenhower draft scheme. When the party realized that the President was determined to run in spite of everybody and everything, it had no choice but to nominate him. Wallace then became the candidate of the new Progressive party, while a Southerner, Governor J. Strom Thurmond of South Carolina, formed the States' Rights Democratic party. The Democrats therefore went into battle divided into three separate parts, the official body unenthusiastically backing a candidate they did not believe in. None of them hoped for victory.

None except Harry Truman. Even if he had to fight alone, he was determined to win. The man who came to the tribune to accept the nomination was no longer the regular guy from Missouri who might have been received with head-shaking commiseration. He was a fighter, an acute tactician. One month earlier, Dewey had promised great reforms and had appropriated the Democratic program. Saying in effect, as Willkie had once indicated, that he would do the same things, only better. Truman very adroitly replied that the Republican party had been in a majority in Congress for the last two years, and that it had done nothing whatsoever. "This do-nothing Congress announces that it is ready to do everything. Very well. I am going to take it at its word, and I shall summon it to Washington for July 28 (which we call Turnip Day in Missouri) and I shall propose to it all the laws it is suddenly showing such a surprising fondness for." It was cleverly turned. Congress met; the atmosphere in Washington was stifling; nothing was done by this "do-nothing session of a do-nothing Congress." Truman had won a point.

The great majority of the press was against him. He decided to appeal directly to the electors, and he undertook a round trip of some 31,700 miles. Three hundred and fifty-six whistle stop speeches addressed to twelve million listeners. His vice presidential running mate, Alben W. Barkley, also did yeoman service in stumping many areas. Truman's speeches were delivered in the stations, while the train stopped. The campaign was directed straight at the Eightieth Congress. It had to be violent. Only repeated attacks could stir the country's political apathy. He had said, "I am going to fight hard. I am going to give them hell." The expectation of a good fight always draws crowds. They came to the railroad stations to listen to "Mr. Missouri." He lashed the Eightieth Congress, and then, when his speech was over, presented his wife and his daughter Margaret: "Here is the boss—and the boss's boss." The Republican newspapers, sure of success, since the public opinion polls gave Dewey 60 percent of the votes, said, "These crowds are made up of people who come as curious spectators, not as electors." They compared the wonderful efficiency of the Republican electoral machine, and Dewey's perfect organization, with Truman's homely, amateur way of carrying on.

Yet the people at the stations cried, "Give 'em hell, Harry." And Harry did so with all his heart. He told the crowds that if they let the Republicans get hold of the White House, they would make America a dependency of Wall Street. He told the workers, "The Republicans voted themselves a cut in taxes and voted you a cut in freedom. The Eightieth Republican Congress failed to crack down on prices. But it cracked down on labor all right." He told the farmers that the Eightieth Congress had given them a "pitchfork in the back," and that a Republican government would abandon the support of farm prices, in order to make economies. To the Negroes, he spoke of their civic rights. He was the first candidate to campaign in the Negro quarter of Harlem. He called the Republicans "gluttons for privilege"; he spoke of cold reactionaries with a calculating machine instead of a heart; he said that it was necessary to choose between a government of the people, by the people, for the people, and a government by the privileged, for the privileged. These resounding speeches awoke some disquiet. But still the bookmakers were giving odds of thirty to one against Truman. Both friends and enemies agreed that Dewey's victory was certain.

Election day arrived. The first results, from Philadelphia and Baltimore, gave Truman a slight advantage. But the Republicans were not worried: the polls could not be wrong. The *Chicago Tribune* brought out a special edition: DEWEY DEFEATS TRUMAN. People waited all night for the final figures. When they came, they utterly confounded the experts. Truman had won 303 electoral votes, and he kept the presidency. Dewey had 189, the Southerner Thurmond 39, and Wallace none whatsoever. The Democrats had regained their majority in the House of Representatives (a margin of 92) and in the Senate (a margin of 12). The unexpected result was heartily welcomed. In life as in the movies, the Americans loved the little man's victory over the giant. Dewey had had a powerful machine at his service; Truman had had to fight single-handed, and almost against his own party. The people cheered courage rewarded. Besides, America rallies to the underdog. Dewey's victory, being certain, would have had nothing exciting about it: Truman's was front-page news. When he came back to Washington, a million admirers covered him with a flood of paper. In the streets, hawkers sold blue buttons reading "I told you so!" This time Truman no longer owed the prophet's mantle to another; he had cut it out for himself.

CHAPTER 21

McCARTHYISM

In the years following World War II, it became increasingly obvious that American foreign policy with regard to mainland Asia was not a brilliant success. As the nation floundered ineffectively to contain Communism in China, critics of the Truman administration charged that American policies were being sabotaged through the activities of disloyal employees. The critics' case seemed to be strengthened by the fact that a very few Americans had actually been recruited by Soviet espionage agents and were passing classified information. However, no firm evidence suggests that any of these agents held significant foreign policy-making positions. When confronted with the charges, President Truman—possibly unwisely—denounced them as "red herrings" concocted for political purposes.

As is suggested in the following reading, these charges came at a critical time. The collapse of the Nationalist Chinese, the announcement of the Russian acquisition, ahead of schedule, of the atomic bomb, the beginning of Russian work on the "H" bomb, and the invasion of South Korea shook the confidence of Americans. "Treason" offered a simplistic explanation for our troubles abroad. The Russians could not possibly construct anything as complex as an atomic device. Our traditional friends, the Chinese, obviously would not turn against us without cause. Traitors in defense plants and in the State Department must be the answer—we had been sold out. No one was better at making these charges and, when pushed for specifics, at replying with additional unproven charges than Senator Joseph McCarthy (R. Wisc.), as both Republicans and Democrats were to discover. He began his demagogic career by attacking President Truman and Secretary of State Dean Acheson, and ended it by assailing Eisenhower and Robert Stevens, the Secretary of the Army. But he was never responsible for the conviction of a single Communist agent.

In viewing this aspect of postwar America, the student should be careful not to focus his attention completely on Senator McCarthy, who was probably the symptom, not the cause of the phenomenon. What lay behind our almost paranoid fear of domestic Communists and their fellow travelers? Why did

Americans find it so difficult to believe that the Soviets could construct an atomic bomb? What was happening to America's self-image in a changing world? Was the "red" menace as great as McCarthy indicated? Was it sufficiently great to justify the tactics used? What alternative steps could have been taken? Why did the issue die down so quickly after McCarthy's censure?

The literature on this topic is immense and usually polemic. One of the most reasoned and, therefore, most devastating attacks on McCarthy, the man and the ism, is Richard Rovere, *Senator Joe McCarthy** (1959). McCarthy is defended by William F. Buckley, Jr. and L. B. Bozell, *McCarthy and His Enemies: The Record and Its Meaning** (1954). Richard Hofstadter analyzes the roots of the movement in "The Pseudo-Conservative Revolt," *American Scholar* (Winter, 1954–1955). *The New American Right** (1956), edited by Daniel Bell, is a collection of essays that deal with the broader implications of McCarthyism. Michael P. Rogin, *The Intellectual and McCarthy: The Radical Specter** (1967), Robert Griffith, *The Politics of Fear: Joseph R. McCarthy and the Senate** (1970), Earl Latham, *The Communist Controversy in Washington* (1966), and Allen Weinstein, *Perjury* (1978), are important works dealing with aspects of the subject.

*Available in a paperback edition.

THE POLITICS OF REVENGE: McCARTHY AND SECURITY

WALTER JOHNSON

After recovering from the initial shock of Dewey's defeat, many Republicans sought revenge. This desire for revenge, capitalizing on the anxieties of living in an atomic age and the aggravations of having to deal with world problems that could not be shelved, created a virulent public mood during the next three years.

Tensions over Truman's Fair Deal domestic problem merged with tensions arising from the Cold War. Spurred by Republican campaign charges in 1946 that he was too lenient toward Communists, and by revelations of a Royal Commission in Canada that Soviet spy rings were in operation there, the President early in 1946 had ordered an investigation of all federal employees. The probe, however, did not quiet the public alarm and two cases in 1949 increased the concern over Soviet espionage. Judith Coplon, a Department of Justice employee, was arrested for passing information about the FBI's counterespionage system to a Soviet agent. But of far greater impact was the Hiss case.

In August, 1948, *Time* editor Whittaker Chambers, a confessed former Communist spy, charged before the House Committee on Un-American Activities that Alger Hiss, a former official of the Department of State and now President of the Carnegie Endowment for International Peace, had been a member of the Communist party between 1934 and 1938. Hiss appeared before the Committee, confronted Chambers, and denied the charge. Then he instituted a libel suit against Chambers. At this point, Truman blundered, increasing the fear that he was not alert to the Communist menace, by telling his press conference that such investigations were a "red herring" to distract the public from the failures of the Eightieth Congress.

Late in 1948, Chambers re-examined his memory and expanded his charge. Hiss had been a member of a Soviet spy ring in the 1930s and had passed confidential documents to Chambers for transmittal to the Russians. Chambers produced copies of secret documents, some of which he alleged were in

SOURCE. Walter Johnson, *1600 Pennsylvania Avenue: Presidents and People, 1929–1959*, pp. 233–238 and 287–295. Copyright © 1960, 1963 by Walter Johnson. Reprinted by permission of Little, Brown and Company.

Hiss's handwriting, while others, he said, were typed on a machine belonging to Hiss. Hiss was accused now, not only of belonging to the Communist party during the depression, a not uncommon affiliation of young intellectuals in that period, but of betraying his country.

Truman stubbornly stuck to his story: the investigation was still a "red herring" and the Committee was just seeking headlines. On December 15, 1948, a New York grand jury indicted Hiss on a charge of perjury for saying that he had not passed on "numerous secret, confidential and restricted documents" and for denying that he had seen Chambers after January 1, 1937. Although the statute of limitations prevented Hiss from being indicted for espionage, the public knew what the indictments meant. The first trial began in May, 1949, but the jury could not agree. The second trial began in November and Hiss was found guilty in January, 1950.

The Hiss case crowded out all other conversation, and Hiss the individual was transformed into Hiss the symbol. An increasing number of people, disturbed over the social changes of the New Deal and holding the Democrats responsible for the crisis with the Soviet Union, made Hiss the representative of the New Deal and Fair Deal eras. To many, Hiss illustrated that Democrats were susceptible to treason. On the other hand, those who felt that Democratic domestic and foreign policies were eminently wise also turned Hiss into "a representation of the Roosevelt-Truman years and pictured the achievements of that era as now under assault from dark reactionary forces. For both these groups, the Hiss symbolism provoked fierce, blinding emotions."

Four days after Hiss's conviction, Secretary of State Acheson, a friend of Hiss and a member of the same law firm as Hiss's brother, was asked if he had any comment on the case. He refused to discuss the legal aspects of the trials but said: "I should like to make it clear to you that, whatever the outcome of any appeal which Mr. Hiss or his lawyers may take in this case, I do not intend to turn my back on Alger Hiss." His conduct would be determined, he explained, by the twenty-fifth chapter of Matthew, starting with verse thirty-four where Christ explained to his followers that the man who turned his back on anyone in trouble also turned his back on Him. The Secretary's position, while courageous and Christian, was politically unwise. It was deliberately misconstrued in the tense, feverish atmosphere of the time and seized upon as additional proof that the Truman Administration underestimated the Communist threat.

The Hiss trials coincided with the collapse of Chiang Kai-shek and the announcement in September, 1949, that the Soviet Union had exploded an atomic bomb. On January 31, 1950, ten days after the conviction of Hiss, the President revealed that the nation was working on the deadly hydrogen bomb. Albert Einstein appeared on television and warned that "radioactive poisoning of the atmosphere and, hence, annihilation of any life on earth has been brought within the range of technical possibilities. . . . General annihilation beckons."

Then, four days later, the British arrested Klaus Fuchs—an atomic scientist who had been sent to Los Alamos in 1944 to help make the atom bomb—for turning over to Soviet agents secret information from 1943 to 1947. "How much more are we going to have to take?" Senator Homer Capehart raged on the floor of the Senate. "Fuchs and Acheson and Hiss and hydrogen bombs threatening outside and New Dealism eating away the vitals of the nation. In the name of Heaven, is this the best America can do?"

On February 9, 1950, Senator Joseph McCarthy spoke to the Republican women of West Virginia. He explained all the difficulties in one sentence: "The reason we find ourselves in a position of impotency is not because our only powerful potential enemy has sent men to invade our shores, but rather because of the traitorous actions of those who have been treated so well by this nation. . . . In my opinion," he added, "the State Department . . . is thoroughly infested with Communists." Acheson, that "pompous diplomat in striped-pants, with a phony British accent," is the most dangerous person in the Department, McCarthy charged.

Reporters present insisted that McCarthy said he had a list of two hundred and five Communists in the State Department. The Senator spoke from notes and later could not find even these. On February 10, at Salt Lake City, he charged there were "57 card-carrying members of the Communist party" in the State Department.

Newspapers headlined the charges, Acheson denied them, and a Senate Committee headed by Millard Tydings investigated. On March 27, Senator Bridges asserted: "The spies of communism in our Government had laid their lines deep, and they are still effective. The wreckage of our diplomatic and military efforts in Europe and Asia is no accident. Stalin is not a superman. He had help from inside our ranks. . . . We must find the master spy, the servant of Russia who moved the puppets . . . in and out of office in this Capital of the United States, using them and using our State Department as he wills." Bridges closed by announcing that the first battle to win the Cold War "must be won in our own Department of State."

Unable to point out any Communists then in the State Department, in a lengthy speech on March 30, McCarthy shifted his attack. Professor Owen Lattimore was "the top Russian espionage" agent in the United States and a man who had long been "one of the top advisers on Far Eastern policy." "He is undoubtedly the most brilliant and scholarly of all the Communist propagandists," McCarthy accused, "and also the most subtle of the evangelists who have deceived the American people about the Chinese Communists." Amidst all the furor created by McCarthy's charge, the fact became obscured that the

Department of State had consulted Lattimore only infrequently during the Truman Administration and generally had ignored his advice.

In addition, the speech contained a blistering attack on the Institute of Pacific Relations, diplomat John S. Service, and Professor Philip Jessup, serving as Ambassador-at-Large to the United Nations, who had helped prepare the State Department's White Paper on China. Although McCarthy's accusation in West Virginia had not mentioned China, the Senator explained on March 30 that the important thing to be determined was "to what extent our far eastern policy has paralleled the Communist party objectives."

The atmosphere of the Senate, one reporter wrote:

. . . is something to remember. No one who sees this show will ever underestimate young Mr. McCarthy again. He is the most formidable figure to hit the Senate, we think, since Huey Long. He has the galleries with him. The Republicans around him beam. Taft and Bridges exchange enthusiastic smiles as he sidesteps hostile questions again and again. . . . It would seem easy to pin down the preposterous utterances, but no; McCarthy is as hard to catch as a mist—a mist that carries lethal contagion.

John Duncan Miller described the situation in *The Times* of London as a revolt of the primitives against the intelligent in the complexities of foreign affairs. And several Washington correspondents reported that Taft remarked: "McCarthy should keep talking and if one case doesn't work out he should proceed with another." Taft immediately protested that this statement misrepresented him. After the Korean intervention, Taft said that Truman had the bad judgment to

assume the innocence of all persons mentioned in the State Department. Whether Senator McCarthy has legal evidence, whether he has overstated or understated his case, is of lesser importance. The question is whether Communist influence in the State Department still exists.

On April 5, 1950, Knowland, although carefully avoiding McCarthy's accusation that Lattimore was a spy, charged:

Yet consistently and insistently Owen Lattimore has played an important part in the undermining of the Republic of China. He has done it in his writings, and in such positions as he has occupied as would permit him to help influence public opinion on United States policy.

After weeks of listening to the charges of conspiracy, Margaret Chase Smith delivered a Declaration of Conscience to the Senate on June 1. She criticized confusion arising from the lack of effective leadership from the White House, of its "complacency to the threat of communism here at home," and " of its petty bitterness against its critics." But she stated:

Certain elements of the Republican party have materially added to this confusion in the hopes of riding the Republican party to victory through the selfish political exploitation of fear, bigotry, ignorance, and intolerance.

On July 17, the Democratic majority on the Tydings Committee submitted its report rebuking McCarthy for making unsubstantiated, distorted charges. McCarthy had no list of Communists in the State Department and "there is not one member of the Communist party or of a 'spy ring' employed in the State Department known to the Secretary of State or other responsible officials of that department." The allegations against Philip C. Jessup were "completely unfounded and unjustified," the report added.

Owen Lattimore was not an employee of the State Department, he was not the "architect of our Far Eastern policy," nor was there evidence to support the charge that he was the "top Russian spy" or any sort of spy. While John S. Service was indiscreet in supplying classified information to *Amerasia,* this was not sufficient "to brand an otherwise competent and loyal employee . . . as disloyal, pro-Communist, or a security risk." And McCarthy's allegation that John Carter Vincent was a member of an espionage ring in the State Department was "absurd."

The charges, the Democrats concluded, were

A fraud and a hoax perpetrated on the Senate of the United States and the American people. They represent perhaps the most nefarious campaign of half-truths and untruth in the history of the Republic.

The report enraged the exponents of the conspiracy thesis and only increased their vituperative attack. Jenner denounced Tydings for conducting the "most scandalous and brazen whitewash of treasonable conspiracy in our history" and insisted that the "crowd of master conspirators" in the State Department had not only "sold out China" but now they were undermining Korea. "The sad thing about it . . . " the Senator declared, "is that those who are being pushed now in Korea are the sons of the mothers of America."

The mood of well-being, repose, and moderation, which came to characterize the first Eisenhower Administration, was not achieved quickly or easily. The acrimony which had made the closing years of the Truman era inglorious and dangerous continued to infect American politics.

On November 6, 1953, Attorney General Herbert Brownell contrasted the Administration's new security program with Truman's, and charged:

Harry Dexter White was known to be a spy by the very people who appointed him to the most sensitive and important position he ever held in Government service.

Since Truman had appointed White, there was a furious outcry. At a stormy press conference on November 11, when asked if he thought Truman knowingly appointed a Communist spy to high office, Eisenhower eased some of the rancor when he replied: "No, it is inconceivable."

A month later, Governor Dewey, after denouncing Truman and the Democrats for "bungling our country" into the Korean war and for the loss of China, said: "Remember that the words Truman and Democrat mean diplomatic failure, military failure, death and tragedy." And, on a speaking tour arranged by the Republican National Committee to commemorate Lincoln's Birthday, Senator McCarthy assailed the Democrats for "twenty years of treason"; "The hard fact is that those who wear the label—Democrat—wear it with the stain of an historic betrayal."

At his press conference on February 10, 1954, the President tried to steer the nation away from this virulent mood. He knew that Democratic leaders would not cooperate in government if Republicans turned party contest into a war of political extermination. To suggest that all Democrats were tinged with treason or were all security risks, Eisenhower said, was "not only completely untrue, but very unwise" since "the Administration needed Democratic votes to get its program through Congress." He then added that it was obvious that he was "not very much of a partisan. The times were too serious . . . to indulge in partisanship to the extreme."

Despite his soothing words, the Administration's security program inflamed partisanship. Having agreed with the extremists in 1952 that there were Communists and security risks in the government, the Eisenhower aides diligently tried to demonstrate that they were ousting such influences. Under Truman, there had been separate loyalty and security programs. The former covered all employees and dismissal occurred when there was a reasonable doubt of loyalty. The latter applied to eleven "sensitive" agencies, including the Departments of Defense and State, and provided for dismissal of employees if their habits—loose talk, drunkenness, and homosexuality, in addition to subversive activities—made them risks to the national security. The Eisenhower Administration eliminated the separation between the two programs, issuing Executive Order 10450 which covered personal habits, integrity, and subversion and applied it to all government positions.

Then began what the Democrats and some non-Democrats called the "numbers game." On October 23, 1953, the White House stated that 1456 government employees had been dismissed or had resigned under Eisenhower's security program. During the next year, the Administration raised the figure to 2200, to 6926, to 8008, and finally stopped the statistics at 9600. While Republican orators clutched the figures with sheer delight, newspapermen clamored for information as to how many were actually dismissed as Communists, former Communists, or fellow travelers. The Alsops denounced it as

"Security-Firing Fakery" and asserted: "The privately admitted purpose of these 'security firings' has been to 'grab the Commie issue away from Sen. McCarthy.' " Under hammering from the press and Democratic Congressmen, Brownell said on February 7, 1954, that the 2200 discharged came under eight or nine categories and by no means were all of them Communists or spies.

The Department of State reeled under the full blast of the hysteria in 1953–1954. Apparently to undercut McCarthy's attacks on the Department, Dulles and his security chief, Scott McLeod, announced that 306 employees had been released for security reasons, and by February, 1954, the figure had reached 534. But, when called before a secret session of a House Appropriations Subcommittee, Department officials explained that only eleven had been dropped for loyalty reasons and no active Communist had been found.

The entire security program was criticized hotly not only by Democratic leaders but by writers, educators, scientists, and lawyers for undermining constitutional rights, forcing conformity of opinion, impeding scientific research and depriving the government of the services of able citizens. And from former right-wing Republican Senator Harry Cain, appointed by Eisenhower to the Subversive Activities Control Board, came devastating criticism. By 1955, he was convinced that the internal security system was doing more harm than good. He charged that the program was brutal and ruthless and was "unnecessarily destroying individuals."

In the spring of 1955, the Administration announced some procedural changes in the security system, including the right of the accused to confront and cross-examine witnesses who supplied derogatory information except when the national security might be jeopardized. The Senate voted unanimously, and the House without debate, for a bipartisan study of the whole security system. With the need to secure cooperation from a Democratic-controlled Congress, no more statistics were issued by the Administration about uprooting security risks. In effect, the Administration now conceded that its security figures had been misleading or false.

The Civil Service Commission admitted that more than 90 per cent of those 9600 employees described as security risks had left the government by regular civil service procedures without hearings to test any security charges. Up to September 30, 1955, only 1016 employees actually had been charged under the security program. And, of these, only 342 were dismissed under security procedures. The interesting fact was that more than 50 per cent of the 9600 had been hired during the Eisenhower Administration.

For the first two years of the new Administration, not only did McCarthy continue his ruthless onslaught on the loyalty of many citizens, but he also tried to usurp the powers of the presidency and wrest control of the Republican party from Eisenhower. From his chairmanship of the formidable Permanent Subcommittee on Investigations, McCarthy immediately launched an attack on the Administration. At first, Eisenhower tried either to ignore the Senator or cooperate with his investigations. It was the President's "passion," his aide C. D. Jackson said, "not to offend anyone in Congress."

When McCarthy announced that a good security officer was needed in the Department of State to clean out Communists, John Foster Dulles complied by appointing Scott McLeod. Such appeasement failed to stop the attacks. McCarthy denounced the appointment of James B. Conant, President of Harvard University, as High Commissioner to Germany. He fought the appointment of Charles E. Bohlen as Ambassador to the Soviet Union as a "security risk" and accused Dulles of "untrue statements" in defending Bohlen.

Throughout these early weeks, McCarthy—with a battery of television cameras recording the hearings—assailed the Information Program of the Department of State. In April he sent his aides, Roy M. Cohn and G. David Schine, on an eighteen-day whirlwind tour through Western Europe to ferret out "subversion" in the information program. McCarthy proclaimed "appalling infiltration" and a number of able people were released by the Department.

In an earlier move to appease McCarthy, the Information Agency on February 19 issued a directive that "No material by any Communists, fellow-travelers, et cetera, will be used under any circumstances." But there was no definition of a Communist or a fellow traveler, or what an "et cetera" was. This produced so much criticism at home and abroad that when Robert Johnson took charge in March as the new director of the Information Agency, he asked Dulles for clearer instructions. Dulles's reply omitted the "et cetera" but ordered the removal of books by those "who obviously follow the Communist line or participate in Communist front organizations" and the withdrawal of any magazine containing "material detrimental to the U.S. objectives." The words "detrimental" and "objectives" again were not defined. While the lists of books and magazines were being drafted, frightened officials overseas removed items that were never to appear on the lists and some books were burned. None of this satisfied McCarthy who had his own list, and who charged on May 5 that "30,000 to 40,000 books by Communists and fellow-travelers" were in the overseas libraries.

While the book episode was raging, Eisenhower's appointee, Robert Johnson, tried to enlist help from the White House only to be told the President was solidly booked for two weeks ahead. Finally, with the aid of writers and publishers, Johnson worked out a policy on books which Dulles approved on July 8. It explained that the Information Agency would not exclude books as Communist or communistic which contained criticism of American policies or institutions: "We must begin with the content of a book. We must examine its special usefulness in terms of our overseas needs." Moreover, books by Communists or Communist sympathizers might be included "if such authors may have written something which affirmatively served the ends of democracy." By this statement, the policy was again essentially the one that had been followed prior to February.

McCarthy stepped up his assault over TV and radio on November 24, 1953, by saying that while Eisenhower was doing "infinitely" better than Truman in ousting security risks, there were a few cases where the batting average was "zero." As to Eisenhower's statement a week before that Communists in government would not be an issue in the 1954 campaign, McCarthy replied bluntly that the "raw, harsh, unpleasant fact" was that Communism would indeed be an issue. Next, he leveled his guns at the Administration's foreign policy and denounced the continuance of mutual assistance to Britain while the British traded with Communist China. Instead of cutting off aid to Britain, the scowling Senator rasped, we are sending "perfumed notes."

With the approval of the President, Dulles now fought back, pointing out that we were dealing with free nations as sovereign equals. The next day Eisenhower, urged by one adviser to mention McCarthy by name, refused, saying: "I will not get in the gutter with that guy." He told the press that to coerce our Allies would be the mark of an "imperialist rather than of the leader." As to Communists in government, the Administration would remove any discovered, but it would protect the basic rights of loyal citizens.

By now, McCarthy was launching an attack on the Army. He asserted that there were "earmarks of dangerous espionage" in the Signal Corps at Fort Monmouth. The Secretary of the Army, Robert Stevens, trying to work with McCarthy, suspended those accused, even though the Federation of American Scientists warned that the suspensions resulted in "a serious disruption of the scientific work at the laboratory." On February 18, 1954, McCarthy, at a hearing, shouted at a distinguished General, Ralph Swicker: "You are a disgrace to the uniform. You're shielding Communist conspirators. . . . You're not fit to be an officer. You're ignorant."

No longer could the Administration ignore McCarthy's attempt to dominate the executive and be master of the Republican party. The Army, with the support of the White House, struck back. On March 3, the President, who considered it inconsistent with the dignity of his office to mention McCarthy by name, stated: "In opposing Communism, we are defeating ourselves if either by design or through carelessness we use methods that do not conform to the American sense of fair play."

On March 11, at the suggestion of Presidential Assistant Sherman Adams, the Army charged that McCarthy, Roy Cohn, and the Subcommittee staff director, Francis Carr, had tried by improper means to force the Army to grant preferential treatment to G. David Schine who had been drafted the previous fall. McCarthy, who now was accusing the Army of "coddling Communists," fired back with forty-six charges.

The Senate Subcommittee voted to investigate the Army-McCarthy charges, with Karl Mundt temporarily replacing McCarthy as the Chairman. The televised spectacle transfixed the nation for thirty-six days. The hearings became, as one newspaperman has written, the national business, the national pastime, and the national disgrace. Among the performers who gained respect was Senator John McClellan of Arkansas, who revealed with rasping logic how the Secretary of the Army had tried to appease the friends of a buck private.

But, above all, there was the image of McCarthy in millions of living rooms, bars, and public places. Scowling, interrupting with "Point of order, point of order, Mr. Chairman," seizing the floor, flinging smears while accusing others of smearing, he became more reckless in his charges. When McCarthy, in a flagrant encroachment on the executive, demanded records of privileged conversations in the White House, the President refused and asserted those rights which "cannot be usurped by any individual who may seek to set himself above the laws of the land."

By now no one, including Eisenhower, was immune to the charges of being soft on Communists. On May 30, McCarthy spoke of "the evidence of the treason that has been growing up over the twenty . . ."—he paused, scowled, and with great deliberation added "Twenty-one years." Now even those Republicans who disagreed with him were treasonable.

As the hearings ground on, McCarthy's popular support was weakened both by his own ruthless tactics as well as by presidential opposition. Still, McCarthy might have preserved some of his following had he not thrown a wild haymaker at Joseph Welch, Chief Army Counsel, and senior partner of a distinguished Boston law firm. Welch's deft questioning infuriated McCarthy. Near the close of the hearings, as Welch led Roy Cohn through a destructive cross-examination, McCarthy interrupted and attacked a member of Welch's law firm for once having belonged to the Lawyer's Guild, "which was named, oh, years and years ago, as the legal bulwark of the Communist party."

With his face white with anger, Welch replied:

Until this moment, Senator, I think I never really gauged your cruelty or your recklessness. . . . Little did I dream that you could be so reckless and so cruel as to do an injury to that lad. . . . I fear he shall always bear a scar needlessly inflicted by you. If it were in my power to forgive you for your reckless cruelty, I would do so, I like to think I am a gentleman, but your forgiveness will have to come from someone other than me.

As McCarthy tried to break in, Welch, with emotion, said: "Let us not assassinate this lad further, Senator. You have done enough. Have you no sense of decency?" When McCarthy tried to ask him about his partner, Welch cut him off with cold scorn and said: "Mr. McCarthy, I will not discuss this with you further. . . . If there is a God in heaven, it will do neither you nor your cause any good."

There was a hush over the room broken suddenly by a storm of applause. McCarthy slouched in his chair, and with bewilderment in his voice turned to someone and said: "What did I do wrong?" "Joseph McCarthy would never know," Eric F. Goldman has written in *The Crucial Decade.* "And that June day, 1954, millions at their TV sets learned once and for all that Joseph McCarthy would never know."

On August 2 the United States Senate voted to form a select committee to weigh a motion of Senator Ralph Flanders to censure McCarthy. On September 27, Senator Arthur Watkins submitted a unanimous report recommending censure. After thirteen days of acrimonious debate, the Senate voted 67 to 22 to censure McCarthy. The arrogant Senator was not censured for attacking the Bill of Rights, for accusing without proof, for dividing the nation or for denying the oldest traditions of the English-speaking heritage, but for abusing the 1951 Senate Subcommittee on Elections and for attacking the special Watkins Committee in language that reflected on the dignity and integrity of the Senate. After the Senate vote, this self-styled man of destiny dwindled into a forlorn figure.

The merit of Eisenhower's approach to the problem of McCarthy will long be debated. While he had disdain for McCarthy, Eisenhower felt that he had to calm public opinion rather than excite it by engaging in a fight with the Senator. Instead, McCarthy was allowed to destroy himself by his own excesses. With his immense prestige, Eisenhower might have been able to isolate McCarthy in 1953 and prevent his outrages. But, while the Senator was playing himself out, countless citizens were subjected to unjust attacks, the machinery of government thrown into confusion, the standards of legislative investigations debased, and an ugly picture of America exported to the world.

CHAPTER 22

THE EISENHOWER YEARS

In November 1952, the American voters, perhaps belatedly reacting to the 1946 slogan of "Had Enough-Vote Republican," handily elected Dwight D. Eisenhower President of the United States. In 1956 they again demonstrated that they still liked Ike and reelected him, although they did not return a Republican majority to either branch of Congress. Eisenhower's two large electoral victories, coupled with his failure to carry his party to victory, have indicated to students of American politics that he owed his election to his own personality and career rather than to any fundamental shift of voters from what had become by the 1950s a normal Democratic party majority. The results of the 1952 and 1956 elections also indicated a growing tendency toward ticket-splitting, and toward the choosing of presidents on other than purely party grounds.

William V. Shannon suggests that one of the reasons that Eisenhower's popularity was not transferred intact to the Republican party was that Eisenhower was in the New Deal tradition whereas his party was not. If this hypothesis is true, we can hardly be surprised that the Eisenhower years saw no great changes in either foreign or domestic policy. Nor should it come as a surprise to learn that Eisenhower, as was indicated in the previous reading, inherited the animosity of one of the assailants of that tradition, Senator Joseph McCarthy, or that the President never had the full support of many of the conservatives of his party (although he was ideologically rather close to them on issues such as balancing the budget). The gulf that separated Eisenhower from Republicans such as William Knowland was not so much their views on how the government should be run but instead their views on the government's role in the life of the nation. Eisenhower accepted the broad outlines of the New Deal, whereas the right wing of the Republican party wished to remove most, if not all, of the continuing influences of the Roosevelt administrations. The same lines of cleavage appear to hold true with regard to foreign policy. Eisenhower believed that the United States should remain involved in world affairs, whereas his conservative critics wavered between demands to "get tough" and the hope that the nation could withdraw to a "Fortress America."

In this early assessment of the Eisenhower presidency, Shannon suggests that "Eisenhower may join the ranks of history's fated good men, the Stanley Baldwins and the James Buchanans." Is such a potentially harsh evaluation valid? If not, how is Eisenhower to be viewed? Is Shannon's analysis of the Eisenhower programs as "holding the line" accurate? If so, how did the Eisenhower era influence the affairs of the 1960s? Why was Eisenhower unable to transform the Republican party along the lines of his political philosophy? Or was he more successful in this respect than Shannon observed in 1958?

There is already a sizable body of literature dealing with the Eisenhower years. Two articles, by Norman Graebner, "Eisenhower's Popular Leadership," *Current History,* Vol. 34 (October 1960), and Oscar Handlin, "The Eisenhower Administration: A Self-Portrait," *The Atlantic,* Vol. 212 (November 1963), are early attempts at analysis. Robert J. Donovan, *Eisenhower: The Inside Story** (1956), is a favorable and valuable early biography, and Marquis Childs, *Eisenhower: Captive Hero* (1958), is equally useful but more critical. More recent and fuller treatments are found in Charles C. Alexander, *Holding the Line: The Eisenhower Era, 1952–1961* (1975); G. W. Reichand, *The Reaffirmation of Republicanism: Eisenhower and the Eighty-third Congress* (1975); E. J. Hughes, *The Ordeal of Power** (1963); Herbert S. Parmet, *Eisenhower and the American Crusades* (1972); Dean Albertson, *Eisenhower as President** (1963); and Arthur Larson, *Eisenhower: The President Nobody Knew** (1968).

*Available in a paperback edition.

EISENHOWER AS PRESIDENT; A CRITICAL APPRAISAL OF THE RECORD

WILLIAM V. SHANNON

Across a divided and militarily defenseless Europe, the shadow of Stalin's armies fell; in Korea, Communist Chinese forces pushed American armies back toward the sea; in the United States, Joseph McCarthy scored his first major political triumph, and the Fulbright Committee investigation began to uncover a vein of corruption in the national administration. It was a grim time for Americans. It was November 1950.

When President Truman summoned General Dwight D. Eisenhower to his private study in the White House one afternoon that month to ask him to return to active duty and become chief of the NATO forces in Western Europe, he called upon one of the few Americans who commanded universal respect and admiration. The image of Eisenhower, the liberator of Nazi-occupied Europe, stood bright and untarnished. He was a symbol of the nation's triumphant and united national purpose in a time when the national consensus was fracturing and the national mood becoming querulous and ugly. Eisenhower's acceptance of his new military assignment ended his brief civilian career as president of Columbia University. It restored him to the center of the public scene where in the decade to follow he was to be the dominant figure. His dominance of the age did not derive from any personal mastery of its diverse forces. A central personality may epitomize the spirit of an era and symbolize its prevailing balance of political forces without necessarily transforming the one or controlling the other. As the decade of the 20's is inextricably linked with Calvin Coolidge and the 30's with Franklin Roosevelt, the 1950's in our political history is likely to be known as the age of Eisenhower.

Although Eisenhower has two years still to serve, his place in history and the significance of his presidency are already becoming clear. Eisenhower is a transitional figure. He has not shaped the future nor tried to repeal the past. He has not politically organized nor intellectually defined a new consensus. When he leaves office in January 1961, the foreign policies and the domestic policies of the past generation will be about where he found them in 1953. No

SOURCE. William V. Shannon, "Eisenhower as President; A Critical Appraisal of the Record," *Commentary,* XXV, November 1958, pp. 390–398. Copyright © 1958 by the American Jewish Committee. Reprinted by permission of the American Jewish Committee.

national problem, whether it be education, housing, urban revitalization, agriculture, or inflation, will have been advanced importantly toward solution nor its dimensions significantly altered. The Eisenhower era is the time of the great postponement. Dwight Eisenhower, the executor and trustee of the programs of his two Democratic predecessors whose contemporary he was (Eisenhower is only eight years younger than Franklin Roosevelt and six years younger than Harry Truman), already looms in history not as the first great figure of a new Republican age but the last of an old Democratic generation.

In assessing Eisenhower's status, it is worth recalling the somber, impassioned national mood which the sudden, savage turn in the Korean war created. . . . The emotions aroused by that war endangered the great double consensus on foreign affairs and domestic affairs which had been in the making since 1933. Eisenhower's historic function when he entered political life two years later was to end the war and preserve that consensus against the attacks of its enemies.

The domestic consensus had emerged out of the violent political struggles and intellectual gyrations of the New Deal period from 1933 to 1938. It rested on an irreversible common agreement that the Federal government has a responsibility to maintain the rudiments of a welfare state. (Social Security, unemployment compensation, and minimum wages were the basic features of this program, and its chief guarantors were trade unions to whom the Wagner Act of 1935 had given firm legal status.) The unionists and their unorganized but sympathetic fellow workers were the guarantors of the concensus because they were the most numerous and, compared to the farmers, the old-age pensioners, and other groups, the most politically dependable of all the New Deal beneficiaries. The Full Employment Act of 1946, the first year of the Truman administration, set a seal of official approval on this consensus but did not extend its range.

The other half of the national consensus, the half on foreign policy, had also begun under Roosevelt but had reached its more significant development during the Truman years. Roosevelt, by his aggressive championing of an internationalist position during the bitter isolationist-interventionist debate of 1940-41, established the basis for a national policy. His actions and his education of the public were esential first steps. He carried it further in his negotiations during the war with various Republican party personalities, looking toward our entry into a world organization. Truman completed this undertaking by leading the country into the United Nations. A genuine bipartisan collaboration during the next five years carried through the Marshall Plan, the Greek-Turkish program, the Berlin airlift, the Point Four program, and other achievements abroad. By 1950, the consensus on foreign policy was well established. It rested on the concept of containment. If Russian aggression in all its forms was firmly resisted, if the military and economic strength of the

West were maintained and increased, and if the neutral, underdeveloped countries were not lost to Communism, it would be possible to avoid a third war and to leave the resolution of the cold war to the slow working of history.

Communist China's entry into the Korean war put the foreign policy consensus in jeopardy. The shocking defeats, the capture of thousands of our troops by the Communists, and the eventual bloody stalemate aroused many doubts and profound dissatisfaction. The scope of the war and its inherent nature intensified popular resentment and bafflement. It was clearly not a major war evoking the instinctive zeal and emotional commitment of the whole population; yet its duration and the thousands of dead and wounded made it more burdensome than the brief "brushfire wars" that the containment policy had seemed to postulate. If it was only a "police action," as President Truman called it, how could the government ask for wartime sacrifices? If it was a glorious struggle on behalf of the United Nations, why did the other UN members leave almost all of the fighting to us?

The anxieties were deep and shaking. The public, half-unconsciously and inarticulately, began the search for an alternative to the existing consensus. First, there was a brief, wild resurgence of the old isolationist impulse in early December 1950 when the drive to the Yalu turned into disastrous defeat. . . . Second, there was the alternative of smashing our way out of the dilemmas of a containment policy by adopting a more venturesome course. This alternative drew upon feelings and posed choices ranging from the proposals for bombing across the Yalu in Manchuria to launching a preventive war "to get the whole thing over with." The popularity of this alternative policy of aggressive venturesomeness reached its height in the spring of 1951 when General MacArthur made his triumphant tour through the United States after his dismissal. This alternative began to fade during the prolonged, anti-climatic MacArthur hearings. There was yet a third alternative. Senator Joseph McCarthy and a few other senators propounded the view that the real source of danger was treason within. The tendency of those who propagated this alternative was to deprecate the importance of the Soviet Union's power and enormously inflate the real but limited and secondary dangers of Soviet espionage and political infiltration within this country. The minimizing of the Soviet Union's menace flattered many naively chauvinistic ideas about our own relative place in the sun; the exaggeration of the espionage-infiltration problem catered to a congeries of notions about foreigners, radicals, and Communists. . . .

As against the alarms and confusions of the isolationist, MacArthurian, and McCarthyite alternatives, Harry Truman and Dean Acheson, the two chief official exponents of the containment policy, made an ineffective defense. Truman was without the resources of rhetoric and the mastery of a grand style which would have enabled a Roosevelt or a Wilson to make an early and overpowering counterattack. Acheson was impaled by his own verbal indiscretions and his starchy public manner. They could only mechanically repeat the familiar platitudes about collective security, the United Nations, and the importance of having allies.

The times called for a man who could restate national purposes, reassert in more winning terms the basic truths underlying the foreign policy consensus, and thereby make possible once again the full concentration of national energies. The situation seemed to require a political figure who would personify the causes that united us rather than those which divided us. It was a situation, in a word, that was historically right for a conservative. The conservative aspiration in politics is always toward the ideal of unity, toward the assertion of proved values and established rationales, and directed toward the deliberate blurring of economic and political conflicts. Even more, the times were right for a certain kind of conservative whose appeal had proved valid in the American past. This was the military hero who had a conservative social background but was basically apolitical and who, although a military man, had the plain, even drab, style suitable in the chief of state of a profoundly civilian country. . . . What was wanted was another Washington, another Grant. What was wanted and what was so splendidly and self-evidently available for the asking, if the asking were insistent enough, was Dwight D. Eisenhower.

The connection between the conservative aspiration (one can scarcely call it, at least in this country, an ideology or a philosophy) and the military hero candidate is more than an expedient alliance. The ideal of national unity dominates the military ethos. Soldiers are trained to defend the existing social order rather than to examine it critically. Military officers see social and economic groups as components in the great design of national strength, not as dynamic participants battling one another in the social arena. If Eisenhower found the conservative Republicans with their dedication to the status quo and their resistance to rapid change more intellectually congenial than the liberal Democrats with their reformist tradition, he was no different from the great majority of his fellow officers. The military services are not a training school for liberals.

The natural affinity between political conservatives and a military hero had deep roots in the American past. George Washington, our first conservative president and also our first soldier president, set the mold. The conservative Whigs managed to elect only two presidents, General William "Tippecanoe" Harrison in 1840 and General Zachary Taylor in 1848. The Republican politicians seeking to consolidate their hold on the country after the Civil War chose General Grant. Each of these men was relatively innocent of political ideas. Their appeal was based on the exploitation of their personality as a symbol of integrity and unity. Their campaigns were usually keyed to a simple idea. Grant, for example, said in 1868: "Let us have peace." Eisenhower, with the air of a man expressing a crystal clear idea, said repeatedly in 1952: "I believe our test should be—what is good for 155,000,000 Americans."

In the fall of 1949, Senator Arthur Vandenberg wrote in a private letter to a friend that he might support General Eisenhower in the next presidential contest. "I think the specifications call for a personality of great independent magnitude who can give our splintering American people an 'evangel' instead of an ordinary campaign," he wrote.

Three years in advance, Vandenberg had forecast Eisenhower's "Great Crusade." It was as the candidate of the more responsible Republicans interested in protecting the foreign policy consensus that the General entered politics. . . . Lacking any alternative to Senator Taft, the Eastern Republicans successfully and plausibly argued with Eisenhower that he would only be carrying out his NATO mission in a different way. By blocking the coming to power of Taft and his neo-isolationist backers, Eisenhower would make certain that a foreign policy oriented toward the defense of Europe and aligned with the principles of the UN would continue to prevail.

Once nominated, Eisenhower necessarily took into account the three principal strains of Republican party criticism of existing foreign policy. Speaking about the Korean war in Peoria, Illinois, he projected the goal of the ultimate withdrawal of American troops from mainland Asia. If there had to be wars there, "let Asians fight Asians." This remark delighted the devout readers of the Chicago *Tribune*. It evoked glowing words of praise from troglodyte politicians like ex-Senator C. Wayland "Curly" Brooks. But it was meaningless. As army chief of staff in 1946-48, Eisenhower had repeatedly and successfully recommended the withdrawal of American troops from Korea. Moreover, it was settled national military policy to avoid stationing troops on the Asian mainland. But this was quite different from disengaging ourselves completely from our interests and responsibilities on that continent. The Peoria speech was only a fugitive gesture to the isolationists.

Eisenhower made more ambiguous gestures in the direction of the aggressive alternative symbolized by General MacArthur. He allowed himself the liberty of condemning the "negativism" of the containment policy and of referring vaguely to the "liberation" and the "rolling back" of the Communist empire. He promised to go to Korea but he left open the question whether he would end the war by extending it to gain a decisive military victory, or try to end it by continuing the armistice negotiations. The campaign rhetoric unfortunately persisted after election day. In his first State of the Union message, Eisenhower "unleashed" Chiang Kai-shek. Secretary of State Dulles wordily threatened the Communists with "massive retaliation" at times and places of our own choosing. The administration strenghtened the government's propaganda forces to wage psychological warfare, seize the strategic initiative, liberate the satellite states by radio broadcasts, and attain various other doubtlessly worthy if uncertain ends. Two crises in the Formosa Straits have demonstrated Chiang Kai-shek is not a free agent; the Hungarian revolution proved the United States had no intention of risking anything to liberate the satellite peoples.

Eisenhower, during the 1952 campaign and for a period thereafter, accommodated himself in small, symbolic ways to the emotional thrust of McCarthyism. He deleted a brief word of praise for General Marshall, his patron, from his Milwaukee speech; he affirmed vigorously his determination to clear the Communists out of government, to encourage the work of the Federal Bureau of Investigation, and to cooperate with the investigating committees of Congress, clearly implying the Truman administration had been remiss, if not treasonable, in these matters. He did not avow belief in the McCarthyite conspiracy theory of the origin of the country's troubles, but to the dismay of some of his admirers in both parties and former colleagues in the Roosevelt and Truman administrations, neither did he disavow it.

Eisenhower's strategy in waging the "Great Crusade" was the only one possible for him given the plasticity of his temperament, his unintellectual cast of mind, and his confident, optimistic nature. He did not separate the sheep from the goats; he welcomed all dissidents to his cause, committed himself in an irretrievable way only to invulnerable platitudes, and hinted genially that in his new synthesis a reconciliation of all divergent elements would be possible. This may not have been the internationalist "evangel" that Vandenberg and his other original supporters had in mind, but it is typical of successful party leaders in our country. Franklin Roosevelt, for example, was able in 1932 to hold the loyalty and quicken the hopes of Huey Long and Bernard Baruch, of Harry Byrd and George Norris. Roosevelt organized his coalition with care and calculation while Eisenhower, gifted with some of the instincts if not the insight and expertise of a successful politician, apparently only did what came naturally to him. If his tactics did not rally a newly broadened and better informed support for the foreign policy consensus, they served at least to deaden and to dissipate the pressures for any serious change from that policy. Eisenhower's fabian tactics carried through successfully the defensive holding action which Truman and Acheson after 1950 could no longer sustain.

As against this negative but vitally important accomplishment, Eisenhower's own positive initiatives in foreign affairs dwindle into insignificance. The Baghdad pact in the Middle East and the SEATO pact in the Far East are pale imitations of the NATO pact in Europe. They have proved irrelevant, if not noxious, diplomatic devices. The administration's ambivalent attitude toward Nasser brought the Atlantic Alliance almost to the breaking point in the Suez affair, but our common interests with Britain are so strong they can survive almost any shock; under Prime Minister Macmillan's soothing ministration, the alliance re-formed itself. . . . Eisenhower has tried the "great man theory" of diplomacy at the summit in Geneva and Dulles has subjected himself to innumerable conferences and journeyings, but no new approaches to the Soviet monolith have developed and none of the old has availed much. Eisenhower settled for truces in Korea and Indo-China, leaving those countries divided and their future unsettled. This is the kind of minimum accommodation between the Communist and non-Communist worlds which the original containment concept had envisaged.

Holding the line and protecting the gains of the past worked well enough in Europe where in the Eisenhower years the situation has remained virtually stable. Secretary Dulles threatened the French with an agonizing reappraisal, but the French were supremely indifferent. So in the end was the Secretary of State. The European Defense Community died, the British and French patched up a reasonable substitute, and the only agonizing was done by the Secretary's Democratic critics. Career diplomats worked out a compromise solution of the Trieste affair, the Russians relinquished their grip on Austria, and the United States kept the line open to Tito in Belgrade. Germany remained divided. Europe remained divided.

In the Middle East and the Far East, however, creative policy making was called for. The situations were less stable and the inherited guide lines of policy were less well developed. Eisenhower had no contribution to make to the hard problems of Arab and Israeli, of African nationalism, of Communist China's menace to Southeast Asia, of Indonesia's interior decay, and of India's economic viability. He held the line and beyond that he could not go. When he got in trouble on a foreign policy issue in these areas of the world, it was usually because he applied the lessons of the postwar past rigidly and almost mechanically. . . .

Eisenhower's clear distinction between a policy and the carrying out of that policy may be simpleminded, but future historians are not likely to find a better or more revealing extemporaneous tribute to the foreign policy consensus. Eisenhower's caretaker attitude is clear. His and Dulles's day-to-day decisions do not matter; only the policy matters, and it has an autonomous life of its own not really greatly dependent on their daily actions and judgments.

When Harry Truman ordered American troops into Korea in June 1950, he did not know that he was killing his Fair Deal domestic program. War and liberalism always go ill together, but when the Korean conflict began few foresaw how it would transform the domestic economic scene and jeopardize the national consensus on domestic policy. . . .

The Korean war, however, not only benefited the Republicans at the polls and made the 82nd Congress of 1951-52 considerably more conservative than its predecessor, but also touched off a severe inflation. Unemployment vanished, farm prices soared, and the high cost of living replaced the threat of joblessness as a key domestic issue.

The emergence of the inflation issue played an important part in Eisenhower's first victory and has been significant in influencing the tone of his administration. The fear of inflation greatly helped him to organize a new majority coalition in the country and end the Republican party's chronic minority status. Before 1952, the Republican party drew its strength principally from three groups. One was the more sophisticated Eastern industrial and financial community and its allies in the press, clergy, and universities; this was an elite group, small in numbers but important in terms of wealth, prestige, and influence in the mass communication industries. By a British analogy, these voters, overwhelmingly but not exclusively Republican, make up what might be called the American Establishment. These were the people who had organized the successful Willkie boom in 1940 and had subsequently more or less accepted Governor Dewey and his associate Herbert Brownell as their political agents. A second group was the less sophisticated, much more numerous but relatively less effective, hard-shelled conservative business and commercial people of the smaller cities and towns of the Midwest. Their idol was Robert A. Taft. These voters gave, at most, grudging acceptance to the great consensus; some hoped for a withdrawal into isolation, others resented labor unions. The strongest conviction they shared was that government cost too much, that the budget should always be balanced, and taxes reduced promptly. The third group were the farmers who had voted predominantly Republican since the midterm election of 1938. These three groups were not enough to make a majority. The Democrats were able to maintain themselves in power with the support of the captive South and the second and third-generation immigrant community voters in the nation's dozen largest metropolitan areas.

Eisenhower cracked the Democratic big cities and the high cost of living was probably his most potent weapon. He made sharp gains among housewives. Moreover, he broke into the ranks of the young voters. During the 1930's and 40's, voters under thirty had been heavily Democratic. By 1952, however, many young war veterans bore a burden of fixed charges, in their mortgaged suburban homes, with appliances bought on the installment plan, driving cars purchased through a finance company. In abstract economic theory, debtors benefit from inflation, but as a practical matter many of these voters felt they were losing in the dollar race. They feared their wages and salaries would not keep pace with rising prices. They voted for Eisenhower.

However, there were other causes bidding for the allegiances of these voters being detached from the old Democratic urban coalition. One of them was McCarthyism. McCarthy had an entree to these voters because, like many of them, he was Catholic and of immigrant ancestry. He was also relatively young and a war veteran. He was a demagogue with a simple issue to exploit who made a biting, raucous, emotional appeal. For these voters, his appeal was quite a new and different experience contrasted to the stodgy, Chamber of

Commerce rhetoric they had been accustomed to hear from Republican orators.

The only real threat to the domestic economic consensus established in the New Deal and perpetuated in Truman's Fair Deal would come from a genuine linkage between working-class and lower-middle-class urban voters, attracted by a non-economic issue like McCarthyism, and the regular Republican voters of the more hard-shelled, conservative, Midwestern school. If the Republican ticket in 1952 had been Taft and Knowland instead of Eisenhower and Nixon, this linkage might have had serious consequences. A right-wing Republican administration much indebted to the emotional dynamism of the McCarthyites for its victory might have attempted a genuine counter-revolution to reverse many of the verdicts of the 30's and 40's embodied in the economic consensus. Eisenhower's nomination forestalled this eventuality. He absorbed the McCarthyite frenzy into his own "Great Crusade" where in subsequent years it died of inanition.

In terms of the internal dynamics of the Republican party, therefore, Eisenhower's victory in November 1952 had several meanings. It meant much of the potential McCarthy following had been detached from his orbit and their fears, dissatisfactions, and status tensions given a different kind of political expression. "I Like Ike" was a harmless substitute for hating the targets McCarthy singled out. The Eisenhower victory meant that millions of lifelong Republican voters were doomed to a new frustration. The "hardshells" hoping for a permanent cut in foreign aid, a crackdown on labor, or a big reduction in taxes and the budget had contributed to a victory that in terms of these objectives had no meaning. The Eisenhower victory also meant that there were now millions of voters momentarily enlisted in the Republican cause who had never been in the party before; they had been attracted by "Ike's" personality, by his promise to bring down the cost of living, and by the desire to escape the Korean stalemate. And finally the victory meant that the predominant Republican wing of the American Establishment was, for the first time in a generation, in power in an administration of its own choosing.

The Eisenhower performance was bound to disappoint at least some of these divergent groups. In practice, it has disappointed them all, and for an odd reason. Upon taking office, Eisenhower, the choice of the more sophisticated Republicans, turned out to have many of the convictions of the most Tory adherents of Taft: he did not share their animus against union labor, but otherwise he was a true disciple of the Old Guard orthodoxy. He believed in the absolute primacy of thrift, he wanted to return government functions to the states, he believed deficit financing was sin, he believed high taxes and government regulations were "stifling free enterprise." Eisenhower in the White House was closer to an Iowa Rotarian than to a Wall Street banker. He was the man from Abilene, Kansas, not the man from Morningside Heights.

The Eisenhower administration vaguely disappointed many in the Eastern elite who had hoped for more positive leadership. Nelson Rockefeller symbolized this discreet discontent when he left the administration and financed a series of reports on public issues urging ambitious programs far more costly than Eisenhower would countenance. The blue-ribbon members of the committee which presented the Gaither Report on national defense filed, in effect, a dissent to Eisenhower's concept of the national interest.

Eisenhower and Agriculture Secretary Benson, committed to the view that subsidies were intrinsically wrong and that what farmers desired above all was the liberation from government marketing and production restraints, did not abolish subsidies, restraints, or surpluses, but they did manage to alienate the farmers, a dwindling but still sizable Republican voting bloc.

The newer Republicans, converted in 1952 in the cities and the suburbs, should have been reassured by the administration's preoccupation with the inflation problem and "the stable dollar." To some extent they were, but they had other tangible concerns such as the schools their children attended and the cost of medical care for their aged parents. The Eisenhower administration, penny-pinched and budget-obsessed, sabotaged the annual legislative drives for Federal aid to schools, cut back the slum clearance program almost to a nullity, and on the whole failed to demonstrate that it was vitally concerned with the needs of the urban and lower-income voters. The latter retained their "liking for Ike," but as early as 1954 and in increasing numbers they, like many farmers, began to re-identify their own economic welfare with the Democratic party. The gap between Eisenhower's popularity and that of the Republican party widened rather than narrowed as his years in the White House progressed.

The hard-shell Republicans who should have been most pleased at the President's unanticipated sharing of their convictions have been disillusioned by his lack of fighting zeal. If the budget were to be balanced at a modest level, income taxes substantially reduced, the balance of functions between the Federal and state governments shifted, and the trend to big government reversed, it would require as many violent political struggles as it took to pass the New Deal in the first place. It would probably be necessary, for example, to pass a national right-to-work law, forbid industry wide collective bargaining, and break the political activities of the labor unions. On no front has Eisenhower undertaken a struggle of this magnitude. If his limited physical strength and his limited intellectual interest in this sort of problem were not sufficient to debar such a conflict, his desire for national unity and harmony would in any case prevent it. The domestic consensus rests secure in his hands.

Arthur Larson, the quondam philosopher of "Modern Republicanism," propounded the thesis in his book *A Republican Looks At His Party* (1956) that the Republican party under Eisenhower's leadership had "for the first time in our history discovered and established the Authentic American Center in politics." The Eisenhower administration expressed an "American Consensus." The steady decay of the Republican party at the state and congressional district level throughout the Eisenhower years is enough to discredit this thesis. Parties which have formulated a widely accepted consensus on the big contemporary issues and are united behind a great leader do not show these alarming signs of disaffection and disrepair.

There is an American Consensus on the issues, but it was developed by Franklin Roosevelt and developed further in some respects by Truman. Eisenhower has been content to leave it undisturbed. His few attempts to return to the "little government" of a bygone day have been abortive. Two statistics alone are enough to account for his defeat: there are 40,000,000 more Americans than there were twenty years ago and more than one-third of all Americans now live in states other than those in which they grew up. The growing population makes the pressure for increased government services irresistible and the mobility of that population makes it equally inevitable that the people look to the Federal government to supply those services as state loyalties disappear and state boundaries become unreal.

Eisenhower did disturb the old political balance of power as distinguished from the consensus on issues, but he had not the energies, the talents, nor the experience to exploit his personal triumphs for his party's advantage.

Eisenhower has been the great leader *manqué*. His dignified bearing, his warm flashing smile, his easy manners made him seem a man with whom most voters could feel at ease, and his hero's reputation made him seem a man in whom they could safely trust their destiny. Has their trust been misplaced? The answer lies in America's margin for error. Eisenhower and his administration have lived off the accumulated wisdom, the accumulated prestige, and the accumulated military strength of his predecessors who conducted more daring and more creative regimes. If our margin for error is as great as it has traditionally been, these quiet Eisenhower years will have been only a pleasant idyll, an inexpensive interlude in a grim century. If our margin for error is much thinner than formerly, Eisenhower may join the ranks of history's fated good men, the Stanley Baldwins and the James Buchanans. Their intentions were good and their example is pious, but they bequeathed to their successors a black heritage of time lost and opportunities wasted.

CHAPTER 23

AMERICA IN THE SIXTIES: THE MAKING OF THE COUNTERCULTURE

The 1960s is a period of great interest to the cultural historian because during these years a widespread revolt against the accepted values and institutions of middle-class American society brought about profound cultural alteration in American life. There have always been nonconformists in this country —people who, in Thoreau's phrase, marched to the beat of a different drummer. But never before the 1960s had the rebellion against the straight world been so widespread, involved so many and such a variety of people, and resulted in such significant cultural changes in so many areas of American life. Radical changes in accepted views and norms are never made easily, and the 1960s were no exception. The period was one of intense social conflict and confrontation. Young hippies with long, stringy hair and handcrafted or surplus military clothing were ranged against older representatives of the Establishment with neatly cropped hair and traditional business suits. Orthodox churchgoers were mystified and disturbed by nonchurchgoing religious enthusiasts who rejected science and reason and championed a new supernaturalism, sometimes including magic and witchcraft. And the traditional American nuclear family was counterposed against communes and unorthodox hippie family arrangements. Such confrontation was characteristic of nearly every major aspect of American life in the 1960s.

The result of the cultural rebellion was the development of a full-blown counterculture, an alternate, competing culture that stood as a counterpoise to the dominant, traditional American cultural matrix. In the following essay, Professor William L. O'Neill provides a provocative discussion of the development of the counterculture and its significance in contemporary America.

Professor O'Neill points out that the counterculture was more than simply a youth culture. Not all the young were rebellious and many people over 30 joined the movement against the cultural Establishment. O'Neill notes that the counterculture arose in the first place because of the defects in the larger culture, particularly in the widespread existence of war, poverty, racial prejudice and bigotry, and various other forms of social injustice. The music and dance, the widespread use of drugs, the style of dress, the communal living patterns, the social and sexual freedom, and the spiritualism, romanticism, and hedonism associated with the counterculture all reflected the adoption of a new value system and the rejection of the grasping, combative, supposedly rational, straight world. These developments, O'Neill suggests, were to be expected; what was surprising was the extent to which the revolt against traditional authority and discipline gained ground in the 1960s.

In reading this essay, the student will want to focus on a number of important questions. First, one should consider the origins of the counterculture. What caused the widespread cultural revolt and why did it come in the 1960s instead of in the 1950s? Second, there is the matter of defining and delineating the counterculture. What are the basic elements that define the counterculture and the dimensions that delineate it? In your view, what is the essential meaning of the counterculture? What is your personal position on the cultural revolt against the established culture? Finally, what has been happening to the counterculture in the years since 1971, when the selection that follows was first published?

The literature on the counterculture and its diverse aspects is varied and provocative. The following works present interesting insights into some of the major counterculture personalites: Lenny Bruce, *How to Talk Dirty and Influence People** (1965); Hunter Davies, *The Beatles: The Authorized Biography** (1968); Tom Wolfe, *The Electric Kool-Aid Acid Test** (1968); Joan Baez, *Daybreak** (1968); Michael Lydon's interview of Janis Joplin, "Every Moment She Is What She Feels," *The New York Times Magazine* (February 23, 1969). Art historian Carl Belz's *The Story of Rock** (1971), is excellent, as is Nicholas von Hoffman's treatment of hippies, *We Are the People Our Parents Warned Us Against** (1968). On the counterculture itself, Theodore Roszak, *The Making of a Counter Culture** (1969), William Braden, *The Age of Aquarius** (1969), and especially Paul Goodman, "The New Reformation," *The New York Times Magazine* (September 14, 1962), are valuable. Also see Charles Reich, *The Greening of America* (1970), and Ronald Berman, *America in the Sixties* (1968).

*Available in a paperback edition.

THE COUNTER-CULTURE

WILLIAM L. O'NEILL

Counter-culture as a term appeared rather late in the decade. It largely replaced the term "youth culture," which finally proved too limited. When the sixties began, youth culture meant the way adolescents lived. Its central institutions were the high school and the mass media. Its principal activities were consuming goods and enacting courtship rituals. Critics and students of the youth culture were chiefly interested in the status and value systems associated with it. As time went on, college enrollments increased to the point where colleges were nearly as influential as high schools in shaping the young. The molders of youthful opinion got more ambitious. Where once entertainers were content to amuse for profit, many began seeing themselves as moral philosophers. Music especially became a medium of propaganda, identifying the young as a distinct force in society with unique values and aspirations. This helped produce a kind of ideological struggle between the young and their elders called the "generation gap." It was the first time in American history that social conflict was understood to be a function of age. Yet the young were not all rebellious. Most in fact retained confidence in the "system" and its norms. Many older people joined the rebellion, whose progenitors were as often over thirty (where the generation gap was supposed to begin) as under it. The attack on accepted views and styles broadened so confusingly that "youth culture" no longer described it adequately. Counter-culture was a sufficiently vague and elastic substitute. It meant all things to all men and embraced everything new from clothing to politics. Some viewed the counter-culture as mankind's best, maybe only, hope; others saw it as a portent of civilization's imminent ruin. Few recalled the modest roots from which it sprang.

Even in the 1950's and very early sixties, when people still worried about conformity and the silent generation, there were different drummers to whose beat millions would one day march. The bohemians of that era (called "beatniks" or "beats") were only a handful, but they practiced free love, took drugs,

SOURCE. William L. O'Neill, *Coming Apart: An Informal History of America in the 1960's,* pp. 233–240, 242–245, 248–249, 251–268, 270–271. Copyright © 1971 by William L. O'Neill. Reprinted by permission of Quadrangle Books.

repudiated the straight world, and generally showed which way the wind was blowing. They were highly publicized, so when the bohemian impulse strengthened, dropouts knew what was expected of them. While the beats showed their contempt for social norms mostly in physical ways, others did so intellectually. Norman Mailer, in "The White Negro," held up the sensual, lawless hipster as a model of behavior under oppressive capitalism. He believed, according to "The Time of Her Time," that sexual orgasm was the pinnacle of human experience, perhaps also an approach to ultimate truth. Norman O. Brown's *Life Against Death,* a psychoanalytic interpretation of history, was an underground classic which argued that cognition subverted intuition. Brown called for a return to "polymorphous perversity," man's natural estate. The popularity of Zen Buddhism demonstrated that others wished to slip the bonds of Western rationalism; so, from a different angle, did the vogue for black humor.

The most prophetic black humorist was Joseph Heller, whose novel *Catch-22* came out in 1960. Though set in World War II the book was even more appropriate to the Indochinese war. Later Heller said, "That was the war I had in mind; a war fought without military provocation, a war in which the real enemy is no longer the other side, but someone allegedly on your side. The ridiculous war I felt lurking in the future when I wrote the book." *Catch-22* was actually written during the Cold War, and sold well in the early sixties because it attacked the perceptions on which that war, like the Indochinese war that it fathered, grew. At the time reviewers didn't know what to make of *Catch-22.* World War II had been, as everyone knew, an absolutely straightforward case of good versus evil. Yet to Heller there was little moral difference between combatants. In fact all his characters are insane, or carry normal attributes to insane lengths. They belong to a bomber squadron in the Mediterranean. Terrified of combat, most hope for ground duty and are free to request it, but: "There was only one catch and that was Catch-22, which specified that a concern for one's own safety in the face of dangers that were real and immediate was the process of a rational mind. Orr was crazy and could be grounded. All he had to do was ask; and as soon as he did, he would no longer be crazy and would have to fly more missions. Orr would be crazy to fly more missions and sane if he didn't, but if he was sane he had to fly them. If he flew them he was crazy and didn't have to; but if he didn't want to he was sane and had to."

The squadron's success depends more on having a perfect bomb pattern than hitting the target. Milo Minderbinder is the key man in the Theater, though only a lieutenant, because he embodies the profit motive. He puts the entire war on a paying basis and hires the squadron out impartially to both sides. At the end Yossarian, the novel's hero, resolved his dilemma by setting out for neutral Sweden in a rubber raft. This was what hundreds of real deserters and draft evaders would be doing soon. It was also a perfect symbol for the masses of dropouts who sought utopian alternatives to the straight world. One day there would be hundreds of thousands of Yossarians, paddling away from the crazed society in frail crafts of their own devising. *Catch-22* was not just black comedy, nor even chiefly an anti-war novel, but a metaphor that helped shape the moral vision of an era.*

Although children and adolescents watched a great deal of television in the sixties, it seemed at first to have little effect. Surveys were always showing that youngsters spent fifty-two hours a week or whatever in front of the tube, yet what they saw was so bland or predictable as to make little difference. The exceptions were news programs, documentaries, and dramatic specials. Few watched them. What did influence the young was popular music, folk music first and then rock. Large-scale enthusiasm for folk music began in 1958 when the Kingston Trio recorded a song, "Tom Dooley," that sold two million records. This opened the way for less slickly commercial performers. Some, like Pete Seeger, who had been singing since the depression, were veteran performers. Others, like Joan Baez, were newcomers. It was conventional for folk songs to tell a story. Hence the idiom had always lent itself to propaganda. Seeger possessed an enormous repertoire of message songs that had gotten him blacklisted by the mass media years before. Joan Baez cared more for the message than the music, and after a few years devoted herself mainly to peace work. The folk-music vogue was an early stage in the politicization of youth, a forerunner of the counter-culture. This was hardly apparent at the time. Folk music was not seen as morally reprehensible in the manner of rock and roll. It was a familiar genre. Folk was gentle music for the most part, and even when sung in protest did not offend many. Malvina Reynold's "What Have They Done to the Rain?" complained of radioactive fallout which all detested. Pete Seeger's anti-war song "Where Have All the Flowers Gone?" was a favorite with both pacifists and the troops in Vietnam.

Bob Dylan was different. Where most folk singers were either clean cut or homey looking, Dylan had wild long hair. He resembled a poor white dropout of questionable morals. His songs were hard-driving, powerful, intense. It was hard to be neutral about them. "The Times They Are a-Changing" was perhaps the first song to exploit the generation gap. Dylan's life was as controversial as his ideology. Later he dropped politics and got interested in rock music. At the Newport Jazz Festival in 1965 he was booed when he introduced a

---

*Lenny Bruce was a more tragic harbinger of change. He was a successful night club comedian who created an obscene form of black comedy that involved more social criticism than humor. Bruce was first arrested for saying "motherfucker" on stage in 1962. Later he was busted for talking dirty about the Pope and many lesser offenses. He may have been insane. He died early from persecution and drug abuse, and then became an honored martyr in the anti-Establishment pantheon. He was one of the spiritual fathers of the yippies.

fusion of his own called "folk-rock." He went his own way after that, disowned by the politically minded but admired by a great cult following attracted as much, perhaps, by his independent life as by his music. He advanced the counter-culture in both ways and made money too. This also was an inspiration to those who came after him.

Another early expression, which coexisted with folk music, though quite unlike it, was the twist. Dance crazes were nothing new, but the twist was remarkable because it came to dominate social dancing. It used to be that dance fads were here today and gone tomorrow, while the two-step went on forever. Inexpert, that is to say most, social dancers had been loyal to it for generations. It played a key role in the traditional youth culture. Who could imagine a high school athletic event that did not end with couples clinging to one another on the dimly lit gym floor, while an amateur dance band plodded gamely on? When in 1961 the twist became popular, moralists were alarmed. It called for vigorous, exhibitionistic movements. Prurient men were reminded of the stripper's bumps and grinds. They felt the twist incited lust. Ministers denounced it. Yet in the twist (and its numerous descendants), bodies were not rubbed together as in the two-step, which had embarrassed millions of schoolboys. Millions more had suffered when through awkwardness they bumped or trod on others. The twist, by comparison, was easy and safe. No partner was bothered by the other's maladroitness. It aroused few passions. That was the practical reason for its success. But there was an ideological impulse behind it also. Amidst the noise and tumult each person danced alone, "doing his own thing," as would soon be said. But though alone, the dancer was surrounded by others doing their own thing in much the same manner. The twist celebrated both individuality and communality. This was to become a hallmark of the counter-culture, the right of everyone to be different in much the same way. The twist also foretold the dominance of rock, to which it was so well suited.

No group contributed more to the counter-culture than the Beatles, though, like folk music and the twist, their future significance was not at first apparent. Beatlemania began on October 13, 1963, when the quartet played at the London Palladium. The police, caught unawares, were hardly able to control the maddened throngs. On February 9, 1964, they appeared on U.S. television. The show received fifty thousand ticket requests for a theater that seated eight hundred. They were mobbed at the airport, besieged in their hotel, and adored everywhere. Even their soiled bed linen found a market. Their next recording, "Can't Buy Me Love," sold three million copies in advance of release, a new world's record. Their first movie, *A Hard Day's Night* (1964), was both a critical and a popular success. Some reviewers compared them with the Marx brothers. They became millionaires overnight. The Queen decorated them for helping ease the balance-of-payments deficit. By 1966 they were so rich that they could afford to give up live performances.

. . . The Beatles were mostly working class in origin but sang with an American accent (like other English rock stars) and dressed in an elegant style, then popular in Britain, called "mod." The result was a deracinated, classless image of broad appeal.

The Beatles did not fade away as they were supposed to. Beatlemania continued for three years. Then the group went through several transformations that narrowed its audience to a smaller but intensely loyal cult following in the Dylan manner. . . . Their music had a great effect on the young, so did their styles of life. They led the march of fashion away from mod and into the hairy, mustached, bearded, beaded, fringed, and embroidered costumes of the late sixties. . . .

. . . The group later broke up. By then they had made their mark, and while strange, it was not a bad mark. Whatever lasting value their music may have, they set a good example to the young in most ways. [John] Lennon's pacifism was nonviolent, even if wildly unorthodox. At a time when so many pacifists were imitating what they protested against, that was most desirable. They also worked hard at their respective arts and crafts, though others were dropping out and holding up laziness as a socially desirable trait. The Beatles showed that work was not merely an Establishment trick to keep the masses in subjection and the young out of trouble.

Beatlemania coincided with a more ominous development in the emerging counter-culture—the rise of the drug prophet Timothy Leary. He and Richard Alpert were scientific researchers at Harvard University who studied the effects of hallucinogenic drugs, notably a compound called LSD. . . . They and many of their subjects became habitual users, not only of LSD but of marijuana and other drugs. They constructed an ideology of sorts around this practice. After they were fired the *Harvard Review* published an article of theirs praising the drug life: "Remember, man, a natural state is ecstatic wonder, ecstatic intuition, ecstatic accurate movement. Don't settle for less."

. . . [Leary's] personal following was never large, but drug use became commonplace among the young anyway. At advanced universities social smoking of marijuana was as acceptable as social drinking. More so, in a way, for it was better suited to the new ethic. One did not clutch one's solitary glass but shared one's "joint" with others. "Grass" made one gentle and pacific, not surly and hostile. As a forbidden pleasure it was all the more attractive to the thrill-seeking and the rebellious. And it helped further distinguish between the

old world of grasping, combative, alcoholic adults and the turned-on, coopera-
tive culture of the young. Leary was a bad prophet. Drug-based mystical
religion was not the wave of the future. What the drug cult led to was a lot
of dope-smoking and some hard drug-taking. When research suggested that
LSD caused genetic damage, its use declined. But the effects of grass were hard
to determine, so its consumption increased.

Sometimes "pot" smokers went on to other drugs—a deadly compound
called "speed," and even heroin. These ruined many lives (though it was never
clear that the lives were not already ruined to begin with). The popularity of
drugs among the young induced panic in the old. States passed harsher and
harsher laws that accomplished little. Campaigns against the drug traffic were
launched periodically with similar results. When the flow of grass was interrupted, people turned to other drugs. Drug use seemed to go up either way.
The generation gap widened. Young people thought marijuana less dangerous
than alcohol, perhaps rightly. To proscribe the one and permit the other made
no sense to them, except as still another example of adult hypocrisy and the
hatred of youth. . . .

In Aldous Huxley's prophetic novel, *Brave New World,* drug use was promoted by the state as a means of social control. During the sixties it remained
a deviant practice and a source of great tension between the generations. Yet
drugs did encourage conformity among the young. To "turn on and drop out"
did not weaken the state. Quite the contrary, it drained off potentially subversive energies. The need for drugs gave society a lever should it ever decide to
manipulate rather than repress users. Pharmacology and nervous strain had
already combined to make many adult Americans dependent on drugs like
alcohol and tranquilizers. Now the young were doing the same thing, if for
different reasons. In a free country this meant only that individual problems
increased. But should democracy fail, drug abuse among both the young and
old was an instrument for control such as no dictator ever enjoyed. The young
drug-takers thought to show contempt for a grasping, unfeeling society. In
doing so they opened the door to a worse one. They scorned their elders for
drinking and pill-taking, yet to outsiders their habits seemed little different,
though ethically more pretentious. In both cases users were vulnerable and
ineffective to the extent of their addiction. Of such ironies was the counter-
culture built.

Another sign of things to come was the rise and fall of Ken Kesey and his
Merry Pranksters. . . .

What really put Kesey at the center of the new culture . . . were the "acid
tests." These were big public gatherings with light shows, rock music, mad
dancing, and of course, acid-dropping. "Can you pass the acid test?" was their
motto. These were the first important multimedia happenings, combining light

shows, tapes, live rock bands, movie and slide projectors, strobe lights, and other technical gimmicks. Their climax was reached at the San Francisco Tripps Festival in January 1966. It was meant to release all the new forms of expression in the cultural underground. Bill Graham, who had managed the San Francisco Mime Troupe, was its organizer. Kesey and the Pranksters gave the acid test. The Tripps Festival was a great success. Several rock groups (The Grateful Dead and Big Brother and the Holding Company) proclaimed the emergence of a new musical genre—acid rock. Graham began staging such affairs regularly in the Fillmore Auditorium in San Francisco. Out of this came the "San Francisco Sound," which made the city a provincial capital in the music industry. Hippie culture, with its drugs, rock groups, psychedelic folk art, and other apparatus, was well and truly launched. . . .

Though Kesey and his friends had different hopes for it, the Tripps Festival proved to be a turning point in the history of rock. Bill Graham and other promoters took the idea and institutionalized it. Rock and light shows attracted big audiences for years afterward and helped launch counter-cultural music groups into the pop culture mainstream. "Acid rock" and such brought deviant values to a national audience. Sex, dope, and anti-social notions became so common that many radio disc jockeys finally gave up trying to censor the music, though TV managed to stay pure. Radio did try to draw the line at revolutionary exhortations. Thus in 1968 many disc jockeys played the Beatles' "Revolution No. 1" because of its counterrevolutionary lyrics ("But if you're carrying a picture of Chairman Mao, you ain't going to make it with anyone anyhow") but did not play the Rolling Stones' rebuttal which insisted that "the time is right for fighting in the streets."

But rock as an idiom was more concerned with social and sexual freedom than politics. The Rolling Stones' subversive appeal was more formalistic than not. The group's real power derived from its sexuality. Mick Jagger hopped about, whacking the stage with a leather belt. Jim Morrison of the Doors was arrested twice for indecent exposure. More articulate than most rock stars, Morrison described his group's function this way: "A Doors' concert is a public meeting called by us for a special kind of dramatic discussion and entertainment." And, further, "We make concerts sexual politics. The sex starts with me, then moves out to include the charmed circle of musicians on stage. The music we make goes out to the audience and interacts with them: they go home and interact with the rest of reality, then I get it all back by interacting with that reality, so the whole sex thing works out to be one big ball of fire." Their listeners took the message perfectly. Morrison was famous in the rock underground for supposedly being able to hold an erection through a two-hour performance. The performers attracted young camp followers known as "groupies." Something like the bobby-soxers of an earlier day, the groupies were more obviously sensual. One legendary (perhaps mythical) team of groupies, known as the Chicago Plaster Casters, carried rock-phallic worship to its logical conclusion by making plaster casts of the performer's sex organs.

But not all rock fans were overstimulated teenie-boppers. At its most pretentious the cult laid great moral responsibilities on the backs of rock groups. When the Beatles released a new album late in 1968 (called simply "The Beatles"), one student critic announced that having transformed the male image and performed other great services, it was now their duty to "forge a cultural revolution." There was broad agreement on this, but rock revolutionaries differed otherwise. . . .

To see how far the youth culture had progressed in a few years, one had only to compare the careers of Joan Baez and Janis Joplin. Miss Baez remained as delicately beautiful and as clear-voiced as ever. In 1964 she and Bob Dylan had been the "fantasy lovers of the folk revival." But by 1968 her vogue was long since gone. She still sang in much the same manner as before. She was even more dedicated to peace and nonviolence. Miss Baez was a tax resister on moral grounds, and she married a draft resister who went to prison rather than accept induction. Yet neither her music nor her beliefs nor her style of life was "relevant" to young people any longer. The place she once occupied was taken by Janis Joplin, a wholly different kind of woman. Miss Joplin was a hard-drinking, tough-talking, ugly but dynamic power singer with roots in the blues tradition. She became famous as the singer for a San Francisco rock band called Big Brother and the Holding Company. A wild, passionate, totally involved performer, she was not much different as a person. Miss Joplin was what the groupies would have become if talented. She did exactly what she pleased, took lovers freely, owned a psychedelic sports car and a closet full of costumes, and, when her reputation eclipsed that of Big Brother and the Holding Company, struck out on her own. "If I miss," she told a reporter, "I'll never have a second chance on nothing. But I gotta risk it. I never hold back, man. I'm always on the outer limits of probability." What was her philosophy of life? "Getting stoned, staying happy, and having a good time. I'm doing just what I want with my life, enjoying it." She burned her candle at both ends and it did not last the night.

Miss Joplin was far more candid than many rock stars. One of their most tiresome habits was insisting on having it both ways. They wanted to be rich and famous while also radical and culturally momentous. What made the Beatles so attractive was that having become rich beyond the dreams of avarice, they abandoned it. And (Lennon excepted) they did not moralize much, however seriously they took themselves. The Rolling Stones, on the other hand, called for revolution in 1968 and the following year made millions with a whirlwind tour of the U.S. As time went on, the commercial aspects increasingly dominated rock. Few went so far as the coalition of groups in St. Louis who refused demands that they offer free, or at least reduced-price, tickets to the needy because doing so would be contrary to the American principle of free enterprise. But time was on their side. . . . As rock became less a movement and more a business, its impact, though not its popularity, declined. It seemed unlikely that rock would soon become a television staple. But some day its fans would be middle-aged, so even that possibility could not be permanently excluded.

The counter-culture's influence on fashion was nearly as great as on rock. Fashions began to change radically even before the hippies and other such groups appeared. . . .

The rebellion against traditional fashion went in two directions, though both were inspired by the young. . . . [One] line of development . . . emphasized brilliant or peculiar fabrics and designs. Here the emphasis was on costuming in a theatrical sense. People wore outfits that made them look like Mongols or cavaliers or whatever. These costumes, never cheap, were often very costly, though not more so than earlier styles. They were worn by others besides the young. What they owed to the emerging counter-culture was a certain freedom from constraint, and a degree of sensuality. Though the mini-skirt became a symbol of rebellious youth, it was so popular that wearing it was not an ideological statement, even if Middle Americans often thought so.

The other direction clothing took was more directly related to counter-cultural patterns. This mode had two seemingly incompatible elements—surplus military garments and handcrafted ones. Army and navy surplus clothing was the first style to be adopted by young people looking for a separate identity. Socially conscious youths began wearing army and navy jacket shirts, and bell-bottom trousers in the early sixties. This was not meant to show contempt for the military, for antiwar sentiment was then at a low ebb, but as a mark of ostentatious frugality in the high-consumption society. As these garments became more in demand, the price went up and more expensive commercial imitations appeared. Wearing them accordingly meant less, but a certain flavor of austere nonconformity stuck to them all the same. They remained favorites of dissenting youths thereafter, even though worn by the merely fashionable too.

The hippies made handcrafted items popular. The implication here was that the wearer had made them, thus showing his independence and creativity. . . . Wearing beads, bangles, leather goods, fringes, colorful vests, and what all showed sympathy for American Indians, who inspired the most common designs, and fitted in with the popular back-to-nature ethic. When combined with military surplus garments they enabled the wearer to touch all the counter-cultural bases at once. Thus these fashions transmitted, however faintly, signals meaning peace, love, brotherhood, noble savagery, community, folk artistry, anti-capitalism and anti-militarism, and later, revolutionary zeal.

This hippie *cum* military surplus mode also had a functional effect. It was a great leveler. . . . In effect, aesthetics were exchanged for ethics. Beauty was no longer related to appearance but to morality. To have the proper spirit, though homely, was to be beautiful. This was a great relief for the poorly endowed and a point in the counter-culture's favor. Yet it enraged adults. Once the association between beads, beards, and military surplus goods on the one hand, and radicalism and dope on the other, was established, Middle America declared war on the counter-culture's physical trappings. School systems everywhere waged a relentless struggle against long hair. To dress this way in many places was a hostile act which invited reprisals. The style became a chief symbol of the generation gap, clung to fanatically by youngsters the more they were persecuted for it, as fiercely resisted by their elders. The progress of the generational struggle could almost be measured by the spread of these fashions.

No doubt older people would have resented the new styles in any case, but the way they emerged made them doubly offensive. They were introduced by young bohemians, mainly in New York and San Francisco, whose deviant attributes were highly publicized. New York hippies were concentrated in a section called the East Village. (Greenwich Village, the traditional bohemian refuge, had gotten too commercial and expensive.) By the mid-sixties a sizable community of radicals, dropouts, youthful vagrants, unrecognized avant-garde artists, and others were assembling there and a variety of cults beginning to flourish. . . .

. . . [The] East Village gained from its proximity to the New York avant garde. The mature counter-culture owed a lot to this relationship, but even in its early stages the East Village suffered from the influx of teenie-boppers and runaways who were to spoil both it and the Haight-Ashbury for serious cultural radicals. The people who were soon to be called hippies meant to build alternatives to the straight world. Against the hostile, competitive, capitalistic values of bourgeois America they posed their own faith in nonviolence, love, and community. Drugs were important both as means to truth and advancers of the pleasure principle. . . .

Hippies lived together, in "tribes" or "families." Their golden rule was "be nice to others, even when provoked, and they will be nice to you." In San Francisco their reservation was the Haight-Ashbury district near Golden Gate Park. They were much resented in the East Village by the natives, poor ethnics for the most part. In the Hashbury, on the other hand, they were welcome at first. Though peculiar, they were an improvement over the petty criminals they displaced. Even when freaked-out in public from drugs, a certain tolerance prevailed. After all, stepping over a drooling flower child on the street was better than getting mugged. Civic authorities were less open-minded. The drug traffic bothered them especially, and the Hashbury was loaded with "narks" (narcotics agents). Hunter S. Thompson wrote that "love is the password in the Haight-Ashbury, but paranoia is the style. Nobody wants to go to jail."

The fun-and-games era did not last long, perhaps only from 1965 to 1966. The hippie ethic was too fragile to withstand the combination of police surveillance and media exposure that soon afflicted it. The first hippies had a certain earnestness. But they were joined by masses of teen-age runaways. Nicholas von Hoffman observed that the Hashbury economy that began as a fraternal barter system quickly succumbed to the cash nexus. It became the first community in the world to revolve entirely around the buying and selling and taking of drugs. Marijuana and LSD were universal; less popular, but also commonplace, were LSD's more powerful relative STP, and amphetamines. "Speed kills" said the buttons and posters; speed freaks multiplied anyhow. To support themselves some hippies worked at casual labor or devised elaborate, usually unsuccessful schemes to make money out of hippie enterprises. Panhandling was popular, so was theft, disguised usually as communism.

Bohemians invariably deplore monogamy, and the hippies were no exception. As one member of the Jefferson Airplane put it, "The stage is our bed and the audience is our broad. We're not entertaining, we're making love." Though committed to sexual freedom on principle, and often promiscuous in fact, the hippies were not really very sexy. Timothy Leary notwithstanding, drugs seemed to dampen the sexual urge. And the hippies were too passive in any case for strenuous sex play. Conversely, the most ardent free lovers, like those in the Sexual Freedom League, had little interest in drugs. Among hippies the combination of bad diets, dope, communal living, and the struggle to survive made for a restricted sex life. Of course the hippies were always glad of chances to shock the bourgeoisie, which made them seem more depraved than they were. Then too, people expected them to be sexually perverse, and the more public-spirited hippies tried to oblige. Like good troupers they hated to let the public down, though willing to put it on.

Hippie relations with black people were worse than might have been supposed. Hippies owed blacks a lot. Their jargon was derived from the ghetto. They admired blacks, as certain whites always have, for being more emotional, sensual, and uninhibited. But there were very few black hippies. Superspade, a beloved Negro drug pusher, was an exception. Most hippies were frightened of blacks. "Spades are programmed for hate" was the way many put it. . . .

In the end it was neither the . . . [motorcycle outlaws] nor the blacks but the media that destroyed hippiedom. The publicity given the summer of love attracted countless thousands of disturbed youngsters to the Hashbury and the East Village in 1967. San Francisco was not burdened with the vast numbers originally expected. But many did come, bringing in their train psychotics, drug peddlers, and all sorts of criminals. Drug poisoning, hepatitis (from infected needles), and various diseases resulting from malnutrition and exposure thinned their ranks. Rapes, muggings, and assaults became commonplace. Hippies had little money, but they were irresistibly easy marks. Hippie girls were safe to assault. They reacted passively, and as many were drug users and runaways they could not go to the police.

So the violence mounted. On the West Coast one drug peddler was stabbed to death and his right forearm removed. Superspade's body was found hanging from a cliff top. He had been stabbed, shot, and trussed in a sleeping bag. On October 8 the nude bodies of Linda Rea Fitzpatrick, eighteen, and James Leroy "Groovy" Hutchinson, twenty-one, were discovered in an East Village boiler room. They had been murdered while high on LSD. Though pregnant, Miss Fitzpatrick had also been raped. That was how the summer of love ended. . . .

At its peak the hippie movement was the subject of much moralizing. Most often hippies were seen as degenerate and representative of all things godless and un-American. A minority accepted them as embodying a higher morality. The media viewed them as harmless, even amusing, freaks—which was probably closer to the truth. But before long it was clear that while the hippie movement was easily slain, the hippie style of life was not. Their habit of dressing up in costumes rather than outfits was widely imitated. So was their slang and their talk of peace, love, and beauty. The great popularity of ex-hippie rock groups was one sign of the cultural diffusion taking place, marijuana another. Weekend tripping spread to the suburbs. While the attempt to build parallel cultures on a large scale in places like the Hashbury failed, the hippies survived in many locales. Isolated farms, especially in New England and the Southwest, were particularly favored. And they thrived also on the fringes of colleges and universities, where the line between avant-garde student and alienated dropout was hard to draw. In tribes, families, and communes the hippies lived on, despite considerable local harassment wherever they went.

Though few in number, hippies had a great effect on middle-class youth. Besides their sartorial influence, hippies made religion socially acceptable. Their interest in the supernatural was contagious. Some of the communes which sprang up in the late sixties were actually religious fellowships practicing a contemporary monasticism. . . .

. . . Teachers of philosophy and religion were struck by the anti-positivist, anti-science feelings of many students. Science was discredited as an agent of the military-industrial complex. It had failed to make life more attractive. Whole classes protested the epistemology of science as well as its intellectual dominion. Students believed the Establishment claimed to be rational, but showed that it was not. This supported one of the central truths of all religion, that man is more than a creature who reasons. Nor was it only the young who felt this way. . . .

Theology reflected the new supernaturalism, just as it had the aggressive secularism of a few years earlier. Harvey Cox, most famous of the contemporary theologians, published a study of the extra-institutional spiritual revival called *The Feast of Fools* in 1969. "God Is Dead" gave way to the "Theology of Hope," after Jurgen Moltmann's book by that title. A German theologian, Moltmann argued that the trouble with Christian theology was that it ignored the future. "The Church lives on memories, the world on hope," he remarked elsewhere. Though he was a Protestant, Roman Catholic theologians in Germany and America agreed with him. Institutional churches responded to the new by absorbing as much of it as they could. Church happenings, rock masses, light shows, and readings from Eastern mystics were used by Protestants and Catholics alike. The home mass gained popularity among Catholics. It gave to formal worship something of the intimate fellowship that the young found so compelling. Thus while church attendance declined from the high levels of the 1950's, this did not mean a decrease in religious enthusiasm. The most striking aspect of the "religious revival" of the 1950's, after all, had been the absence of devotion. Going to church then was more a social than a religious act. In the late sixties faith was expressed by not going to church.

There were many ways of responding to this spiritual revival. Orthodox churchgoers were offended by it, and even more by the efforts of their denominations to win the inspirited young. More flexible religious leaders saw it as a great opportunity. Secular radicals and educators were more often depressed by it. Men whose lives were dedicated to the pursuit of truth through reason were not about to become shamans. If it was true that science and scholarship had not yet brought the millennium, this did not seem good cause for abandoning them.

The most surprising man to protest this new turn was Paul Goodman. Goodman's life and work were more nearly of a piece than most people's. He was a secular anarchist, but while hoping to wreck the old order, he believed that the old tools—reason, expertise, science—would still be needed. Hence, though he was one of the chief intellectual mentors of the counter-culture, its growing spiritualism, indeed anti-intellectualism, disturbed him.

. . . [Goodman emphasized that mere] confrontation was not the answer to society's ills, especially when done hatefully. Gandhi's great point had been that the confronter aims at future community with the confronted. Yet many New Leftists did not regard their enemies as members of the same species. "How can the young people think of a future community when they themselves have no present world, no profession or other job in it, and no trust in other human beings? Instead, some young radicals seem to entertain the disastrous illusion that other people can be compelled by fear. This can lead only to crushing reaction."

The young knew nothing of society's institutions, how they worked, where they came from, what had made them what they were. For many, history began in 1968. . . . They didn't trust people over thirty because they didn't understand them and were too conceited to try. "Having grown up in a world too meaningless to learn anything, they know very little and are quick to resent it." The most important thing to the young was being together, en masse if possible. At the rock festivals they found the meaning of life which, as they explained it, consisted of people being nice to each other. A group of them passing a stick of marijuana behaved like "a Quaker meeting waiting for the spirit." And, Goodman concluded, "in the end it is religion that constitutes the strength of this generation, and not, as I used to think, their morality, political will, and common sense."

Goodman's argument was an exceptionally brave one. No one who had done less for the young could in good conscience have spoken so bluntly of them. And religion as an organizing principle for making sense of the serious young seemed useful. But it didn't help to distinguish what was durable and what was merely fashionable in the counter-culture. The term itself was hard to define as it embraced almost everything new and anti-Establishment, however frivolous. On its deepest level the counter-culture was the radical critique of Herbert Marcuse, Norman O. Brown, and even Paul Goodman. It also meant the New Left, communes and hippie farms, magic, hedonism, eroticism, and public nudity. And it included rock music, long hair, and mini-skirts (or, alternatively, fatigue uniforms, used clothes, and the intentionally ugly or grotesque). Most attacks on the counter-culture were directed at its trivial aspects, pot and dress especially. Pot busts (police raids), often involving famous people or their children, became commonplace. The laws against pot were so punitive in some areas as to be almost unenforceable. Even President Nixon, spokesman for Middle American morality that he was, finally questioned them. Local fights against long hair, beards, and short skirts were beyond number. The American Civil Liberties Union began taking school systems to court for disciplining students on that account. New York City gave up trying to enforce dress codes. It was all the more difficult there as even the teachers were mod. At one school the principal ordered women teachers to wear smocks over their minis. They responded by buying mini-smocks. . . .

The greatest event in counter-cultural history was the Woodstock Festival in Bethel, New York. It was organized on the pattern of other large rock festivals. Big name groups were invited for several days of continuous entertaining in the open. A large crowd was expected, but nothing like the 300,000 or 400,000 youngsters who actually showed up on August 15, 1969. Everything fell apart in consequence. Tickets could not be collected nor services provided. There wasn't enough food or water. The roads were blocked with abandoned autos, and no one could get in or out for hours at a time. Surprisingly, there were no riots or disasters. The promoters chartered a fleet of helicopters to evacuate casualties (mostly from bad drug trips) and bring in essential supplies. Despite the rain and congestion, a good time was had by all (except the boy killed when a tractor accidentally drove over his sleeping bag). No one had ever seen so large and ruly a gathering before. People stripped down, smoked pot, and turned on with nary a discouraging word, so legend has it. Afterward the young generally agreed that it was a beautiful experience proving their superior morality. People were nicer to each other than ever before. Even the police were impressed by the public's order (a result of their wisely deciding not to enforce the drug laws). . . .

The rock festival at Altamont that winter [, however,] was . . . [a] disaster. It was a free concert that climaxed the Rolling Stones' whirlwind tour of the U.S. They called it their gift to the fans. Actually it was a clever promotion. . . . Little was done to prepare the site. The police didn't have enough notice to bring in reserves, so the Stones hired a band of Hell's Angels as security guards (for $500 worth of beer). The Stones did their thing and the Angels did theirs.

The result was best captured by a *Rolling Stone* magazine photograph showing Mick Jagger looking properly aghast while Angels beat a young Negro to death on stage. A musician who tried to stop them was knocked unconscious, and he was lucky at that. Before the day was over many more were beaten, though no others fatally. Sometimes the beatings were for aesthetic reasons. One very fat man took off his clothes in the approved rock festival manner. This offended the Angels who set on him with pool cues. No one knows how many were clubbed that day. The death count came to four. Apart from Meredith Hunter, who was stabbed and kicked to death, they mostly died by accident. A car drove off the road into a clump of people and killed two. A man, apparently high on drugs, slid into an irrigation canal and drowned. The drug freak-outs were more numerous than at Woodstock. The medical care was less adequate. . . .

It remained for *Rolling Stone,* the rock world's most authoritative journal, to tell the whole story of what it called the Altamont Death Festival. The violence was quite bad enough, but what especially bothered *Rolling Stone* was the commercial cynicism behind it. That huge gathering was assembled by the Stones to make a lucrative film on the cheap. They could have hired legitimate security guards, but it cost less to use the Angels. (At Woodstock unarmed civilians trained by the Hog Farm commune kept order.) They were too rushed for the careful planning that went into Woodstock, too callous (and greedy) to pour in the emergency resources that had saved the day there. . . .

. . . Ralph Gleason of the *San Francisco Chronicle* explained Altamont this way: "The name of the game is money, power, and ego, and money is first as it brings power. The Stones didn't do it for free, they did it for money, only the tab was paid in a different way. Whoever goes to the movie paid for the Altamont religious assembly." . . . Here the gullibility—innocence, perhaps —of the deviant young was responsible. Because the rock bandits smoked pot and talked a revolutionary game, they were supposed to be different from other entertainers. Even though they made fortunes and spent them ostentatiously, their virtue was always presumed. What Altamont showed was that the difference between a rock king and a robber baron was about six inches of hair.

If Altamont exposed one face of the counter-culture, the Manson family revealed another. Late in 1969 Sharon Tate, a pregnant movie actress, and four of her jet-set friends were ritually murdered in the expensive Bel-Air district of Los Angeles. Though apparently senseless, their deaths were thought related to the rootless, thrill-oriented life style of the Beautiful People. But on December 1 policemen began arresting obscure hippies. Their leader, Charles Manson, was an ex-convict and seemingly deranged. Susan Atkins, a member of his "family," gave several cloudy versions of what had happened. On the strength of them Manson was indicted for murder. . . .

Life with the Manson family was a combination of hippieism and paranoia. Manson subscribed to the usual counter-culture values. Inhibitions, the Establishment, regular employment, and other straight virtues were bad. Free love, nature, dope, rock, and mysticism were good. He believed a race war was coming (predicted in Beatle songs) and armed his family in anticipation of it. . . . Of course hippies were not murderers usually. But the repressed hostility, authoritarianism, perversity, and mindless paranoia that underlay much of the hippie ethic were never displayed more clearly. The folkways of the flower children tended toward extremes. At one end they were natural victims; at the other, natural victimizers. The Manson family were both at once.

Taken together the varieties of life among deviant youths showed the counter-culture to be disintegrating. What was disturbing about it was not so much the surface expression as its tendency to mirror the culture it supposedly rejected. The young condemned adult hypocrisy while matching its contradictions with their own. The old were materialistic, hung up on big cars and ranch houses. The young were equally devoted to motorcycles, stereo sets, and electric guitars. The old sought power and wealth. So did the young as rock musicians, political leaders, and frequently as salesmen of counter-cultural goods and services. What distinguished reactionary capitalists from their avant-garde opposite numbers was often no more than a lack of moral pretense. While condemning the adult world's addiction to violence, the young admired third-world revolutionaries, Black Panthers, and even motorcycle outlaws. The rhetoric of the young got progressively meaner and more hostile.

This was not so bad as butchering Vietnamese, but it was not very encouraging either. And where hate led, violence followed.

. . . [But there were hopeful signs in the counter-culture toward the end of the decade. One was] the surge of student interest in environmental issues. . . . These were not fake problems, like so many youthful obsessions, but real ones. They would take the best efforts of many generations to overcome. No doubt the young would lose interest in them after a while as usual. Still, it was better to save a forest or clean a river than to vandalize a campus. No amount of youthful nagging was likely to make adults give up their sinful ways. It was possible that the young and old together might salvage enough of the threatened environment to leave posterity something of lasting value. The generations yet unborn were not likely to care much whether ROTC was conducted on campus or off. But they will remember this age, for better or worse, with every breath they take.

. . . [The] counter-culture's decline ought not to be celebrated prematurely. It outlasted the sixties. It had risen in the first place because of the larger culture's defects. War, poverty, social and racial injustice were widespread. The universities were less human than they might have been. The regulation of sexual conduct led to endless persecutions of the innocent or the pathetic to no one's advantage. Young people had much to complain of. Rebellious youth had thought to make things better. It was hardly their fault that things got worse. They were, after all, products of the society they meant to change, and marked by it as everyone was. Vanity and ignorance made them think themselves free of the weaknesses they saw so clearly in others. But adults were vain and ignorant too, and what's more, they had power as the young did not. When they erred, as in Vietnam, millions suffered. The young hated being powerless, but thanks to it they were spared the awful burden of guilt that adults bore. They would have power soon enough, and no doubt use it just as badly. In the meantime, though, people did well to keep them in perspective.

. . . [Another important development of the 1960's] was the rise of an adult counter-culture. Americans have always been attracted to cults and such. No enthusiasm, however bizarre, fails to gain some notice in so vast and restless a country. Crank scientists and religious eccentrics are especially welcomed. In the 1960's this was more true than ever, and there seemed to be more uniformity of belief among the cults than before. Perhaps also they were more respectable. . . .

. . . [During the 1960's there] were literally thousands of groups dedicated to better mental health through de-sublimation, often sponsored by businesses and universities. In a sense what they did was rationalize the counter-cultural ethic and bend it to fit the needs of middle-class adults. For some, expanding their consciousness meant little more than weekend tripping with, or more commonly without, drugs. If most didn't give up work in the hippie manner, they became more relaxed about it. Some thought less about success and more about fun. Some found new satisfaction in their work, or else more satisfying work. The range of individual response was great, but the overall effect was to promote sensuality, and to diminish the Protestant Ethic. . . .

While it was difficult in 1969 to tell where the counter-culture would go, it was easy to see where it came from. Artists and bohemians had been demanding more freedom from social and artistic conventions for a long time. The romantic faith in nature, intuition, and spontaneity was equally old. What was striking about the sixties was that the revolt against discipline, even self-discipline, and authority spread so widely. Resistance to these tendencies largely collapsed in the arts. Soon the universities gave ground also. The rise of hedonism and the decline of work were obviously functions of increased prosperity, and also of effective merchandising. The consumer economy depended on advertising, which in turn leaned heavily on the pleasure principle. This had been true for fifty years at least, but not until television did it really work well. The generation that made the counter-culture was the first to be propagandized from infancy on behalf of the pleasure principle.

But though all of them were exposed to hucksterism, not all were convinced. Working-class youngsters especially soon learned that life was different from television. Limited incomes and uncertain futures put them in touch with reality earlier on. Middle-class children did not learn the facts of life until much later. Cushioned by higher family incomes, indulged in the same way as their peers on the screen, they were shocked to discover that the world was not what they had been taught it was. The pleasure orientation survived this discovery, the ideological packaging it came in often did not. All this had happened before, but in earlier years there was no large, institutionalized subculture for the alienated to turn to. In the sixties hippiedom provided one such, the universities another. The media publicized these alternatives and made famous the ideological leaders who promoted them. So the deviant young knew where to go for the answers they wanted, and how to behave when they got them. The media thus completed the cycle begun when they first turned youngsters to pleasure. That was done to encourage consumption. The message was still effective when young consumers rejected the products TV offered and discovered others more congenial to them.

Though much in the counter-culture was attractive and valuable, it was dangerous in three ways. First, self-indulgence led frequently to self-destruction. Second, the counter-culture increased social hostility. The generation gap was one example, but the class gap another. Working-class youngsters resented the counter-culture. They accepted adult values for the most part. They had to work whether they liked it or not. Beating up the long-haired and voting for George Wallace were only two ways they expressed these feelings. The counter-culture was geographical too. It flourished in cities and on campuses. Elsewhere, in Middle America especially, it was hated and feared. The result was a national division between the counter-culture and those adults who admired or tolerated it—upper-middle-class professionals and intellectuals in the Northeast particularly—and the silent majority of workers and Middle Americans who didn't. The tensions between these groups made solving social and political problems all the more difficult, and were, indeed, part of the problem.

Finally, the counter-culture was hell on standards. A handful of bohemians were no great threat to art and intellect. The problem was that a generation of students, the artists and intellectuals of the future, was infected with romanticism. Truth and beauty were in the eye of the beholder. They were discovered or created by the pure of heart. Formal education and training were not, therefore, merely redundant but dangerous for obstructing channels through which the spirit flowed. It was one thing for hippies to say this, romanticism being the natural region of bohemia. It was quite another to hear it from graduate students. Those who did anguished over the future of scholarship, like the critics who worried that pop art meant the end of art. These fears were doubtlessly overdrawn, but the pace of cultural change was so fast in the sixties that they were hardly absurd.

Logic seemed everywhere to be giving way to intuition, and self-discipline to impulse. Romanticism had never worked well in the past. It seemed to be doing as badly in the present. The hippies went from flower power to death-tripping in a few years. The New Left took only a little longer to move from participatory democracy to demolition. The counter-cultural ethic remained as beguiling as ever in theory. In practice, like most utopian dreams, human nature tended to defeat it. At the decade's end, young believers looked forward to the Age of Aquarius. Sensible men knew there would be no Aquarian age. What they didn't know was the sort of legacy the counter-culture would leave behind. Some feared that the straight world would go on as before, others that it wouldn't.

CHAPTER 24

THE AMERICAN WOMAN

In Carl Degler's important interpretive study of American history, *Out of Our Past*, one of the sections on early America is entitled "A Paradise For Women." Professor Degler argues persuasively that in the colonial period women enjoyed greater freedom, more rights, and higher esteem and status than their counterparts in the Old World. He goes on to suggest that this relatively superior position for women has been characteristic of the American experience down to modern times. But whatever their position relative to other women in the world, American women in recent years have expressed extreme dissatisfaction with their lot and have prompted a serious reevaluation of their role in American life. The questioning, ferment, and protest, in addition to profound social and economic adjustments since World War II, have resulted in a good deal of change—in constitutional and legal rights for women, in the ways in which women view themselves and are viewed by men and by the larger society, and, most noticeably, in the language (e.g., "chairwoman" or "chairperson" instead of "chairman"). The magnitude and ultimate meaning of these changes are presently indeterminable, but it is clear that the process of change will continue apace for some years to come.

In this selection, William Chafe summarizes briefly the significant developments in women's history in the mid-twentieth century and attempts to determine what the prospects are for improvement in women's status in the immediate future. Professor Chafe contends that major changes have occurred in the last three or four decades not so much because of conscious efforts to raise female consciousness and to counter male prejudice but because of basic alterations in American institutions and society. In his discussion, World War II looms large as a disrupter of traditional patterns of life and a catalyst for the creation of new modes of behavior and activity. Chafe does not pretend that the changes he describes have produced sexual equality nor does he claim that there is universal agreement even on the significance of the changes that have occurred. However, he does contend that a firm foundation has been laid for the continuation of the movement toward greater freedom and equality for women.

In reading this selection, students should keep the following questions in mind. First, in Professor Chafe's view, what is the primary way in which social change occurs? Do you agree? Second, why was World War II so important in bringing change in the area of women's status? Third, if Professor Chafe is correct about the relative inefficacy of trying to change attitudes about race and sex prior to changes in behavior, what is the real role of feminist groups in the improvement of women's position? What should women—and men—be doing to try to further the freedom and equality of women?

Like blacks and other special groups, women have generally been neglected in the study and writing of the history of this nation, but the developments of recent years have stimulated a keen interest in the role of women in American life, past and present. A good beginning point is Page Smith's historical survey, *Daughters of the Promised Land** (1970). William L. O'Neill, *Everyone Was Brave: The Rise and Fall of Feminism in America** (1969), and William Chafe, *The American Woman: Her Changing Social, Economic, and Political Roles, 1920–1970* (1972), treat women's history from the late-nineteenth century to the 1970s. A brief but useful survey of the changing role of women is Carl N. Degler, "Revolution Without Ideology: The Changing Place of Women in America," *Daedalus,* 93 (Spring 1964). An outstanding collection of pioneering essays in women's history is provided by Gerda Lerner, *The Majority Finds Its Past: Placing Women in History* (1979). Interpretations of the women's liberation movement from different perspectives are presented in Kate Millet, *Sexual Politics** (1970); Germaine Greer, *The Female Eunuch** (1971); Shulamith Firestone, *Dialectic of Sex** (1970); Norman Mailer, *The Prisoner of Sex* * (1971); and Midge Decter, *The New Chastity and Other Arguments Against Women's Liberation* (1972).*

*Available in a paperback edition.

FUTURE PROSPECTS

WILLIAM H. CHAFE

How does social change occur? The question has been implicit throughout the preceding discussion, and the answer to it may hold the key to much that has been said here. There are two fundamental responses to the query. The first is based on the premise that attitudes determine behavior and that ideology is the crucial variable affecting the process of change. According to this argument, people act on the basis of their values or beliefs. Hence a change in society can come about only through persuading the public that a given set of values is wrong and must be modified. The second position—far more skeptical —operates on the assumption that attitudes, especially those involving emotional matters such as race or sex, almost never change except under compulsion and that behavior is a more promising fulcrum for change than attitudes. As Gordon Allport has observed in his study of prejudice, "the masses of people do not become converts [to racial equality] in advance; rather they are converted by the *fait accompli.*" Thus social scientists have observed that white workers lose some of their bias against racial minorities when forced to work alongside them, but if the same workers had a choice beforehand, the contact would never occur and the bias would remain intact.

Although the interplay of attitude and behavior is far more complicated than the above paragraph indicates, the distinction provides a useful conceptual device for analyzing the recent history of women. It has seemed to me that attitudes toward woman's place have been so deeply imbedded within the process of living itself that any direct attempt to transform those attitudes through persuasion or ideological confrontation was doomed to failure. The suffragists believed that they had made significant progress toward equality through acquisition of the franchise, but they seriously overestimated the impact of the ballot on the structure of relationships between the sexes. Women might vote, but as long as they followed the lead of their husbands and fathers in the world outside the home, the reform meant relatively little. The real obstacle to equality was the division of spheres between men and women, and the Nineteenth Amendment did not substantially alter that. Males

SOURCE. William H. Chafe, *The American Woman: Her Changing Social, Economic, and Political Roles, 1920–1970,* pp. 245–254. Copyright © 1972 by Oxford University Press. Reprinted by permission.

continued to be reared in one way, females in another, and attitude and behavior reinforced each other. In a society with few models of "independent" women to emulate, only a small percentage of college girls were willing to risk failure in the female world of marriage and motherhood in order to prove their worth in the male world of business and the professions. The idea that the two sexes should fulfill different roles and responsibilities was buttressed by institutions such as the family and transmitted from generation to generation through the socialization process. Feminists might protest against discrimination and urge equality, but their agitation had little effect. Only a substantial upheaval could modify the existing division of labor between the sexes.

It was for that reason that World War II assumed so much importance. The event of war, by definition, disrupted traditional patterns of life and propelled men and women into new activities. In the years prior to 1940, employment of married women had been frowned upon as unseemly, and a violation of woman's place. The war made such attitudes irrelevant, and caused women's work to be defined as a national priority. As a result of the crisis, almost 7 million women joined the labor force for the first time, three out of four of them married. Most observers expected that women would go back to the home when the fighting stopped, but once in the labor force, female workers decided to remain on the job. With the passage of time, the number of employed married women grew steadily—partly as a response to inflation and rising family aspirations, but partly also because of a desire by many women to establish an identity beyond the home. Before the war, it had been almost unheard of for a middle-class wife or mother to work. Thirty years later, the labor force contained 60 per cent of all wives from homes with an annual income of more than $10,000, and more than half the mothers of children from six to seventeen years of age. If the nation—including women—had been asked in 1939 whether it desired, or would tolerate such a far-reaching change, the answer would undoubtedly have been an overwhelming no. But events bypassed public opinion, and made the change an accomplished fact. The war, in short, was a catalyst which broke up old modes of behavior and helped to forge new ones. As a result, work for middle-class women has become the rule rather than the exception, and the content of women's sphere has been permanently altered.

It would be a mistake, of course, to view a job as a panacea for women, or as a solution to the problem of inequality. Today, as fifty years ago, most employed women hold second-echelon jobs which pay low wages and offer little possibility for advancement. Although 70 per cent of all female college graduates are in the work force, nearly 20 per cent are employed in clerical, sales, or factory positions, and the median income of women with degrees is only 51 per cent of that earned by men with a comparable education. Nor can it be said that the woman with a job is necessarily more fulfilled, or happier than the woman who does not work for pay. Many wives enjoy the roles of homemaker and mother, and find a full measure of satisfaction in child-rearing, volunteer activities in the community, and an absorbing family life. Poll data suggest that most Americans—including women—still believe that a woman's *primary* responsibility is in the home, especially during the early years of child-rearing. Thus the dramatic shift in women's economic activities has not immediately transformed the norms governing the appropriate roles of men and women.

Nevertheless, employment has operated as an effective engine of change in the lives of women. To begin with, holding a job has involved women in a role —that of breadwinner—which by all accounts is most salient in defining the differences between the sexes. If, as the feminists claim, one of the principal obstacles to equality is the division of labor between men and women, departing from the home to take a job represents at least a step toward closing the gap between male and female spheres, and creating a new and different kind of life for women. Over and over again during the 1940's and 1950's, female workers spoke of enjoying their jobs, and valuing the social companionship and sense of personal recognition which accompanied employment. In a society where housework is denigrated by men and women alike (despite the efforts of advertisers), the opportunity to take a paying job has represented for many a broadening of experience, a move away from sexual apartheid. Much of women's work might be monotonous and boring, but it is no more so than washing dishes or hanging clothes.

More important, perhaps, the transformation of women's economic role has led to a series of "unanticipated" consequences in relations between the sexes. As more and more women have taken jobs, responsibilities within the home have been redistributed between husbands and wives, women increasingly expect to fill a diversity of roles, and the models available to young children have altered so that daughters of working mothers grow up exhibiting greater assertiveness and less attachment to the values of traditional femininity. To some extent, the changes reflect long-term trends such as the development of the companionate family. Yet every study made by social scientists indicates that female employment acts as an important spur to the greater sharing of domestic tasks. Most married women workers find it difficult to carry a full-time job outside the home and still shoulder the burden of household management. If husbands are to enjoy the benefits of a second income, justice requires that they assume at least some of the responsibilities previously borne by the wife. The process may be resisted at first, but it is not difficult to reconstruct. What begins as a "favor" gradually becomes a routine, then an obligation and duty. The increased overlapping of sexual spheres could not have been foreseen when married women first entered the labor force in large numbers, but it represents one of the most significant byproducts of women's increased economic activity.

Finally, the change in women's economic role has provided a necessary precondition for the revival of the drive for equality. Historians have noted that the ideology of the American Revolution represented in large part the articulation on a level of conscious principle of a set of conditions which already existed in practice. Phrased in another way, ideology requires a base in reality which can be used as a point of departure for raising people's consciousness to the existence of a problem and the presence of a program which applies to it. The woman's movement failed to enlist popular backing for much of the period after 1920, because, as long as most women internalized society's conception of their proper place, they had no experience which would permit them to see the relevance of feminist ideas to their own lives. Once the war dislocated women from conventional patterns of behavior, however, and set in motion a different cycle of behavior, a new set of expectations concerning women's sphere gradually evolved. The altered content of women's lives highlighted the disparity between the myth and reality of woman's place, and provided an important incentive for closing the gap. As more and more women joined the labor force, they gained personal knowledge of discrimination and the need to correct it. In addition, the presence of a working wife in the home appeared to have a liberalizing influence on male attitudes. In sex as in race, direct experience with a feared reality has proved an effective way of dispelling prejudiced or uninformed attitudes.

None of this, of course, means that feminist goals have been reached or that the process of change has advanced far enough for women to achieve full equality with men. The future of the feminist program depends a great deal on the fate of the family. According to many contemporary women's rights advocates, female "servitude" is rooted in the distinctive roles played by men and women in the nuclear family and can be eliminated only by the creation of alternative institutions and life styles which are more equalitarian in nature. Yet anthropologists have observed that every culture has familial arrangements based on a sexual division of labor. In most cases, women accept responsibility for "expressive" tasks such as child-rearing and men take charge of "instrumental" tasks such as earning a living or providing a defense against attack. Although such distinctions have clearly been muted in modern technological societies, they have not been totally abolished anywhere, and even in the collective kibbutz communities of Israel, sociologists have noted a revival of nuclear family forms. Thus it would seem that any further movement toward equality in America will occur through additional modification of the existing family structure rather than through the establishment of totally new social institutions.

A second and related obstacle to the realization of feminist goals is the degree to which women continue to exhibit behavioral characteristics that differ from those of men. Psychological surveys indicate that girls are more likely to be ingratiating, dependent, sympathetic, and submissive than boys, and to have appreciably less achievement motivation. Such characteristics are as likely to appear in female college students as in those without a higher education. In one test, different groups of college women were given identical sets of articles to read, some bearing the name John McKay, others Joan McKay. The students consistently judged the work associated with the female author as less worthwhile and persuasive than the same work associated with a male author. Reviewing the results, Dr. Philip Goldberg, administrator of the test, concluded that "women are prejudiced against female professionals, and regardless of the actual accomplishments of these professionals, will firmly refuse to recognize them as the equals of their male colleagues." A similar study measuring attitudes toward a female in medical school found that 65 per cent of the women respondents demonstrated a definite "motive to avoid success" in contrast to only 10 per cent of the men. For the most part, such attitudes reflect the fact that women are still brought up to expect that they will not succeed as well as men, and as new socialization patterns take hold, the discrepancy in self-image between the sexes will undoubtedly narrow. But for a time yet, it seems likely that women will be predisposed to take second place in any competition with men and to accept as "normal" the discriminatory treatment of some employers.

Finally, there is the nagging problem of why more women have not pursued careers. At a time when the socio-economic background and marital status of women workers have been transformed, and more than 70 per cent of female college graduates are employed, the proportion of women in business and the professions has changed hardly at all. Much of the reason can be traced to problems we have already discussed—overt discrimination, the expectations transmitted through child-rearing patterns, the lack of professional role models, and the discontinuity in the married woman's career life caused by giving birth to one or more children. Perhaps the most subtle reason, however, is the role stress which develops when a woman seeks to combine a career with marriage and a family. During the last three decades, millions of families have struck "role bargains" which permit wives and mothers to take jobs outside the home while their husbands or others assume responsibility for a share of the domestic tasks. But a job has limits. The time it consumes, the energy it requires, and the rewards it brings can all be fairly well defined in advance, and in most cases the bargain is based on the assumption that the woman is an incidental wage-earner, that her *primary* role is still in the home.

A career, in contrast, requires a commitment of energy and spirit which is inconsistent with such an arrangement. The doctor or lawyer is often faced with a situation in which professional responsibilities must take priority over family responsibilities. If the person is a man, the problem is usually mitigated by the presence of a woman in the home to take up the slack and "carry on" until life returns to normal. If the career person is a woman, however, the man in the home must make the temporary sacrifice. In a strictly equalitarian society, the stress should be similarly tolerable in both cases. But in a society which maintains the assumption that a wife's aspirations come after her husband's, the predicament generates severe tension and makes far more difficult the task of negotiating a satisfactory role settlement. Thus despite some significant changes in relationships between the sexes, most potential professional women still face a profound marriage-career conflict—a conflict which mirrors how far the society still must go to reach equality and which highlights the extent to which even "liberated" individuals remain attached to traditional ideas of male and female roles.

It is precisely in such areas that feminists face their greatest challenge and their greatest opportunity. As we have seen, a great many changes can take place as a matter of course, without conscious intent or direction. But if married women are to sustain a commitment to a career, demand full equality (and mutual sacrifice) in the home, and ensure that their children do not inherit invidious sexual stereotypes, they must be guided by a high degree of ideological energy and awareness. By calling attention to instances of discrimination, and demonstrating that an issue of principle is involved when women are denied certain career opportunities, the woman's movement can help to provide that energy. Enough women have departed from their traditional sphere to create a potential constituency for an effective movement toward equality. Now, the problem is to mobilize the constituency and create a wider consciousness of the meaning of women's rights.

But whatever the fate of feminism per se, it seems clear that history is on the side of continued change in women's status. Although the nuclear family itself may not be replaced, the distribution of responsibilities within it continues to undergo substantial alteration. And while female children still demonstrate less desire for achievement than male children, social scientists have noted a growing trend to treat youngsters the same regardless of sex and to avoid differentiating between the roles assigned them. "Today we may be on the verge of a new phase in American family history," Robert Blood has observed. "Employment emancipates women from domination by their husbands and secondarily raises daughters from inferiority with their brothers. . . . The classic differences between masculinity and femininity are disappearing as both sexes in the adult generation take on the same roles in the labor market." Such conclusions are perhaps exaggerated, especially the assertion that men and women occupy the *same* roles in the labor market. But the basic thrust of the statement rings true. The doubling of nursery school enrollments from 1965 to 1970, the number of women now foregoing immediate marriage and child-bearing after college, the fact that two out of three new jobs during the 1960's went to women—all provide dramatic reinforcement for the impression of change. At schools like Vassar, the percentage of graduates applying to professional schools skyrocketed at the beginning of the 1970's, and even crime statistics showed a trend toward closing the gap between the sexes. Arrests for prostitution have declined sharply, but the number of women charged with burglary, robbery, and other "major" crimes has soared—an indication to criminologists that women are becoming full partners with men and are no longer merely accomplices in the world of crime.

In the end, of course, conclusions on any subject so complicated and important depend a great deal on the perspective of the observer. It seems quite justifiable, from a feminist point of view, to argue that no meaningful shift in status has occurred among American women during the past fifty years. Very few observers will dispute the fact that women are frequently treated as "sex objects," that they are still expected to place their aspirations behind those of their husbands, and that those who hold jobs are underpaid and exploited. On the other hand, important shifts in behavior have taken place and it seems that the changes bear directly on some of the root causes of sexual inequality: the definition of male and female spheres, the role models we provide our children, the permissible horizons available to men and women. If the thesis presented here is correct—that attitudes toward woman's place run too deep to be changed through direct conversion—then the only alternative means of change is to break into the cycle of behavior which perpetuates the status quo and initiate a new cycle which will undermine the structural basis for traditional views of male and female roles.

It is just such a process which I believe has taken place in the years since 1940. With World War II as a catalyst, a dramatic change has occurred in women's economic role, generating a series of "ripple effects" which ultimately have reached into such crucial areas as home life and child-rearing practices. No one can claim that equality has been achieved as a result of these changes, but it may be that a foundation for seeking equality has been established. As the nation approaches the last quarter of the century, no aspect of contemporary life exhibits greater flux than relations between the sexes. And if the final balance sheet is not yet in, there is good reason to believe that the movement toward greater freedom for women will not soon come to a halt.

CHAPTER 25

THE AMERICAN DILEMMA

From the beginning, there has been, in Gunnar Myrdal's phrase, "an American Dilemma." The dilemma, growing out of centuries of antiblack racism and maltreatment, is how to square American attitudes and behavior with the principles of freedom and equality on which this nation is founded. Those who would seek to solve the dilemma, who would create open, positive relations between blacks and whites and identify creative roles for blacks in national life, invariably run up against the invisible wall of history. For the "American Dilemma" is the product of history, and there is no way to roll back the pages of time so that the errors of the past can be removed from the pathway to racial justice and harmony. Nowhere is this better demonstrated than in the attempts of the nation's courts over the past three decades to end school segregation and to ensure racial equality in American education. It was inevitable that the courts would encounter trouble of gigantic proportion as they sought to solve what the author of the following selection calls America's "insoluble race problem."

In this selection, J. Harvie Wilkinson, law professor, newspaper editor, and former clerk to Justice Lewis F. Powell, discusses the complex problems confronting the high court in the 1960s and 1970s. Unlike the more clear-cut issue that had faced the court in the *Brown* v. *Board of Education* case, the questions of busing and of affirmative action in education involve the clash of fundamental principles and of the legitimate aspirations of various groups of people. There are no easy solutions for the problems relating to these issues, and Wilkinson points out that although the courts have achieved some success, they have also suffered failure. He maintains, for example, that court-imposed busing has seriously harmed a number of school systems across the country and he warns that the courts have been preoccupied with how many blacks and whites are in school together to the detriment of sound educational practice. In concluding remarks, Wilkinson suggests that in general blacks are making substantial gains, that white racism is declining to some degree, and that progress is being made toward racial justice. But he notes that we as Americans, black and white, still have a long way to go.

The student should try to approach this selection as objectively as possible, attempting to keep an open mind and to put aside preconceived notions and prejudices. As you read the selection, keep the following questions in mind. First, what is the essential nature of the racial dilemma in American schools? Second, what are the major causes of the dilemma? Third, what solutions are the courts trying? What are the difficulties in making these solutions work? What solutions do you have to the dilemma? Are you optimistic or pessimistic about the chances for better relations between blacks and whites? Why?

The bibliography on this subject is large and is rapidly expanding. On the monumental Supreme Court case of 1954 see Richard Kluger, *Simple Justice: The History of* Brown v. Board of Education *and Black America's Struggle for Equality* * (1976). The history of segregation and the civil rights movement is presented in Anthony Lewis, *Portrait of a Decade* * (1964); C. Vann Woodward, *The Strange Career of Jim Crow* * (1974); D. L. Lewis, *King: A Critical Biography* (1970); and Charles Silberman, *Crisis in Black and White* * (1964). On black activity in the past two decades, see S. A. Levitan et al., *Still a Dream: The Changing Status of Blacks Since 1960* (1975).

*Available in a paperback edition.

BUSING AND DESEGREGATION IN THE 1970s

J. HARVIE WILKINSON III

It was an ugly, worn, but still functional piece of machinery that stopped by the roadside that fall morning to take Robin Smith to high school. Its coming was part of the early morning rhythm for the Smith family, a half-noticed reminder to Robin's father, the town dentist, that it was high time to be off. But following that school bus into town was greatly annoying; it made endless stops, as did the cars piled behind it, all thanks to state law. Yet on other, less hurried days, the bus had a faintly endearing qaulity, reminding Mr. Smith of his own childhood friends and frolics on the way to school. Back then the old school bus had been quite a necessity; not all families owned cars and the new county high school was quite a way off.

Neither the Smiths nor the millions of other Americans riding and honking at school buses in 1954—certainly not the justices of the United States Supreme Court—had any idea that this creaky piece of daily routine would become the flash point of domestic politics in the early 1970s, the symbol of America's ceaseless attempt to solve its insoluble race problem. Busing, as all races, ages, and classes understood, rubbed the raw nerve endings of American life. It posed the most vicious questions. Must the children of today atone for yesterday's wrongs? How much must white America compromise its own interests for its mistreated minority? And who should make the compromise: North or South, rural or urban areas, working class neighborhoods or the more affluent suburbs? How much social reform might the judiciary shoulder? To what extent must educational policy be tailored to race? For all such questions, the yellow school bus and its short, hissing derivative—busing—now became the transcendent symbol. . . .

. . . Student busing, suggested by some as the most promising answer to the racial separateness of the 1970s, was for others so freighted with political, social, and educational costs as to be no answer at all. Indeed, one wonders whether there will ever be any such thing as an answer. In the 1960s, we felt certain that there was. The fear of the 1970s is that there is not, that no solution

SOURCE. J. Harvie Wilkinson III, *From* Brown *to* Bakke: *The Supreme Court and School Integration: 1954–1978,* pp. 131–135, 161–165, 169–170, 173–177, 184–189, 191, 307–310. Copyright © 1979 by Oxford University Press. Reprinted by permission.

fair to both races, supported by both races, and advantageous to both races can be humanly devised.

The problem is that we are no longer certain what kind of question public school desegregation really is. Twenty years ago we were convinced it was a matter of showing southern school segregation to be morally wrong. But with busing, good moral arguments exist on both sides. To the extent that desegregation has become less a moral question, or at least more a moral standoff, is it also less clearly a constitutional requirement the Supreme Court is entitled to impose? . . .

. . . [T]he task of the Court in the 1970s was far more complex than in the two preceding decades. "Nothing in our national experience prior to 1955," admitted Chief Justice Burger, "prepared anyone for dealing with changes and adjustments of the magnitude and complexity encountered since then." In the 1950s the object was simply to enroll a few Negro children in formally all-white schools. By the mid-1970s the Court was asked to transform the face of urban education, to reshape the metropolitan apartheid into which the country had so regrettably lapsed. Not only were the logistics of such an effort more awesome by far than anything in the Court's southern, and largely rural, phase. The Court was now tackling a national, not a regional problem. And popular support for bold action was, to put it mildly, difficult to discern. . . .

The first of the great school busing cases to reach the Supreme Court was *Swann* v. *Charlotte-Mecklenburg Board of Education*, in 1970. [Finding Charlotte's board of education in constitutional violation because of its failure to provide a completely unitary system of education, the Court mandated that school authorities undertake widespread busing to bring racial ratios in the schools to specified levels. Busing and other means must be used, the Court insisted, to secure the highest possible degree of actual desegregation.] . . .

. . . [*Swann* cast the busing issue in a new light.] Traditionally, busing had been democratically conceived and democratically implemented. Consolidated schools, increased access to special resources, and safer transportaion all were educational aims a goodly number of citizens might be expected to support. Control of bus routes by the school board, itself an elected body or a group responsible to such a body, helped assure convenience and economy in the planning of routes. Busing to desegregate, on the other hand, was both involuntary and inconvenient. It generally had to be judicially imposed. Not only was the federal judiciary less attuned to local wishes. Its goal of desegregation presupposed inconvenience: that schools nearer home be bypassed for schools farther away, if racial balance was thereby improved. . . .

* * * * *

The Supreme Court in *Swann* drove the yellow school bus down the road of racial reform. And a bumpy journey it would prove to be. Why, one wonders, did the Court choose busing among all the alternatives available? Why, moreover, was that choice unanimous? Why, lastly, had several justices even swallowed their personal misgivings to join the opinion? . . .

There was more to the Court's approval of busing than integrating the South. *Green* had whetted the Court's appetite for numbers. Black-white percentages at last gave the Court a concrete measuring rod, an objective determinant of a school board's good faith. If one's goal for schools was statistical racial balance, busing seemed the most direct way to achieve it. In fact, busing seemed the only way to achieve it in the urban metropolis where the races lived largely apart.

But something more profound motivated the Court's probusing stance in 1971: a mystical force in the catacombs of the Supreme Court known as the spirit of *Brown*. *Brown*'s legacy was a special race consciousness, an understanding among justices that blacks were henceforth to enjoy constitutional priority. *Brown* had been the gateway to the modern era in constitutional law, a catalyst to reform in criminal justice, in the relationship of state to federal courts, and in the law's protection of the poor, all of which were intended, among other things, to benefit blacks. The race cases soon developed their own internal hierarchy. While justices might disagree, for example, over Civil Rights protests or selection of juries, to dissent in a school case was very close to sacrilege. . . . Never mind that school issues in the 1970s differed from those of 1954. *Brown* had the Court bewitched. For the tenure of the new Burger Court to begin with a setback in school desegregation would have been a dreadful omen for many that the hard-won gains since *Brown* were about to be rolled back. . . .

＊　＊　＊　＊　＊

The first justice to openly challenge *Swann* was Lewis F. Powell, Jr., of Richmond, Virginia. Powell was not appointed to the Court until after *Swann*; indeed, in *Swann,* he had submitted an *amicus* brief on behalf of Virginia in opposition to forced busing. . . .

By most measures of opinion in the aftermath of *Brown,* Powell was very much a moderate. That meant he was also a gradualist. . . .

Once on the Court, Powell was not long in leaving his mark on school desegregation. Though the occasion was the 1973 Denver school case, Powell's opinion had little to do with Denver and almost everything to do with *Swann*. "To the extent," wrote Powell, "that *Swann* may be thought to *require* large-scale or long-distance transportation in our metropolitan school districts, I record my profound misgivings. Nothing in our Constitution commands or encourages any such court-compelled disruption of public education."

The words had not come easily. If few issues concerned Powell more than busing, on few was he less eager to write. He knew the solitary statement of a Southerner so soon after appointment would raise eyebrows. In his freshman term, he refrained from writing in another school case for just that reason. But in Denver, the time had come. Powell personally shepherded the opinion through ten different drafts, seeking firm but unemotive language. He remembered *Dred Scott* and *Plessy* and the dim corners to which history consigned judicial frustration of black aspirations. And he pondered the spirit of *Brown*. In the end, he decided to bet that court-ordered busing was the wrong way to solve America's race problem.

His view of race was a patient one. "It is well to remember," he cautioned, "that the course we are running is a long one"; the racism that persisted for generations would take generations to overcome. Inequality of opportunity among men was a natural state; courts could go only so far in combatting it. What he could not accept was race as the basis of unequal status. But to believe that a system of accustomed advantages for the children of certain members of the society might suddenly be upturned was folly. Hope for the Negro lay in gradual progress along many fronts: in voting, jobs, housing, and education. But busing was precipitous, calamitous, visionary. It was wrong, he protested, to place on today's schoolchildren the full, crushing burden of historical atonement. To Powell, history alone was not controlling. What practical sense, he began asking, did busing make today?

Had America somehow lost perspective on race? The tingling moments of the Civil Rights struggle, the Montgomery bus boycott, the marches to Washington and from Selma, the Greensboro sit-ins, Meredith and Mississippi, the tiny bands of black students crossing segregated thresholds: all spoke so palpably and eloquently of injustice, a fact few Americans in the quiet of conscience could deny. But were black demands for busing as justly based? And were neighborhood schools quite the evil as lunch-counter and back-of-the-bus segregation? Was *Swann*'s insistence on "the greatest possible degree of actual desegregation" a plea for integration for integration's sake? With *Swann* and busing, had the Civil Rights movement lost its purity and entered a more sterile and mechanical phase, where the form of racial justice had overtaken the substance? Had it come to be that the cart had been put before the horse, and that who was in school together and in what proportions was now more important than what was learned there?

Powell worried that the race issue, in the fractious form of forced busing, might eclipse quality of instruction as the focus of public schools. Busing, he argued, was "likely to divert attention and resources from the foremost goal of any school system: the best quality education for all pupils." . . .

* * * * *

. . . It hardly seemed timely, thought Justice Powell, amidst rising concern and falling indicators of public school performance to turn the attention of communities "from the paramount goal of quality in education to a perennially divisive debate over who is to be transported where."

There was evidence that some blacks shared Powell's priorities, that the frantic quest for racial balance had left both races numb. "At first [blacks] fought to get into white schools to get the same things the whites were getting," remarked Henry Pruitt in 1977, principal of the Englewood Middle School in New Jersey, which had become 80 percent black after fourteen years of desegregation. "[N]ow some of them are saying we can go back to 'separate but equal' as long as we can get quality education. . . . This integration stuff is kind of passé now. All the parents want to know from me is what kind of education are their kids getting.". . .

[The opponents of busing centered their arguments on the desirability of maintaining the neighborhood school.] The grand justification for neighborhood schools is their inculcation of a sense of personal identity. Each life needs its points of anchor and ports of call. These were once found close to us: in our family, our neighborhood, our place of work and worship, and our school. They should, above all, be warm, personal, durable, dependable. Justice Powell, for one, feared they no longer were:

Today, we are being cut adrift from the type of humanizing authority which in the past shaped the character of our people.

I am thinking, not of governmental authority, but rather the more personal forms we have known in the home, church, school, and community. These personal authorities once gave direction to our lives. They were our reference points, the institutions and relationships which molded our characters.

We respected and grew to maturity with teachers, parents, neighbors, ministers, and employers—each imparting their values to us. These relationships were something larger than ourselves, but never so large as to be remote, impersonal, or indifferent. We gained from them an inner strength, a sense of belonging, as well as of responsibility to others.

This sense of belonging was portrayed nostalgically in the film "Fiddler on the Roof." Those who saw it will remember the village of Anatevka in the last faint traces of sunset on Sabbath eve. There was the picture of Tevye, the father, blessing his family, close around their dining room table. They sang what must have been ancient Hebrew hymns, transmitted from family to family through untold generations. The feeling of individual serenity in the common bond of family life was complete.

The threat to traditional institutions seems clear enough: the increasing divorce rate, the automation replacing artisanship in work, the turn from the church, the retreat of individual home ownership before the high rise. To lament such trends is to be a sentimentalist. Yet Powell viewed them with disquiet, fearful that we, as a people, might be losing our rootedness, our unifying bonds. He recalled earlier days, less vulnerable to technological change and great social reform. For him, the issue of busing was clear: whether students whose friendships and loyalties had arisen out of their experience at certain schools were to be sacrificed to a social experiment of dubious worth:

Neighborhood school systems, neutrally administered, reflect the deeply felt desire of citizens for a sense of community in their public education. Public schools have been a traditional source of strength to our Nation, and that strength may derive in part from the identification of many schools with the personal features of the surrounding neighborhood. Community support, interest, and dedication to public schools may well run higher with a neighborhood attendance pattern: distance may encourage disinterest. Many citizens sense today a decline in the intimacy of our institutions—home, church, and school—which has caused a concomitant decline in the unity and communal spirit of our people. I pass no judgment on this viewpoint, but I do believe that this Court should be wary of compelling in the name of constitutional law what may seem to many a dissolution in the traditional, more personal fabric of their public schools.

The Court admitted grudgingly in *Swann* that neighborhood schools made educational sense. "All things being equal, with no history of discrimination," the Court noted, "it might well be desirable to assign pupils to schools nearest their homes." The advantages, especially in the elementary years, seemed obvious. . . .

[Where students were bused in large numbers to nonneighborhood schools,] . . . a sense of belonging often failed to take root. "The school loyalty problem," noted the Louisville *Courier-Journal,* "seemed sharpest at Shawnee, the inner-city [high] school whose white majority is bused in and changes each year. The turnover was 79 per cent this year; at pep rallies some Shawnee students reportedly boo their own school to show loyalty for the old schools to which they will return next year."

Alienation was not unique to Shawnee. Toward the end of Louisville's second year of busing, many students complained of feeling no "ownership" in schools to which they were transported. Bused students—white and black —were observed to act more belligerently in schools away from their own neighborhoods, as if they had something to prove. . . .

One may argue for bus schedules that permit extracurricular participation and for busing plans that assign elementary or high school students to the same school throughout. . . . But will any plan really overcome the estrangement of those bused in? The perception by the student of his school as a component of his own neighborhood, the proximity of the school to home, the easy access of parents to the faculty, the school as the recreational hub of the surrounding community, may be what creates student loyalties and ties. For judicial edicts to break such communal bonds was a weighty moral step, no matter how lofty the proclaimed constitutional ends. . . .

* * * * *

. . . [As busing came to engage the attention and emotions of the entire nation, not just those of the South, it prompted the raising of a question of the greatest magnitude,]: whether school integration itself was a genuinely worthwhile goal. That question, previously, had been safe to ignore. *Brown* said only that segregation by law was not right, and around that modest but powerful proposition a national consensus built. Yet the consensus that maintained that enforced segregation was always wrong was something less than one that held that integration was always required or right. . . .

[Although the social sciences had pushed strongly for integration in the 1950s and 1960s, they grew skeptical in the 1970s.] . . . Integrated schools, proponents would claim, would boost black aspirations and self-esteem, raise black achievement levels and college-career prospects, and reduce racial prejudice. Blissful results only were forecast, unhappy ones often ignored. But by the 1970s, the unhappy possibilities began to receive more serious attention. Might not integration heat up racial tensions instead of relaxing them? Might black self-confidence not be greater in an all-black school than in an integrated one? And did putting the races under the same school roof or even in front of the very same teacher really boost minority achievement?

To all such questions, sociologist David Armor, in an article entitled "The Evidence on Busing"(1972), gave rather pessimistic answers. Studies of community busing programs in five northern and western cities had shown, said Armor, that integration had little positive effect. Not one study was able to demonstrate "that integration has had an effect on [minority] academic achievement as measured by standardized tests.". . .

Doubt was the byword of social science in the 1970s. Professor Nancy St. John concluded in 1975 after reviewing 120 school desegregation studies that "biracial schooling must be judged neither a demonstrated success nor a demonstrated failure." Years of studying its effects both on academic achievement and racial attitudes, she noted, had "netted such inconclusive results." State-imposed segregation, the Court had held in *Brown,* gave Negroes "a feeling of inferiority as to their status in the community that may affect their hearts and minds in a way unlikely ever to be undone." But was it not possible, St. John suggested, that court-imposed desegregation did the very same thing? Planned desegregation, she noted, "focuses attention on racial differences and, unless very carefully managed, makes minority group children the object of curiosity and study, if not hostility. They are further stigmatized if they are singled out for remedial help, if they are tracked into a low-status program, or if they are the only children who arrive and leave by bus."

A self-styled committed integrationist, St. John could not be accused of an antibusing bias. And other observers confirmed that the "present mood [of social scientists toward school integration] is one of less certainty. There is growing doubt that the hopes many have had for the outcomes of school desegregation can be fully achieved. . . . Desegregation does not appear to be the panacea many hoped it would be. . . . If we are to achieve any of the several objectives that school desegregation is meant to achieve, we will have to abandon the simplistic notion—now largely discredited by available evidence—that the mixing of the races *in itself* will invariably have positive educational and social consequences." No one, of course, urged a return to pre-*Brown* days. Yet as leading thinkers of the 1950s helped discredit rigid segregation, integration as an inflexible requirement now likewise has come under heavy intellectual assault.

None of the new skepticism was intended to portray integration as a failure. Only that it was ever so complicated, that it might convey to a black child either hope or discouragement, fulfillment or emptiness, a sense of worth or worthlessness, a feeling of being wanted or of being merely trouble. And the relevant new question was not whether integration was per se good or bad, but under what conditions it could be made to work. . . .

Often periods of reaction are also periods of despair. But the countercurrents of the 1970s, though vigorous, were not altogether disillusioning. For some, the faith of the fifties bore marvelous fruit. E. L. Bing, an assistant school superintendent in Tampa, Florida, sensed it every day. "The longer the [black] youngsters have been a part of the integration process, the more articulate they seem to become," said Bing in 1977. "Now I can walk into a school and talk to a group of black kids and they can express their ideas in complete, understandable sentences. They no longer talk in fragments and monosyllables. Believe me, that's a long way from where we were before desegregation."

Experimentation need not await academic approval. In the end, sociology was often corroborative of common sense. No special wisdom was needed to confirm that a teacher with a personal interest in students of all races helped make integration a success. Sam Horton, principal of Thomas Jefferson High School in Tampa, watched integrated couples stroll arm-in-arm through his hallways and groups of blacks and white study together under the campus palms. Horton's formula was straightforward enough. He abolished the course in black history, replacing it with an American history course, designed to "bring in the contributions of all ethnic groups." And he disbanded separate "culture clubs," such as the Black Student Union and Latin American Club.

"Initially," he explained, "those kinds of clubs were good for the minorities. They allowed the kids to adapt to a new environment without getting lost or losing their identity. But I found that the longer that kind of thing stays, the more divisive it becomes. I think if you're going to integrate a school, it has to be integrated all the way down the line." . . .

Out of the confusion of social science, one conclusion did emerge: merely tossing whites and blacks together in court-contrived ratios might do more harm than good. Yet the Supreme Court retained an obsession with how many black and white bodies were in the same school together, not with how they related, or what transpired in the classroom. Though identical racial balances were not required in all schools, racial ratios reflecting school district populations were the "starting point" and by far the most important point in court-ordered transportation. But this mathematical approach, undeviatingly applied, wrought havoc in some American cities: Atlanta, Memphis, Richmond, Boston, Pasadena, to name but a few. "For too long," noted Professor St. John, "courts, legislatures, schoolmen, and social scientists have been obsessed with questions of quantity rather than quality, with mathematical ratios, quotas, and balance, rather than with the education process itself. The real task—to translate desegregation into integration—still remains." . . .

* * * * *

As a boy, I liked to visit courthouses. I would sit against some tree on courthouse greens in rural Virginia, watching and observing by the hour. Exactly why I did this, I don't rightly know. Perhaps, in their slow stir lay the most pleasant somnolent sensations. Sometimes a few sparrows pecked about; the sun-bleached bulletins seemed immune to all sense of urgency or time. On the front lawn stood the statue of the valiant Confederate infantry-man or a cannon, long mute. On a nearby bench, a few farmers might spit tobacco or swap pleasantries on the trip to town. The courthouse brought together community life: the judge was there and the country clerk and the treasurer, sheriff, and state's attorney. I was so young—and my sense of things so settled—I scarcely noticed they were always white. Watching, I must have felt a peace of mind and setting many Americans had long forgotten or professed not to care for. Yet the quiet of those courthouse greens was also the quiet of eternal custom, the sum of unspoken racial understandings that life's lots had been irrevocably cast.

Brown disturbed the calm of the courthouse. Along with better roads, television, new political trends, and population growth. And, of course, I was growing older. Those quiet little places no longer seemed the same. But things were changing for the better too. Before *Brown,* there was but one possible verdict on race relations in the South. *Brown,* of course, had not set race relations right. The new order never follows neatly the destruction of the old. But at least now the hopeful case can be plausibly advanced. Before *Brown* there was no hope, only the still courthouse air.

The effort to change the world of the courthouse later spilled over to more dubious initiatives, the two most notable being busing and racial numbers in affirmative action plans. On busing the evidence is not all in, nor is it all on one side. But what there is suggests that only in the most select circumstances can busing be exepcted to succeed. Both busing and affirmative action goals suffered practical drawbacks. More important, each clashed with legitimate competing ideals: the desire for neighborhood schools and color-blind admissions. Against such opposing values, the drive for racial equality began to stall. The single-mindedness of national purpose gave way to a decade of accommodation and compromise. First the Court in *Milliken* v. *Bradley* served notice that the aspirations of the majority counted constitutionally too. Then, in *Bakke,* that competing moral claims must be brokered and negotiated.

The long voyage from *Brown* to *Bakke* has been one from optimism and confidence to confusion and doubt. School integration has entered a period of seeming contradiction: productive in one setting, disappointing somewhere else. Harmony in one school, tension in another. White flight in one city, stability elsewhere. Black academic progress here, but not there. To generalize nationwide now seems foolish. Rather, one must work to understand the particulars that explain diverse results.

From *Brown* to *Bakke* has been a maturing journey also. Findings in the education cases laid bare the depth of American prejudice and made clear the true dimensions of our difficulties. We now seem to be many sad and wise days away from those happy forecasts of playground bliss. What we better understand is our own lack of understanding. School integration has taught us at home what Vietnam did abroad: how much eludes the American capacity to reshape. That is hardly surprising. Public education represented so many different things to many different people. To some, schools were symbols of democracy, equal opportunity, upward mobility for the dispossessed. To others they were places for promoting intellectual excellence. To still others, places for class compatability and social exclusion. Many regarded public schools as they did housing, as extensions of advantage and choice in their own private lives. When these conflicting preconceptions of public education combined with the emotions of race, a monstrous problem confronted the courts. Why were quick results ever expected? Was school integration thought somehow to be less complex a problem or one more manageable than others in this vexing age? Was the specter of prejudice, so prominent in our history, one that anyone would have thought capable of vanishing before Supreme Court decree?

Yet white racism is receding, at least in its coarser forms. This is true of public attitudes as well as under the law. Talk of absolute segregation has given way to talk of tolerance levels and tipping points. And each of these changes is progress of a sort. Life for the small but growing black professional class has been greatly enriched. It may even be, as William Julius Wilson thinks, that "class has become more important than race in determining black life-chances." But one should not speak too soon. Race has been too much a part of our past not to be part of our foreseeable future. Solutions that make race immaterial or minorities equal or understanding total are not now in sight. A quarter century after *Brown,* American life has become a bit fairer, black opportunities slightly greater, black contributions somewhat more significant. If talk of racial millennia now seems foolhardy, chances for further gradual improvements in black status seem bright.

Yet the nature of racial progress, at least in education, affords little reason to boast. Those making the decisions on school integration were too often not those whose lives were affected by these decisions. Genuine self-sacrifice has been rare; white magnanimity something of a myth. In the early days after *Brown,* the nation told the South what to do for the Negro. This same eagerness to watch others pay the price of progress continued into the 1970s. Many of the most forceful advocates of forced busing held their own children back. Integration itself often left the suburbs and the affluent relatively untouched. And those who devised generous affirmative action goals were not those who bore their real costs. Nowhere was the nature of racial reform better illustrated than with the courts. Judges could spearhead school integration, because they would not risk re-election. Direct personal accountability and sacrifice could, once again, be escaped.

In the end, however, the school cases sharpen one's sense of the Supreme Court as a pragmatic institution. For only five years during the past quarter century (1968–1973), did the Court demand substantial integration. More often it pleaded, mediated, mollified, or even withdrew. In almost all the landmark school cases, white racial sensibilities weighed heavily. In *Brown* and *Swann* they influenced the tone of the Court's opinion; in *Brown II, Milliken,* and *Bakke* the actual result.

The decisions involved the extent to which rule by law can alter popular racial beliefs. They ranged from *Plessy* (law cannot change popular attitudes), to *Brown I* (it can and will), to *Brown II* (but it must bear them in mind), to *Green* and *Swann* (but not forever), to *Milliken* (but, after all, law cannot function in the teeth of intense popular dissent). The Court's perambulations on this score are understandable. Its central dilemma is that of an institution protecting minority rights in a nation of majority rule. Its members feel not just their special obligation to protect minorities but the lurking inconsistencies of judicial activism with democratic notions of self-governance. Due to this tension, the Supreme Court's decisions on race and education may never steer any clear course.

These final observations have stressed complexity and confusion, gradualism and pragmatism, contradiction and compromise. Such notes will certainly strike some as indifferent or dour. Yet they are not so intended. The goal of racial justice remains luminous as ever. Better lives for blacks—and, indeed, for all oppressed peoples—remains a grand and worthy end. Yet the clash of moral forces before the Court has shifted since *Brown*. Justice was no longer the monopoly of any outlook or race in the education cases of the 1970s. Progress had to be sought in ways majorities of both races might perceive as fair. The limits as well as the potential of law had to be explored. The old courthouse had come to signify both the real progress of blacks in America and that stubborn sediment in human habit and behavior of which all racial reform, sooner or later, would have to take account.

CHAPTER 26

THE AMERICAN DREAM IN THE LATE TWENTIETH CENTURY

When the American nation was born in 1776, to the ringing phrases of Thomas Jefferson's magnificent Declaration of freedom and opportunity, a vista of a new society was presented to the world. In America change and growth were to be expected and ordinary men and women could dream of and often achieve a better life for themselves and their posterity. When the country celebrated its Centennial in 1876, America was still a young nation, vibrant, productive, full of confidence and energy. Thousands of immigrants would flock to the country's shores in subsequent years, convinced that America was indeed the last best hope. But by the time of the nation's Bicentennial in 1976, things had changed and the national mood had altered. The nation no longer seemed so productive or so successful; Americans were no longer so buoyant or so confident that aggressive pursuit of goals would result in success. The country appeared to be engulfed in a national malaise and one wondered whether the American Dream was dead.

In the selection that follows, Eric F. Goldman, one of America's most distinguished historians, seeks to assess, in broad perspective, the nation's experience in the 100 years since 1876. He focuses his discussion around the idea of the American Dream, the essence of which he finds expressed in the Declaration of Independence. Professor Goldman suggests that around 1960 more Americans were closer to realizing their individual American dreams than ever before. Then the bottom appeared to drop out; the nation seemed to be repeatedly confronted with insurmountable problems of awesome proportions, and American optimism and confidence were replaced with doubt and pessimism. It seemed in the Bicentennial year, in contrast to 1776 and 1876, that the nation had little to celebrate. But Goldman notes that American tradition runs deep, and he is unwilling to pronounce the death knell of the American Dream.

In reading this selection, students should consider the following questions. First, what is "The Idea" which Goldman identifies as the well-spring of the great American document, the Declaration of Independence? In what ways was the Declaration more than merely a statement of independence from England and a call for political democracy? Second, what does Professor Goldman consider the fundamental national purpose of our country? How is national success measured? What has been America's greatest achievement and contribution over the years of national existence? Third, what is Professor Goldman's assessment of America's last 100 years? From your personal experience and your unique perspective, how do you predict the future of the American Dream?

Many of the works cited for Chapter 27 of this volume contain material and perspectives useful in a consideration of the selection that follows. See also Carl N. Degler, *Affluence and Anxiety: America Since 1945* (2nd ed., 1975); William E. Leuchtenburg, *A Troubled Feast: American Society Since 1945* (1973); and Godfrey Hodgson, *America in Our Time* (1976). Phineas J. Sparer, ed., *America: Heritage and Horizons* (1976), is very valuable, particularly the essay by Ashley Montagu, "America—Present and Future."

THE U.S. EXPERIENCE—THE LATER YEARS

ERIC F. GOLDMAN

I appreciate the compliment of appearing in the M.L. Seidman Memorial Lecture Series associated with Memphis State University. The series has established a reputation for being one of the nation's distinguished forums of free-wheeling and yet responsible thinking.

I'll try to repay the compliment of the invitation not by making a formal speech, full of pronunciamentoes and eternal wisdom, but rather by asking you to come with me, as it were, into the workshop of my own present thinking, some very tentative and troubled thinking indeed.

My focus, naturally, is the Bicentennial which, if it is to mean anything at all, calls for the long overview, the hour of inventory and stock-taking. In doing that, we must, I believe, start with a blunt statement. The Bicentennial is not a real success. It is closer to a disaster in the fundamental sense of the nature of the response it is provoking. There is even plenty of evidence that the Bicentennial observance is making many a thoughtful American feel downright uncomfortable.

Some of the reasons for this reaction are plain. Several months ago a former student of mine, knowing of my connection with the establishment of the national Bicentennial Commission, fixed an eye on me and said, "Sir, just what is there to celebrate?" It made me ponder. We are hardly in an exultant period of the Republic. Of just what shall we sing? Of Watergate and Vietnam? Or corruption in both political and corporate life making daily headlines? Of cities crumbling so fast that a recent mayor's conference warned of "oncoming disaster"? Of a public school system, for generations the life blood of this democracy, now descended to a level where a large proportion of high school graduates cannot read, cannot count, and cannot write a clear sentence? Of additional reports on the schools indicating that, to quote the *New York Times*, "crime and violence have become the norm throughout the nation"? Of a recession ending with a U.S. government prediction of at least 6% unemployment and 6% inflation extending into the late 1970s? Of an America the Beautiful from sewage-laden sea to shining oil slicks?

SOURCE. Eric F. Goldman, "The U.S. Experience—The Later Years," in Phineas J. Sparer, *America: Heritage and Horizons,* pp. 33–49. Copyright © 1976 by Memphis State University Press, Copyright © 1977 by Eric F. Goldman. Reprinted by permission.

Then too, much of the Bicentennial celebration itself is enough to make wise men weep and so many of us, wise or not, wince. At times it is difficult to decide whether the worst is the rampant commercialization or the merely banal and ridiculous. Junk, junk, and more junk, James Michener sighs as he observes gaudy, shoddy "Minute Men" salt and pepper shakers. Up and down the country fife and drum corps, dressed in fake colonialism, fife and drum in celebration of events that were unimportant when they happened and have now reached a kind of higher meaninglessness. Books and pamphlets pour from the presses in unabashed vulgarity and silliness.

A President of the United States, later somewhat hectically retired to San Clemente, thought well of a plan for producing red, white and blue ice cream. We did produce red-white-and-blue toilet seats and "Bicentennial decked" coffins. A football league launched a $25,000 essay contest on the subject of the football league's relationship to the Bicentennial. Well, at least those essays ought to be short.

But all of this, dreary as it is, is not the basic explanation of the nation's reaction to the Bicentennial. Consider our first big birthday party, the Centennial of 1876. In that year the country was grinding through not merely a recession but a severe depression. In the White House sat the amiable, utterly ineffectual Ulysses S. Grant, long competing only with Warren Harding in historians' polls at the absolute bottom of American Presidents. Scandals in Grant's administration kept breaking month after month and in the fall of 1876 the United States had its one and only Presidential election which, beyond doubt, was literally bought. As for tacky commercialization, our genius for that was already in full flower. The James Micheners of 1876 had full reason to sigh as the 1876 tazzas and lambrequins burst across the country.

Yet this is the more important fact: The Centennial of 1876 was an unquestioned triumph. The public really responded. It was "the greatest, most enjoyable party the nation has ever given," one of its historians has written, "and one remembered long after many of the troubles of Grant's seedy years." The reason is simple: The center of the celebration was the Philadelphia Exposition and the actual official name of that was the "International Exhibition of Arts, Manufactures, and Products of the Soil and Mine." In short, it was a spectacular array of the results of technological genius in that period—primarily American—and it was an enormously impressive show, including everything from an elaborate assortment of nuts and bolts of great ingenuity to the first patented systems for dressmaking, on to the giant Corliss engine which was revolutionizing industry at that time and of course to the first public exhibition of the telephone. The observance was complete down to its apocryphal story about the Emperor Dom Pedro of Brazil coming to the Centennial, picking up Alexander Graham Bell's receiver, listening and hearing words, and saying,

"My God, it talks!" He didn't say it, but it certainly was in the spirit of the Centennial—that pride of Americans in technological progress.

This, people were saying, is America's great achievement, invention, ingenuity, innovation that is going to offer more and more economic and social opportunities to more and more citizens. Americans have meant many things by freedom but most especially they have meant the freedom to get ahead in income and social status. Despite the many unhappy circumstances of the 1870s, the public could respond to the Centennial because the observance was saluting one route for a national getting-ahead in a way that seemed eminently realistic.

The Centennial, in its own way, was at the crux of the meaning of the Declaration of Independence for 1876 or 1976. It was talking about and projecting what I am going to call—to properly emphasize it—"The Idea" behind the Declaration. Of course it is stated in the cathedral prose of the Preamble itself. The trouble is we know that Preamble so well we tend to glide over it, not realizing what we are really reading, and we certainly glide over its audacity, its sweeping demands and its vaulting promise.

Let me read a few of the sentences to you, sentences that I would like you to listen to as if you had never heard them before. "When in the course of human events, it becomes necessary for one people to dissolve the political bonds which have connected them with another . . . a decent respect to the opinions of mankind"—what a master of the English language Mr. Thomas Jefferson was!—"a decent respect to the opinions of mankind requires that they should declare the causes." The causes? "We hold these truths to be self-evident, that all men are created equal, that they are endowed by their Creator with certain unalienable Rights, that among these are Life, Liberty and the pursuit of Happiness." Government exists to advance these rights and if it does not, the citizen has a right to revolt against it.

Full significance of these words will be suggested if you realize that Jefferson was actually taking over some basic ideas from the British philosopher, John Locke. But Locke said, "life, liberty and property." Jefferson changed "property" to the far more exciting, challenging, insidious phrase, "pursuit of happiness," which can have endlessly expansive meaning. So here is the heart of The Idea and what a shimmering, crimson-shot idea it was. It was not merely a declaration of independence from England, not even merely an appeal for political democracy. It cut far, far deeper into the fundamentals of a man's whole conception of himself and of his relations with other human beings.

Note that for some six thousand years of recorded history in most societies poor and ordinary men had been expected to remain poor and ordinary. Their children were to follow in the same or similar occupations and to live in much the same status. Upper-class families were expected to remain upper-class families. Now here is a document trumpeting: "*No.* Nothing has to be fixed about class lines. Everything is to be fluid; everything is to make plain"—in the words of an old American folk saying that came from the spirit of the Declaration—"There are no little people. They are as big as you are, whoever you are." The Declaration held up a vista of an unprecedented society, one in which ordinary men would walk in the tonic air of self-respect and could expect more and more income and status for themselves. More and more, and not only for themselves but especially for their children. No wonder the Declaration has proved a world force, exciting peoples on every continent, especially in the lands of Asia and Africa where society has been so frozen for so long.

In the United States The Idea was woven into American history and kept helping to bring about fundamental changes. To speak of the most basic fact, we started off a nation under the Constitution in which, as a result of state qualifications for voting, large numbers were disenfranchised because they did not have enough property or because they were of the wrong religion. It was The Idea of the Declaration, so powerful a catalytic, that did much to bring about in the early nineteenth century suffrage for all white males and then gradually extended it still further.

Or, in the early nineteenth century, the nation's few public schools gave few chances for an ordinary kid to get even an elementary education. The application of The Idea's central dynamic—opportunity to get ahead—was a principal factor in erecting the sweeping American system of tax-supported public education, first for elementary school, then high school, then college and graduate school.

Probably the most important influence of The Idea came when our nation after the Civil War entered rampant industrialization and urbanization. The whole "progressive," "liberal" reform movement that culminated in the New Deal amounted to an effort to use government on the federal, state and local levels to protect and extend opportunities for the less advantaged person. And it was Franklin Roosevelt, the climactic figure in it, who so appropriately said when asked to characterize his philosophy, "I'm a Democrat, an Episcopalian, and a follower of Thomas Jefferson."

The America of The Idea reached at least a temporary apogee in the years around 1960. We had a sheer economic boom such as no nation anytime, anywhere, had come anywhere near equaling. We had what might be called a prosperity psychosis in the United States—a whole generation, never having known depression, assuming that prosperity was the natural way of life. Something of the feeling of the Centennial of 1876 was being recreated by a new outburst of the brilliance of American technology. During World War II we invented what those of you in the business and engineering fields will recognize as "R & D"—"Research and Development," meaning that you take a hefty part of the profits of an industry and plow them back in order to mass produce new products. And we were getting conspicuous results from that, ones that conspicuously offered hope of constantly heightening standards of living.

Let me especially stress to you that around 1960 (I repeat "around," the specific date is just a convenient peg) we had a sense of an increase in status opportunities in this country again such as no people, anywhere, has ever known. It is necessary to distinguish between income and status. Sometimes in the United States they mean the same thing; having more money often gives you more status. Sometimes they're quite different. For example, in 1960 many American families preferred that their child become a supermarket assistant manager rather than a plumber, although the plumber might make considerably more money. The clue is in the status phrase "white collar" and "blue collar."

I discovered the other day in talking with a group of young people that the special meaning of the phrases seems somehow to be lost. Let me ask here of some of the younger members of the audience. Do "white collar" and "blue collar" have meaning for you? No? Yet for decades they have been a talisman of status—rising from the blue-collar group, where you work with your hands, to the white-collar group, where your hands remain clean and your tie stays on. Whatever the language may be today, the same status drive connoted by them has been and is a tremendous force in American life. To get across that white-collar line—ah, that was what the millions sought—most particularly for their children. They worked for it, scrimped for it, spent a lifetime achieving it.

Some kinds of facts have a way of getting buried in history. One of them is a simple statistic of the year 1954. Then, the U.S. Government announced that for the first time in our history more Americans made their living from a "service job" rather than a "production job"—the white-collar job being that assistant manager of the supermarket or the person employed in teaching, the medical field, in sales, or the thousands of other non-manual tasks. With the general labor population of the United States shifting, from production to service jobs, obviously many more felt the status satisfaction of being white-collar.

At the same time came the effects of a piece of legislation which, in its own way, has been the silent revolutionist of modern America. As World War II was being won, President Franklin Roosevelt faced the problem of the millions of veterans who would be returning to civilian life. After previous wars, the usual procedure had been to give veterans a money bonus. But that was not promising. Many veterans spent the money and wanted more; besides, there was the danger of mass unemployment. FDR's expert group worked out the basic concepts of legislation which came to be known as the "G.I. Bill of Rights." It has many provisions but the two most important gave a veteran the right to financial support for further education or to a low-cost loan to start a small business.

A number of experts believed most veterans would choose the low-cost loan; experts can be wrong. Overwhelmingly, veterans picked the further education. The Korean War came and Congress kept extending the G.I. Bill to more veterans. The legislation brought about what in many ways was the most important "status-revolution" of modern America because if getting from blue-collar to white-collar was so important, the most generally assumed way to do it was to acquire a college education.

I know I speak to an audience of which, among the younger, there are many who do not think it remarkable that they are in a college though they may come from middle-class, lower middle-class, or ordinary worker backgrounds. Times have indeed changed. The simple fact of the matter is that until the G.I. Bill went into operation only a small percentage of families were able to send their children to college. College was a distinctly upper-class thing, and the nation was sharply divided between being the college and the non-college person. What the G.I. Bill did was to make a college degree possible for the masses; in case after case, the first person in long generations of an American family achieved an AB. Then he wanted to make sure that his children went to college. One of my more interesting experiences in Washington was to read some of the letters that had come in from G.I. AB's. Typically, they said, in effect, I'm the first one of my family who's a somebody and watch my children!

And then, in the years around 1960, there was the breakthrough of the minorities. When the word "minority" is used these days, it is often associated largely with blacks or Puerto Ricans. But, percentage-wise, these groups were smaller "minorities" in the traditional American sense of the word. In long-time American usage, the majority, the so-called "typical American," has been a white, Protestant, Anglo-Saxon, "Anglo-Saxon" meaning generally a person of Western Europe origin. He was the WASP. And it was commonplace for discriminations to be made not only against people of color but against many millions of the other "minorities." One of the biggest of such "minorities" was created at the turn of the twentieth century by a huge flood of immigrants from southern and eastern Europe, most of whom were Catholics. The word "ethnic" may have its literal meaning but when it is used today, it usually refers to these Catholic migrants from southern and eastern Europe.

In a very real sense, American history has consisted of a broad canopy of economic and social opportunities into which new groups have been admitted or forced their way. At the beginnings, the canopy was occupied largely by Englishmen and a few similar stocks. During the nineteenth and early twentieth centuries, the Irish and the Jews began claiming sizeable territory under the canopy for themselves. By the post-World War II period, the canopy was well occupied by all kinds of Americans but with two critically important groups still subjected to notable obstacles in their pursuit of income and status —the blacks and, to a much less but significant extent, the ethnics.

In the later post-World War II era, the years around 1960, came the breakthrough. Everyone talks of the "Black Revolution." There was also the "Ethnic Revolution." Typically, Vince Lombardi, an ethnic of Italian immigrant stock, had been a star, as you know, on the famous Fordham Rams, very football savvy, an extremely effective coach. But, as Lombardi would say, when it came time for the hiring of a bigtime coach, "they'd pick a WASP and Lombardi, because he was named L-O-M-B-A-R-D-I, would be the assistant coach." As the 1960s came in, Lombardi became the head coach of the Green Bay Packers and went on to his chosen glory. The exuberance of the ethnic breakthroughs was caught by another descendant of the turn-of-the-century migration, the ethnic bricklayer's son, Yogi Berra, who's a favorite of mine for many reasons. Berra was told that a Jew had been elected Mayor of Dublin, which was true, and he observed, "Only in America could such a thing happen." All over America, in occupations ranging from high executive posts in industry to the better secretarial jobs, ethnics enjoyed a new feeling of expanding acceptance and achievement.

Status breakthroughs, economic boom—the years around 1960 brought what must be called a revolution of expectations for ordinary Americans. The Idea behind the American Revolution seemed to be producing to a wondrous degree. Never, anywhere, had a nation expected so much of the present and future in terms of monetary real income, dignity and self-respect and status.

Then, suddenly it happened. I suspect that a hundred years from now, at the Tricentennial, historians will look back and declare the years of the early 1970s—more specifically, 1973–74—a major watershed in the American experience. Three specifics will be deemed the triggers of the new era—Vietnam, Watergate, and a special kind of recession. For what they did was to shake severely, if not to undermine, assumptions on which the revolution of expectations had rested.

I must be brief about these assumptions and omit entirely some of significance. One that cannot be omitted is this: The assumption that the world was going to let us alone while we did all these wonderful things for ourselves. We believed it so firmly that it was a kind of an American Law of History. Human beings everywhere and at all times want peace and democracy; they want to get ahead to middle-class living and by techniques that preserve the respectability of the middle-class way. Consequently the history of man is a long, slow swing to a world that consists entirely of middle-class democracies like ours. Once in a while trouble comes when an evil leader takes over a nation and forces it along a different path—the German Emperor of the World War I era or the fascists and Communists of more recent times. Then all we have to do is to slap such leaders down. With the imposters gone, the natural instincts all people will take them along the way toward peace and middle-class democracy. Foreign policy itself is something we have, like measles, and get over with as quickly as possible. As I say, this was a very, very comforting Law of History. It meant that we were the future, we were on the right track, foreign peoples really weren't going to bother us for long. We could concentrate on the business of the revolution of expectations in America.

The headlines blared—the fall of Vietnam, in which we suffered a peculiarly humiliating and jolting defeat. It was only one, if the most serious, of a whole series of events in the early 1970s which shouted that much of the rest of the world was not interested in peace and middle-class democracy, even less in respectable ways of change, and still less in being an imitation of ourselves. In fact, some observers began to emphasize that this whole idea of a middle-class democracy is something quite new in the world, existing for only six or seven centuries in the 6,000 years of recorded history. Moreover, they were saying, "Today middle-class democracy is a little island in a vast sea of one kind or another of totalitarianism."

Assumption number two? We've assumed that our political system was a good, sound, workable one. Oh yes, there were always crooked politicians and stupid ones and ones who were woeful ciphers, but basically ours was a practical system. What we had not noted is that we'd been very lucky with respect to the part of the political system that mattered most, the Presidency. As some unheralded wag has said, "God takes care of fools, drunkards, and the United States." We have been extraordinarily lucky in the sense that out of the long line of Presidents—whom we persist in choosing in the most rococo of ways—we achieved ones who innocently presided over cesspools, like Warren Gamaliel Harding, the nothings such as Rutherford B. Hayes, the simply inadequate like a Zachary Taylor or a Calvin Coolidge. But the worst of them was tolerable. Then our luck ran out and we got Richard Nixon.

At first, still very sure of our political system, we told ourselves, Yes, we put the wrong man in, but look how effectively our system got rid of him. The House Judiciary Committee voted the impeachment counts, the Supreme Court ordered the White House tapes released, and Nixon had no choice but to be impeached or resign. But on second thought many an American was not so sure of our political system. What if Nixon had committed the same unlawful acts but not made tapes of his conversations? What if, when he first scented trouble, he had burned the tapes? How sound, really, was the American political system? The revelations of the dangerous activities of the FBI, the CIA, and other governmental agencies—all part of the general Watergate atmosphere—hardly tended to quiet the doubts and questionings. So again, another shaken assumption.

And what of the assumption that America was so much the land of abundance, so blessed with natural resources, that we could support an endlessly increasing standard of living? Of course you recall the sense of shock that went through the United States in 1973 when the Arabs clamped down their oil embargo. The effect of that too was permeative in American thinking and the worry was not diminished by the continuing evidence of other serious shortages or potential shortages.

Assumption number four—American and its "minorities." One group after another would be brought under the canopy of opportunity; gradually we would all be stirred in the Melting Pot and everybody would join in the Big Barbecue. No wonder we believed this so firmly; it had worked to a remarkable extent for almost two centuries. When the black revolution got under way, we assumed the process would continue for the blacks too. I remember laboring fervently in Washington on the civil rights legislation, the poverty program, and other governmental programs of the 1960s intended primarily to lift the black man. I was the typical American—I'm not attributing these assumptions only to other people, I'm attributing them in considerable measure to myself too. I assumed that if we gave the blacks adequate education, job training, a greater atmosphere of non-discrimination, it would be the same story. The black man would be like the Irishman, the Jew, and the ethnic and would move into the mainstream of American life with reasonable smoothness. Well, the jolt came in the late 1960s and early 1970s. Whether we weren't doing enough or whether the problem had different dimensions or both, the process was scarcely working well. It was, in fact, playing a considerable role in what everyone was calling the "urban crisis" and it gave a large section of the public the feeling that vital centers of the nation were disintegrating into shambles.

Finally, a fifth assumption, that there's endless room in America for an endless status striving. The millions go to college, the millions become white-collar. With the coming of the severe recession of 1973–75—and this is why I say it was a peculiar recession—we discovered that in a number of cities unemployment meant that some jobs were quite available but people did not want them; they wanted professional work. Yet in a number of fields we had too many professionals for the available openings. Take, for example, the law. This year we will graduate some 30,000 lawyers for some 15,000 openings. In general, as one scholar who has devoted his career to the history of U.S. education remarked to me ruefully, "We seem to be getting like India, where everybody has a PhD and walks around with a peanut butter sandwich in his dispatch case because he has no job and no papers to carry."

Still more assumptions strained if not shattered—The Idea behind the Declaration of Independence, so expansive and alluring, can seem not to be doing very well these days. It is this which, at bottom, is bringing so ambivalent a response to the Bicentennial. Yes, the tourists are present by the millions, also the fireworks and the fife-and-drums but little beyond that. We are in the midst of a national doubting and queasiness which is sufficiently pronounced that perhaps it had better be called a national malaise. Talk of the decline of American civilization, not to speak of the decline of all Western democratic society, is common and among some of the more responsible members of Western society.

The malaise is so deep that more than a few thoughtful commentators are saying that the American Dream, as we have known it for two centuries, is done. Perhaps, and perhaps not—I do not presume to be sure. I do think it should be added that whatever our present woes, we are still an enormously rich nation, in talent as well as resources. Whatever the degree of malaise, there is still, very deep in the American tradition—look inside your own mind and emotions—the dogged belief that America is and must remain the land of expanding opportunities for the ordinary man. And before the gloom becomes any thicker, perhaps we should recognize that The Idea which has been so powerful in the American experience has never been any one set of techniques. It was a goal. It did not tell you just how to get that ever better tomorrow for ever more Americans; it said you should strive for it. Moreover, it never prescribed any particular level of expectations; it said you had a right to expectations, necessarily adjusted to the possibilities and problems of the era.

If you will think along these lines, you will note the extent to which today all kinds of new or at least different techniques are being discussed in all the troubled fields, whether education, foreign policy, or race relations. Many of the approaches are still in the thoroughly murky stage, but things are decidedly stirring. You will note too that, if these various discussions have any one common theme, certainly it is this: Let's cut down not on expectations but on the extent of the expectations which Americans had in the booming, soaring years around 1960.

No state was more a symbol of the-sky-is-the-limit than California. It is symbolic that California today has a governor, Edmund Brown, Jr.—I say this totally nonpolitically, he is not my candidate for President—whose chief theme is lowered expectations and who enjoys a whopping eighty-seven percent approval rating in his state. After all, you know, there was something a bit bombastic, frenetic, overly boomeroo and exuberant—like a very young man declaring that the world was his oyster—about the super expectations of 1960.

If in fact the present stirrings in America represent a search for changed techniques within the context of lowered expectations, we may simply be at another highly productive stage in the long and varied history of The Idea. Such a stage would hardly be inappropriate for the 200th anniversary. It could represent not the decline of American civilization buts its maturing.

CHAPTER 27

THE AMERICAN CHARACTER

The attempt to define the American character has profitably engaged the energies of both foreigners and Americans from the earliest years of the nation to the present. The exact reason for this keen interest is difficult to determine. It seems logical to assume that, in part, it stems from the felt need of Americans to define some form of homogeneous behavior among the heterogeneous people who have made up this nation. If Americans do not have a composite character, then they must have a number of characters that might augur ill for their possession of a unitary set of national goals and standards. Yet nations whose mixed origins are much further back in antiquity apparently do not worry nearly as much about their national character.

In this essay, Professor David Potter, an outstanding student of American self-portraiture, suggests that there are two principal strains in the national character. He names these two divergent traits after those who first described them. To Potter, the Jeffersonian trait shows up in the Americans' almost devoutly idealistic individualism, whereas the Tocquevillian trait is toward a conformist, materialistic existence. Obviously, with two such divergent traditions operating, it becomes extremely difficult to find a single image that represents American character.

In considering this essay, a number of questions must be faced. Is there a definable, distinguishable American character? If Potter is correct in his concept of two conflicting traditions, what has been the effect of the conflict on the American character? How does this concept relate to a contemporary problem such as the racial question? How can an understanding of the tensions inherent in a people's traditions help in understanding and, thus, in solving the nation's problems?

In addition to the works cited in Potter's essay, the interested reader also should see works by the distinguished American anthropologists Margaret Mead, *And Keep Your Powder Dry** (1942), and Clyde Kluckhorn, *Mirror for*

*Man** (1954). See also Max Lerner, *America As a Civilization** (2 vols., 1957), and the three volumes of Daniel J. Boorstin's *The Americans—The Colonial Experience** (1958), *The National Experience** (1965), and *The Democratic Experience** (1973). Louis Hartz in *The Liberal Tradition in America** (1955), discusses the political implications of the American experience, and David Potter's *People of Plenty** (1954), offers a provocative interpretation of the effect of abundance on the American people.

*Available in a paperback edition.

THE QUEST FOR THE NATIONAL CHARACTER

DAVID M. POTTER

Unlike most nationality groups in the world today, the people of the United States are not ethnically rooted in the land where they live. The French have remote Gallic antecedents; the Germans, Teutonic; the English, Anglo-Saxon; the Italians, Roman; the Irish, Celtic; but the only people in America who can claim ancient American origins are a remnant of Red Indians. In any deep dimension of time, all other Americans are immigrants. They began as Europeans (or in the case of 10 per cent of the population, as Africans), and if they became Americans it was only, somehow, after a relatively recent passage westbound across the Atlantic.

It is, perhaps, this recency of arrival which has given to Americans a somewhat compulsive preoccupation with the question of their Americanism. No people can really qualify as a nation in the true sense unless they are united by important qualities or values in common. If they share the same ethnic, or linguistic, or religious, or political heritage, the foundations of nationality can hardly be questioned. But when their ethnic, religious, linguistic, and political heritage is mixed, as in the case of the American people, nationality can hardly exist at all unless it takes the form of a common adjustment to conditions on a new land, a common commitment to shared values, a common esteem for certain qualities of character, or a common set of adaptive traits and attitudes. It is partly for this reason that Americans, although committed to the principle of freedom of thought, have nevertheless placed such heavy emphasis upon the obligation to accept certain undefined tenets of "Americanism." It is for this same reason, also, that Americans have insisted upon their distinctiveness from the Old World from which they are derived. More than two centuries ago Hector St. John de Crèvecoeur asked a famous question, "What then is the American, this new man?" He simply assumed, without arguing the point, that the American is a new man, and he only inquired wherein the American is different. A countless array of writers, including not only careful historians

SOURCE. David M. Potter, "The Quest for the National Character," in John Higham, ed., *The Reconstruction of American History,* Hutchinson and Co., Ltd., 1962, pp. 197–220. Copyright © 1962 by Hutchinson and Co., Ltd. Reprinted by permission of Hutchinson and Co., Ltd.

and social scientists but also professional patriots, hit-and-run travellers, itinerant lecturers, intuitive-minded amateurs of all sorts, have been repeating Crèvecoeur's question and seeking to answer it ever since.

A thick volume would hardly suffice even to summarize the diverse interpretations which these various writers have advanced in describing or explaining the American character. . . . But it is probably safe to say that at bottom there have been only two primary ways of explaining the American, and that almost all of the innumerable interpretations which have been formulated can be grouped around or at least oriented to these two basic explanations, which serve as polar points for all the literature.

The most disconcerting fact about these two composite images of the American is that they are strikingly dissimilar and seemingly about as inconsistent with one another as two interpretations of the same phenomenon could possibly be. One depicts the American primarily as an individualist and an idealist, while the other makes him out as a conformist and a materialist. Both images have been developed with great detail and elaborate explanation in extensive bodies of literature, and both are worthy a close scrutiny.

For those who have seen the American primarily as an individualist, the story of his evolution as a distinctive type dates back possibly to the actual moment of his decision to migrate from Europe to the New World, for this was a process in which the daring and venturesome were more prone to risk life in a new country while the timid and the conventional were more disposed to remain at home. If the selective factors in the migration had the effect of screening out men of low initiative, the conditions of life in the North American wilderness, it is argued, must have further heightened the exercise of individual resourcefulness, for they constantly confronted the settler with circumstances in which he could rely upon no one but himself, and where the capacity to improvise a solution for a problem was not infrequently necessary to survival.

In many ways the colonial American exemplified attitudes that were individualistic. Although he made his first settlements by the removal of whole communities which were transported bodily—complete with all their ecclesiastical and legal institutions—he turned increasingly, in the later process of settlement, to a more and more individualistic mode of pioneering, in which one separate family would take up title to a separate, perhaps an isolated, tract of land, and would move to this land long in advance of any general settlement, leaving churches and courts and schools far behind. His religion, whether Calvinistic Puritanism or emotional revivalism, made him individually responsible for his own salvation, without the intervention of ecclesiastical intermediaries between himself and his God. His economy, which was based very heavily upon subsistence farming, with very little division of labor, also impelled him to cope with a diversity of problems and to depend upon no one but himself.

With all of these conditions at work, the tendency to place a premium upon individual self-reliance was no doubt well developed long before the cult of the American as an individualist crystallized in a conceptual form. But it did crystallize, and it took on almost its classic formulation in the thoughts of Thomas Jefferson.

It may seem paradoxical to regard Jefferson as a delineator of American national character, for in direct terms he did not attempt to describe the American character at all. But he did conceive that one particular kind of society was necessary to the fulfillment of American ideals, and further that one particular kind of person, namely the independent farmer, was a necessary component in the optimum society. He believed that the principles of liberty and equality, which he cherished so deeply, could not exist in a hierarchical society, such as that of Europe, nor, indeed, in any society where economic and social circumstances enabled one set of men to dominate and exploit the rest. . . . In fact, only a society of small husbandmen who tilled their own soil and found sustenance in their own produce could achieve the combination of independence and equalitarianism which he envisioned for the ideal society. Thus, although Jefferson did not write a description of the national character, he erected a model for it, and the model ultimately had more influence than a description could ever have exercised. . . .

Jefferson's image of the American as a man of independence, both in his values and in his mode of life, has had immense appeal to Americans ever since. They found this image best exemplified in the man of the frontier, for he, as a pioneer, seemed to illustrate the qualities of independence and self-reliance in their most pronounced and most dramatic form. Thus in a tradition of something like folklore, half-legendary figures like Davy Crockett have symbolized America as well as symbolizing the frontier. . . . In American politics the voters showed such a marked preference for men who had been born in log cabins that many an ambitious candidate pretended to pioneer origins which were in fact fictitious.

The pioneer is, of course, not necessarily an agrarian (he may be a hunter, a trapper, a cowboy, a prospector for gold), and the agrarian is not necessarily a pioneer (he may be a European peasant tilling his ancestral acres), but the American frontier was basically an agricultural frontier, and the pioneer was usually a farmer. Thus it was possible to make an equation between the pioneer and the agrarian, and since the pioneer evinced the agrarian traits in their most picturesque and most appealing form there was a strong psychological impulse to concentrate the diffused agrarian ideal into a sharp frontier focus. This is, in part, what Frederick Jackson Turner did in 1893 when he wrote *The Significance of the Frontier in American History*. In this famous essay Turner offered an explanation of what has been distinctive in American history, but it is not as widely realized as it might be that he also penned a major contribution to the literature of national character. . . .

A significant but somewhat unnoticed aspect of Turner's treatment is the fact that, in his quest to discover the traits of the American character, he relied for proof not upon descriptive evidence that given traits actually prevailed, but upon the argument that given conditions in the environment would necessarily cause the development of certain traits. Thus the cheapness of land on the frontier would make for universal land-holding which in turn would make for equalitarianism in the society. The absence of division of labor on the frontier would force each man to do most things for himself, and this would breed self-reliance. The pitting of the individual man against the elemental forces of the wilderness and of nature would further reinforce this self-reliance. Similarly, the fact that a man had moved out in advance of society's institutions and its stratified structure would mean that he could find independence, without being overshadowed by the institutions, and could enjoy an equality unknown to stratified society. All of this argument was made without any sustained effort to measure exactly how much recognizable equalitarianism and individualism and self-reliance actually were in evidence either on the American frontier or in American society. There is little reason to doubt that most of his arguments were valid or that most of the traits which he emphasized did actually prevail, but it is nevertheless ironical that Turner's interpretation, which exercised such vast influence upon historians, was not based upon the historian's kind of proof, which is from evidence, but upon an argument from logic which so often fails to work out in historical experience.

But no matter how he arrived at it, Turner's picture reaffirmed some by-now-familiar beliefs about the American character. The American was equalitarian, stoutly maintaining the practices of both social and political democracy; he had a spirit of freedom reflected in his buoyance and exuberance; he was individualistic—hence, "practical and inventive," "quick to find expedients," "restless, nervous, acquisitive." Turner was too much a scholar to let his evident fondness for the frontiersman run away with him entirely, and he took pains to point out that this development was not without its sordid aspects. There was a marked primitivism about the frontier, and with it, to some extent, a regression from civilized standards. . . .

An essay like this is hardly the place to prove either the validity or the invalidity of the Jeffersonian and Turnerian conception of the American character. The attempt to do so would involve a review of the entire range of American historical experience, and in the course of such a review the proponents of this conception could point to a vast body of evidence in support of their interpretation. They could argue, with much force, that Americans have consistently been zealous to defend individualism by defending the rights and the welfare of the individual, and that our whole history is a protracted record of our government's recognizing its responsibility to an ever broader range of people—to men without property, to men held in slavery, to women, to small enterprises threatened by monopoly, to children laboring in factories, to industrial workers, to the ill, to the elderly, and to the unemployed. This record, it can further be argued, is also a record of the practical idealism of the American people, unceasingly at work.

But without attempting a verdict on the historical validity of this image of the American as individualist and idealist, it is important to bear in mind that this image has been partly a portrait, but also partly a model. In so far as it is a portrait—a likeness by an observer reporting on Americans whom he knew —it can be regarded as authentic testimony on the American character. But in so far as it is a model—an idealization of what is best in Americanism, and of what Americans should strive to be, it will only be misleading if used as evidence of what ordinary Americans are like in their everyday lives. It is also important to recognize that the Jefferson-Turner image posited several traits as distinctively American, and that they are not all necessarily of equal validity. Particularly, Jefferson and Turner both believed that love of equality and love of liberty go together. For Jefferson the very fact, stated in the Declaration of Independence, that "all men are created equal," carried with it the corollary that they are all therefore "entitled to [and would be eager for] life, liberty, and the pursuit of happiness." From this premise it is easy to slide imperceptibly into the position of holding that equalitarianism and individualism are inseparably linked, or even that they are somehow the same thing. This is, indeed, almost an officially sanctioned ambiguity in the American creed. But it requires only a little thoughtful reflection to recognize that equalitarianism and individualism do not necessarily go together. Alexis de Tocqueville understood this fact more than a century ago, and out of his recognition he framed an analysis which is not only the most brilliant single account of the American character, but is also the only major alternative to the Jefferson-Turner image.

After travelling the length and breadth of the United States for ten months at the height of Andrew Jackson's ascendancy, Tocqueville felt no doubt of the depth of the commitment of Americans to democracy. Throughout two volumes which ranged over every aspect of American life, he consistently emphasized democracy as a pervasive factor. But the democracy which he wrote about was far removed from Thomas Jefferson's dream.

"Liberty," he observed of the Americans,

is not the chief object of their desires; equality is their idol. They make rapid and sudden efforts to obtain liberty, and if they miss their aim resign themselves to their disappointment; but nothing can satisfy them without equality, and they would rather perish than lose it.

This emphasis upon equality was not, in itself, inconsistent with the most orthodox Jeffersonian ideas, and indeed Tocqueville took care to recognize that under certain circumstances equality and freedom might "meet and blend." But such circumstances would be rare, and the usual effects of equality would be to encourage conformity and discourage individualism, to regiment opinion and to inhibit dissent. . . .

At the time when Tocqueville wrote, he expressed admiration for the American people in many ways, and when he criticized adversely his tone was abstract, bland, and free of the petulance and the personalities that characterized some critics, like Mrs. Trollope and Charles Dickens. Consequently, Tocqueville was relatively well received in the United States, and we have largely forgotten what a severe verdict his observations implied. But, in fact, he pictured the American character as the very embodiment of conformity, of conformity so extreme that not only individualism but even freedom was endangered. Because of the enormous weight with which the opinion of the majority pressed upon the individual, Tocqueville said, the person in the mintority,

not only mistrusts his strength, but even doubts of his right; and he is very near acknowledging that he is in the wrong when the greater number of his countrymen assert that he is so. The majority do not need to force him; they convince him.

"The principle of equality," as a consequence, had the effect of "prohibiting him from thinking at all," and "freedom of opinion does not exist in America." Instead of reinforcing liberty, therefore, equality constituted a danger to liberty. . . .

Tocqueville was perhaps the originator of the criticism of the American as conformist, but he also voiced another criticism which has had many echoes, but which did not originate with him. This was the condemnation of the American as a materialist. . . . In the interval between the publication of the first and second parts of Tocqueville's study, Washington Irving coined his classic phrase concerning "the "the almighty dollar, that great object of universal devotion throughout the land." But it remained for Tocqueville, himself, to link materialism with equality, as he had already linked conformity. . . .

For more than a century we have lived with the contrasting images of the American character which Thomas Jefferson and Alexis de Tocqueville visualized. Both of these images presented the American as an equalitarian and therefore as a democrat, but one was an agrarian democrat while the other was a majoritarian democrat; one an indepenedent individualist, the other a mass-dominated conformist; one an idealist, the other a materialist. Through many decades of self-scrutiny Americans have been seeing one or the other of these images whenever they looked into the mirror of self-analysis.

The discrepancy between the two images is so great that it must bring the searcher for the American character up with a jerk, and must force him to grapple with the question whether these seemingly antithetical versions of the Americans can be reconciled in any way. Can the old familiar formula for embracing opposite reports—that the situation presents a paradox—be stretched to encompass both Tocqueville and Jefferson? Or is there so grave a flaw somewhere that one must question the whole idea of national character and call to mind all the warnings that thoughtful men have uttered against the very concept that national groups can be distinguished from one another in terms of collective group traits.

Certainly there is a sound enough basis for doubting the validity of generalizations about national character. To begin with, many of these generalizations have been derived not from any dispassionate observation or any quest for truth, but from superheated patriotism which sought only to glorify one national group by invidious comparison with other national groups, or from a pseudoscientific racism which claimed innately superior qualities for favored ethnic groups. Further, the explanations which were offered to account for the ascribed traits were as suspect as the ascriptions themselves. . . .

Some thinkers of a skeptical turn of mind had rejected the idea of national character even at a time when most historians accepted it without question. Thus, for instance, John Stuart Mill as early as 1849 observed that

of all vulgar modes of escaping from the consideration of the effect of social and moral influences on the human mind, the most vulgar is that of attributing diversities of character to inherent natural differences.

Sir John Seely said, "no explanation is so vague, so cheap, and so difficult to verify."

But it was particularly at the time of the rise of Fascism and Naziism, when the vicious aspects of extreme nationalism and of racism became glaringly conspicuous, that historians in general began to repudiate the idea of national character and to disavow it as an intellectual concept, even though they sometimes continued to employ it as a working device in their treatment of the peoples with whose history they were concerned. To historians whose skepticism had been aroused, the conflicting nature of the images of the American as an individualistic democrat or as a conformist democrat would have seemed simply to illustrate further the already demonstrated flimsiness and fallacious quality of all generalizations about national character.

But to deny that the inhabitants of one country may, as a group, evince a given trait in higher degree than the inhabitants of some other country amounts almost to a denial that the culture of one people can be different from the culture of another people. To escape the pitfalls of racism in this way is to fly from one error into the embrace of another, and students of culture—primarily anthropologists, rather than historians—perceived that rejection of the idea that a group could be distinctive, along with the idea that the distinction was eternal and immutable in the genes, involved the ancient logical fallacy of throwing out the baby along with the bath. Accordingly, the study of national character came under the special sponsorship of cultural anthropology, and in the 'forties a number of outstanding workers in this field tackled the problem of national character, including the American character, with a methodological precision and objectivity that had never been applied to the subject before. After their investigations, they felt no doubt that national character was a reality—an observable and demonstrable reality. . . .

Still confronted with the conflicting images of the agrarian democrat and the majoritarian democrat, the investigator might avoid an outright rejection of either by taking the position that the American character has changed, and that each of these images was at one time valid and realistic; but that in the twentieth century the qualities of conformity and materialism have grown increasingly prominent, while the qualities of individualism and idealism have diminished. This interpretation of a changing American character has had a number of adherents in the last two decades, for it accords well with the observation that the conditions of the American culture have changed. As they do so, of course the qualities of a character that is derived from the culture might be expected to change correspondingly. Thus, Henry S. Commager, in his *The American Mind* (1950), portrayed in two contrasting chapters "the nineteenth-century American" and "the twentieth-century American." Similarly, David Riesman, in *The Lonely Crowd* (1950), significantly sub-titled *A Study of the Changing American Character,* pictured two types of Americans, first an "inner-directed man," whose values were deeply internalized and who adhered to these values tenaciously, regardless of the opinions of his peers (clearly an individualist), and second an "other-directed man," who subordinated his own internal values to the changing expectations directed toward him by changing peer groups (in short, a conformist).

Although he viewed his inner-directed man as having been superseded historically by his other-directed man, Riesman did not attempt to explain in historical terms the reason for the change. He made a rather limited effort to relate his stages of character formation to stages of population growth, but he has since then not used population phase as a key. Meanwhile, it is fairly clear, from Riesman's own context, as well as from history in general, that there were changes in the culture which would have accounted for the transition in character. Most nineteenth-century Americans were self-employed; most were engaged in agriculture; most produced a part of their own food and clothing. These facts meant that their well-being did not depend on the goodwill or the services of their associates, but upon their resourcefulness in wrestling with the elemental forces of Nature. Even their physical isolation from their fellows added something to the independence of their natures. But most twentieth-century Americans work for wages or salaries, many of them in very large employee groups; most are engaged in office or factory work; most are highly specialized, and are reliant upon many others to supply their needs in an economy with an advanced division of labor. Men now do depend upon the goodwill and the services of their fellows. This means that what they achieve depends less upon stamina and hardihood than upon their capacity to get along with other people and to fit smoothly into a co-operative relationship. In short the culture now places a premium upon the qualities which will enable the individual to function effectively as a member of a large organizational group. The strategic importance of this institutional factor has been well recognized by William H. Whyte, Jr., in his significantly titled book *The Organization Man* (1956)—for the conformity of Whyte's bureaucratized individual results from the fact that he lives under an imperative to succeed in a situation where promotion and even survival depend upon effective inter-action with others in an hierarchical structure.

Thus, by an argument from logic (always a treacherous substitute for direct observation in historical study), one can make a strong case that the nineteenth-century American should have been (and therefore must have been) an individualist, while the twentieth-century American should be (and therefore is) a conformist. But this formula crashes headlong into the obdurate fact that no Americans have ever been more classically conformist than Tocqueville's Jacksonian democrats—hardy specimens of the frontier breed, far back in the nineteenth century, long before the age of corporate images, peer groups, marginal differentiation, and status frustration. In short, Tocqueville's nineteenth-century American, whether frontiersman or no, was to some extent an other-directed man. Carl N. Degler has . . . [demonstrated] very focibly that most of our easy assumptions about the immense contast between the nineteenth-century American and the twentieth-century American are vulnerable indeed.

This conclusion should perhaps, have been evident from the outset, in view of the fact that it was Tocqueville who, in the nineteenth century, gave us the image which we now frequently identify as the twentieth-century American. But in any case, the fact that he did so means that we can hardly resolve the dilemma of our individualist democrat and our majoritarian democrat by assuming that both are historically valid but that one replaced the other. The problem of determining what use we can make of either of these images, in view of the fact that each casts doubt upon the other, still remains. Is it possible to uncover common factors in these apparently contradictory images, and thus to make use of them both in our quest for a definition of the national character? For no matter whether either of these versions of the American is realistic as a type or image, there is no doubt that both of them reflect fundamental aspects of the American experience.

There is no purpose, at this point in this essay, to execute a neat, pre-arranged sleight-of-hand by which the individualist democrat and the conformist democrat will cast off their disguises and will reveal themselves as identical twin Yankee Doodle Dandies, both born on the fourth of July. On the contary, intractable, iresolvable discrepancies exist between the two figures, and it will probably never be possible to go very far in the direction of accepting the one without treating the other as a fictitious image, to be rejected as reflecting an anti-democratic bias and as at odds with the evidence from actual observation of the behavior of *Home americanus* in his native haunts. At the same time, however, it is both necessary to probe for the common factors, and legitimate to observe that there is one common factor conspicuous in the extreme—namely the emphasis on equality, so dear both to Jefferson's American and to Tocqueville's. One of these figures, it will be recalled, has held no truth to be more self-evident than that all men are created equal, while the other has made equality his "idol," far more jealously guarded than his liberty.

If the commitment to equality is so dominant a feature in both of these representations of the American, it will perhaps serve as a key to various facets of the national character, even to contradictory aspects of this character. In a society as complex as that of the United States, in fact, it may be that the common factors underlying the various manifestations are all that our quest should seek. For it is evident that American life and American energy have expressed themselves in a great diversity of ways, and any effort to define the American as if nearly two hundred million persons all corresponded to a single type would certainly reduce complex data to a blunt, crude, and oversimplified form. To detect what qualities Americans share in their diversity may be far more revealing than to superimpose the stereotype of a fictitious uniformity. If this is true, it means that our quest must be to discover the varied and dissimilar ways in which the commitment to equality expresses itself—the different forms which it takes in different individuals—rather than to regard it as an undifferentiated component which shows in all individuals in the same way. Figuratively, one might say that in seeking for what is common, one should think of the metal from which Americans are forged, no matter into how many shapes this metal may be cast, rather than thinking of a die with which they are all stamped into an identical shape. If the problem is viewed in this way, it will be readily apparent that Tocqueville made a pregnant statement when he observed that the idea of equality was "the fundamental fact from which all others seem to be derived."

The term "equality" is a loose-fitting garment and it has meant very different things at very different times. It is very frequently used to imply parity or uniformity. The grenadiers in the King of Prussia's guard were equal in that they were all, uniformly, over six feet six inches tall. Particularly, it can mean, and often does mean in some social philosophies, uniformity of material welfare—of income, of medical care, etc. But people are clearly not uniform in strength or intelligence or beauty, and one must ask, therefore, what kind of uniformity Americans believed in. Did they believe in an equal sharing of goods? Tocqueville himself answered this question when he said, "I know of no country . . . where a profounder contempt is expressed for the theory of the permanent equality of property."

At this point in the discussion of equality, someone, and very likely a businessman, is always likely to break in with the proposition that Americans believe in equality of opportunity—in giving everyone what is called an equal start, and in removing all handicaps such as illiteracy and all privileges such as monopoly or special priority, which will tend to give one person an advantage over another. But if a person gains the advantage without having society give it to him, by being more clever or more enterprising or even just by being stronger than someone else, he is entitled to enjoy the benefits that accrue from these qualities, particularly in terms of possessing more property or wealth than others.

Historically, equality of opportunity was a particularly apt form of equalitarianism for a new, undeveloped frontier country. In the early stages of American history, the developed resources of the country were so few that an equality in the division of these assets would only have meant an insufficiency for everyone. The best economic benefit which the government could give was to offer a person free access in developing undeveloped resources for his own profit, and this is what Americans did offer. It was an ideal formula for everyone: for the individual it meant a very real chance to gain more wealth than he would have secured by receiving an equal share of the existing wealth. For the community, it meant that no one could prosper appreciably without activities which would develop undeveloped resources, at a time when society desperately needed rapid economic development. For these reasons, equality of opportunity did become the most highly sanctioned form of equalitarianism in the United States.

Because of this sanction, Americans have indeed been tolerant of great discrepancies in wealth. They have approved of wealth much more readily when they believed that it had been earned—as in the case, for instance, of Henry Ford—than when they thought it had been acquired by some special privilege or monopoly. In general, however, they have not merely condoned great wealth; they have admired it. But to say that the ideal of equality means only equality of opportunity is hardly to tell the whole story. The American faith has also held, with intense conviction, the belief that all men are equal in the sense that they share a common humanity—that all are alike in the eyes of God—and that every person has a certain dignity, no matter how low his circumstances, which no one else, no matter how high *his* circumstances, is entitled to disregard. When this concept of the nature of man was translated into a system of social arrangements, the crucial point on which it came to focus was the question of rank. For the concept of rank essentially denies that all men are equally worthy and argues that some are better than others—that some are born to serve and others born to command. The American creed not only denied this view, but even condemned it and placed a taboo upon it. Some people, according to the American creed, might be more fortunate than others, but they must never regard themselves as better than others. Pulling one's rank has therefore been the unforgivable sin against American democracy, and the American people have, accordingly, reserved their heartiest dislike for the officer class in the military, for people with upstage or condescending manners, and for anyone who tries to convert power or wealth (which are not resented) into overt rank or privilege (which are). Thus it is permissable for an American to have servants (which is a matter of function), but he must not put them in livery (which is a matter of rank); permissible to attend expensive schools, but not to speak with a cultivated accent; permissible to rise in the world, but never to repudiate the origins from which he rose. The most palpable and overt possible claim of rank is, of course, the effort of one individual to assert authority, in a personal sense, over others, and accordingly the rejection of authority is the most pronounced of all the concrete expressions of American beliefs in equality.

In almost any enterprise which involves numbers of people working in conjunction, it is necessary for some people to tell other people what to do. This function cannot be wholly abdicated without causing a breakdown, and in America it cannot be exercised overtly without violating the taboos against authority. The result is that the American people have developed an arrangement which skillfully combines truth and fiction, and maintains that the top man does not rule, but leads; and does not give orders, but calls signals; while the men in the lower echelons are not underlings, but members of the team. This view of the relationship is truthful in the sense that the man in charge does depend upon his capacity to elicit the voluntary or spontaneous co-operation of the members of his organization, and he regards the naked use of authority to secure compliance as an evidence of failure; also, in many organizations, the members lend their support willingly, and contribute much more on a voluntary basis than authority could ever exact from them. But the element of fiction sometimes enters, in terms of the fact that both sides understand that in many situations authority would have to be involked if voluntary compliance were not forthcoming. . . .

It is in this way that the anti-authoritarian aspect of the creed of equality leads to the extraordinarily strong emphasis upon permissiveness, either as a reality or as a mere convention in American life. So strong is the taboo against authority that the father, once a paternal authority, is now expected to be a pal to his children, and to persuade rather than to command. The husband, once a lord and master, to be obeyed under the vows of matrimony, is now a partner. And if, perchance, an adult male in command of the family income uses his control to bully his wife and children, he does not avow his desire to make them obey, but insists that he only wants them to be co-operative. The unlimited American faith in the efficacy of discussion as a means of finding solutions for controversies reflects less a faith in the powers of rational persuasion than a supreme reluctance to let anything reach a point where authority will have to be invoked. If hypocrisy is the tribute that vice pays to virtue, permissiveness is, to some extent, the tribute that authority pays to the principle of equality.

When one recognizes some of these various strands in the fabric of equalitarianism it becomes easier to see how the concept has contributed to the making, both of the Jeffersonian American and the Tocquevillian American. For as one picks at the strands they ravel out in quite dissimilar directions. The strand of equality of opportunity, for instance, if followed out, leads to the theme of individualism. It challenged each individual to pit his skill and talents in a competition against the skill and talents of others and to earn the individual rewards which talent and effort might bring. Even more, the imperatives of the competitive race were so compelling that the belief grew up that everyone had a kind of obligation to enter his talents in this competition and to "succeed." It was but a step from the belief that ability and virtue would produce success to the belief that success was produced by—and was therefore an evidence of—ability and virtue. In short, money not only represented power, it also was a sign of the presence of admirable qualities in the man who attained it. Here, certainly, an equalitarian doctrine fostered materialism, and if aggressiveness and competitiveness are individualistic qualities, then it fostered individualism also.

Of course, neither American individualism nor American materialism can be explained entirely in these terms. Individualism must have derived great strength, for instance, from the reflection that if all men are equal, a man might as well form his own convictions as accept the convictions of someone else no better than himself. It must also have been reinforced by the frontier experience, which certainly compelled every man to rely upon himself. But this kind of individualism is not the quality of independent-mindedness, and it is not the quality which Tocqueville was denying when he said that Americans were conformists. A great deal of confusion has resulted, in the discussion of the American character, from the fact that the term individualism is sometimes used (as by Tocqueville) to mean willingness to think and act separately from the majority, and sometimes (as by Turner) to mean capacity to get along without help. It might be supposed that the two would converge on the theory that a man who can get along by himself without help will soon recognize that he may as well also think for himself without help. But in actuality, this did not necessarily happen. Self-reliance on the frontier was more a matter of courage and of staying power than of intellectual resourcefulness, for the struggle with the wilderness challenged the body rather than the mind, and a man might be supremely effective in fending for himself, and at the same time supremely conventional in his ideas. In this sense, Turner's individualist is not really an antithesis of Tocqueville's conformist at all.

Still, it remains true that Jefferson's idealist and Tocqueville's conformist both require explantion and that neither can be accounted for in the terms which make Jefferson's individualist and Tocqueville's materialist understandable. As an explanation of these facets of the American character, it would seem that the strand of equalitarianism which stresses the universal dignity of all men, and which hates rank as a violation of dignity, might be found quite pertinent. For it is the concept of the worth of every man which has stimulated a century and a half of reform, designed at every step to realize in practice the ideal that every human possesses potentialities which he should have a chance to fulfill. Whatever has impeded this fulfillment, whether it be lack of education, chattel slavery, the exploitation of the labor of unorganized workers, the hazards of unemployment, or the handicaps of age and infirmity, has been the object, at one time or another, of a major reforming crusade. The whole American commitment to progress would be impossible without a prior belief in the perfectibility of man and in the practicability of steps to bring perfection nearer. In this sense, the American character has been idealistic. And yet its idealism is not entirely irreconcilable with its materialism, for American idealism has often framed its most altruistic goals in materialistic terms—for instance of raising the standard of living as a means to a better life. Moreover, Americans are committed to the view that materialistic means are necessary to idealistic ends. . . .

If the belief that all men are of equal worth has contributed to a feature of American life so much cherished as our tradition of humanitarian reform, how could it at the same time have contributed to a feature so much deplored as American conformity? Yet it has done both, for the same respect of the American for his fellow men, which has made many a reformer think that his fellow citizens are worth helping, has also made many another American think that he has no business to question the opinions that his neighbors have sanctioned. True, he says, if all men are equal, each ought to think for himself, but on the other hand, no man should consider himself better than his neighbors, and if the majority have adopted an opinion on a matter, how can one man question their opinion, without setting himself up as being better than they. Moreover, it is understood that the majority are pledged not to force him to adopt their opinion. But it is also understood that in return for this immunity he will voluntarily accept the will of the majority in most things. The absence of a formal compulsion to conform seemingly increases the obligation to conform voluntarily. Thus, the other-directed man is seen to be derived as much from the American tradition of equalitarianism as the rugged individualist, and the compulsive seeker of an unequally large share of wealth as much as the humanitarian reformer striving for the fulfillment of democratic ideals.

To say that they are all derived from the same tradition is by no means to say that they are, in some larger, mystic sense, all the same. They are not, even though the idealism of the reformer may seek materialistic goals, and though men who are individualists in their physical lives may be conformists in their ideas. But all of them, it may be argued, do reflect circumstances which are distinctively American, and all present manifestations of a character which is more convincingly American because of its diversity than any wholly uniform character could possibly be. If Americans have never reached the end of their quest for an image that would represent the American character, it may be not because they failed to find one image but because they failed to recognize the futility of attempting to settle upon one, and the necessity of accepting several.